CLOSER *to* TRUTH

CLOSER *to* TRUTH

Challenging Current Belief

ROBERT LAWRENCE KUHN

McGraw-Hill

New York   San Francisco   Washington, D.C.   Auckland   Bogotá
Caracas   Lisbon   London   Madrid   Mexico City   Milan
Montreal   New Delhi   San Juan   Singapore
Sydney   Tokyo   Toronto

Library of Congress Cataloging-in-Publication Data

Closer to truth : challenging current belief / [edited by] Robert Lawrence Kuhn.
   p. cm.
  ISBN 0-07-135996-6
  1. Science—Social aspects.   2. Science and civilization.   3. Closer to truth (Television program)   I. Kuhn, Robert Lawrence.

Q175.55 .C58 2000
303.48'3—dc21

00-028176

McGraw-Hill

A Division of The McGraw·Hill Companies

1 2 3 4 5 6 7 8 9 0 DOC/DOC 0 9 8 7 6 5 4 3 2 1 0

ISBN 0-07-135996-6

Printed and bound by R. R. Donnelley & Sons Company.

Jacket art and art on part openers by Todd Siler.

McGraw-Hill books are available at special quantity discounts to use as premiums and sales promotions, or for use in corporate training programs. For more information, please write to the Director of Special Sales, Professional Publishing, McGraw-Hill, Two Penn Plaza, New York, NY 10121-2298. Or contact your local bookstore.

 This book is printed on recycled, acid-free paper containing a minimum of 50% recycled, de-inked fiber.

Contents

PART FOUR: TECHNOLOGY & SOCIETY

PART FIVE: UNIVERSE & MEANING

Contributors

PAUL R. ABRAMSON (Chapters 9 and 10), a leading authority on human sexuality and on matters relating to sex and the law, is a professor in the Department of Psychology at the University of California, Los Angeles (UCLA). He is the author of many books, including *With Pleasure: Thoughts on the Nature of Human Sexuality* (with S. D. Pinkerton) and *Sexual Nature/Sexual Culture* (also with Pinkerton).

W. FRENCH ANDERSON (Chapters 7 and 8) is the director of the Gene Therapy Laboratories at the University of Southern California (USC) School of Medicine, where he is a professor of biochemistry and pediatrics. He is recognized as a leading pioneer of gene therapy—he has been called "the father of gene therapy"—perhaps the most revolutionary medical advance in recent times. He is the current national champion for his age group in karate.

FRANCISCO J. AYALA (Chapters 7, 23, 24, and 28), profiled in the *New York Times* as the "Renaissance man of evolutionary biology," is the Donald Bren Professor of Biological Sciences at the University of California, Irvine (UCI), where he specializes in evolutionary genetics and the philosophy of biology. He has published twelve books and is a past president of the American Association for the Advancement of Science.

GREGORY BENFORD (Chapters 3, 13, 20, 25, and 28) is both a recognized scientist and a best-selling science fiction novelist. He is a professor of plasma physics and astrophysics at UCI, where he specializes in galactic jets, quasars, and pulsars. He has written more than thirty books, including *The Martian Race, Sailing Bright Eternity, If the Stars Are Gods, COSM,* and *Against Infinity,* and is considered one of the most scientifically accurate science fiction writers.

BARRY BEYERSTEIN (Chapters 2, 5, and 6) is a professor of neuropsychology at Simon Fraser University in Canada. He is a leading skeptic, a member of the Executive Council of the Committee for the Scientific Investigation of Claims of the Paranormal (CSICOP), and a frequent contributor to the *Skeptical Inquirer* magazine.

EDWARD DE BONO (Chapters 14, 21, and 22) is a pioneer and leading authority in creative thinking and the direct teaching of thinking. During the past thirty years, he has written over fifty books including *Six Thinking Hats, De Bono's Thinking Course,* and his pathbreaking *Lateral Thinking: Creativity Step by Step.* His systems for teaching creativity have been adopted by school systems and corporations in many countries around the world. He is the originator of the concept of lateral thinking, a term attributed to him in the *Oxford English Dictionary.*

TODD BOYD (Chapter 16) is a professor of critical studies in the School of Cinema-Television and has been in the Department of African-American Studies at USC. He is an internationally recognized expert on film and popular culture and is considered a "public intellectual" on matters of race, class, and gender. His recent book is *Am I Black Enough for You?: Popular Culture from the 'Hood and Beyond.*

WARREN S. BROWN (Chapter 4), a professor of psychology at Fuller Theological Seminary, in Pasadena, California, is the director of research at the Psychophysical Laboratory, where he works with brain-damaged patients. *Whatever Happened to the Soul?: Scientific and Theological Portraits of Human Nature,* which he coedited with Nancey C. Murphy (Chapters 26 and 27) and H. Newton Malony, denies the dualist notion that the soul has an independent existence and is considered a significant contribution to contemporary Christian thought.

CHARLES BUCHANAN (Chapter 25), a physics professor at UCLA, teaches an interdisciplinary seminar with professors from the biological and social sciences called "Science and the Human Condition," which brings quantum theory and cosmology down to earth. He is an experimental physicist specializing in high-energy physics.

VERN BULLOUGH (Chapters 9 and 10), a professor at California State University at Northridge, is a medical historian who specializes in the study of sexual practices and taboos and the sociology of diverse groups of "sex workers." He has written or edited more than fifty books, including *Sexual Attitudes: Myths and Realities; Human Sexuality: An Encyclopedia;* and *Frontiers of Sex Research.*

STEPHEN J. CANNELL (Chapters 11 and 12), is one of the most prolific producers and writers in television, having created or cocreated forty network television series, including *The Rockford Files, Baretta, Hunter, The Commish,* and *The A-Team.* He has produced over a thousand hours of television and written over four hundred of the episodes himself. Also a major novelist—his national best-sellers include *The Devil's Workshop, King Con,* and *The Plan*—Stephen is dyslexic and an accomplished spokesperson on the subject of dyslexia.

DAVID J. CHALMERS (Chapters 1, 2, and 3) is one of the leaders in the emerging field of consciousness studies. He is a professor of philosophy at the University of Arizona, where he codirects the Center for Consciousness Studies. His book, *The Conscious Mind: In Search of a Fundamental Theory,* takes a new position on the fundamental nature of consciousness.

BRUCE CHAPMAN (Chapters 17 and 18), a specialist in public policy with a long career in government service, is the founder and president of the Discovery Institute, a public policy think tank in Seattle that promotes representative government, free markets, and individual liberties. From 1981 to 1983, he was the director of the United States Census Bureau, and later he served in the Reagan White House. He has received the State Department's Superior Honor Award.

PATRICIA SMITH CHURCHLAND (Chapters 23 and 24) is a professor of philosophy at the University of California, San Diego, where she focuses on the foundations of neuroscience and psychology. Her books include *On the Contrary: Critical Essays, 1987–1997* (with Paul M. Churchland); *Neurophilosophy: Toward a Unified Science of Mind-Brain; The Computational Brain* (with Terrence J. Sejnowski); and *The Mind-Brain Continuum* (co-editor with Rodolfo Llinás).

MIHALY ("MIKE") CSIKSZENTMIHALYI (Chapters 11, 12, and 13) is considered the leading academic authority on both creativity and happiness. Now at the Claremont Graduate University, he has been professor and head of the Department of Psychology at the University of Chicago. His books have helped define the field: *Flow: The Psychology of Optimal Experience; Finding Flow; Creativity: Flow and the Psychology of Discovery and Invention;* and *The Evolving Self.*

ARTHUR S. DE VANY (Chapter 8) is a professor of economics at UCI, where he specializes in complex systems and the economic organization of telecommunications, motion pictures, and power generation. He is a former professional athlete and a lifelong fitness buff, whose unusual theories are set out in a forthcoming book entitled *Evolutionary Fitness.*

EDWARD FEIGENBAUM (Chapters 14 and 21), a pioneer in artificial intelligence, is often called "the father of expert systems." He is the Kumagai Professor of Computer Science at Stanford University, where he is coscientific director of the Knowledge Systems Laboratory. He is a coeditor (with Julian Feldman and Paul Armer) of *Computers and Thought,* and coeditor of the four-volume *Handbook of Artificial Intelligence.*

TIMOTHY FERRIS (Chapters 23 and 24) is the best-selling author of eleven books, including *Coming of Age in the Milky Way* (winner of the American Institute of Physics Prize), *The Mind's Sky: Human Intelligence in a Cosmic Context,* and *The Whole Shebang: A State-of-the-Universe(s) Report.* A generalist scholar, he is emeritus professor at the University of California, Berkeley, and his film, Life Beyond Earth, was a major PBS special.

WENDY FREEDMAN (Chapters 26 and 27), an astronomer based at the Observatories of the Carnegie Institution in Pasadena, California, is the principal investigator for a critical Hubble Space Telescope project to determine the age of the universe. Along with this work, her fundamental contributions in the areas of extragalactic distance scale and the stellar populations of galaxies are internationally recognized.

ROBERT FREEMAN (Chapters 11, 12, and 16) is Dean of the College of Fine Arts at the University of Texas, Austin, and one of the world's leading music intellectuals, educators, and public spokespeople for music education. He has been chief executive of two major music schools: the New England Conservatory of Music and the Eastman School of Music. An accomplished pianist and musicologist, he has received numerous awards, including a Fulbright Fellowship and a Woodrow Wilson Fellowship.

FRANCIS FUKUYAMA (Chapters 15, 19, and 20), a professor of public policy at George Mason University and a consultant to the RAND Corporation, is recognized as one of the leading geopolitical thinkers in the world. His seminal book, *The End of History and the Last Man*, has been called one of the most important works of philosophical history since Marx and has stimulated enormous interest and controversy. He is the author of *Trust: The Social Virtues and the Creation of Prosperity* and *The Great Disruption: Human Nature and the Reconstitution of Social Order.*

GEORGE GEIS (Chapter 19) is an adjunct professor in the Anderson School of Management at UCLA, where he specializes in strategies for the digital economy. He has written articles and books on business management and technology, consults for multinational corporations, and tracks the progress of technology as president of TriVergence.

ROCHEL GELMAN (Chapter 24) is a psychology professor at UCLA, specializing in cognitive and language development and learning theory. She is a leader in the study of the thought processes of infants and young children. She was named a 1998 recipient of the William James Fellow Award of the American Psychological Society and serves on its board of directors.

BARBARA MARX HUBBARD (Chapters 17 and 18) is a futurist, citizen diplomat, social architect, and global politician. She is a cofounder of the Foundation for Conscious Evolution, a founding member of the World Future Society, and the author of many books, including *The Revelation: A Message of Hope for the New Millennium; Conscious Evolution: Awakening the Power of Our Social Potential;* and *The Hunger of Eve.*

RHODA JANZEN (Chapters 13 and 16), twice the poet laureate of California (1994 and 1997), has published more than a hundred and fifty poems and has won numerous prizes in poetry, including the William Butler Yeats National Poetry Competition. She is in the English Department at UCLA, where she received the 1999–2000 Distinction in Teaching Award.

SARU JAYARAMAN (Chapters 17 and 18) is the national founder of WYSE (Women and Youth Supporting Each other), a mentoring program to empower young inner-city girls. While an undergraduate at UCLA, she was recognized as one of the top three students in the nation. She has a master's degree in public policy from Harvard and is now studying for a law degree at Yale Law School.

JOHN KAO (Chapters 11, 12, and 13), a psychiatrist, Harvard M.B.A., and entrepreneur, is an authority in the intersecting fields of corporate creativity, new media, and entrepreneurial management. He has taught courses in business creativity at Harvard and Stanford Business Schools and is the author of many books on that topic, including *Jamming: The Art and Discipline of Business Creativity.*

STEVEN KOONIN (Chapters 23 and 25) is vice president and provost of the California Institute of Technology (Caltech), where he is also professor of theoretical physics. He has served on a number of national advisory committees and is a fellow of the American Physical Society, the American Association for the Advancement of Science, and the American Academy of Arts and Sciences.

BART KOSKO (Chapters 15, 19, 21, and 22) is a leading authority in the new field of fuzzy logic and theory. He is a professor of electrical engineering at USC and the author of *Fuzzy Thinking; Fuzzy Engineering; The Fuzzy Future: From Society and Science to Heaven in a Chip;* and the futuristic novel *Nanotime.* His research interests include adaptive systems, neural networks, and biocomputing.

GEORGE KOZMETSKY (Chapters 15 and 20) is an authority on the relationship between technology and society. He is a cofounder and former executive vice president of Teledyne, Inc., and the founder of the IC^2 ("Innovation, Creativity, and Capital") Institute, a think tank at the University of Texas at Austin, where he was dean of the College of Business Administration and the Graduate School of Business. He has received numerous awards, including the National Medal of Technology.

RAY KURZWEIL (Chapters 11, 12, and 16) is a world-renowned inventor, computer scientist, entrepreneur, and best-selling author. He founded four technology companies, which include speech recognition devices, computer-based music keyboards, and reading machines for the blind. He has received numerous awards, including MIT's Inventor of the Year. He is the author of *The Age of Intelligent Machines* and *The Age of Spiritual Machines: When Computers Exceed Human Intelligence.*

LEON LEDERMAN (Chapters 25, 26, 27, and 28) won the Nobel Prize in physics in 1988 for contributing to the body of evidence that explains the fundamental structure of matter. A national spokesperson for particle physics, he is director emeritus of the Fermi National Accelerator Laboratory (Fermilab) in Batavia, Illinois, and the author of *The God Particle: If the Universe Is the Answer, What Is the Question?* (with Dick Teresi) and *From Quarks to the Cosmos* (with David N. Schramm).

ANDREI LINDE (Chapters 25, 26, and 27), a professor of physics at Stanford University, is one of the originators of inflationary cosmology and cosmological phase transitions—the startling explanation that describes the universe as a self-reproducing metauniverse, continually and randomly giving birth to new universes. He is the author of one hundred and fifty papers and two books, *Inflation and Quantum Cosmology* and *Particle Physics and Inflationary Cosmology*. His 1982 paper suggesting the new inflationary universe scenario became the most often cited paper of the year in physics.

JOHN H. MCWHORTER (Chapters 17 and 18) is a professor of linguistics at the University of California, Berkeley. Specializing in Creole languages and sociolinguistics, he has written and spoken widely about the Ebonics controversy—that is, the use of black English in education—and affirmative action. He is also the author of *Spreading the Word: Language and Dialect in America* and *The Word on the Street: Fact and Fable About American English*.

MARVIN MINSKY (Chapters 15, 19, and 20), the Toshiba Professor of Media Arts and Sciences at the Massachusetts Institute of Technology (MIT), is one of the founders of the field of artificial intelligence. He was the cofounder and longtime director of MIT's Artificial Intelligence Laboratory. His new book, *The Emotion Machine*, describes the role that emotions play in our mental processes.

GRAHAM T. MOLITOR (Chapters 14, 21, and 22) is vice president and legal counsel of the World Future Society and president of Public Policy Forecasting, a private consulting company. He is the author of numerous articles and books on the future, and the coeditor (with George Thomas Kurian) of the *Encyclopedia of the Future*. He was director of candidate research for Governor Rockefeller's presidential campaigns and a lobbyist for the food industry.

RICHARD MOUW (Chapter 18) is the president of Fuller Theological Seminary, where he is also a professor of Christian philosophy and ethics. On the editorial boards of several publications, he is the author of ten books, including *The God Who Commands; Uncommon Decency; Christian Civility in an Uncivil World*; and *Consulting the Faithful*. He is the chairman of the Commission on Accreditation for the Association of Theological Schools.

NANCEY C. MURPHY (Chapter 26 and 27) chairs the Theology Division at Fuller Theological Seminary and is also a professor of Christian philosophy there. She is a leading scholar in the relationship between science and religion. Her books include *On the Moral Nature of the Universe: Theology, Cosmology, and Ethics* (with George Ellis); and *Theology in the Age of Scientific Reasoning*.

BRUCE C. MURRAY (Chapters 15, 19, 21, 22, and 28) is a professor of planetary science and geology at Caltech and a leading authority on space exploration. He was the director (chief executive) of the Jet Propulsion Laboratory, NASA's 5000-person center for unmanned space exploration, from 1976 to 1982. He is a cofounder (with Carl Sagan) and the president of The Planetary Society, the largest public-participation organization concerned with space exploration. He has authored seven books, including *Navigating the Future*.

SHERWIN NULAND (Chapters 7, 8, 10, and 14) is clinical professor of surgery (gastroenterology) at Yale University School of Medicine, where he also teaches medical history and bioethics. His best-selling books—*How We Die, How We Live,* and *The Mysteries Within: A Surgeon Reflects on Medical Myths*—are remarkable portraits of death and life and have been called resonant works of moral philosophy. He won the 1994 National Book Club Award for Nonfiction (*How We Die*).

CLIFFORD AND JOYCE PENNER (Chapters 9 and 10) are sex therapists, educators, and speakers. Working as a team, they have written eight books, including *Men and Sex: Discovering Greater Love, Passion, and Intimacy with Your Wife* (winner of the Christian Booksellers Association Gold Medallion) and *What Every Wife Wants Her Husband to Know About Sex.* Clifford Penner is a clinical psychologist with a Ph.D. in psychology, and Joyce Penner is a registered nurse with a master's degree in psychosomatic nursing.

DEAN I. RADIN (Chapters 4, 5, and 6), one of the world's leading parapsychology researchers, is the author of *The Conscious Universe: The Scientific Truth of Psychic Phenomena.* He has carried out his research at the Consciousness Research Laboratory at the University of Nevada (where he was director), Princeton, SRI International, the University of Edinburgh, and for the United States government. He has served three terms as the president of the Parapsychological Association.

MARILYN SCHLITZ (Chapters 1, 2, 5, and 6) is the director of research at the Institute of Noetic Sciences, in Sausalito, California, a leading research and membership organization devoted to interdisciplinary and diverse studies of the mind and consciousness. Trained as an anthropologist, she has conducted important investigations in parapsychology, including remote viewing, intentionality, and healing at a distance.

JOHN R. SEARLE (Chapters 1, 2, 3, and 4), the Mills Professor of Philosophy at the University of California, Berkeley, is considered one of the leading philosophers of mind. He is the author of numerous works on the philosophy of language and the philosophy of mind, including *The Mystery of Consciousness, The Rediscovery of the Mind, The Construction of Social Reality,* and *Minds, Brains and Science.*

TODD SILER (Chapters 13 and 16) is an internationally recognized artist whose science-based works are held in numerous private and public collections worldwide, including major museums. He is also a writer and educator, and the first visual artist to receive a doctorate from MIT (in psychology and art). He has written two best-selling books, *Breaking the Mind Barrier* and *Think Like a Genius.*

BRIAN SKYRMS (Chapter 14) is a professor of philosophy and social science at UCI, where he directs the interdisciplinary program in history and philosophy of science. He specializes in game theory and decision making and is the author of many articles and books, including *Evolution of the Social Contract* and *The Dynamics of Rational Deliberation.*

GREGORY STOCK (Chapters 7, 8, 9, 20, and 22) is the director of the Program on Medicine, Technology, and Society at UCLA, where he examines such transformational technologies as genetic engineering. He is also a visiting senior fellow at UCLA's Center for the Study of Evolution and the Origin of Life. A biophysicist with a Harvard M.B.A., he is the author of *Metaman: The Merging of Humans and Machines into a Global Superorganism* and *The Book of Questions.*

CHARLES TART (Chapters 4, 5, and 6), a core faculty member of the Institute of Transpersonal Psychology in Palo Alto, California, is internationally known for his psychological work on the nature of consciousness, as one of the founders of the field of transpersonal psychology, and for his research in scientific parapsychology. His two classic books, *Altered States of Consciousness* and *Transpersonal Psychologies,* became widely used texts. His online journal TASTE—www.issc-taste.org—is devoted to transcendent experiences that scientists have reported.

FRANK J. TIPLER (Chapters 26, 27, and 28) is a professor of mathematics and mathematical physics at Tulane University, where his interests center on cosmology, particularly the fate of the universe. His two books have stimulated much controversy: *The Anthropic Cosmological Principle* (with John D. Barrow), and *The Physics of Immortality: Modern Cosmology and the Resurrection of the Dead.*

ALLAN J. TOBIN (Chapter 7) is the director of the Brain Research Institute at UCLA, where he is also a professor of neurology in the medical school and a professor of physiological science in the College of Letters and Science. A leading researcher on epilepsy, Huntington's disease, and juvenile diabetes, he is also the scientific director of the Hereditary Disease Foundation.

JAMES TREFIL (Chapters 1, 3, 5, and 6) is the Clarence J. Robinson Professor of Physics at George Mason University and the author of more than twenty books, including *Reading the Mind of God, From Atoms to Quarks, Sharks Have No Bones; Science Matters: Achieving Science Literacy* (with Robert M. Hazen); and *Are We Unique?* A regular contributor to many publications, including *Smithsonian Magazine,* he is also a commentator for National Public Radio.

NEIL DE GRASSE TYSON (Chapters 17, 23, and 24) is a visiting research scientist in the Department of Astrophysics at Princeton University. He is also director of the Hayden Planetarium of the American Museum of Natural History, in New York. He is the author of several popular books on science, including *Just Visiting This Planet, Merlin's Tour of the Universe,* and *Universe Down to Earth,* and is interviewed often in the media.

ROY WALFORD (Chapter 8), one of the leading authorities on the biology of aging, promotes dietary restriction as the key mechanism for retarding aging and disease. He has been a professor of pathology at UCLA Medical School for thirty years, and was the physician inside Biosphere 2. He has published numerous articles and books on aging, including *The 120-Year Diet* and *The Anti-Aging Plan.*

FRED ALAN WOLF (Chapters 1, 2, 3, and 4) is a physicist, writer, and international lecturer on consciousness and the new physics. He is an award-winning author of eight books, including *The Spiritual Universe, The Dreaming Universe, Parallel Universes,* and *The Eagle's Quest: A Physicist's Search for Truth in the Heart of the Shamanic World.* In 1982, Wolf won the American Book Award for Science softcovers for *Taking the Quantum Leap.*

ROBERT LAWRENCE KUHN is the creator and host of the *Closer to Truth* public television series. He is the author or editor of more than twenty books, including the *Handbook for Creative and Innovative Managers* and the *Library of Investment Banking.* He is the president of The Geneva Companies, a leading merger and acquisition firm for private, middle-market businesses. Since 1989, he has worked with enterprises in the People's Republic of China, including the Science and Technology Ministry and China Central Television (CCTV). He is the executive producer of *Capital Wave,* the first series on mergers and acquisitions broadcast on Chinese television, and *In Search of China,* a Public Broadcasting Service (PBS) documentary (he is the author of the companion book of the same title). He has a bachelor of arts in human biology (Johns Hopkins), a doctorate in anatomy/brain research (UCLA), and a master's degree in management (MIT Sloan Fellow). He is a senior research fellow at the IC^2 Institute of the University of Texas, Austin, and was a research affiliate in psychology and brain science at MIT and an adjunct professor (corporate strategy) at the Stern School of Business of New York University.

Acknowledgments

There are many people to thank for their participation and support in the protracted process of imagining, creating, planning, producing, writing, editing, thinking about, talking about, wondering about, and worrying about *Closer to Truth*—the ideas, the television series, and the book. Most are friends, family and mentors, with whom I have spoken of these matters over the years. The simplest way to acknowledge their contributions is to make a list—and be sure to arrange it alphabetically: David Antion, Stephan Chorover, Carmine Clemente, Jerome D. Frank, George Geis, Rick Harriman, David Jon Hill, Yuji Ijiri, Brian Knowles, George Kozmetsky, Aaron Kuhn, Adam Kuhn, Daniella Kuhn, Dora Kuhn, Lee Kuhn, Louis Kuhn, Bruce Levy, James Loper, Jack Martin, Samantha McDermott, Pamela McFadden, George Merlis, Ed Miskevitch, George Morgenstern, James Mosso, Gene Nichols, Stanley Rader, Lionel Schaen, John Schlag, Diana Serviyarian, Alan Shapiro, Michael Shepley, Jacqueline Slater, Roberta Smith, James Tabor, Cal Thomas II, Don Tillman, Tedd Tramolini, David Troob, Karen Troyan, Denis de Vallance, Adam Zhu, George Zimmar, and of course all the participants on the television show and contributors to the book. I am pleased to present the artistry of one of our contributors, Todd Siler, a friend from MIT days, whose drawings introduce each of the Parts. His painting on the book jacket, *Deciphering the Neural Rosetta Stone,* epitomizes the essence of *Closer to Truth* (and hangs in my office). A special thanks to Sara Lippincott for her editorial assistance and stimulating comments; at McGraw-Hill, my editor Griffin Hansbury for his vision and diligence, and to Amy Murphy for her support; Mel Rogers, president of KOCE-TV, the PBS station in Huntington Beach (Orange County), California, for his belief in the concept and help with the name; Niki Vettel for developing the *Closer to Truth* television series as a new genre of programming called knowledge affairs; and Bruce Murray for his ideas and development of the *Closer to Truth* website (www.closertotruth.com).

Introduction

Mind & Brain, Health & Sex, Creativity & Thinking, Technology & Society, Universe & Meaning—what organizing theme might bring together such subjects? The answer: a personal take on topics that color the human condition at this particular period in our development. The contributors to this book—participants in the *Closer to Truth* television series—are among the leaders in their fields; the informal, unrehearsed discussions, taken from the shows' transcripts, give a good sense of state-of-the-art thinking at current intellectual frontiers. Each year I hope to take a fresh look at advances in three of my favorites: consciousness, cosmology, and creativity. My bet is that what I like, you like.

Closer to Truth is made up of patterns, not proofs—patterns formed by the topics and informed by the contributors. The series is concerned with what it means to be human in the new millennium—with our continuing search for collective destiny and individual purpose. It deals with the mysteries of mind, matter, and meaning, bringing together prominent thinkers, scientists, scholars, and artists to discuss what is happening at the leading edge of science and the humanities. It tests conventional wisdom and seeks truth wherever it may change, seeing the humor as well as the import of tradition-breaking ideas.

Closer to Truth is feel and flavor more than fact and logic, experience and emotion more than reason and analysis. It's not *the* Truth, not even Closest to Truth. It's more process than conclusion; the discussions reflect educated opinion but no certainty, no smugness. There's a welcome measure of ambiguity, complexity, and even occasional confusion. Remember, we give no assurances about truth, just a promise to get you closer.

Challenging current belief is the prism, the conceptual lens, through which advances in knowledge are viewed. It does not matter whether the challenges are obvious or obscure, simple or complex, voiced by few or accepted by many. When challenges are defensible, they act as a scalpel to dissect the latest thinking in the field, teasing apart and exposing critical issues. Often current belief is bimodal, with opposing though widely held views (for example, whether consciousness does or does not exist apart from a physical brain).

Topics do not develop linearly; arguments do not flow smoothly. The books the contributors have written are linear and smooth, but these conversations are not. The dialogues in *Closer to Truth* complement these more canonical works, which I recommend to you for further reading (see the Contributors listing).

In each chapter, we listen to five experts from diverse fields or perspectives engaging one another in the competitive marketplace of ideas. The transcripts are presented essentially raw, except for verbal cleanups, some restructure, occasional bracketed editorial interpolations, and footnotes where they are felt to be necessary. Enjoy the head-to-head spontaneity, the tang of the original discourse. It's fascinating how the group dynamics move these leading thinkers to express themselves in ways dissimilar from their iteratively edited writings, revealing strong passions and subtle nuances not commonly heard. What emerges is personality; it's fun to meet the people who are challenging truth, changing truth, making truth—to watch them navigating with less control than they normally have when they are giving talks to their colleagues in symposia or crafting their unfailingly elegant books.

My own role as host of these programs was broad-brush—picking the subjects, selecting the guests, moving the talk along. My introductions and conclusions to each of the chapters in the book are more mini-essays than analytical outlines; they position or summarize the ideas, highlighting issues and reflecting my particular, perhaps peculiar, orientation. I have some good fun here, and so do the participants, taking the topics seriously but (we hope) not ourselves.

So *Closer to Truth* should be seen as a work in progress, with no deadline. There is no artificial surety, no cosmetic harmony. Though the book proceeds linearly, the reader need not. Enter and exit at any point. Select by personal interest, not numerical order. Each chapter stands more or less on its own, presenting the take of its diverse contributors. Yet there is order to the sequence, from *Brain & Mind* to *Universe & Meaning*—from consciousness to cosmology—reflecting the shape of the series, now and in the future. I make no apologies for overlap in the discussions: look for greater dimension and deeper grain; see subjects from various viewpoints; watch for curves in the road. Comments do not fit together neatly as if pieces in a puzzle. *Closer to Truth* may mean pieces too few or pieces too many; chapters are not manicured or neat but reflect the real-time current thinking of these real-world current thinkers.*

---

*At the end of most chapters, there are Outtakes—what we all said when the lights went down and the cameras turned off, after the shows were over (or so we thought, because the sound, fortuitously, was still being recorded).

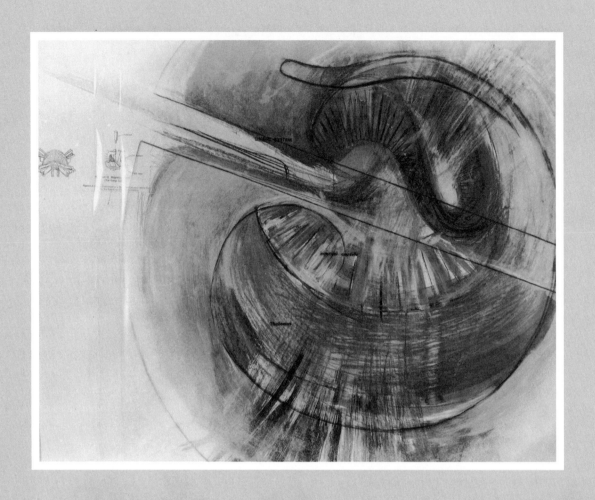

PART ONE

BRAIN & MIND

Cerebreactors: Powers of the Mind and Brain and Intuition in Moments of Cerebral Fusion. (Courtesy of Todd Siler.)

CHAPTER 1

What Is Consciousness?

Are you conscious? How do you know? What is consciousness—our thoughts, feelings, hopes, and dreams; the hidden voice of our private selves; our inner identity? What might consciousness consist of? All of us think we can understand consciousness, but none of us can explain it—therein lies its mystery. Think about yourself reading these words, and at the same time, observe yourself thinking. This is *self*-awareness, the interior mental experience we call consciousness. But why should you be self-aware at all? Is there something special about consciousness—something unique to human beings, something not found in computers, something of the mind not in the brain? Many scientists, taking the so-called reductionist approach, believe that the inner voice we all experience is simply the illusion of selfhood, manufactured by our brain functions. These people subscribe to *materialism,* the philosophy that only the physical is real and that nothing nonphysical can exist. But there are a few scientists who wonder whether consciousness may be a fundamental part or property of existence—like matter, energy, space-time—and whether some obscure form of stuff may constitute our private selves. Then there are many people who believe in the existence of an independent, metaphysical spirit or soul, which is somehow an attribute of all human beings and, in concert with the human brain, forms the human mind. These people—traditional theologians are an example—espouse *dualism,* the philosophy that two radically different forms of "stuff" exist in the world: mind, the essence of which is thought, and matter, the essence of which is extension in space and time. Dualism traces its roots to the ancients but was famously expounded by the seventeenth-century mathematician and philosopher René Descartes, who also said, "I think, therefore I am," thus asserting the primacy of consciousness. Materialism and dualism have been the two principal combatants in the philosophical tug of war commonly known as the *mind-body* problem. But there are related (and somewhat less respectable) belief systems such as *idealism,*

which asserts that mind is the reality and matter the illusion, and *solipsism*, which holds that the self is the one and only true reality. (Modern variances of materialism, such as eliminative reductionism and functionalism, are discussed in the books written by our guest contributors.) Why is consciousness so fascinating? And why is it such a hot topic these days, with an academic journal devoted solely to consciousness studies, a proliferation of popular books on the subject, and a series of interdisciplinary conferences at the University of Arizona? To provide you with some insights, we enlisted the help of two philosophers, two physicists, and an anthropologist who is an expert on extrasensory perception. Remember, we give no assurances about truth—just a promise to get you closer.

PARTICIPANTS

Dr. David Chalmers, a philosopher at the University of Arizona, is the author of *The Conscious Mind: In Search of a Fundamental Theory.* Dave wonders whether consciousness may be just as fundamental as matter and energy.

Dr. Marilyn Schlitz is research director of the Institute of Noetic Sciences, a center devoted to an integrated understanding of consciousness. Marilyn believes that consciousness extends beyond the individual body and brain.

Dr. John Searle, a leading philosopher of mind at the University of California, Berkeley, is the author of many books, including *The Mystery of Consciousness* and *The Rediscovery of the Mind.* John believes that while consciousness is a real phenomenon, it arises solely from the brain.

Dr. James Trefil, a professor of physics at George Mason University, is the author of *Are We Unique? A Scientist Explores the Unparalleled Intelligence of the Human Mind.* Jim offers the mainstream scientific view that consciousness consists entirely of electrochemical activity within the brain.

Dr. Fred Alan Wolf, a nonmainstream theoretical physicist, is the author of *The Spiritual Universe: One Physicist's Vision of Spirit, Soul, Matter, and Self.* Fred suspects that consciousness may be the "real reality" and matter a dream-like illusion.

ROBERT: John, you're one of the leading philosophers of mind. Why is consciousness such a mystery?

JOHN: We don't know how to explain it. Compare consciousness to physics. We're doing pretty well in physics, even though we have some puzzling areas, like quantum mechanics. But we don't have an adequate theory of how the brain causes conscious states, and we don't have an adequate theory of how consciousness fits into the universe.

ROBERT: Why is consciousness suddenly so hot?

JOHN: Well, in a way, the puzzling thing is why hasn't consciousness *always* been hot? It's the single most important fact about our existence, except for life itself. Consciousness is the most descriptive thing about human beings. So what happened to consciousness? There was a period of nearly a hundred years—most of the twentieth century—when the scientific consensus believed that there was no way to construct a scientific theory of consciousness. William James and many of the leading thinkers in the late nineteenth century assumed that there was just nothing useful one could say about it. So what has happened recently, I think, is not that we've suddenly discovered consciousness, but that we've rediscovered something we should have been studying all along. We have gone back to what is a normal preoccupation of curious, self-perceptive human beings: How does our own consciousness work? What makes consciousness hot now is that we've overcome the silliness of a certain era, when people thought you couldn't really say anything about it.

ROBERT: We haven't fully overcome prejudice against the subjective. Many scientists still feel that studying consciousness just spends our money and wastes our time.

JOHN: But they don't dominate the scene the way they once did.

MARILYN: Certainly consciousness has been hot, and within our own culture we're just beginning to wake up to this idea. What is unique about this moment in human history is that, for the first time, we have a convergence of worldviews. We have available all of the wisdom traditions—sacred texts from different cultures—that previously only a handful of people could access. Now you can download it all on the Internet. If you add the advances we're making in the neurosciences and cognitive sciences to the teachings of the wisdom traditions, the result is an unprecedented interface between two diverse ways of knowing and being in the world. We're suddenly being compelled to reevaluate the significance of consciousness and to confront the notion that our subjective and our objective dimensions are probably one and the same.

ROBERT: Dave, over the last ten years, what have you seen change in our perception of consciousness?

DAVE: The central change is a shift in science. Many scientists are now willing to take subjective data seriously, as legitimate data. Inner feelings and awareness are appreciated as real and manifest in the world. You have to take your own states of consciousness at least as seriously as, say, pointer readings on physical meters. Electronic recordings of the brain are data, but so also are accounts of inner experiences—all these are data, too. Many scientists are now prepared to consider consciousness as a real phenomenon, as something that can be connected to everything else. But that's what science is about; it's about building connections among different phenomena.

ROBERT: John, what are some of the traditional explanations for consciousness? Don't critique them now; you'll get your chance later.

JOHN: That's hard to resist—critiquing them. The standard view, the one that the man and woman in the street believe, is usually dualism. Dualism is the idea that in addition to the physical world there's a separate mental world—an independent mental reality of consciousness that's not part of the ordinary physical world. In opposition to dualism is materialism, which is the prevailing view among professional experts—psychologists, philosophers, neurobiologists. And materialism is the idea that the material world is all there is, and either consciousness has to be reduced to brain states or computational states or something absolutely physical like that, or else it doesn't really exist at all. So the big choice today is between dualism, which says that we live in two separate worlds, a mental world and a physical world, and materialism, which says no, it's all physical.

ROBERT: Zombies, Dave. What are zombies, and what do zombies have to do with consciousness?

DAVE: Zombies don't exist. That's what's interesting about them. Zombies are hypothetical creatures. They're physically identical to you and me; they look the same. They walk, they talk, they behave; they're incredibly sophisticated, just like we are—but they aren't conscious. They have no inner lives, no awareness, no subjective experiences. This is what makes these strange, spooky beings zombies. Again, the interesting thing about zombies is that they

don't exist. We're not zombies. And that's precisely what we want a science of consciousness to explain. *Why* aren't we zombies? Why are we conscious beings? Why did nature produce self-aware beings like us? We humans are much more than this interesting physical structure of body and brain; we have subjective inner lives.

ROBERT: Your recent book, *The Conscious Mind,* makes a claim that consciousness is as much a fundamental building block of reality as is matter, energy, space, and time. Do you really believe that? Or are you just tweaking us a bit?

DAVE: Coming at the question of consciousness as a scientist, taking the scientific worldview, I ask simply, "What do we want to explain?" Let's start with the data. There are two kinds of data about consciousness. There's third-person data—what we observe about others: physical presences, biological structures, behavior, complex language, reactions, and the like. But then there's also first-person data—what we observe about ourselves—and this data we have to take incredibly seriously. Included here are the internal subjective sensations that are highly personal—such as, what the mind "feels like" to us, the complex experience of vision, mental immersion, and thought. So data about consciousness can be bifurcated into third-person data and first-person data, and I think there's reason to believe that these are irreducible to each other. What we want a science of consciousness to do is to take both persons seriously: the third-person data about brain and behavior and the first-person data about the mind and consciousness. We need to take inner experience as seriously as outer behavior and connect them up in a systematic theoretical paradigm. And that's what we need for a true science of consciousness.

ROBERT: Marilyn, as an anthropologist, you're a leading researcher in parapsychology, which is the scientific study of anomalous, sometimes startling, mental phenomena. How does parapsychology reflect on the nature of consciousness?

MARILYN: I think that we can assume that there's a physical, material basis to consciousness; all we have to do is take a sledgehammer and bang somebody over the head to see a reduction in consciousness. The key question

---

Most cultures believe that we're also capable of transcending this physical, material aspect of our being, that our consciousness is capable of stretching or expanding . . .

---

takes the next step and asks whether consciousness is anything more than what is physically or materially determined. Most cultures believe that we're also capable of transcending this physical, material aspect of our being, that our consciousness is capable of stretching or expanding—stretching out into the world, expanding beyond our bodies. There's a great deal of evidence in parapsychological research that suggests that there's some nonlocal exchange of information—such as between two people (i.e., telepathy)—that at the very least extends our definition of materialism. Though any kind of dualism may provoke skepticism, statistically significant data from parapsychology begins to support some kind of dualistic model, which John [Searle] mentioned before.

ROBERT: Lest he be miscast, John didn't mention dualism with much joy, but we'll let him have at you later.

ROBERT: Jim, you're a physicist who has written a book on consciousness, *Are We Unique?* What do you think—are we unique, and is consciousness a part of our uniqueness?

JIM: I think it's possible to be a good twenty-first century materialist who thinks that the brain is a physical, chemical system that operates according to known, or at least knowable, laws and still think that there's something different about human consciousness—something remarkable that can't be reproduced by machines and hasn't been seen in animals. This was the "uniqueness" question I approached in my book. And I must tell you, it was a question about which, as a scientist, I had a deep emotional concern. How do you reconcile the scientific view of a human being as basically a machine with the first-person experience that Dave [Chalmers] talked about: the sure sense of my inner self that I am not a machine? That's one of the things I try to get at.

ROBERT: And that's a fundamental issue of human existence. Fred, you're also a physicist, trained in theoretical quantum physics. Yet you've written extensively on the spiritual essence of the universe and on the spiritual nature of human beings. Give us your take on consciousness. Dualism? Materialism? Where do you stand?

FRED: I choose "C," none of the above. We may be missing the boat here by adopting a view that one of these categories must be correct, whether empirical objectivity and physical materialism on the one hand or the rather archaic and simplistic dualistic models on the other. Possibly, there's a third choice—a choice that says that there's something beyond all materialism, beyond the physical world, out of which *all* reality, the whole of existence, projects. This would overwhelm traditional dualism—and I take this view not as a mystic but as a quantum physicist. I think that our most modern understanding of the physical world suggests that there may be an ineffable realm, a mystical realm, an "imaginal" realm, out of which the physical world pops into existence. Kind of like what [the German physicist and pioneer of quantum mechanics] Werner Heisenberg suggested when he brought the notion of consciousness into physics—when he said that it's the observer who creates the observed simply by the act of observation. So I answer the question of consciousness not by speculating about what it is, but by specifying what it does.

ROBERT: Let's get back to basics. Let's get some traditional characteristics of consciousness.

JOHN: The obvious characteristic is the one we all experience when we wake up in the morning. There are these qualitative, subjective states of sensation or personal feelings or inner awareness. For every consciousness state, there's something that it "feels like" to be in that consciousness state. So we know what it is to taste beer, and we know that tasting beer is different from feeling an itch, and that both sensations are different from smelling roses, which is nothing like the sensation of eating steak, and all of these are different from thinking about mathematics. Now, all of these things we "feel like" are conscious states; they all have this qualitative, subjective, inner character. So consciousness is what happens when you wake up in the morning from a dreamless sleep, and it continues throughout the day until you go to sleep again, or get hit on the head, or die, or otherwise become unconscious.

ROBERT: But don't all those "feel-like" states of the mind relate directly to physiological states of the brain?

JOHN: Of course they do. In my worldview, there isn't any question that consciousness is caused by brain processes. Anytime I have any doubts about that, all I have to do is take an aspirin, or drink too much whiskey, and I detect immediately the effect on my consciousness of changes in my brain.

ROBERT: Marilyn, what about this clear correspondence between mental states of the mind and physical states of the brain? When you drink too much alcohol, you do feel a little dizzy; when you get hit on the back of the head, you do see stars. Don't these facts undermine arguments for the dualistic nature of consciousness?

MARILYN: We make certain assumptions, and right now—at this point in human history, in this culture—we have a materialist worldview and a physicalist, reductionist approach to existence, whereby all explanations are reduced to fundamental physical properties. Therefore the questions that scientists commonly ask today about the nature of consciousness derive from this materialist worldview. They ask physical kinds of questions. The physical nature of consciousness is very real, but perhaps we need a broader definition of what is physical. If you look at the wisdom traditions—Buddhism, for example—you see a materialist model, too, but this kind of materialism defines matter to be much more encompassing than what we currently maintain within the physicalist model that defines Western science.

ROBERT: Dave, why do you talk about "easy problems" and "hard problems" in the study of consciousness?

DAVE: There are many different problems of consciousness. Even the word *consciousness* doesn't mean the same thing to all of us. When I'm talking about consciousness, I mean this. When you're talking about consciousness, you mean that. So there are many problems. Problem one has to do with behavior. How is it that we're able to get around in the world, to respond appropriately? For example, I look at you and say, "That's Robert." I can behave towards you; I can point at you; I can talk about you.

ROBERT: Nicely, I hope.

DAVE: Only if you're having a good day. But that's what we might call the relatively easy problem of consciousness: How is it that I can behave toward you in this conscious way? Now, the hard problems of consciousness are the problems of first-person subjective experience. While I'm doing all this sensing, acting, and behaving—looking at you, talking to you, talking about you—I'm also having inner, subjective experiences of you. It "feels like" something.

ROBERT: Simple as it sounds, this "feels-like" question is fundamental for understanding the true nature of consciousness.

DAVE: Right. I have internal visual images of you; I have thoughts about you running through my mind, maybe even with a little emotional affect attached. But why is all this internal stuff going on? Why is there a first-person inner life at all? Granted, it's probably connected, in some way, in my brain. But why *is* it that my brain processes produce these sub-

jective experiences of inner awareness? That's the hard problem.

ROBERT: Dave, do you see Jim [Trefil] over there? Usually he's a nice guy. But in his book about consciousness, here's what he wrote about you, and I paraphrase: If consciousness were a football game, you, Dave Chalmers, would forfeit right after the opening kickoff. In other words, he's saying that you seem to have thrown up your hands and given up too quickly in simply rejecting the mainstream materialist view. Now, maybe the metaphor should have been rugby [Dave is Australian], but you get the point.

DAVE: Jim said that?

JIM: The point is that there's a standard saying in the sciences that extraordinary claims require extraordinary proof. And so when you want to say, as Dave does, that we have to create this new category of reality which is somehow related to consciousness—or if you want to say that there's this other kind of dimension or this undetected part of our world—the first thing I want to know is, well, OK, why am I forced to consider this extreme possibility? Unless I see data saying that there's no way that I can avoid this unlikely scenario—that there's no way to explain all the things we're talking about just on the basis of the physical brain alone—then I'm not going to take that next step. Until I see proof of that, I'm not going to look beyond the physical.

FRED: You can't even explain physics without going beyond the physical! That's the answer, and it's very clear. If we talk about quantum mechanics, we have to talk about a quantum wave function, something that is clearly not material, not substantive, yet necessarily has to exist in order to explain the simplest physical phenomena.

JOHN: But isn't there a rather simple verbal shift that will at least get us to the point where we can address the same question? The traditional categories of the mental and the physical, as they're commonly used in popular speech and even in much of the sciences, are essentially seventeenth-century categories. And they're really out of date. What we're interested in is "how does the world work?" Now, one of the things I think we do know about the world is that consciousness exists. It's a *real* phenomenon in a real world, and it's a biological phenomenon caused by processes in the brain. Maybe consciousness is caused by some new kind of brain systems; we don't know that yet. But certainly consciousness is caused in the brain. By the way, Jim, I was amazed that you were seeming to deny consciousness to animals. Let's get serious here; there isn't any doubt that my dog Ludwig is conscious.

JIM: So's my dog.

ROBERT: We're now going to compare dogs?

JIM: No, but the point I was making was this. Everyone has his or her own idea of how the brain will ultimately be determined to produce

---

I think consciousness is an emergent property.

---

consciousness. My own particular idea comes from complexity theory—from what are called emergent properties. I think consciousness is an emergent property. Consciousness requires lots

of neurons conveying electrical information to be stuck together in brains, and like it or not, dogs have fewer neurons than the hundred billion that humans have. This is very much like what John [Searle] said—that these categories of consciousness are a seventeenth-century concept. We have this one word *consciousness,* and it has to describe everything.

ROBERT: I agree that this same word has to subsume every possible collection of neurons, whether found in humans, dogs, or worms. We don't yet know enough about the issue of mental awareness—let alone self-awareness—across species, and this is a problem, though I'm not sure it's *the* problem. Jim, do you think there's a significant difference between human consciousness and whatever exists of a similar nature in nonhuman animals?

JIM: Yes, I think so. At least you can make that argument. Someplace along the evolutionary track, you get to a certain complexity, and suddenly the properties of a system become fundamentally different. And such emergence has happened many times on the curious path to human beings—or to mammals or sea cucumbers.

JOHN: There are all kinds of differences between human and animal consciousness, but the essential thing is what Dave [Chalmers] was pointing to—namely, that they both have subjectivity, they both have these qualitative, inner experiences—and that's what we are all trying to explain. How do these qualitative inner experiences fit into the rest of the universe? And what I'm suggesting is that the traditional categories are not the way to pose the question.

DAVE: There's no question that a really deep connection exists between the brain and consciousness. If you duplicate my brain in reality, you're going to duplicate my consciousness in reality. You affect my brain, you affect my consciousness. The real question is, What is it about the brain that can explain consciousness? You can tell stories about how the neurons interact within the brain, such as how the prefrontal cerebral cortex produces motor responses [i.e., what happens in the brain to cause movements like fingers playing a piano]. This will explain only how I behave. It will explain how I can talk to you, and how I react to your constant questioning, and so on. Physical processes are really good for explaining physical structure and physical behavior. But once we get to consciousness, it seems that we're dealing with a whole new class of problems. It's no longer a problem about the structure and behavior of physical objects—it's now about the internal qualitative feel of inner mental awareness. And here is where the standard method of physical explanations may well need to be amended.

JOHN: [To Dave Chalmers] Do you believe in levels of consciousness? Is a mouse conscious? A fly? A virus? A piece of wood?

DAVE: I think there are degrees of consciousness, and there are very different kinds of consciousness. We humans have a particularly complex consciousness, as expressed by our language and as represented by our concepts. And we are conscious of ourselves. Now take a dog. A dog may well be conscious of the world around it—the internal hunger, the external food, fire hydrants, other dogs. But it may not be conscious of itself in the same complex, self-aware way that humans are. Go on to a fly. A fly is still sort of looking out at the world, and it may have some really simple kind of visual perceptual field. I don't see a reason to deny a simple kind of consciousness to a fly. The farther down you go

on the chain of animal complexity, the more diminished the degree of consciousness, but it's very much an open question.

ROBERT: Fred, how do you envision degrees of consciousness?

FRED: I'm not sure if the degree of consciousness ever diminishes. I'm not even sure that we humans are so super-conscious ourselves. I look at an anthill and I'm amazed at how human-like these simple creatures behave. The real question is trying to define what we mean by consciousness. This is the really crucial point that scientists need to think about. How do we define consciousness? What are the models we can use to approach the question? Materialism is not going to work. Pure subjectivity [i.e., idealism, the philosophical theory that only the mental is real and the physical is an illusion] is also not going to work. But something that somehow encompasses the two might work. This synthesis is what has to be brought about. Quantum mechanics might be the place to start to look. But even quantum mechanics is not going to be the final answer.

JOHN: I don't see the problem. Definitions sometimes come in two kinds: There's the detailed, comprehensive, technical definition that you give at the end of an investigation; we are nowhere near being able to do that for consciousness. But there's also the commonsense definition, where you simply identify the target of an investigation; that's rather easy. Let's try the commonsense definition here: Consciousness consists of these qualitative, subjective, inner states. You pinch yourself and you produce an altered state of consciousness—that is, you feel a pain that you didn't feel before. Now, that's what we're trying to explain. Eventually, of course, if we had a perfect science of the brain, we'd be able to give a comprehensive, scientific definition of consciousness. It would be like moving from the definition of water as a colorless, tasteless liquid to water as the molecule H_2O with a precise bonding structure. Regarding consciousness, we're still in the "colorless, tasteless liquid" phase. But there's no fundamental problem.

ROBERT: Would that comprehensive, scientific definition of consciousness include the possible need for a separate entity or independent category?

JOHN: No separate entity, not for me. I don't know about an independent category—but the point is that we want to be able to recognize that consciousness is a real feature in a real world. It's a biological phenomenon. It's real in the same sense that digestion or photosynthesis are real biological phenomena. We're not going to get rid of consciousness, or show that it doesn't really exist, or that it's all an illusion.

MARILYN: Let's build on that idea. If consciousness is a construct as much as it is a process, as we begin to try and do science on consciousness, we need to recognize the dichotomy between the first-person and the third-person data that Dave [Chalmers] offered us and expand it. We have our first-person subjectivity—that inner experience. We have the third-person objectivity, which we can study using electrodes and Positron Emission Tomography (PET scans) and different kinds of physiological monitoring techniques. But there is another "person." I believe we must include in any appreciation of consciousness the second-person perspective, which is the *relational* aspect of consciousness. All of our concepts, our symbols, the meaning systems by which we can even have this conversation, are based on a shared set of cultural assumptions. I'd like to use this second-person perspective to

comment on what Jim [Trefil] said, that until there are data to support the notion that there's something more than a physical brain state of consciousness, he won't be willing to buy it. I would say that a key to understanding consciousness is the problem of the second person. I seek the liberation of the second person in the study of consciousness. I believe that a second-person perspective provides a fresh set of assumptions, a new cognitive framework, in which we can formulate our opinions, ask our questions. And so I would submit that there are data out there suggesting that consciousness is more than just the brain—or at least suggesting that the brain's capacities are far more than what we've currently reduced them to. But because our worldview—our Western scientific way of thinking—limits our assumptions, we interpret those data with a particular set of filters, which may limit our ability to actually get closer to truth about what is the nature of reality.

JIM: But now you're introducing the interaction between two brains, which of course is much more complex than the processes within a single brain itself.

MARILYN: But you can't have consciousness without a multiplicity of beings from all levels of psychological strata.

JOHN: It seems to me that you can have subjective states of awareness even if you're Robinson Crusoe on a desert island. You don't need a second-person perspective for consciousness. The point that Dave [Chalmers] was making— I was trying to make the same point—is that consciousness is a first-person mode of existence. Of course, you can't have a fully developed consciousness, of the kind we have, without second-person activities as well. You need language, which you can't have unless you can interact with other consciousnesses. Nor can you explain consciousness without appealing to the third-person fact that we have objectively existing brains in our skulls. But the actual existence of conscious states—the actual feeling of a pain, or the taste of the beer—these are first-person experiences.

ROBERT: Are you using a third-person analysis of biological processes to equate, say, gastric secretions in the stomach to consciousness "secretions" in the brain?

JOHN: Yes, absolutely. That's the point I'm making. Maybe we can create consciousness artificially in some machine, but as far as we know to date, it exists only in human brains and in certain animal brains. And it's probably not worthwhile worrying about how far down the biological strata consciousness goes. Since we don't know how consciousness works in our brain, we're not yet ready to worry about how it works in flies.

ROBERT: Dave, do you agree with the gastric secretions analogy?

DAVE: The difference as far as stomachs are concerned is that you can tell a physical story to make it transparently clear just why you find those gastric secretions there. You tell a physical story about the brain—how the neurons hook up to one another, how brain areas are wired together—and you can say that this is what produces consciousness, and probably it does, but does that explain *why* it produces consciousness? No. Consciousness seems to be an irreducible, further fact that seems to be tacked on to the story somewhere. What we need in the science of consciousness is an explanatory theory that connects brain processes and mental self-awareness.

JIM: Doesn't that depend on what kind of explanation it turns out to be? Look at where we're starting. It's like sitting around in the year 1600 and arguing about electronics four hundred years in the future. We have no idea what the science of complexity is going to tell us about how the brain is organized.

ROBERT: I think it's fashionable to underestimate how much we do know about the brain and overestimate how much there is yet to know. I'm not sure whether what there's yet to know will qualitatively increase our understanding of the neural basis of first- or second-person consciousness.

JOHN: We do have one fact we can start with. We know that it happens—we know that the brain produces consciousness. Now, from the fact that we know that the brain does it, we can at least formulate a well-defined question: How does the brain do it? That's the basis on which we have to proceed. Of course, it may turn out that our existing neurobiological paradigms are inadequate to explain the special essence of consciousness and maybe we need some complete scientific revolution. But we have to recognize that, one, consciousness exists, and two, consciousness is caused by the brain.

ROBERT: John, tell me about those who would take issue with you and deny altogether the very existence of consciousness. The brain is real, they contend, but consciousness is not. What are their best arguments? I want you to honestly be your own opponent here.

JOHN: I've dealt with these guys for years; I don't have any problem telling you their arguments.

ROBERT: I'm listening carefully.

JOHN: OK, here we go. Their argument goes as follows: Science demonstrates that the way the world works is entirely physical or material. Nothing exists that is not physical. Therefore if some people still believe that consciousness requires something else to exist—something in addition to the physical, some touchy-feely, airy-fairy kind of stuff like Searle kind of talks about—then it must be unscientific and hence imaginary. Consciousness can't be anything like that. So consciousness is in fact an illusion—an artificial, artifactual, deceptive illusion generated by . . . (and here follows whatever your favorite theory is). Nowadays the favorite theory is "by computer programs in our brains," and these programs, we're told, is all that consciousness ever was. How about that? Was that honest enough?

DAVE: For much of this century, science has been afraid of subjectivity. Science is meant to be objective, right? No subjective elements allowed.

For much of this century, science has been afraid of subjectivity.

But consciousness is subjective by its very nature, so some people conclude, by *a priori* definition, either that science can't touch consciousness or that consciousness doesn't exist.

ROBERT: It's interesting how the latest brain theory always employs the latest technology—modern mechanisms as modern metaphors. At the beginning of the century, the brain was likened to a telephone exchange, with wires plugging and unplugging. Later it was likened to electronic circuits, then simple computers, then holograms. Remember the hologram period of brain theory, where all parts of the brain stored all the same memories? Recently, the metaphors have grown more intricate, with parallel computing, and now even quantum physics and complexity theory.

JOHN: Look back all the way to the Greeks. Greek thinkers thought that the brain was a kind of catapult.

FRED: There's something very important that we're leaving out. Even the notion of a subject is questionable. Take Buddhism's concept of consciousness: There is no subject. It's something that arises momentarily, spontaneously, and then disappears.

ROBERT: Fred, is consciousness a useful concept?

FRED: Well, sociologically, we need to understand consciousness, because we build pictures of the world based upon how we envision the world. If we can understand how brains are conditioned by certain ways of seeing, if we can understand how differences in perceiving can yield differences in actions, then I think we've come a long way. Take some mundane examples: In advertising, how do images and ideas affect the minds of the audience? In politics, why did we choose this candidate and not that one? In Hollywood, why do we like that movie star and not this one? All of these attitudes have to do with the nature of our human consciousness.

ROBERT: Jim, wouldn't many of your fellow physicists believe that research funds spent on consciousness would be more productively employed in building larger accelerators?

JIM: No, I think there's a pretty good recognition that the study of the brain, in which I embed the study of consciousness, is the real frontier for the next century. What happened, as John [Searle] alluded to, is that we now think we understand how to ask the questions. We start with neurons. We understand a little bit about how the brain works and we see how we can understand a whole lot more. And that's why, in the scientific community, brains are hot.

MARILYN: At this point, I don't think we do know the right questions to ask about consciousness. I think we're just beginning to formulate some questions, let alone come up with any answers about the nature of this great mystery.

ROBERT: John, do you think that the wisdom traditions and religion can make significant contributions to the study of consciousness?

JOHN: I'm open-minded. My theory is, use any weapon you can lay your hands on, use any data you can find. If you can get interesting data from mystics or swamis or people in altered states,

---

. . . when ultimately we solve the problem of consciousness, we'll have done it by examining actual biological mechanisms.

---

that's fine by me; just use all the weaponry you can. But I think that when ultimately we solve the problem of consciousness, we'll have done it by examining actual biological mechanisms. You're going to have to get deep into the thalamo-

cortical system and find out how these critical brain processes work.

ROBERT: But once we do, when we have finally worked out a comprehensive biological mechanism of consciousness, will you then be satisfied that consciousness is completely explained?

JOHN: Absolutely!

ROBERT: Marilyn, will you be satisfied by biology alone?

MARILYN: I would say that a complete explanation of consciousness will require an integrated research agenda. Surely we acknowledge the physical dimensions that John [Searle] and Jim [Trefil] refer to, but we also need to recognize that consciousness can't be completely explained in isolation from other people—there's a social, cultural dimension. Going further, I also think there's compelling data to suggest that consciousness also includes a *transpersonal* component, something beyond individual awareness. The mystics and sages of all the ages haven't all been deluded; their insights and visions can't all be categorically rejected. Ultimately, a complete explanation of consciousness is going to have to accommodate these various perceptions.

ROBERT: It seems we've found a fundamental disagreement here.

JOHN: I don't think there's any out-of-brain consciousness.

ROBERT: And you do, Fred?

FRED: I'm convinced there is. I rely not only on my readings of the traditions of many cultures and religions, but also on some extraordinary experiences that I personally have had with shamans in various parts of the world.

ROBERT: Jim, no out-of-body consciousness for you, right?

JIM: I'll keep an open mind, but right now I don't see why we need it.

DAVE: John says that consciousness is caused by the brain, that consciousness arises from the brain. But I think there can be subtle problems with cause and effect. Cause and effect are often different things. So even if consciousness does arise from the brain, it isn't at all clear that consciousness must therefore be reducible to the brain. One must keep these two separate domains distinct, even if interwoven, in their fundamental natures.

ROBERT: A summary question: Fast-forward a hundred years. What has happened to consciousness?

JOHN: In a hundred years, and I hope before that, we're going to know how the brain does it. As we talk here, there are very confident people working on precisely this question: By what processes, exactly, do human and animal brains cause consciousness? And I think we're going to know the answer to that.

MARILYN: We'll recognize the limits of a strictly physical, materialist model. We'll have begun to embrace some of the expanded aspects of our being so that we can grapple with the serious social problems that we're facing today.

JIM: I think we'll understand the brain in terms of neurons, and we'll understand how this phenomenon of consciousness arises from that.

ROBERT: Fred, I hope you don't agree with these guys.

FRED: Well, I don't entirely disagree, but I'll reverse it. What we're going to understand in a hundred years is possibly how consciousness creates brains! And how brains arise from the messiness of reality.

DAVE: I think we'll be closer to creating a sort of fundamental principle connecting physical processes and processes of conscious experience. When we have a simple set of fundamental principles—like the laws of physics—then we'll have a theory of consciousness.

ROBERT: CONCLUDING COMMENT

You are not a zombie, and you know it. What it means to be conscious directly affects what it means to be human. The strongest current theory is that consciousness is a complex, emergent property of the brain—a property not easily, or perhaps not ever, reducible to simple states of the brain. This means that consciousness "emerges" from all the complex electrical and chemical activities in our brains, something like an atomic bomb "emerges" from a critical mass of uranium, or a molecule of water "emerges" from two atoms of hydrogen and one atom of oxygen. So while consciousness is produced by the brain, we may never know quite how. But I can't shake the thought that consciousness may also be something else—a more fundamental description of self-aware beings like us, a special part of reality. With philosophers and physicists disagreeing among themselves, it is good that the study of consciousness is becoming a scientific field of great promise. For now, this divergence of opinion is what brings us closer to truth.

OUTTAKES

FRED: *I love all your thinking.*

DAVE: *That was good fun.*

MARILYN: *John, where did you do your academic work?*

JOHN: *I started at Wisconsin, but then I went to Oxford. I was nineteen and I stayed there forever.*

MARILYN: *Well, the best thing you got from there was a wife, huh?*

JOHN: *That's right.*

CHAPTER 2

Do Brains Make Minds?

What are you thinking about right now? Perhaps you're deciding whether to continue reading this book or to pay a bunch of bills gathering on your desk. Where are you thinking that thought? In your brain? In your mind? This is the crux of the *mind-body problem:* What is the relationship between the thoughts in our minds and the brains in our heads? This is one of the fundamental issues in philosophy and it has enticed thinkers for centuries. Is gray matter all that matters, or is "mind stuff" different in kind from "brain stuff"? Is there something unique and nonmaterial about the human mind, something not crammed into our craniums? Today, the relationship between brain and mind is the subject of intense scientific debate. What is special about the human brain compared with, say, the brains of chimps or dolphins? Or compared with the artificial brains of computers? Modern brain research—that is, neuroscience—provides a deep understanding of our processes of cognitive thought, sensory perception, emotional feelings, and behavioral actions. But can neuroscience explain love and hate, ambition and altruism, music and art? Can neuroscience solve the mind-body problem? We have five expert views.

PARTICIPANTS

Dr. Barry Beyerstein, a brain scientist, is a professor of neuropsychology at Simon Fraser University in Canada. Barry is a skeptic who does not believe in anything nonphysical.

Dr. David Chalmers is co-director of the Center for Consciousness Studies at the University of Arizona. Dave believes that correlations between brain states and mental events do not prove that brain causes mind.

Dr. Marilyn Schlitz is an anthropologist and parapsychologist at the Institute of Noetic Sciences. Marilyn asserts that we can have experiences outside the brain.

Dr. John Searle, the author of many books about the mind such as *Minds, Brains and Science,* is the Mills Professor of Philosophy at the University of California, Berkeley. John focuses on the problem of how the brain causes experiences.

Dr. Fred Alan Wolf, a theoretical physicist, is the author of The *Dreaming Universe: A Mind-Expanding Journey into the Realm Where Psyche and Physics Meet.* Fred speculates that reality is more spiritual dream than physical manifestation.

ROBERT: Barry, you're a materialist who believes that only the physical is real. Does that mean you believe that the mind is the output of the brain, just as urine is the output of the kidneys?

BARRY: The brain and the kidneys are both physical organs. Both have anatomical structures and physiological processes that generate particular things. And, yes, the output of one is urine and the output of the other is thought.

ROBERT: John, your book *The Rediscovery of the Mind* helped to return the mind to the front burner of intellectual inquiry. How do you assess the increasing confidence—some might call it arrogance—of neuroscientists like Barry, who are virtually asserting that they have solved the mind-body problem?

JOHN: Well, I don't detect any arrogance—though I'm sorry that Barry's so down on kidneys. But I do think he would agree that we have a long way to go in understanding how the brain works. Most of the neuroscientists I know are very cautious about the progress we've made in understanding the brain, and in fact progress has been very slow. It's laborious to try to understand how the brain does anything. It may even be a little overoptimistic to state that we now can explain sensory perception, much less emotions. We don't really understand how percep-

tion works. We can more or less track the visual system from the back of the eye through the midbrain to the cerebral cortex at the rear surface of the brain. Maybe we can figure out what's going on in the midbrain, but when we get to the visual areas of the cerebral cortex, though we can relate certain simple perceptions to neuron function, unifying these perceptions into visual awareness gets to be mysterious.

ROBERT: Any solutions here to the mind-body problem?

JOHN: There are really two mind-body problems. One is the overall philosophical question: What are the general relationships between the mind and the brain? And I think we can now say what those are: Brain processes cause mental states and mental states are realized in the brain. But the second mind-body problem is what Dave [Chalmers] calls the hard problem: How exactly does it work? How do brain processes cause mental states? And we don't know the answer to that.

ROBERT: Marilyn, you're director of research at the Institute of Noetic Sciences and have conducted some of the leading experiments in parapsychology. And you've produced strong, if controversial, evidence for rather startling abilities of the human mind to apprehend images in ways not explainable by neuroscience. How do you assess the claims being made by many scientists that the mind is strictly the physical output of the brain and nothing more?

MARILYN: I would take the position of a radical empiricist, in that I am driven by data, not theory. And the data I see tells me that there are ways in which people's experience refutes the physicalist position that the mind is the brain and nothing more. There are solid, concrete data that suggest that our consciousness, our mind, may surpass the boundaries of the brain. So I think it's important that we keep a balanced perspective.

ROBERT: Dave, your book *The Conscious Mind* makes the controversial case for "mind" and "consciousness" being a primary element of reality, like mass and energy, and not an epiphenomenon, or secondary phenomenon, arising meaninglessly from the brain. What would it take for you to reverse your position—change your mind, as it were—and discard the mind as a primary element of reality and realize that you should have been a good old materialist all along, like Barry [Beyerstein], believing that mind is just the output of the brain as urine is just the output of the kidneys? What kind of data would you have to see?

DAVE: Well, I started out life as a materialist, because materialism is a very attractive scientific and philosophical doctrine.

ROBERT: Materialism is the philosophical position that only the physical is real, and anything else, like mind or consciousness, are just artifacts or illusions. What you can't know through the normal senses cannot exist.

DAVE: Brain research is going to give us better and better correlations between states of the brain and events in the mind. That's what we're

seeing now; it's beginning to happen. We find these kinds of strong correlations in many areas. Take the visual cortex, which is associated with certain kinds of visual experiences. Areas of brain function and different states of consciousness are indeed coming together. But finding correlation is not the same as finding an explanation, a reduction of mind to brain.

ROBERT: I take it you mean that correlation is not cause. Correlations of brain states with mental events can't reduce the mental to the physical. To claim that there is nothing in the mind not generated by something in the brain would be a philosophical leap too far.

DAVE: To truly bridge the gap between the physical nature of brain physiology and the mental essence of consciousness, we have to satisfy two different conceptual demands. It's not yet looking very likely that we're going to reduce the mind to the brain. In fact, there may be systematic reasons to think there will always be a gulf between the physical and the mental.

ROBERT: Are you saying that neuroscientists will never be able to bridge the gap between mind and brain? Is there no evidence that can be discovered or produced that would convince you that mind and consciousness are just the output of brains and brain cells? Are you saying that such proof is impossible?

DAVE: Well, I think all the evidence is going to be about correlation, not about cause. So we're going to have input/output, if you like—input to the brain, output to the mind. But the really interesting question is, How do you get from input to output?

ROBERT: I want to push you; this is fundamental. Are you saying that it's logically impossible for any data in brain research to make you change your mind and accept materialism?

DAVE: All the data are about correlation. The question of whether correlation, however strong, is in itself an explanation or reduction isn't a scientific question; it isn't an empirical question. It's strictly a philosophical question.

ROBERT: So, again, you're determining that it's philosophically impossible for brain to explain mind, for mind to be reduced to brain? Brain research can never make you a materialist?

DAVE: Brain research is providing more and more data about the correlations. But how you interpret the data will always be a philosophical question.

ROBERT: Barry, are you more open-minded than Dave? Could you envision any data that could make you reject materialism? Could any imaginable evidence convince you that radical physicalism is not the right description of the world but that there is something more to the human mind than what resides in the human brain?

BARRY: Actually, I agree with Dave [Chalmers]. At its heart, the mind-body problem is a philosophical question. Yet I go back to what Gertrude Stein said: "Difference isn't a difference unless it makes a difference." I can't see anything that we need to bring in from the outside to explain anything in neuroscience. I'm going to push the materialist position as far as it will go. It's conceivable that someday I could come up against something that doesn't fit the neuroscience model of mind, and if that happens, then I'll have to change my mind.

ROBERT: Fred, as a physicist, you've written books on what you call "the spiritual universe"

and "the dreaming universe." What convictions do you have that don't fit Barry's worldview of the strictly neuroscience model of mind?

FRED: Almost nothing fits. In many ways, I agree with Dave [Chalmers] that there's really no way that materialism is going to explain consciousness. Sure, they're correlated—it's a necessary correlation, just like an automobile can go from one place to another because there's a driver inside. But I see reality differently. Reality to me is more like a dream—I see a dreaming reality. I envision a dreamer, or a great spirit, of which we're all a part. Reality as a dreamer dreaming a dream. And I think that using this model we can achieve some real scientific breakthroughs, rather than attempting to reduce everything down to the simplest level.

ROBERT: John, does this sound like a ghost in the machine to you?

JOHN: I think this whole debate so far is totally misconceived, and I can't resist saying a little bit why. Of course we're going to find correlations, just as we did with the germ theory of disease.

I think this whole debate so far is totally misconceived . . .

But then the next step—again, just as with the germ theory of disease—is reduction, to find out cause. [Ignaz] Semmelweis in Vienna, with his obstetrics patients, first found a correlation; then he found causation. First you find a correlation, then you find a causal relation and a causal mechanism. Now, this is precisely how we're going to do it in brain research. Once we move from correlation to cause in neuroscience, then all these old-fashioned categories, like materialism [only the physical is real] and dualism [some nonphysical entity is needed to explain mind], will fall by the wayside.

ROBERT: Will states of the mind ultimately be reducible to states of the brain?

JOHN: No, but for a kind of trivial reason. Consciousness is not going to be reducible to brain states because it has a first-person ontology, by which I mean that consciousness exists only from the point of view of some agent or organism that experiences it. In this sense, states of the mind are subjective, while states of the brain are objective. So we can't get a reduction of mind to brain in the classical philosophical sense, but we can still get a solid, satisfying scientific explanation. That's all I think any of you guys really want.

ROBERT: Marilyn, do you agree with me that John is a closet materialist?

MARILYN: I'm not sure he's in the closet at all; I think he's out in the open. For me, there's a compelling body of data [from parapsychology and extrasensory perception research] suggesting that we can supersede our brain—that we can move our awareness, our sense of self, out into the world beyond our bodies, in ways that are not reducible to states of the brain. If we're ever going to have a complete science of the mind and brain, this extraordinary data will have to be accommodated by the neuroscience perspective. I don't know what we'll end up with.

ROBERT: I hear Marilyn saying something remarkably strong. If neuroscience ever hopes to form a true picture of reality, of how mind and brain constitute consciousness, it has to include data from parapsychology and allied

fields. Science as it is currently constituted will never get there.

MARILYN: A complete science has to speak to all the data, including the internal sense of everyday experience, rather than assuming that we can fit everything into a purely physical scheme that simply reduces mind to brain. A reductionist model just doesn't include all the data.

JOHN: Well, I hear Marilyn saying something even stronger than that—namely, that you can have experiences outside the brain.

MARILYN: Yes.

JOHN: I don't see any evidence of that. We have our hands full trying to figure out what goes on in the brain. If I had a theory of how the brain causes experience, I would feel that that was a pretty good day's work. Then, if somebody wants to go and figure out how there can be experiences outside the brain, OK, but that's for tomorrow.

ROBERT: Why should we wait? If you feel there's even a remote possibility that we can have experiences outside the brain, and perhaps collect quantifiable, scientifically determined evidence to verify this claim, then your whole approach to the mind-body problem must suddenly shift. You have a radically new subject. Aren't you postponing what could be revolutionary?

JOHN: If you had some really conclusive data, sure. But there's nothing in the neuroscience literature offering conclusive data for out-of-body conscious experiences. You don't want to exclude the possibility *a priori,* but if I'm a neuroscientist with a job to do, I'm going to spend my time figuring out how the brain does it. And if somebody can then give me solid data demonstrating that there's stuff going on outside the brain, that's terrific. That would mean there are diseases that aren't caused by the germ theory.

ROBERT: I agree that scientists are more likely to do good science by remaining in their own disciplines. If you're a pathologist, you're best off staying within pathology. Neuroscientists are no different. But science sometimes requires a few fearless souls—no metaphysics intended—to step outside the common order and risk failure, even ridicule. What Marilyn is saying, and Fred as well, is that there's a whole world of consciousness outside neuroscience, and that unless you consider this data, you're not going to truly understand the nature of the mind or the construction of reality.

JOHN: Let the people who are absolutely convinced that they have solid data for out-of-body conscious experiences do the research on what they think are worldview-changing occurrences. But those of us who have a well-defined research project—namely, how the hell does the brain do it?—should concentrate on this vital, scientifically clear work. We know that the brain does it; let's figure out how. After that, if you believe that you can corroborate mental stuff going on outside the brain, then fine. As for me, I'm very skeptical about it. I've never seen anything that's even remotely supportive—but let's keep an open mind about it.

ROBERT: Do I sense a slight pejorative tinge in your phrase "out-of-body"?

JOHN: That's what Marilyn is talking about, right?

MARILYN: If we want to accommodate the full nature of human experience, and to fully understand who we are as unique human beings, then we have to move out of this box that limits our inquiries—we have to move beyond the easy questions. We have to expand our search to include the personal, introspective observations that people make in every culture, every day of their lives.

FRED: I just want to say that there's an assumption here that John is making—and all of us are, to some extent—that the subjective "I" is within the body. This is not a clear evidential statement. It seems obvious, but it's absolutely not provable. You cannot scientifically prove that your "I" is in your body. There's no scientific evidence for that.

BARRY: Look, if I manipulate your brain [give

Look, if I manipulate your brain . . . your consciousness is going to change.

---

you coffee, alcohol, drugs], your consciousness is going to change.

FRED: That may be, but you don't know that.

JOHN: The point I'm making is that the "I" that I live with is in my body.

FRED: You don't know that.

JOHN: Well, "I" see.

FRED: You believe that's true.

JOHN: I wake up in the morning and there isn't any question whose body this "I" is in. If I can figure out how that mechanism works, that would be terrific. Whoever can explain that [how one's mental sense of self is formed from the billions of neurons in one's head] should get the Nobel Prize.

FRED: What if you were to wake up in another reality? What if you suddenly realized that your "I" was in an alternate reality?

JOHN: Terrific! Have you ever had that experience?

ROBERT: Even if Fred's "I" has had such alternative-reality wakings and realizations, the easiest explanation is that Fred was just dreaming. (Fred likes to dream.) That's what dreams are—sensations of alternate realities that are artifacts constructed by states of the brain, usually while you're asleep.

FRED: That's not the point. As long as you have a paradigm you're always going to try to define things within that paradigm. What I'm saying is, your paradigm ain't big enough. We

---

. . . your paradigm ain't big enough.

---

need to go beyond the egocentric, "I"-centered worldview that a subject exists only in a body.

ROBERT: Let's come back down to bodies on earth. Let's talk about comparative anatomy—specifically, how the human brain compares with the brains of various animals. If brain is the sole cause of mind, we should be able to plot some additional data points by investigating the correlations between mind and brain in other

species. Barry [Beyerstein], describe briefly the relationship between the human brain and the brains of chimps or dolphins.

BARRY: The basic floor plan of the mammalian brain is remarkably similar, from the human brain down through the rest of the mammalian chain. But what differentiates human brains from the brains of other animals is probably the most interesting part—and, I think, one of the most profound pieces of evidence in favor of the idea that the brain is the organ of consciousness. If you compare brains, as comparative neuranatomists and evolutionary biologists do, what you find is that as the brain develops—gets larger, more complicated, and more interconnected—new mental processes emerge that didn't exist prior to that. Take the dolphin brain and the human brain, for instance. Huge parts of our brains—that is, the higher sections of the cerebral cortex—are devoted to vision, which is to be expected, since vision is our primary sense. In dolphins, brain areas devoted to vision are relatively smaller—which is again to be expected, since vision is not the primary sense of dolphins, whose environment is the ocean. Dolphin brains have a larger area devoted to hearing, since dolphins live in a world requiring a three-dimensional auditory sense, which they use for active echolocation; and their brains are structured accordingly, with huge areas devoted to that.

ROBERT: How about the relative size of the dolphin brain compared with the human brain?

BARRY: The dolphin brain is a little larger. So size isn't everything.

ROBERT: Would you say a dolphin is conscious?

BARRY: Yes, I think so. There's much good research on higher mental processes in dolphins such as problem-solving.

ROBERT: Let's review the facts. The dolphin brain is larger than the human brain, with more auditory than visual territory. In this context, what about the output of the dolphin brain versus the output of the human brain, say, in terms of social accomplishment or mental activity? Doesn't there seem a mismatch here, a disconnect? Either dolphins are a whole lot smarter than we think or there may be something really interesting going on in the human brain. Fred, what's your feeling about this?

FRED: This is a very difficult question.

ROBERT: Should I ask you only easy ones?

FRED: We have thumbs, which allows us to manipulate the world better than dolphins can. And we have consciousness in our thumbs.

ROBERT: Now you sound like Dave [Chalmers]—seeing consciousness in lots of strange places.

FRED: I don't believe that consciousness is limited to the brain. I think there's consciousness in the body. Whatever consciousness does, it's adapted in the dolphin to form that kind of entity. It's not that a dolphin has consciousness; it's that consciousness has a dolphin. Consciousness also has a Fred Wolf, which appears momentarily and disappears—

ROBERT: Is there something special about dolphins and Fred Wolf that spawns such attention from consciousness?

FRED: Consciousness also has a Robert Kuhn. It has a John Searle. Consciousness has it all. It seems to me that this model of reality, because it encompasses more, can help us explain something. We need to go back and look at the ways in which ancient peoples first began to think about consciousness.

ROBERT: Dave, we discussed this in the previous program [Chapter 1], but it's worth going into here: Do you see consciousness as different in humans and animals?

DAVE: I think humans and animals have a lot in common. They all perceive, learn, remember, act on the world, in broadly similar ways. I think they're all conscious. What's different in humans is that we have language.

ROBERT: And language engenders self-consciousness?

DAVE: Language gives us a set of concepts that come along with that. Take the word *I*. When we got the word *I*, we got self-consciousness and also the articulated set of concepts that goes with it.

ROBERT: If language in general and the concept of *I* in particular constitute a fundamental difference between human and animal cognition, how do you account for language in humans? Especially since the brains of humans and animals are so similar and the dolphin brain is even larger than the human brain.

DAVE: I think the human brain is a lot more developed. It's learned to make many fine-grained distinctions. Somewhere along the line, something happened in the evolution of our brains that gave us the ability to speak.

BARRY: The floor plan is similar; it's the small differences that distinguish the human brain from the brains of other mammals.

ROBERT: There's no mystery to language. Neuroscientists can locate where language is generated by the brain. Stroke victims can be lucid but totally unable to speak if the traumatic insult was to one of these specific language areas.

JOHN: There isn't any question about it. For most people, language is located on the left side of the brain. Humans have specialized language areas in the brain that don't exist in other primate brains.

DAVE: Apes and parrots use language in very simple ways, and it's interesting to see them doing that. A parrot can be trained to talk. Apes use signs, and they can communicate by pointing. But none of these rudimentary activities is like the human version of complex, articulated language.

ROBERT: Marilyn, do you see qualitative differences between humans and animals?

MARILYN: What intrigues me about your question is the notion of extended capacities. There are creatures, like bats and dolphins, who have the ability to echolocate, by means of resources we don't use in our repertoire of capabilities. In a dog, the olfactory senses are highly developed. All of this leads me to wonder what capacities of the human brain are going untapped. What capabilities might allow us to actualize certain unrecognized aspects of our experience that go far beyond the constraints that the materialist box would impose on us?

ROBERT: Are you saying that the small anatomical difference between human and animal brains is precisely related to the sharp differences between human and animal mental activity?

MARILYN: I wouldn't reduce it to that.

ROBERT: But that's what everyone else seems to be saying.

MARILYN: I simply don't know. Ultimately, at the end of the day, if it turns out that we can reduce it all to the brain, I would say, "Fine!" My point is that we really don't have enough information about what the capacities of the brain are to understand how a purely physical model of reality would accommodate such a broad range of human experiences, including parapsychological phenomena such as out-of-the-body experiences. We don't know the potential of what our experiences might become if we could really harness and utilize our brains.

ROBERT: But John, you're saying that the fact that the human brain has a language area is the one key factor that differentiates human beings from animals?

JOHN: Well, there are other differences, but if you had to say in one sentence what the difference is between humans and animals, as far as consciousness and mental life is concerned, it's language. Once you have language, you can get all kinds of experiences you can't get otherwise. Animals can have pair-bonding, but they can't, in our sense, fall in love. They can't have a love affair, because for that you need a vocabulary. They can't suffer the angst of postindustrial man under late capitalism. Now, I have that angst all the time, but I couldn't have it without language.

MARILYN: You haven't met my dog.

JOHN: The point is that the ability to structure experience linguistically gets you a kind of self-referential capacity. That is to say, you can have words that refer to the emotions of which that word is a component part. As a French philosopher said, "Very few people would ever fall in love if they had never read about it." Nowadays, you need to see it on television or in the movies. In order to fall in love, you need a vocabulary—a whole scenario—that goes with it. And this is true, cross-culturally, of all human beings.

ROBERT: So you're reducing the fundamental difference between humans and animals to language?

JOHN: It's not "reducing."

ROBERT: I'm trying to make you a reductionist.

JOHN: No, I'm not a reductionist. It's an extension. What I'm saying is . . . I love Ludwig—that's my dog. He's wonderful and we communicate well. But when it comes to doing philosophy, poor thing, he can't even keep up with me. To do philosophy, you have to be able to talk.

MARILYN: But we shouldn't privilege one way of knowing over another. It's obvious that there are things that are unique about human abilities as compared with those of dogs or birds or ants. But in the same way that our human differences make for a more interesting human soup, the multiple ways of knowing among species add to the repertoire of what makes life so interesting and rich. It's really about the diversity of ways of knowing. And humans are not necessarily superior on this kind of social evolutionary ladder to dogs or any other creature.

JOHN: If Ludwig could talk, the first thing he'd say is, "How come you humans can't smell at all?"

MARILYN: Exactly.

ROBERT: I think all of you are being too politically correct.

JOHN: I'm accused of that?

ROBERT: Well, in terms of mental output, the difference between humans and animals far exceeds the small anatomical and physiological differences we see in their respective brains. And I think that's not been explained.

JOHN: Human and animal differences are huge, but they're made possible by those anatomical differences.

ROBERT: That's a philosophical point of view, not an experimental one.

JOHN: We have people who've suffered damage to parts of their brains, and they go back to existences that are like Ludwig's.

ROBERT: Yes, but humans who can't see or hear are just as conscious, and can be just as literate, as anyone else.

DAVE: Here's a better difference. Let's see what humans can do without the aid of culture. A lot of what makes us as smart as we are is the cultural apparatus and substructure that we've built up in our society. Culture is largely made possible through language and through communication. With culture, we're all smart. We can stand on the shoulders of our ancestors and we can see everything. Now suppose you bring me up in the wild, without culture, without much in the way of language, then you'll see how smart I am intrinsically.

JOHN: Is this a personal confession?

DAVE: None of us would be anything much without culture.

JOHN: When we say "language," we don't just mean making noises through our mouths, but also things like money, property, marriage, government. The stock market. Interest rates. Congress. Elections.

ROBERT: You mean that all of these things that are culturally constituted or socially instituted can be traced back down to language?

JOHN: Absolutely. You can't have any of them without language. The capacity for expressing yourself in spoken words and storing linguistic data in written words is a tremendous revolution. Given that, culture becomes possible.

ROBERT: In philosophical terms, then, language is necessary for the development of human thought and collective human culture—but is it sufficient?

JOHN: No, but we have constructed language in such a way that it's sufficient for us. By itself, language is not sufficient. But as we have evolved thousands of years from the earliest forms of language, we have simultaneously evolved human civilization in all its color and variety. Language alone isn't sufficient; you've got to have this development. It's a kind of bootstrapping effect that we've used to build human culture—all done with our marginally better brains.

ROBERT: So we have animals and humans on the same general spectrum of consciousness.

Now consider computers—massively parallel supercomputers—and go out numerous generations. The big question of the moment is, Can computers become conscious?

JOHN: I've been in an argument with these people, and the short answer is no, because if you define a computer in the classic sense as a device that manipulates formal symbols—usually zeroes and ones—then that by itself is not enough for consciousness and mental life, because such manipulations are a purely formal operation.

ROBERT: Why can't formal operations, at some level of complexity, generate consciousness?

JOHN: It's the difference between syntax as a bunch of symbols and semantics as meaning. There's a one-sentence proof of this. It's kind of a long sentence, but anyway . . . imagine that you're the computer, and imagine a task that you don't know how to perform. I don't know how to speak Chinese.

ROBERT: Go to your Chinese Room.

JOHN: I imagine myself locked in a room, and I have a rule book in the form of a computer program that enables me to answer questions put to me in Chinese. So the Chinese symbols come in, and I look up in the rule book what I'm supposed to do in response to each symbol, and the rule book gives me other Chinese symbols. I look at a symbol that comes in, and I look up what symbols I'm supposed to respond with, and I give back those Chinese symbols as answers. To people outside the room, it might appear as if I understood Chinese. But I don't understand a word of Chinese, because all I have are the symbols—the syntax. Now—this is the point; it's the end of the sentence—if I don't understand Chinese, even though I'm implementing the program for understanding Chinese, then neither does any other digital computer on that basis, because that's all any computer can do. The computer is a device for manipulating formal symbols.

ROBERT: Dave, what do you see when you look inside a computer? Do you see syntax but no semantics, symbols but no meaning?

DAVE: Look inside a brain; you see a bunch of neurons interacting. Do you see any semantics in that? Somehow, and we don't know how, all those neurons interacting give rise to a conscious, meaningful mind. I don't see a difference in principle between carbon-based neurons, which are wet, and silicon-based chips, which are dry.

JOHN: OK, I'll tell you exactly the difference. The brain is a causal mechanism. "Computation" does not name a causal mechanism. It names a formal symbolic mechanism that can be implemented in a causal mechanism.

DAVE: A computer is a causal mechanism.

JOHN: You mentioned silicon. Computation has nothing to do with silicon. Computation is an abstract formal process that we, currently, in our backward technology, have found ways to implement in silicon. I have no objection to the idea that silicon might be conscious, but silicon has nothing to do with computation. Computation needs an abstract, formal symbolic process that we can implement in any medium whatever.

DAVE: I think the interesting thing about artificial intelligence is that what matters to the mind

is not the meat [i.e., brain tissue and cells]. It's not what the mind is composed of that's meaningful, it's the patterns, the infrastructure, which that meat constructs. Replace the meat in my brain, neuron by neuron, with silicon chips [assuming that each chip is functionally the

---

. . . what matters to the mind is not the meat.

---

same as the neuron it replaces]. What will happen? You're still going to have a causal mechanism for mind, but it will be a different causal mechanism. Even though this neuron-by-neuron, chip-by-chip replacement has created a new silicon-based structure, that structure is going to be the same kind of structure and cause the same kind of results.

ROBERT: Might not this chip-for-neuron replacement transform a conscious being into your favorite zombie, who would appear to do everything that the formerly conscious being did—react, behave, and so on—but now without self-awareness?

DAVE: You mean, is my consciousness going to fade out along the way, winking out incredibly slowly as each neuron is replaced by each chip? Why should it?

JOHN: Let's look closely at what you're saying. If you had one causal mechanism, the brain, and you replaced it with another causal mechanism made of silicon, whether or not the silicon would be conscious is an empirical, factual question, not something we can settle *a priori*. I think that's fine.

ROBERT: Please elaborate on what you think is fine.

JOHN: I think it's fine to hypothesize that you can create consciousness in some medium other than meat.

ROBERT: To hypothesize is one thing. To be able to do it in the real world is something else. Do you think it would ever be possible to create consciousness in some medium other than brains?

JOHN: I don't think so. I think it's out of the question.

ROBERT: You don't *think* you can?

JOHN: My statement is a factual thesis, not a philosophy proof. The philosophy proof goes as follows: Just having the formal symbols, abstract zeros and ones, by itself, isn't sufficient to guarantee the presence of consciousness.

DAVE: Any computer is more than zeros and ones. Any computer is not just symbols. It's about voltages and chips interacting with one another—

JOHN: Computation is not defined in terms of voltage.

DAVE: Computers are more than computation, more than zeros and ones.

ROBERT: But what is the brain doing that's so fundamentally different? Maybe, in addition to electrical impulses zipping around, the brain also works by broad electrical field transmissions. Maybe it also works by bathing neurons in an information-influencing chemical soup. What is the essential difference between carbon-based brains and silicon-based computers that can cause the qualitatively enormous difference we're calling consciousness?

JOHN: Let me give you an actual example. We don't know much about the brain, but we do know a little bit about how certain drugs affect the brain. We know that if you put cocaine into your brain, it has a dramatic effect. It messes up the neurotransmitters [i.e., chemicals that transmit information between individual neurons].

FRED: This isn't answering the question.

JOHN: I'm precisely answering the question. And the answer is this: cocaine affects certain neurotransmitters—

FRED: So what?

JOHN: Now, I can do a computer simulation of that with my own home computer.

FRED: So what?

JOHN: What I'm trying to tell you is that if I ingest cocaine, it actually causes a change in my conscious state, whereas—

FRED: You don't know that. You take cocaine and you may change in a certain way. But there are people who take cocaine and don't have any experience at all.

DAVE: Who's to say that a cocaine-induced experience cannot be present in a computer?

JOHN: The point is that the formal simulation of the cocaine experience in a computer is not sufficient to give it a cocaine high.

ROBERT: Fred, you're convinced that at some point in the future a computer can become conscious?

FRED: I think it will have to be a different kind of computer.

ROBERT: A quantum computer, massively parallel, orders of magnitude more powerful than anything imaginable today. You name the computer. I don't care what kind of computer. Do you foresee a time when your computer will be a better friend than your current dog?

FRED: Not only do I see that, but I think I'll become a better human being as a result of having a better friend.

ROBERT: So you'll have a pet, a companion, which is a computer, and you'll relate to it better than to your current dog?

FRED: Maybe better. But maybe in a more expanded sense.

ROBERT: Let's ratchet up the argument. When pet computers become orders of magnitude more powerful still—say, a trillionfold—will they then become better companions than your wife? Maybe I should ask her that about you? Maybe it will take only a thousandfold improvement to replace you—just kidding.

FRED: Both my wife and I will be better companions to each other as a result of what's coming.

ROBERT: John, how does your dog Ludwig compare to computers?

JOHN: We talk about computers a lot, Ludwig and I. I think that there's no PC that's ever going to replace Ludwig. The reason is very simple: I know that Ludwig is conscious and I know that a computer is not. And this conclusion has nothing to do with computing power. You can expand the power all you want, hooking up as many computers as you think you need, all in parallel, and they still won't be conscious, because all they'll ever do is shuffle symbols. Computers don't have the causal powers of brains. So, no; no computer as currently defined is going to replace my dog, because computers aren't conscious.

ROBERT: You're looking in the brain for some causal mechanism not present in current computers. But Fred is saying there'll be different kinds of computers.

JOHN: If we change the definition of a computer, then what are the computers? If "computer" means anything that can compute—add two plus two and get four—then you and I are computers. Because we can do that.

ROBERT: But artificial intelligence, defined broadly as nonbiological intelligence, will never replace Ludwig?

JOHN: Well, if you build me an artificial dog that has the same kind of power to cause doggy consciousness, then you can have an appointment. I see no objections.

ROBERT: Then you have no problems in creating artificial consciousness?

JOHN: But computation, as it's currently defined, is never going to do that. Now, Fred says, "Well, we can change the definition, get a different kind of computer." Fine, but we already have a different kind of computer—you and me.

ROBERT: But now we're talking about duplicating our brains in another physical form—in silicon, or gallium arsenide, or some new material.

JOHN: Or in whatever. Look, the brain is a machine. Whatever we know, we know that. And if by "machine" you mean a physical system capable of performing functions, then the brain is a machine. So we already have a conscious machine. You have one, I have one; it's called a brain.

ROBERT: Dave [Chalmers], do you agree with that?

DAVE: I think that what matters to consciousness is the structure. So if you took my neurons and replaced them by silicon chips, you're going to have a conscious machine. The PCs we have today aren't even close.

ROBERT: Expand computer power as much as you like.

DAVE: The PC has potential. If you can get a computer to take on any structure you like, and if consciousness is generated by structure, then by definition that kind of structure is going to eventually give you consciousness.

ROBERT: So eventually computers can become better companions than people?

DAVE: I don't know if we want our companions, or our pets, to be that smart.

MARILYN: We'll never be able to equate human beings with computers. We're not machines. I disagree profoundly with the notion that we're just physical, mechanical objects. Humans are unpredictable. We're capable of a vast repertoire of messy things called emotions.

We have the potential for intense kinds of transcendent experiences that will never be within a computer's repertoire. So we need not fear our position as human beings—and that's not to say

---

We're not machines. I disagree profoundly with the notion that we're just physical, mechanical objects.

---

that someday computers won't be wonderful companions. Dogs aren't the same as humans, either. So down the road we may well have computers as pets.

ROBERT: I hear two radically different views flying around. The first, more popular among scientists, states that although no computer is like the brain today, if we are clever enough, and patient enough, after a certain period of time we can create John Searle's consciousness in some nonbrain physical material. But Marilyn is saying that no matter how clever we are, no matter how patient we are, it's never going to happen; no manufactured physical matter is ever going to produce human-level consciousness.

MARILYN: There's also a cosmological dimension that's fundamental to this entire issue, and it relates to one's personal belief system. If the assumption is that human beings are purely physical entities, produced on an assembly line, then maybe we could equate human beings and computers. But I think that the uniquenesses and individuality of our human personalities is what makes us really vital and interesting.

ROBERT: We'll now take predictions. A hundred years from today, what is the new relationship between the mind and the brain?

BARRY: There won't be a new relationship. We'll surely know a great deal more about what goes on in the brain when any specific mental experience occurs. But a hundred years from now, there will still be groups like ourselves sitting around and fighting just as we have been fighting. And people will still hold to each of these same opposing opinions.

DAVE: We'll have a really good set of correlations between processes in the brain and thoughts in the mind—which brain systems go with which mental process. We'll have a set of abstract principles to explain the correlations. I also think that computers will have minds that aren't wholly different in kind from ours.

FRED: As we begin to meld mechanical things, so-called hard silicon reality, with physiological things, so-called soft carbon reality, the distinction between a material device like a computer and a mental device like a human being will not be as demarcated as it is now. And we'll have, I believe, clearly intelligent artificial devices.

MARILYN: As a culture, we'll become so dissatisfied with this prevalent mechanistic metaphor that has deprived us of the poetry of being unique human beings that we'll throw the whole materialistic philosophy into the trash bin. As for computers, they'll take care of day-to-day matters, giving us plenty of time to excel in those things that make us uniquely human.

JOHN: In fifty years, we will know the neurological correlates of consciousness. In a hundred years, we'll know which of those correlates are actually causal—we'll know the causal mechanisms that produce consciousness.

ROBERT: CONCLUDING COMMENT

It seems a paradox. The more some explain mental activity in the purely physical terms of neuroscience, the more others contend that mental activity cannot be reduced solely to electrical impulses and flowing chemicals, while still others wonder anew whether minds have existence outside the physical. Can neuroscience ultimately explain all mental activity, reducing mind to brain? Or is demoting the mind a vacant boast, philosophically naïve and hopelessly deficient? Does the mind maintain an independent existence—beyond the brain and outside the physical—as a fundamental, irreducible element of reality? Perhaps the answer goes far beyond us. Perhaps we are forever limited, simply because we are forced to use the mind to explain the mind—this is our enduring paradox. It's conflict like this that carries us closer to truth.

OUTTAKES

MARILYN: I think that was way too complex.

BARRY: I thought we got some lively stuff.

FRED: Dave, I didn't realize that you and I agree.

DAVE: Nor did I.

JOHN: I think you both ought to worry about that.

CHAPTER 3

Strange Physics of the Mind?

Why are some physicists suddenly so interested in the human mind? Is mind as real as matter? A few have even begun wondering whether mind may be the "real reality" and matter a deceptive illusion. What is it about mental activities that causes such smart people to offer such wild speculations? Part of the reason is the weird implications of two fundamental theories that have changed forever our sense of reality: quantum mechanics, which injects uncertainty into the subatomic scale, and relativity, which unifies space and time on the large-scale structure of the universe. But can theories of physics explain mechanisms of the mind? Can the behavior of atoms determine the behavior of people? Can the structure of the universe describe how we think, feel, and know? We assembled an impressive group of physics-friendly guests to guide us through some remarkable territory.

PARTICIPANTS

Dr. Gregory Benford is a professor of physics at the University of California, Irvine, where he specializes in plasma and astrophysics. Greg is also a well-known writer of science fiction, in which he has used quantum mechanics to create a whole new universe.

Dr. David Chalmers is a professor of philosophy and co-director of the Center for Consciousness Studies at the University of Arizona. Dave believes that the mind cannot be explained by brain alone.

Dr. John Searle is a leading philosopher of mind at the University of California, Berkeley. John asserts that the mind comes only from processes in the brain and there is no special need to invoke quantum physics.

Dr. James Trefil is a professor of physics at George Mason University and a prolific science writer. Jim claims not to be bothered by the "quantum weirdness" of the subatomic world.

Dr. Fred Alan Wolf is a theoretical physicist and author of books on the relationship between quantum physics and consciousness. Fred says some extraordinary things about reality.

ROBERT: Fred, your books, such as *Taking the Quantum Leap* and *Parallel Universes,* have all discussed how quantum mechanics might radically reform our understanding of reality. Do you really believe that mind is more fundamental than matter, or are you just having fun with us?

FRED: Maybe a little bit of both. I'm interested in being a kind of gadfly to stir up materialists—those people who believe that only the physical is real—so that they begin to rethink this fundamental problem once again. But I do believe that mind plays a far more important role in the way the universe is constructed than has previously been thought in any mechanical model.

ROBERT: Jim, as a physicist, you've written many broad-based books on science, among them *Science Matters: Achieving Scientific Literacy.* Do you think that what Fred [Wolf] says is literate?

JIM: It's very articulate, of course; Fred is a very articulate guy. Many physicists get uncomfortable, though, when people take physical theories like quantum mechanics and then draw conclusions from them that aren't supported by the theory itself. And most physicists would say that the idea of observers affecting the universe and other such ideas having this wide a context aren't really supported by our views of quantum mechanics.

ROBERT: Greg, you're a practicing physicist and a science fiction writer, whose recent novel, *Cosm,* describes the accidental creation of another universe, where time is speeded up. How seriously should we take your fiction as a description of reality?

GREG: I would hope you'd take it somewhat seriously, because one writes novels in order to make points. But I always try—and I think every scientist always tries—to convey the attitude that science has toward what constitutes proof. We should be sensitive to the style with which we offer our conclusions, because there's a culture of science—

ROBERT: That process of building on past knowledge, rigorously assessing data, logically analyzing hypotheses, requiring repeatability and independent replication—

GREG: Yes. There's a culture of science and we should always keep it in mind.

ROBERT: John, as the renowned author of numerous books on the mind, such as your recent *Mind, Language, and Society,* are you pleased or dismayed to watch strange physics perhaps remystifying the mind?

JOHN: I don't think anybody has succeeded in remystifying the mind. Physicists are as capable of talking nonsense as anyone else. And more non-sense today is talked about quantum mechanics

---

Physicists are as capable of talking nonsense as anyone else.

---

than almost any other subject, except maybe computers. But I'm not dismayed, no.

ROBERT: Dave, reviewers of your book *The Conscious Mind* claim that you see consciousness almost everywhere you look in the universe. Do you take that as a criticism or compliment?

DAVE: I don't know about panpsychism, but I think it's good to open up the idea—at least, after a few drinks late at night. The serious point here is that we don't understand the mind.

ROBERT: Panpsychism is the theory that consciousness or "psychic stuff" is to be found literally everywhere, including in the lowest forms of single-celled life and even in ordinary inanimate matter. Is this what you would advise us mortals to consider?

DAVE: I don't know whether the mind is everywhere. But here are two problems to consider. Problem one: We don't understand the mind; we don't understand the mind's place in physical

---

Maybe there's mind right at the very basis of physical reality.

---

reality. Problem two: We don't understand the intrinsic nature of physical reality. So there can

seem to be an attractive notion—some of the time—that we might try to solve these two problems at once. Maybe there's mind right at the very basis of physical reality. I don't know whether that's the case.

ROBERT: Does this mean that you can envision mind as being more causative of physical reality than physical reality is causative of mind?

DAVE: Mind might well be more fundamental to the universe than is commonly believed. We already know from physics that the world is a weird place. We already know from philosophy that the mind is a weird place. Who knows about a world of mind?

ROBERT: Fred, you focus on dreams. Your book *The Dreaming Universe* takes a fresh look at envisioning reality. Though many people take dreams as an incidental part of life, not much related to anything, you imagine dreams to provide some rather original insights into the structure of reality. Tell us about your theory of dreams.

FRED: The basic idea is that in a dreaming brain there are superpositions—that is, overlapping aspects of our world picture coming together and forming new pictures or new visions. This reminds me of—or is a metaphor for—what happens in quantum physics when we look at overlapping possibilities forming new possibilities. Such superpositioning seems to be how the universe may be constructed, based on a quantum mechanics model. So it seems that dreaming could be a natural place to look at where the mind and quantum mechanics interact and affect the physical world—in terms of how we make pictures of that physical world. My model basically uses dreams as the prism to look at different kinds of pictures—what might be called archetypal pictures, which form at the deepest level of our subconsciousness, even before we become aware of them.

ROBERT: "Archetypal" meaning some fundamental, structural thought or image that pervades the mental activity of numerous people, perhaps all humanity; archetypes are usually subconscious and always transpersonal.

FRED: Yes, there are universal archetypes that seem to be present among the myths and images of virtually all peoples and cultures, according to certain models of psychology. Carl Jung is the main proponent of this point of view. These archetypes are formed in sleep, during deep sleep, during this form of sleep we call dreaming. And there seems to be clear indications that we dream in order to form structure of the world, to give form to our understanding of our surroundings. For example, it's known that the fetus, from the time when the brain begins to develop in the womb, spends something like eighteen hours a day dreaming. This is measured by the rapid eye movement that research has shown accompanies dreaming.

ROBERT: Jim, do you think that Fred is dreaming here?

JIM: I have problems with the metaphor. The theory of dreams is as it may be. We don't know much about dreams or why they function—but the idea of two independent things coming together to form a radically new third thing. . . . Yes, [superposition] is part of quantum mechanics. It's also part of waves in your bathtub, and no one says that the universe is a bathtub. This way of speculating bothers me, though I know Fred is very much aware of these distinctions. But when these ways of speculative thinking get propa-

gated, I suddenly have students telling me that quantum mechanics means the world has to be a certain way. If this were ten years ago, they'd be saying that quantum mechanics proves that we shouldn't live in a patriarchal society. I've heard the quantum mechanics/dreaming argument, among others, before. I agree with John [Searle] that you get a lot of nonsense being talked about quantum mechanics.

ROBERT: Does quantum mechanics generate consciousness? Can the way the world works at the subatomic level—uncertainty, superpositioning, duality, and the like—be directly causative of the way self-awareness works at the organism level, which to our knowledge is associated only with brains? This is the general view of, among others, Roger Penrose, the English mathematician and physicist, who speculates that quantum mechanical effects deep inside brain neurons might engender the kind of baffling first-person experience we call consciousness. But can what goes on in the microstructure of the universe be responsible for creating all the unique characteristics of human mental life?

FRED: There's a new model of quantum physics indicating that there might be a way to generate self-reference from a quantum system. The system not only has to observe something outside of itself, it also has to observe itself observing outside of itself. And that forms a quantum state in what is called the parallel-worlds model, or the many-worlds hypothesis, of quantum physics. It's a very interesting idea, because it allows one to feed back, in a linear way—which physicists never thought was possible [and most still don't].

ROBERT: There are indeed mainstream theoretical physicists—if such an animal as a mainstream theoretical physicist exists anymore—who do contemplate parallel universes, but strictly in a physical sense. The consensus view is that even if parallel worlds do exist in some way, there would still be no congress possible between them.

JIM: Quantum mechanics is the science that deals with what goes on at the level of the atom and inside it. When you look at quantum mechanics, it is, as David [Chalmers] said, weird. I mean, it's just weird.

ROBERT: Weirdness like observer-created reality, wave-particle duality, superposition, nonlocality, the uncertainty principle, time flowing backward as well as forward, and other such counterintuitive notions.

JIM: Quantum mechanics doesn't correspond with our intuition. But our intuition is based on the macro world in which we live. And the idea that when you descend to the world of the atom, that somehow it should be the same as the world we're used to, is in itself weird. Why should the micro world work the same way as the macro world? They don't have to work the same way, any more than when you go to another country the natives all have to speak English. So when we get inside the atom and find that it doesn't behave as we might expect—

If you want to play the quantum game, you have to play by the quantum rules.

---

and we can't describe it in terms of colliding baseballs—that doesn't mean that therefore we have to give up all our other ideas about the universe. The strangeness of the subatomic world just tells us that when we go to this other realm, the rules are different. If you want to play the quantum game, you have to play by the quantum rules.

DAVE: There are some particularly strange things about quantum mechanics. For example, quantum mechanics tells us that an electron can be in two places at once. Now, that's not a problem; that's just a little bit weird. But what happens when someone makes an observation? If an observer comes in, with a conscious mind, then that electron can only be in one place at one time. That's the thing that's hard to understand.

JIM: It's the interaction.

DAVE: Put it this way: if people want to find a role for mind in physical reality, if they already have a bias to do so, quantum mechanics would be exactly the place to look.

JIM: Because it's a place where our intuition breaks down.

FRED: Jim [Trefil] just made a very important point. "It's the interaction," he said. I totally disagree with that. It's not the interaction that does it, because interactions fit within the framework of quantum mechanics, and they lead to more weirdness. In order to get from that pool of weirdness to a single actual observation, something has to change radically and suddenly. It's not the interaction that does it. It's the *observation* that does it. And [Werner] Heisenberg made that point a long time ago when he said that it's the observation that creates the path of an arrow.

JIM: But what I'm saying is, the problems you run into are always from mixing metaphors— from imposing our classical [macroscopic] ideas on the atomic world, where they don't belong. If you look at the atomic world, it's an interactional place; that's what it is.

ROBERT: John, are physicists trying to take over what traditionally has been philosophers' sphere of influence?

JOHN: I don't think this is a case of physicists trying to take over from philosophers. Neurobiology is a focal point, and although we know a great deal about how the brain works, we're still at a stage where we welcome all speculations. But the idea that we're going to find consciousness at the level of the wave function in quantum mechanics is, so far, without any experimental support whatever. There's a real difficulty with this idea. As far as we know, consciousness exists only in human and animal brains. And they have a very specific kind of anatomy: They have neurons. The problem with quantum mechanics is that it's everywhere, absolutely everywhere. So if you're going to find consciousness in the collapse of the wave function, let's say, or in superpositioning, then you're going to have to conclude that the universe is in every place "conscious."

ROBERT: The collapse of the wave function is how we get from the micro world of all this weirdness (i.e., quantum indeterminacy) to the macro world where everything is in its place. When we measure, or observe, something, we collapse its wave function.

FRED: There's something very interesting here. The classical world is a clearly defined world in which causality seems to be the rule. The quantum world is probabilistic in nature, and causality is not clear. The question is, How do we get from the quantum to the classical? If you look at the parallel-worlds model that I mentioned earlier

and discussed in *The Dreaming Universe,* you find that in many self-referencing systems, classical physics reappears. A system can have knowledge of simultaneous things that, according to the laws of quantum mechanics, it shouldn't be able to know. It can know things in violation of the uncertainty principle, provided that it doesn't put that information out into the outside world. I take that to be a metaphor for how we make up stories about ourselves. We can know things about ourselves that we can never know about somebody else. That's trivial, but the things that we know are personal stories about how we got from A to B, whereas for somebody else the blanks have to be filled in.

ROBERT: Dave, you've postulated that information—I assume in some pure, idealistic form—may be the underlying essence of reality. Could you tell us about that?

DAVE: Let's think about the way physics really works. Basically, physics tells us about relationships between things. For example, there are two different states that an electron might have, and it might have this or that effect on another particle. Physics doesn't tell us what these electrons are in themselves; it tells us only about the relations between the differences here which make a difference elsewhere. Physics is silent about the intrinsic nature of reality. Basically, it tells us about bits. Zeros and ones, if you like—on or off, this state or that state. Whenever you have information, though, it deals with intrinsic nature—descriptions or categories. Is something red or is it blue, opaque or transparent, and so on. What we're really looking for, down deep, is the intrinsic nature of physical reality. And I might speculate that the intrinsic nature of physical reality could have something to do with the intrinsic nature of mind.

ROBERT: Greg [Benford], when you sketched first thoughts about your book *Cosm* and made parallel universes its core concept, what was going on in your head? Was quantum mechanics involved in your mental creativity?

GREG: Gee, I hope not. It's an interesting question, though: Where does creativity come from? I tend to believe that we are mostly builders of analogies. All the time, we ask ourselves, "Does this thing look like that thing—or does it look like that other thing?" If it looks more like that other thing, go there; follow it; build on it. Building analogies and following trails of thought are the most common form of creativity, and that's what I did in this novel. I thought about the calculations that have arisen in the last ten years about being able to create a whole universe in a laboratory, and I wondered what might happen if this could actually be true. And then I wondered, What if someone were to do it by accident? The mechanism for universe creation has been shown to be a quantum mechanical event that began as a microscopic event in the real world.

ROBERT: In the real world?

GREG: Yes, in the real world. The creative leap was to suppose that a quantum mechanical event could appear in the real world on a large scale. This isn't as farfetched as it may initially seem, since our current universe was once a quantum mechanical object. That was a long time ago, of course, and we weren't there.

ROBERT: Fred was there.

GREG: Of course, Fred [Wolf] may have been there—he looks a lot like Jehovah. If our entire universe emerged out of a quantum mechanical event far smaller than an atomic particle, why

couldn't such a thing happen again? But this doesn't mean that I want to imply that quantum mechanics is often operating on the macroscopic levels of our common, classical world. Look at it this way: *Cosm* is a novel that uses a colossal metaphor like the creation of the cosmos and then imagines all the dust that flies— what happens to society when it turns out that ordinary untenured faculty members can actually create universes.

ROBERT: Do they get tenure for that?

GREG: It looks like she's going to get tenure; it's amazing what you have to do to get tenure these days. But there's a danger here in these quantum mechanical musings. Let's put it another way: I had a lot of fun painting a French impressionist portrait of a cow—but don't try to get milk out of it. Similarly, don't try to squeeze everything out of quantum mechanics, because quantum mechanics doesn't work well as a metaphor in the large-scale world. John [Searle] is always saying this, and I quite agree. And just in case you may not be following all that we're saying here, don't think that you alone don't understand quantum mechanics, because we physicists don't understand much of quantum mechanics either.

ROBERT: Let's take a specific, strange aspect of quantum mechanics called nonlocality. What is nonlocality in quantum mechanics, and does it help explain some of the more mystical traditions of humanity? Fred, I'm wandering into your territory.

FRED: Nonlocality means that something that happens over here occurs because something happened over there, when there is seemingly no physical means by which the something-over-there could effect the something-over-here.

So, how did the something-over-here become what it is when the something-over-there did what it did, since there's no possible physical connection between the two? That's what we call nonlocality.

ROBERT: It's also called "spooky action at a distance." It might have been called pseudo-science, because it would seem to be impossible, but in quantum mechanics we learn that what seems impossible may be quite ordinary.

FRED: Nonlocality is possible because the original objects—the one over here and the one over there—interacted before they separated, and they formed what is called a single state. And even though they are now separate, they still behave as a single state.

JIM: This phenomenon is called quantum entanglement. You start with two particles that are near each other and have some interaction, and when they separate they retain—if you like to think about it in this way—a "memory" of the original interaction. This is one of the more surprising predictions of quantum mechanics, and it was verified experimentally in the 1960s. It's the only case I know of in science where you had a theory that everyone believed was true, made a prediction based on that theory, conducted the experiment, verified the prediction—and everybody was upset. Because what it confirmed was that you can never visualize what is going on in the quantum world. And we're primates; we deal in visual systems. We all think of these elementary particles as baseballs flying about or billiard balls bumping into each other—I do, I don't deny it. We think of things that way, and then we get into these paradoxes, and we find things that don't make any sense, nonlocality being one good example. Actually, nonlocality, if you describe it correctly—and it's

a long argument, beyond our scope here—isn't a paradox. It's just impossible to visualize; it's something that doesn't fit the classical view.

ROBERT: Fred, help us with nonlocality. What's an example that we can relate to?

FRED: Pretend you're looking at a pair of dice, seemingly ordinary dice. But notice that you can't see any spots on them. Yet if I pick up one of them—this act is called "observation"—it can suddenly change: Look, now it has red spots on it! Well, that's interesting. Observation is affecting the reality of the die. That's the metaphor here. It gets even more interesting when I take two dice, let them interact, and then pull them apart. Now, when I observe the die over here, making its spots appear, then spots also appear on the second die, over there. And if I make an observation again and the one over here changes and has black spots on it, so does the second die, over there—now it, too, has black spots. In other words, my observation of one immediately affects the other.

ROBERT: A nice illustration of nonlocality, but it hardly proves that reality is a dream. So what does this tell me about the nature of things?

FRED: Nonlocality tells you that there's an order in the universe that may complement and supersede the simple mechanical order we've been conditioned to accept.

ROBERT: Can quantum mechanics be involved in any of the strange occurrences that some claim are supernatural? Consider synchronicity—coincidences; the seemingly nonrational association of events; the juxtaposition of events for no obvious physical reason—which was popularized by the mystical psychoanalyst Carl Jung. Recently, certain physicists and people involved in parapsychology have wondered whether quantum mechanics might be the underlying cause of these kinds of synchronicities. . . . John [Searle], you're laughing at me.

JOHN: We have two mysteries for one again. The problem is that these kinds of bizarre coincidences that you get in real life are distinctly odd statistically, whereas quantum mechanics is pervasive and distinctly predictable statistically. The kind of mystical phenomenon you're talking about is, for example, a mother suddenly imagining her son in a car accident, and—my God!—she finds out an hour later that he was in fact in a car accident at that very time . . . so there must be some explanation. Now, here's the explanation as to why these seemingly odd occurrences should be quite normal and expected. Given that all of us have billions of conscious states in the course of our lives, it's not at all surprising that you occasionally get these odd correlations. But the idea that these strange events are connected somehow with quantum mechanics is not correct. They aren't remotely like quantum mechanics. Quantum mechanics is absolutely a pervasive feature of the world at the most micro and fundamental level. So I don't see the connection between quantum mechanics and these occurrences; I've never seen anybody make the connection work.

FRED: I think, to be fair to John, that one does have to stretch the implications of quantum mechanics to apply it here. I agree with you all on this. Quantum mechanics is not the end of the story here, but it's important to wonder what quantum mechanics is telling us. Quantum mechanics is exhibiting some features that look a lot like synchronicity and other features that look a lot like nonlocality. Now go back to these experiences that human beings have, that seemed totally unexplainable before quantum

mechanics. What I and others are saying is that maybe quantum mechanics has something to contribute. But maybe we need a new theory; maybe we need something bigger than just quantum mechanics. I think synchronicity is another ordering parameter of the universe.

ROBERT: What is your description of synchronicity?

FRED: Synchronicity is when two events take place, in which a clear meaning is associated with the juxtaposition, but it's a coincidence that cannot be explained causally—that is, by one event's effecting, or causing, the other. So synchronicity can be defined as a meaningful but noncausal relationship between two or more events.

JOHN: Do you assign this meaning after the events take place?

FRED: I presume you do.

JOHN: That's very important to me. Because how can you assign meaning to things or events if you don't know that they're going to occur? You have no way of predicting them. For example, there's a famous tale about a woman who was discussing her creativity, and was having visions of a scarab or something like a gold bug, and suddenly a similarly colored beetle flew into the screen of a window where Carl Jung was working with a patient. This is what he would call a synchronicity. When I hear psychologists tell stories, they're always filled with remarkable synchronicities.

ROBERT: I agree. The balancing question is how many of the innumerable synchronicity-type events that could have conceivably occurred did *not* occur? And when the ultrarare synchronicity-type events do occur, are their appearances really anything more than random coincidences amidst the overwhelming number of similar events that did not occur?

JIM: Isn't this what my old statistics instructor used to call the "golf ball on the fairway" fallacy? You hit a golf ball onto the fairway, and ask, "What's the chance that my golf ball will hit any particular blade of grass?" That chance is basically zero. But the ball must land on *some* blade of grass, of course. So you go over to the ball afterward and say, "Look at this! The odds that my ball would land on this specific blade of grass are astronomical!" But in fact the ball has to land somewhere.

ROBERT: Another problem is the "expectation bias": Do synchronicity-type events occur more to those people who believe in them? If so, we should be suspicious, though I suppose that one could always argue that "believers" can generate or attract more synchronicity-type events than can "nonbelievers."

FRED: The universe is an interesting place; and so is the mind.

ROBERT: Jim, what evidence could convince you that Fred's worldview has legitimacy?

JIM: Let's talk some more about synchronicity. A good-sized sample of people would have to faithfully write down all the visions they have, and then independent analysts would assess how many of them were clearly and meaningfully coincident. But you have to define in advance what "clearly and meaningfully coincident" means—this is what John [Searle] was saying. Assigning meaning in advance is a very important part of this test. Only then can you determine whether the

result is greater than chance. If you have a million visions and only one of them is clearly meaningful, that hardly seems more than coin-flipping chance.

ROBERT: But what if the results of your experiment, designed in your way and assuming sufficient trials and repetition, demonstrated statistically significant, nonrandom occurrences of synchronicity?

JIM: I would accept that there was something going on that had to be explained, something beyond mere chance. And then I would start looking for explanations.

ROBERT: Let's reverse the results. Would a negative outcome of your experiment constitute a logical proof that there was no strange, synchronous connection to the one "clearly meaningful, noncausal event" even though it was statistically a random occurrence?

JIM: No.

ROBERT: The principles of logic and statistics can make causal connections unlikely but not impossible.

FRED: But the question is, What does it mean to "explain" something like synchronicity? The problem today, in our scientific way of thinking, is that "explanation" means a cause-and-effect relationship. If we can't fit something into a cause-and-effect relationship, we surmise that we haven't explained it. This is the notion I'm challenging. Synchronicities, I'm saying, are another form of order, which is noncausal or acausal. Synchronicities don't fit the causal model, so we're unable to explain them in the same way we're accustomed to explaining normal things.

JIM: What I'm saying is that we haven't yet established that there's something to be explained.

ROBERT: Let's change direction. In the development of consciousness as a field of scientific study, how important is quantum mechanics?

DAVE: At this moment in our investigations of consciousness, we're concentrating on neuroscience. These are the early days, when we're linking the chemical and electrical processes in the brain with the mental and psychological processes we know and love in our conscious experience. It's like the early days of physics, when scientists were concentrating on processes at the macroscopic level. Similarly, once we come to understand these neuroprocesses in the brain [at the cellular and subcellular levels], then we can go farther and develop detailed speculations—maybe even explanations—for what underlies that level. Maybe fifty or a hundred years from now there will be working theories describing how quantum mechanics or some other part of physics contributes to the fundamental theory of mind. For now, I think it's a little early.

ROBERT: I'm always skeptical when I hear of some special new brain locus, or focal point, where mind is said to emerge from brain. We know that electrical impulses, which carry information flows in the brain, are generated at the synapses between the billions of neurons. Fred [Wolf] wonders about the role of glial cells, which are the much more numerous nonneurons in the brain, involved in supporting the biochemical environment. And others, like Roger Penrose, speak about the tiny microtubules inside neurons and speculate about how quantum effects might take place there. At our present level of understanding, I think it's dangerous to assign the mind-brain interface, as it were, to any specific physical location.

JOHN: But it's a good idea to start with what we know for a fact. We know for a fact that our brains are conscious brains. We know, as far as we know anything, that a table is not conscious. But there's just as much quantum mechanics in a table as there is in our brains. So if you're going to look for consciousness at the level of quantum mechanics, you'd better start talking about the special features of brain anatomy—because as far as we know, the brain is the only place where consciousness actually occurs in the real world. Tables are not conscious.

ROBERT: Fred, you've spent your entire career talking about the relationship between quantum mechanics and mind. Why should we care about such an abstract subject?

FRED: For a very good reason. Today we live in a culture that has a particular view of how things work. And unfortunately—or fortunately, depending on your bias—we have a highly mechanical orientation. People who are born in a certain way, or who live in certain circumstances, may think of themselves as handicapped or victimized for the rest of their lives

---

. . . by changing the way you observe things, you can possibly change yourself . . . Everything can benefit from a quantum metaphor . . .

---

because, mechanically, that's the way they seem to be constructed. The quantum metaphor, the quantum story, changes all that. It says that observation affects, changes, alters reality. This means that by changing the way you observe things, you can possibly change yourself. So I think that everything can benefit from a quantum metaphor—ourselves, our families, our culture, our world, and possibly even our universe.

ROBERT: Can quantum mechanics affect free will?

GREG: I really don't think so. It actually sounds more useful for a therapist than a physicist. Trying to explain free will by reference to quantum mechanics is much like playing tennis with the net down. It looks interesting at first,

---

Trying to explain free will by reference to quantum mechanics is much like playing tennis with the net down.

---

but after a while it loses its zip. I don't think we make progress by compounding the levels of mystification. You have to get some kind of predictive value out of a scientific idea. This [speculation] just seems to be worsening the problem, not bettering it.

ROBERT: So you want to discard all the quantum mechanics discussions of the mind?

GREG: No, but you shouldn't ask quantum mechanics to solve philosophical problems, which it cannot do. A philosopher can tell you why.

DAVE: The relationship between quantum mechanics and mind is an important issue for us, because it relates to what we are as human beings. We want to know what we are. Are we souls, which live forever, or get passed from body to body, or to other creatures, down the generations? Are we just bags of neurons that rot when we die? Or does it turn out that our consciousness is actually composed of fundamental physical entities? Or maybe we're mental entities that were around at the time of the Big Bang. I think the answer would make a huge difference to our worldview. And if a quantum physics view of mind turns out to be right, that would force us to reconstruct the entire picture of ourselves. But just because a quantum mechanism would be extremely important for understanding mind, that doesn't mean it's right.

JOHN: We should care about these issues, because we want to know how the world works. And the most fundamental theory we have about how the world works is quantum mechanics. Now we're tempted to think, Well, quantum theory is going to explain a whole lot of other things, like consciousness and free will. I'm very skeptical about such attempted explanations. I don't think any of that is going to happen. But we would like to know how the world works, and we'd like to know how we work. If knowing how the world works at the most fundamental level will help us to explain how we work—great! If not, all the same, it's something we should know about as well.

JIM: I agree that there's a fundamental desire to know who we are. If the quantum mechanics metaphor helps people in their lives, as Fred was suggesting, then by all means use the metaphor—but don't try to pretend that it has anything to do with the quantum mechanics that's part of physics.

ROBERT: In advanced discussions of consciousness, some physicists are starting to talk about the nature of time as described by relativity theory. How do you see the relationship between time and consciousness?

DAVE: I don't know. You might try to make some link. Relativity says that time can flow at different speeds. Consciousness, we all know, does flow at different speeds—in some states of consciousness time flows faster and in other states slower. Personally, though, I think that's biologically explainable. I don't see a relationship between that and the physics of relativity. Some say otherwise, and I wish them well.

ROBERT: Greg, how important is a sense of time in our sense of ourselves?

GREG: Time is adjustable, as evolution has engineered it. If you're in the middle of an auto accident, time hasn't changed, though your perceptions of time, during and after, will be different from normal experience. But the fundamental nature of time is something that physics has not truly figured out yet. It may not be comprehensible. It may be that time is one of the fundamentals of the universe, behind which there is no other actor.

ROBERT: But when time is ultimately understood, do you think it will have some close relationship to the nature of consciousness?

GREG: No.

FRED: I think it will. I think that our sense of self, even the nature of our soul, is that we are time-based creatures. Thought itself is time, and the relationship between thought and time is far more intimate than we can presently understand.

JOHN: But that's true of anything in the universe. Everything has a temporal dimension to it. There's nothing special about consciousness in terms of time. What's special about consciousness is that sometimes psychological time doesn't match real time. This is an interesting question, but seems more likely to be solved, as Dave [Chalmers] was suggesting, by understanding how psychology and the brain works.

ROBERT: So relativity has little impact on consciousness?

JOHN: I don't think it has any special connection. Here's our problem now: We don't understand consciousness, so we're thrashing around desperately, seeing whether we can lay our hands on something that will explain it. But I would go back to the brain. There we have a mechanism that we actually know something about, and we know that it's where consciousness is taking place. And of course, like everything else, brains exist in time. So do feet exist in time, but thinking about "feet in time" doesn't much help us to understand the nature of feet—or to understand consciousness.

DAVE: When it comes to the problem of time, maybe the key lies in the order of explanation. Time may be going the other way. Here's a problem about time. Time seems to pass. Time seems to flow—"flows like a river," people sometimes say. Physics can't make sense of this concept: "Time flows like a river." So we're going to have to understand how we sense time in our consciousness.

ROBERT: Is time a fundamental aspect of the universe independent of consciousness, or must time be understood through consciousness?

DAVE: Maybe it could turn out that the very sense of time flowing doesn't correspond to something that's independent of mind. Maybe that sense is just a construct in our mind.

JIM: When physicists talk about time, they don't talk about what you're talking about—the essence of time. They talk about measuring it—measuring periodic events. So we can measure intervals of time but never define time. Physicists don't define space, either. We talk about how to measure distance, but we don't say what space is.

ROBERT: But could time be, in essence, a construct of the human mind? Could space and time be dependent on consciousness?

JOHN: The way we conceptualize time may be derived from characteristics of our own consciousness rather than our own consciousness being derived from the way we understand time.

FRED: But there's something interesting going on in terms of how the brain operates in external, or physical, time. You can actually observe and map chemical and electrical events taking place in the cerebral cortex of the brain and compare these physiological markings with events that people say are happening to them at the same moment. And what we find is that "brain time" does not correspond precisely to "external time." In fact, time reversals can occur.

JIM: That's right.

FRED: This would indicate that we don't clearly understand time and consciousness as a one-to-one mapping of one onto the other. It may be that we need two physical events in order to have a single consciousness experience.

ROBERT: Are you hinting that there may be a more fundamental relationship in the universe combining consciousness and time?

FRED: Yes, but not according to the popular view—defining the sense of time as physical events happening one after another. It may be that several events are required to cause a consciousness experience, and that this consciousness occurs somewhere in between them.

JIM: I agree that the brain is not a very good clock.

JOHN: You need to make a distinction between the perception of time and the time of the perception. And what we've found, with all kinds of interesting experiments, is that you don't get an exact match. The runner thinks he began to run when he heard the starter's gun, but we have good evidence showing that he in fact started before he could have heard the sound, before the conscious mind could have registered the sound of the gun. This is a fascinating piece of experimental data. I don't know if it's right, but it's good stuff for philosophers, psychologists, and neurobiologists to work on. But I don't see problems of time and consciousness as suitable for relativity theory.

FRED: No, not relativity theory, but perhaps a quantum model might explain it.

ROBERT: I want a prediction. One hundred years from now, what will be the accepted relationship between modern physics and the human mind?

FRED: Physics and mind will both be seen as approximations of a deeper reality. The separation between mind and matter will be seen as an artifact that came about through an accident of history, and this will reflect a deeper unity.

GREG: A hundred years from now, I suspect we'll say that although physics can explain the working of the brain, it still can't make detailed predictions about what people are going to do. Probably never.

DAVE: It's possible that in the next hundred years something really surprising will happen that will make us look at the whole mind-brain problem in a new way. More likely, we'll have a bunch of detailed, speculative theories, more detailed than we have now, but still with no consensus.

JOHN: In a hundred years, we'll have finally gotten over our traditional vocabulary that says there's the mental and the physical and they're in two different realms. This distinction is already obsolete, just as it's obsolete to think that there's a distinction between machines and other kinds of physical systems. My guess about the future is that we'll come to accept quantum mechanics in the same way we now accept relativity theory. We'll just grow out of our obsession that everything has to behave like middle-size physical objects—why should it? We now know from relativity that space and time are not the way we thought they were, so why should subatomic particles be the way we thought they were? Regarding our understanding of the mind, I think we'll have a biological account of the brain and how it produces consciousness—and it will have about the same relation to quantum mechanics as does any other part of biology such as disease or photosynthesis.

JIM: I think John's right. We'll understand the brain, in terms of neuroscience and in terms of complexity theory. And quantum mechanics will be what it is today; it's not going to change very much, and we're still not going to like it.

ROBERT: CONCLUDING COMMENT

So modern physics has persuaded a few scientists that quantum mechanics engenders mind, a few others that physical systems can never fully explain mental states so that mind cannot be built by matter alone, and still others that a spirit or a soul or even a dream is needed to explain consciousness. The theories are fascinating, even if not convincing. Is consciousness a fundamental essence of the universe, the real stuff of reality? The easy answer is: Nice, but no. But could matter and mind both be derived from the same fundamental stuff, whatever that may be? I think we'll be astonished by whatever sits as the ultimate building block of reality. We should be more astonished that human beings can even conceive of it. It's dreaming like this that transports us closer to truth.

OUTTAKES

FRED: *You all say the most unexpected things. I thought I had you pegged.*

JIM: *You're not going to let people get away with saying that quantum mechanics shows that consciousness is our ultimate reality?*

DAVE: *Quantum mechanics doesn't prove that, but quantum mechanics, more than other areas of physics, leaves that possibility open.*

ROBERT: *Part of the concept of the* Closer to Truth *show is to take ideas—like quantum* mechanics and consciousness—that media pros have said cannot possibly be shown on television and—

DAVE: —and prove them right! But still, you can't let them kill off the concept for the next thirty years.

DAVE: Is there a good place to eat around here? Let's pick someplace interesting.

GREG: There's a good Italian restaurant right across the street.

CHAPTER 4

Can Science Seek the Soul?

Do you have a soul? Are you a soul? What is a soul? Why do so many people in so many cultures believe in an immortal soul, while so many scientists do not? In lives often capricious and filled with despair, belief in an immortal soul offers hope for the forlorn and comfort for the bereaved. This spiritual essence, which is somehow associated with each human being, is said to transcend death, offering a promise of better tomorrows than todays. But given the remarkable advances in neuroscience—the physics, chemistry, and biology of understanding how the brain senses, thinks, feels, and behaves—most scientists are materialists, who believe that only the physical is real. Materialists reject dualism, denying that any independent, nonphysical component—call it a soul—is part of our makeup. Can science seek the soul? History records ancient and protracted conflict between science and religion, and the battles still rage. To hear from all sides, we invited five soul-savvy experts.

PARTICIPANTS

Dr. Warren Brown is a professor of psychology at Fuller Theological Seminary in Pasadena, California, where he is director of research at the Psychophysical Laboratory. A committed Christian, Warren surprises us by denying the necessity of a traditional Christian soul.

Dr. Dean Radin, an experimental psychologist, is the former director of the Consciousness Research Laboratory at the University of Nevada. Though Dean believes that scientific research validates extrasensory perception and other psychic phenomena, he, too, doubts that good evidence supports the existence of a soul.

Dr. John Searle, the Mills Professor of Philosophy at the University of California, Berkeley, and the author of numerous books about the mind, takes a rigorous approach to consciousness and a dim view of a disembodied soul.

Dr. Charles Tart, a professor of psychology emeritus at the University of California, Davis, is now at the Institute of Transpersonal Psychology, in Palo Alto. Charles believes that we need both science and spirituality to make us human.

Dr. Fred Alan Wolf, a theoretical physicist, is an international lecturer and author of many books on physics and the mind. Fred envisions spiritual underpinnings to all existence.

ROBERT: Charles, your recent book, *Body, Mind, Spirit,* propounds the importance of spirituality. What's the relationship between the existence of the soul, if such a noncorporeal entity exists, and spirituality?

CHARLES: Spirituality is predicated on the idea that human life is more than just a short-term show here and now, with nothing ever to happen after we die—that there are long-term consequences. This idea can have enormous impact on how people live their lives. Personally, I don't think the deciding factor should be belief—that we should just either believe in souls or spirituality or not believe in them. I think we should look at the evidence that there is something that transcends death, that transcends the physical body. And I find there's some evidence for just such an assertion, which makes spirituality much more interesting to me than if it were just a belief.

ROBERT: And if solid evidence could demonstrate life beyond death, and/or mind beyond the body, how would that affect our lives?

CHARLES: It would affect our lives a great deal. Suppose you know you're going to die in a short while. What are you going to do with your last hours?

ROBERT: I'm going to do more shows [and books] like this. Do you think that's a good investment for the *really* long term?

CHARLES: I think it is.

ROBERT: Fred, your book *The Spiritual Universe* claims to use scientific methods to prove that the soul exists. How can you use physical methods to prove the existence of something that's not physical?

FRED: First of all, we have to define what we mean by a soul. If we can get a definition that lends itself to some scientific test of probability, then we could prove its existence. I think we already have enough groundwork to start the search: there's enough in the way the physical universe is constructed to indicate the presence of something called soul. Where I begin looking for this soul is in the nature of quantum mechanics, or quantum physics, which says that there may be spiritual underpinnings to the physical world.

ROBERT: Warren, you're a neuroscientist and a psychologist—and also a committed Christian. You've coedited a book called *Whatever Happened to the Soul?* So tell us, what happened?

WARREN: The position we take in the book is that the idea of the soul as a separate metaphysical entity isn't necessary to explain humankind. That doesn't mean that God doesn't exist or that there's no spiritual world. But it does mean that you don't have to add a nonphysical element to our physical nature in order to explain what it means to be human.

ROBERT: Denying the existence of an immortal soul doesn't sound like Christian orthodoxy, even to my unordained theological ears.

WARREN: Right. Most Christians would probably find the negation of immortal souls a tough road to travel, but this is what I would call nonessential theology. That belief is not a critical point for most Christian theology.

ROBERT: John, you've been a leader in the rediscovery of the mind, the title of one of your many books. But rediscovering the mind does not mean defending the existence of the soul?

JOHN: It depends on what you mean by the soul. There are different definitions of "soul," and so because of this confusion I don't find the notion of soul much use. There is Aristotle's notion of soul, which is a kind of principle of organization of the body. And I have no objection to that. And if by "soul" you just mean "mind," I'm all for it. But there's another definition of soul—which we get from Descartes, and dualists, and so on—which says that there's this thing attached to your body, and when your brain and body are destroyed this thing is going to cut loose and have a life of its own. Now, that's very comforting to believe, but I've never seen any evidence for it. All the experiences I've ever had were caused by processes in my brain. And it's kind of depressing, but it turns out, as far as I can tell, that when my brain goes, those

experiences go. I'm not going to have any soul after the destruction of my brain, any more than I'm going to have any digestion after the destruction of my stomach.

ROBERT: Dean, your book *The Conscious Universe* claims to apply scientific methods to the investigation of the paranormal, or psi phenomena. Can the same kinds of methodologies be used to assess the soul?

DEAN: Yes, these same kinds of methodologies can be, and actually have been, applied to search for after-death phenomena. Now you might think that as a parapsychologist I would be highly sym-

---

. . . I'm fairly doubtful that, so far, we have any good evidence for something like a soul—something that actually survives bodily death.

---

pathetic to the idea of the existence of a soul, but in fact I'm fairly doubtful that, so far, we have any good evidence for something like a soul—something that actually survives bodily death.

ROBERT: In the early days of parapsychology, research focused on after-death survival and out-of-body and near-death experiences. There were many investigations of mediums and seances, where supposed spirits of the dead would come back to communicate with the living. Such survival research is no longer the focus of parapsychology. Why?

DEAN: It's true that parapsychology began pretty much as a study of mediumistic phenomena. But within a matter of a decade or less, it had transitioned into laboratory studies of phenomena like telepathic communication between a medium and what was thought to be the departed loved one. The reason for the transition was that if telepathy proved to be a real phenomenon, it would cast enormous doubt on just what or whom a medium was actually communicating with.

ROBERT: It isn't easy—even if you believe in psi—to distinguish between a medium reading the minds of the living relatives or truly communicating with the dead. So has survival research, at least in this technical sense, become less important to this question?

DEAN: No, I think it's still very important. It just turns out to be extremely difficult to find a valid empirical way of testing for survival that excludes the possibility of telepathy.

ROBERT: Do you agree with that, Charles?

CHARLES: I want to qualify that a little bit. When you look at the old mediumistic research, of course you find a lot of nonsense there. But occasionally an ostensible communicator says very specific things about his or her past life—things that could not possibly have been known to the medium. So you've got to postulate either that there's a surviving soul of some sort that can communicate, or that the medium has great psychic abilities to pull this information out.

ROBERT: There is a lot going on here. First, you are assuming that such "very specific things" could truly not have been known by normal means, even through subconscious communication—which must be shown to be statistically significant amidst the innumerable clutter of ordinary specific things that would

not be so surprising. Next, if you could jump this first hurdle, I would agree that you still have the serious logical problem of not being able to eliminate the possibility that the medium was apprehending the surprising information through strong psychic ability and not through communication with a surviving after-death spirit or soul. Such psychic knowing would include not only telepathy, where the medium would read the minds of living people, but also clairvoyance, where the medium would somehow sense the surprising information directly without any person needing to know it, and irrespective of whether it was past or present.

CHARLES: This dual track for knowing makes the question of proving survival per se very difficult. On the other hand, if some people have minds that can access any information in the cosmos, without any known bodily limits, that's the sort of mind we think might survive death, isn't it? So, survival research is not a dead issue, if I may use that word—it's just a complicated issue.

ROBERT: Warren, how have you approached the soul from a scientific point of view? You run a neurophysiological lab, and you're interested in brain damage; you confront fundamental interactions of brain and mind when working with your patients. In addition, and equally important to our discourse here, you have a strong commitment to evangelical Christianity—the received Christian tradition, the Old and New Testaments. How do these different lines of knowledge and/or belief all come together in a scientific search for the soul?

WARREN: One thing you know from neurophysiology is that brain damage or brain malfunction causes changes in states of consciousness, awareness, and even, in a number of situations, in people's understanding of their own spirituality. An easy example is temporal lobe epilepsy, where a person can, in some circumstances, have an experience that seems quite religious. But we know that these experiences are in fact embodied in their physical brains, and there's no need to postulate a soul to explain the phenomenon.

ROBERT: How do you reconcile your views on a nonessential or nonexistent soul with your Christian belief?

WARREN: For this view of a nonexistent soul to stand within Christian theology, you do have to agree, or to postulate, that God exists, that God is spiritual, that our spirituality represents our ability to be in a spiritual relationship to God. But it's not necessary to postulate that we possess a spirit, another entity that influences or determines our behavior and our experiences.

ROBERT: Charles, one of your more well-known books is *Altered States of Consciousness*. In temporal lobe epilepsy, Warren is talking about a particular kind of altered state, which has at times been shown to cause religious experiences.

WARREN: Associated with religious experiences, not shown to cause them.

ROBERT: I accept the careful distinction. So, Charles, bring us up to date on your use of altered states to demonstrate the existence of worlds beyond the physical, especially in this context of brain research providing us with incontrovertible evidence that there are physical causes for seemingly spiritual experiences.

CHARLES: We're mixing up several things here. My interest in altered states is to make

clear that the mind can work in very different patterns. And these very different patterns—whether meditative states, drug-induced states, hypnosis, dreams, and the like—are good for some things and bad for other things. Collectively, they give us different views of the world. But in terms of proving that there's something beyond the physical, or even that these altered states are more than merely subjective phenomena or brain-based phenomena, altered states provide no such proof per se. Altered states give you a great experience, and they may give you a conviction, but that's not the same as proving that the mind is something more than the body.

ROBERT: Can you take the next step and seek proof of a new reality beyond the physical?

CHARLES: This is where you get into parapsychological research, where you set up experiments. In the materialist worldview, it's assumed that the physical senses give us all there is to know about the nature of the world, and that it's impossible for people to communicate without the senses. So you do the careful experiments to see whether you can get some nonsensory communications among people. Or whether people can learn about or affect things at a distance. Do you get a statistically significant effect in your experiments? This is your basic parapsychological approach. And we do get extraordinary data frequently enough that, as a scientist, I have no doubt that sometimes a human mind can do things that we can't attribute to anything we know about neurophysiology or conventional physics. This basic scientific finding says to me that I should consider ideas about spirituality more seriously, because there's actual evidence for it. This isn't a philosophical position, it's experimental science; the mind can do things that the brain can't do.

ROBERT: You like to think of yourself both as a tough-minded scientist and as someone seriously interested in the spiritual. How do you reconcile the two worldviews?

CHARLES: I'm a human being and I have many facets, and if I identify exclusively with any one of them I'm leaving out part of my humanity. But I don't want to be fooled, OK? I don't want to believe things just because they make me feel good. I want the best science possible to check on the possibility of certain beliefs. On the other hand, I don't want to fall into scientism—into taking the latest physical theories as if they were revealed truth and believing that since we know so much about everything, we don't have to pay attention to any contradictory evidence. I believe that we do have evidence that mind can transcend what we know about the physical body and brain. To me, that's a vital underpinning for spirituality.

JOHN: Well, some people think we have such evidence. I have serious doubts that we have any solid evidence showing that the mind can transcend the brain. What we do have, and I hope Charles would agree with this, is a long history—particularly in our civilization, but in other civilizations as well—of all kinds of strange experiences that people have. There's no question that people have mystical experiences. They have all kinds of altered states of consciousness. But so far, nothing follows. And I think Charles would agree with that. Just from having these kooky experiences, nothing whatever follows.

ROBERT: "Kooky" is a pejorative term.

JOHN: OK, sorry—these unusual experiences. Actually, I don't mind calling these experiences kooky. To me, it's not pejorative. I love kooky

experiences. But some people might think it's pejorative. The interesting question is, Do we have solid evidence that some guy can sit on this side of the room and bend spoons on the other side? I would want a stricter scientific methodology employed in these cases, because the kind of cases I know where people purport to bend spoons are very unconvincing.

FRED: We're looking in the wrong direction. The assumption everybody here is making is that only the physical is real. It's now clear that what's physical can't even be contained in the physical. For example, a magnetic field exists in space and time, and there's no physicality to a magnetic field. It's not mass and it's not energy, in that sense, yet we describe it and construct metaphors for it—it's wavy, it has lines of force, and so on—because description and metaphor is what we do. So we have a metaphor for the body—that it's a massive thing—and everything else has to be contained within it. But there's clear evidence of a subjective nature, of a spiritual essence, which indicates that people have memories of things that they could not possibly remember from their life experiences. Spoon bending may or may not be phony; I don't know about that. But there's evidence for spiritual connections that transcend the individual "I."

ROBERT: Fred, you've sought the nature of soul by searching some of the Eastern traditions and religions. Why should we, as we begin the twenty-first century, look to ancient traditions to give us knowledge about what we are?

FRED: Because of what Lenin said about the Russian Revolution: "One step forward, two steps back." You need to look back in time in order to see where we've been going. It turns out that there are ancient spiritual traditions—for example, Cabala [the esoteric interpretation of the Hebrew scriptures by rabbinical mystics], or the beliefs of the ancient people of Chaldea, around the Tigris and Euphrates—that depict the nature of spirit and soul and consciousness in a way reminiscent of how quantum physics would speak of the vacuum of space. The vacuum of space as the home of the soul or the spirit. Are vibrations in the apparent nothingness of space the consciousness effervescence of which we all partake? And the memories that we all have? We think, Oh, that's only my memory. But your brain is a million years old; it has its own memories.

ROBERT: Warren, you seem a little amused by all this. How would you evaluate Fred's view of collective memories?

WARREN: Well, it's on a level that, within my area of science, is just very difficult to deal with. One can postulate ancient, nonphysical entities as being a part of who I am now, in that sense. I certainly would suggest that God exists and that there is a spiritual universe. And what we have in ancient religious traditions are some changing attempts to represent that spiritual universe. But whether those ancient traditions have anything directly to do with my self and my consciousness—that's a big leap for me.

ROBERT: Charles [Tart] and Fred [Wolf], in your writings both of you seem to dethrone, or delegitimize, science-centered materialism, based on the following argument: Science has lost its right to explain the world with any overarching authority, since science has caused more bad things than good things throughout history. The argument continues that we need to look to other systems of knowing rather than traditional science to help us comprehend reality. But doesn't your argument confuse morality with reality? My opinion—which I do give from

time to time—is that it doesn't matter what science produces. Results are irrelevant; truth is amoral.

CHARLES: You're putting me in a box where I'm not going to let you put me, Robert. I have nothing against science, and I don't attribute the bad things in the world to science—I never

---

I have nothing against science . . . What I object to is scientism.

---

have. What people do with the truths discovered by science is a matter of morality and intelligence. That's a different issue. What I object to is scientism.

ROBERT: Scientism being a belief system in which science and the scientific method are virtually omniscient, able to discern all truth.

CHARLES: What I object to is science always being an open-ended process—always saying, "Let's keep looking at the data," "Here's what we make of it," "This is our best guess at the time." What I object to is when these "best guesses" turn into a religion. Consider a situation where someone has a spiritual experience—and I've counseled many such people—and he or she mentions the experience in front of someone who's "scientific," and the listener says, "That's impossible! You must be crazy!" That attitude I don't like. That dismissal of people's actual experiences is not good science. It's arrogance in the guise of science. That's scientism.

FRED: My major concern, coming out of the ranks of science, has been my own arrogance.

How arrogant I was, to put down other people's ideas that didn't agree with my scientific view. When I went around the world and spent time with indigenous peoples and tribes, I realized that my arrogance just didn't fit in. Like the man in the story by H. G. Wells, I thought that in the country of the scientifically blind, the one-eyed man would be king. In fact, I was the one who was blind. I was intellectually incapacitated. As long as I held on to my scientific view, I couldn't see. I thought I saw everything; I didn't see anything. So I had to give up much of what I previously held as real, in order to see what these people saw. And when I was finally able to attain this new vision, it totally changed my view of science. And I began seeing science as a tool— not the be-all and end-all of the universe, but a tool to help us begin to dig deeper into the nature of what it means to be a human being. I don't think we've arrived at that point yet. I don't think we're quite awake yet. I think we're all still asleep—dreaming, hoping, wishing— mechanically relying on our intellect to lead us out of the morass in which we constantly find ourselves. When we can use our heart and our spirit as well as our brain, that's when science will begin to adapt to a new world order.

ROBERT: Charles, how does spirituality affect people's lives? You deal with "transpersonal psychology." What does that mean?

CHARLES: Human beings have a need for meaning. They have a need for feeling that they're part of something larger than themselves. Biological gratification is not enough. Some of the kinds of meanings humanity has created have been unreasonable. We need something deeper. Our traditional religions used to provide meaning for people, telling them, "You don't just exist alone; you're part of a big picture of the world—and there are things you should do and things you shouldn't do." These traditional religions aren't working for a lot of people anymore, because they're based too much on beliefs, many of which don't fit in with what we know scientifically about the world. We need a practical spirituality that is consistent with our scientific knowledge.

ROBERT: What does "practical spirituality" mean?

CHARLES: Practical spirituality isn't just a set of ideas but also involves the heart; however, the heart must be an educated heart. For example, one of the practical spiritual ideas that has revolutionized my personal life is the understanding that emotions can be trained to be intelligent, to tell us something about the world. Emotions need to be balanced with intelligence, intuition, and the like. I agree with Fred [Wolf] here.

JOHN: I don't see this opposition that you make between biology and nature on the one hand and spirituality on the other, because this human need for meaning and transcendence is as much biologically based as any other human need. That is, it's part of our genetic structure, and part of our culture. Sure, we would like to find things that transcend the stupidity and mediocrity of most everyday existence. But I don't see a conflict between these natural longings and the rest of nature. Transcendent needs are part of nature.

FRED: The problem with that view [i.e., the desire for transcendence is entirely generated by personal biology] is that it leads to separation, to isolation, to aloneness, to feelings of not being part of something—whereas our natural inclination is to be part of a community.

JOHN: These are old categories, like science versus nonscience, mind versus body. These categories are obsolete.

FRED: I agree.

JOHN: It's just knowledge. Let's find out how the world works. Sometimes, when society is satisfied enough about how some part of the world works so that you can get a grant for

---

As long as we get at the truth, who cares if it's science?

---

doing research on it, then people are willing to call it science. I don't care if they call what I do "science." It doesn't matter. As long as we get at the truth, who cares if it's science? And if we have all kinds of strange phenomena, they're worthy of study.

ROBERT: Don't you find it fascinating that biological systems, in your terms, have a need for meaning? Did that evolve?

JOHN: Absolutely fascinating. And of course it evolved. There isn't any doubt about it. There isn't any doubt that human beings, with our pathetic forty-six chromosomes and a hundred billion neurons, have evolved this tremendous intellectual capacity for transcending the stupidity and mediocrity of most of the things that fill our ordinary lives. That's what makes life interesting.

DEAN: Right. And so the key question is, What is the nature of the scientific evidence that supports spirituality? And by spirituality, I assume

we mean something like transcending the ordinary boundaries of space and time.

ROBERT: What evidence of such spirituality can meet the traditional standards of science?

DEAN: I was struck by John's remark earlier, about spoon bending. Of course the scientific evidence for spoon bending is very, very poor. In popular culture, spoon bending is all that most people know about psychic research. But in fact there's a huge body of additional research, much of it published in mainstream journals, which says that there are anomalies out there, affirmed by strong scientific evidence, that support ideas of spirituality.

JOHN: I welcome all the facts we can lay our hands on. I certainly don't want to suggest that we shouldn't accumulate all these data, but there's a mistake that I think we want to avoid. We shouldn't assume that these data of anomalous phenomena are either fraudulent or else conclusive proof of the supernatural. There are all kinds of other possibilities. We have the "Clever Hans" history in the nineteenth century, Hans being a horse that appeared to do arithmetic, but it turned out that he was getting unconscious cues from the trainer. That was neither fraudulent nor did it demonstrate some supernatural power on the part of the horse. I take any anomalous data as just more evidence—more stuff with which we can work. If I don't take it as evidence of a supernatural realm, neither do I take it as necessarily fraudulent.

WARREN: There's a larger problem here—the nature of God's action in the universe. But I don't think it's necessary to require the action of a soul within the psychological or mental mechanisms of a human being. We can understand all that human beings think and do as an embodied physical process, the complex workings of the brain, an emergent function of the kinds of things that the brain does.

ROBERT: Are there ethical implications of despiritualizing the soul?

WARREN: My coeditors and I had to address this issue in our book, *Whatever Happened to the Soul?* If you make human consciousness and free will a cognitive process, you have the problem of dealing with the cognitively impaired. So we ask about the essence of soul within the Christian religion, and we say that what "soul" is meant to convey is the nature and experiences of "personal relatedness."

ROBERT: Are you saying, in your rather unconventional Christian view, that "soul" is more an adjective than a noun—a modifier of other things rather than a thing in itself?

WARREN: Yes. "Soul" is really an adjectival term; it connotes "soulish" or "soulishness."

ROBERT: Define "soulishness," with a practical example.

WARREN: Soulishness is personal relatedness. An application is when an individual who has diminished cognitive capacity is supported in a human community; here the soulishness or personal relatedness support is asymmetrical. The community can support an individual with diminished capacity, even though the handicapped person cannot reciprocate.

ROBERT: Are there ethical or spiritual implications of this asymmetric relationship?

WARREN: The ethical implication is that the community has a responsibility to maintain soulishness, a relatedness to the individual who has less capacity for reciprocating. The spiritual implications—and the ultimate example—is the concept of grace. Grace is God's relationship with us at a level at which we are not capable of symmetrically relating back. We stand in an asymmetrical relationship with God.

ROBERT: Charles, how does Warren's description of soulishness articulate with your own view of spirituality?

CHARLES: It's too abstract. I want to bring this discussion back to a more concrete level. If you're a Christian, prayer is a central aspect of your spirituality. Now, from a conventional scientific point of view, if the mind is nothing but electrochemical processes in the brain, when you pray you're talking to yourself, and that's the end of it. Maybe it makes you feel better, but then neuroscience will develop a drug that will make you feel better [quicker], too.

WARREN: This is why I say that the real prob-

. . . the real problem goes back to the nature of God's action in the universe.

---

lem goes back to the nature of God's action in the universe.

ROBERT: Fred, how have people reacted to your book on the spiritual universe?

FRED: I've received very good responses—particularly from scientifically inclined people who feel that they've lost a sense of the spiritual. They want spirituality in their lives, but they feel that science has pulled the rug out from under their feet. They're looking to books like mine to help reconcile their spiritual longings with their scientific understanding.

ROBERT: Charles, you have a Web site where scientists can explore their own spirituality.

CHARLES: That's right. TASTE [an acronym for The Archives of Scientists' Transcendent Experiences] is an online journal devoted to transcendent experiences that scientists have reported. On the Web site [www.issc-taste.org], scientists can anonymously post their own spiritual experiences in a psychologically and professionally safe space, without fear that they'll be laughed at. Scientists have spiritual experiences, too—and, following on Fred's point, they should know that there can be a reality to such experiences. Over the years many scientists, once they've realized I'm a safe person to talk to, have told me about unusual experiences they've had—but who later said, "Strange, it was incredible, it changed my life—except I thought, This must be crazy, it just can't be so." Too often I was the first and only person they ever told about their experiences, for fear of ridicule from their colleagues and adverse effects on their career. Such fears have, unfortunately, too much of a basis in fact—it's the social conditioning of our times. I want to change that.

ROBERT: You've said that scientists today occupy a social role like that of "high priests," proclaiming what is and isn't "real," and consequently what is and isn't valuable and sane.

CHARLES: Unfortunately, the dominant materialistic and reductionistic climate of contemporary science (what sociologists long ago named

scientism, an attitude different from the essential process of science), rejects and suppresses a priori both having and sharing transcendent, transpersonal, and altered states (or "spiritual" and "psychic," to use common words, in spite of their too vague connotations) experiences. From my perspective as a psychologist, this rejection and suppression distorts and harms scientists' and laypersons' transcendent (and other) potentials, and also inhibits the development of a genuine scientific understanding of the full spectrum of consciousness.

ROBERT: John, how do you react to reports of transcendent experiences?

JOHN: As I was suggesting earlier, there's no question that people have all sorts of interesting, fascinating, strange experiences, and this ought to be a matter of great interest to us. But just from the existence of the experience by itself, nothing follows. It doesn't follow that these people are in communication with the navel of the universe, or that there's a separate realm that's not part of the world we live in.

ROBERT: But to comprehend fully the human condition, we have to explore these transcendent experiences.

JOHN: Absolutely. It's absolutely crucial to take all the data. And part of the data that we have about human life is that people have all sorts of experiences that transcend ordinary, everyday mediocrity. This isn't something to be lamented or sneered at. It's something to be cherished and investigated.

WARREN: I'm not sure that "nothing follows" from a spiritual experience. From most of these experiences—particularly the ones related in culture and literature—a great deal follows.

Changes can occur, such as in people's beliefs and belief systems, how they conduct their lives, and how they relate to other people. I totally agree that from a scientific perspective of assessing reality, nothing follows—but from a personal perspective, a great deal follows.

JOHN: Nothing follows that could help us understand existence or reality.

WARREN: Exactly. But much follows in terms of personal perspective.

JOHN: I agree with that. When I say "nothing follows," this means that if I have a mystical experience in which I sense the existence of God, for example, it does not follow that God exists in reality. My experience is just an experience.

WARREN: From a scientific point of view, I agree.

JOHN: From any point of view. I may have had the experience, and it may have been an interesting experience, but nothing follows about reality.

ROBERT: Warren, help us understand how your concept of soulishness works in real people.

WARREN: Soulishness, as I've said, is personal relatedness—deep and rich levels of personal relatedness. The interaction between a therapist and a client, for example, is really dealing with the soulishness of that client, with the interpersonal experience of relatedness. Soulishness is not something "out there"—it's relatedness to other people, relatedness to the world.

ROBERT: Charles, does Warren's [Brown] soulishness equate to your transpersonal psychology?

CHARLES: No. It's good what he has there, but transpersonal psychology is about those experiences that seem to go beyond our biological limits. And to me the question is, Is this possible?

ROBERT: The question is fundamental: Can the reach of the mind exceed the boundaries of the brain? Or are these mystical experiences simply triggered by random or chaotic biological processes in the brain?

CHARLES: I can program my computer to suddenly print out "I have contacted the great Central Processing Unit in the sky, and now I know all knowledge." And we would quite rightly regard that statement as nonsense. It's just an arbitrary arrangement of electrons within the computer. If a person comes to me and says, "I've had a mystical experience. I've been in touch with a higher being, and have received certain truths—"

ROBERT: You'd get a doctor to prescribe a tranquilizer?

CHARLES: Well, if I were the doctor, would I prescribe a tranquilizer, or would I ask if there were a possibility that the mystical experience might be worth looking into? I think we have enough laboratory evidence so that I wouldn't just dismiss these experiences as brain simulations of unrealities. There could be a nonphysical being; there could be communication through some extrasensory mechanism like telepathy, or something like that.

JOHN: I would reject the idea that if you have these intense experiences, either you're in touch with the universe or you need a tranquilizer. There are all kinds of other possibilities as well.

ROBERT: I'm just worried about not giving the person that tranquilizer. Who knows what could happen?

CHARLES: Well, having such an experience could be dangerous, but remember, our baseline is that life is dangerous to begin with. We're not always safe. But if people have such mystical experiences, and I tell them that there might be some reality there, how those people handle the experiences is a totally separate question. Is the person going to deal with a transcendent happening in a sane, mature way, or is he or she going to get inflated by the experience and go crazy with it?

JOHN: The way we think of therapeutic problems is already corrupted by our philosophical, religious, and scientific tradition. For example, we think that there's a mind and a body and therefore there are diseases of the mind and diseases of the body—and that's already a massive confusion. And it does an enormous amount of harm. For example, consider the placebo effect. You give a patient a sugar tablet, and if the patient gets better, then the assumption is that there was nothing wrong in the first place. It doesn't follow. You can have some very serious illnesses that are helped by placebo effects, and the assumption that therefore "there was nothing wrong with you" is based on the mind-body dualism that we should be militant against.

WARREN: I agree with that. I think the placebo effect is the best illustration of "something follows" in terms of what may result from my beliefs—where there's a real physical outcome as expressed by my bodily immune system. So even if "nothing follows" in terms of making a metaphysical statement about God, these mystical experiences can clearly cause something that follows them.

ROBERT: But those are two different categories in which something may or may not follow from mystical experiences. The first category deals with the external world, the essence of the universe, the nature of reality—here's where John [Searle] says "nothing follows." The second category is the psychophysical aspects of the mind-body and how the mind affects the body—here's where Warren says that "something follows." It's important to keep the two categories separate.

WARREN: Correct. My comments focused on the category of psychophysical interactions, where something does follow from mystical experiences. What doesn't follow are any necessary statements about the existence of God or a spirit realm.

FRED: As human beings, we seek meaning in life, and if that meaning is eroded or destroyed by any system—whether scientism, religion, or philosophy—we're in danger. We need to be open to possibilities.

DEAN: There's a third category with which we can assess whether something or nothing follows from mystical experiences. We've been talking about the metaphysical and the psychophysical aspects of strange experiences. There's also the category of just pure physics; because if somebody said that he had an amazing experience where he somehow understood things apprehended from far away without any sensory communications, I would wonder whether there was something funny about physics. I would not wonder so much about metaphysics or psychology. I would focus on what we can study in a physics laboratory—and then suddenly these strange experiences can have consequences that do follow.

FRED: There's always something funny about

. . . physics is not the end of our understanding—it's really just a beginning.

———————————————

physics, because physics is not the end of our understanding—it's really just a beginning.

ROBERT: In summary, let's project forward a hundred years. What more has happened to the soul?

CHARLES: We'll have evidence that one mind can communicate with another, with no known channel to account for it—and this will be recognized as a mechanism for prayer.

JOHN: A hundred years from now, we'll know enough about the brain so that the anomalous stuff we're stuck with today will no longer seem so mysterious to us.

DEAN: Actually, I completely agree with John [Searle], but I also believe that our advanced knowledge will redefine what we think of the soul.

WARREN: I agree, but there will still be some mystery in the universe. We won't be able to scientifically approach the idea of God's action in the universe.

ROBERT: Are there any more mysteries that will remain?

FRED: All of the above. There will still be mystery, as we begin to realize that there's something about us that's not just brain, not just mind—

and not just self, yourself, himself, herself, ourselves, but that there's a unity to us all, of which each of us is a reflection. That unity will become very real for us.

ROBERT: CONCLUDING COMMENT

The question of nonphysical souls, immortal or any other kind, may be more complex than commonly assumed. Scientists and theologians, it seems, are found on both sides of the Great Divide. I limit myself to a single question: Can science seek the soul? Is it within the realm of the scientific method to even address this question? My answer is yes, and no. Yes, in that the accumulating discoveries of brain function eliminate artificial mysteries, previously the province of the soul. No, in that there may remain certain kinds of knowledge that the scientific method cannot assess. Some say that we should combine science and theology harmoniously—but sometimes dichotomy, not harmony, brings us closer to truth.

——————————————— ———————————————

OUTTAKES

CHARLES: *Robert, I'm not sure I agree with your concluding statement—that there are some things the scientific method can't look into.*

ROBERT: *I'd be nervous if you agreed with everything I said.*

DEAN: *As soon as we understand something, we call it science.*

ROBERT: *Things may exist in the reaches of reality that can never be understood.*

FRED: *You're all beginning to sound like me.*

CHAPTER 5

What Is Parapsychology?

Can claims of extrasensory perception, or ESP as it is commonly called, be studied as a science? Can assertions of psychic phenomena be subject to the scientific method of experimental design, statistical significance, and independent replication? The controversial field is called parapsychology, and if you can read minds, see the future, or sense unusual things, we have some parapsychologists who would like to meet you—and test you. But critics—who call themselves skeptics—assert that the entire field is virtually all pseudoscience, without serious merit, just capitalizing on uncritical media and a gullible public. Parapsychology, according to skeptics, should be debunked. Parapsychology, according to proponents, is the scientific study of the paranormal, also known as psi phenomena. It is the careful investigation of events—like mental telepathy, clairvoyance, or other bizarre manifestations—that seemingly cannot be accounted for by natural law or knowledge. The claim that parapsychology is a real science excites some but annoys others. Is parapsychology a new science or an old fraud? Here we brought together some leading parapsychologists and skeptics. They joust and we judge.

PARTICIPANTS

Dr. Barry Beyerstein, a neuropsychologist at Simon Fraser University in Canada and a leading skeptic, is a regular contributor to the *Skeptical Inquirer* magazine. Barry explains how skeptics approach parapsychology.

Dr. Dean Radin, an experimental psychologist who has conducted ESP experiments, is the author of *The Conscious Universe.* Dean believes that ESP research demonstrates what he calls "the scientific truth about psychic phenomena."

Dr. Marilyn Schlitz, trained as an anthropologist, is the research director of the Institute of Noetic Sciences and a leading scientist in parapsychology. Marilyn presents careful experiments supporting the existence of psychic phenomena.

Dr. Charles Tart, a research pioneer in scientific parapsychology, is the author of over 250 articles published in professional books and journals, including *Science* and *Nature.* Charles is a spiritual seeker who believes that one of his virtues as a scientist is that he hates to be fooled.

Dr. James Trefil, a professor of physics at George Mason University, is a prolific author and commentator on science in the national media. Jim views parapsychology through the critical eyes of a mainstream scientist.

ROBERT: Dean, why do you think that the scientific method can be applied to the investigation of psychic phenomena? Skeptical critics claim that ESP is more wishful thinking or ancient superstition than serious science, with a touch of modern fraud tossed in now and then.

DEAN: Science consists of two general areas: there is the act of measurement, which is the

---

. . . it's quite true that we don't have very good theories about why psychic phenomena happen.

---

empirical side of science, and there is the development of mechanisms, which is its theoretical side. When people ask the question, "Is parapsychology scientific?" they're almost always thinking about the theoretical side. And it's quite true that we don't have very good theories about why psychic phenomena happen.

ROBERT: Do you mean that even those scientists who are convinced of the reality of psychic

phenomena cannot construct convincing fundamental mechanisms—theories—to explain its underlying cause?

DEAN: Yes. But on the measurement side, it's very clear that the scientific method can be brought to bear on these phenomena.

ROBERT: We're going to examine that assertion. Charles, you've been a parapsychologist for forty years; you're one of parapsychology's founders. Can you describe the field and give some sense of its import for human understanding?

CHARLES: Parapsychology is our modern name for what was originally called psychical research. It began as an organized field of inquiry in the nineteenth century, when there was much conflict between science and religion. Science seemed to be explaining more and more of the world, and it threatened to throw out religion totally. But a few scientists thought that religion was not all nonsense. They wondered whether it was possible to apply the methods of science, which had worked so well in the physical sciences, to examine the strange or unusual happenings associated with religion and to find out whether those phenomena are actual fact or just superstition. Parapsychology is the modern evolution of those early investigations.

ROBERT: Barry, you're a neuroscientist and a skeptic. I know what a neuroscientist does—you study the brain. What does a skeptic do?

BARRY: A skeptic is someone who demands reasonable evidence and reasonable logic to back up extraordinary claims. I wouldn't call parapsychology a pseudoscience, as long as it uses the same experimental controls, the same

---

I wouldn't call parapsychology a pseudoscience, as long as it uses the same experimental controls . . .

---

techniques, and the same mathematical and statistical procedures that are used within mainstream science. We can disagree about the adequacy of the evidence—that's what I'm skeptical about—but I don't claim that it's all fraud or pseudoscience. The key is the amount of evidence and the availability of that evidence for skeptics to check.

ROBERT: We're going to give you some evidence right now. Marilyn, the Institute of Noetic Sciences is a leading center of research on the mind and unusual phenomena. Could you describe your own most compelling experiments where human "senders" influenced the physiological responses of human "receivers" at a distance, without any intervening sensory communications?

MARILYN: We were interested in evaluating the extraordinary claims made by healers in different cultures. Were those healers somehow able to influence the physiology of people at a distance, under conditions where recipients didn't even know that senders were trying to affect them? Since such investigations are very difficult to conduct in a field setting, we moved into the laboratory. The experiment monitored the measurable effects of autonomic nervous activity, which is the part of our physiology that functions automatically.

ROBERT: Like heart rate, breathing, peristalsis.

MARILYN: That's right. So I would invite you into the lab and I would monitor various attributes of your physiology.

ROBERT: I'm nervous already.

MARILYN: We can calm you. . . . Then we would start monitoring your galvanic skin response, the electrical activity of your skin, which is the same method used in lie detectors—

ROBERT: I'm not coming near you.

MARILYN: Oh, you have something to hide, do you? Here's the procedure. You, as the recipient-subject, sit in one room while we're monitoring your physiology. Then we invite a sender-healer to sit in a distant room, and there's absolutely no sensory communication between the two of you. We ask this healer, at specific random moments, to influence your physiology at a distance. So, for example, he or she might try to calm you, by employing psychical projections of serenity. We then compare your autonomic nervous system activity during the test periods, when the healer is attempting to calm you, with your autonomic nervous system during the control periods, when everything is the same except the healer is not sending. We call these experiments "intentionality at a distance."

ROBERT: As the recipient, I wouldn't know when the healer was trying to exert influence—intentionality—at a distance?

MARILYN: Exactly. You'd have no idea when these influence periods occur; they're randomly distributed throughout the session. We've now compiled about forty experiments that were set up under this kind of protocol. Overall, the results are highly compelling. There are strong statistical data to support the idea that there's some kind of exchange of information between the sender and the recipient, even though under these conditions there's no sensory contact.

ROBERT: Have you had nonbelievers—skeptics—auditing the experimental design, the data, and the statistical analysis?

MARILYN: The most recent experiments I've done were with a professor from England, Richard Wiseman, who's a card-carrying member of the skeptical community. He was very interested in doing experiments together, and the first project we did was in his lab, under his conditions. Everything was identical—same equipment, same randomization procedures, same subject population—except that I worked with half the people and he worked with half the people. The result was that we both replicated our initial findings: I got statistical significance and he didn't. This result was compelling to us, in terms of what effect the expectations of the researcher might have on the results. We then invited Richard to come over to my laboratory and set up the same experiment—and, again, we replicated the effect a second time. These experiments suggest that not only is there

an effect but it can happen under conditions where skeptics and proponents work together. And they further suggest that there may be some way in which the belief systems or expectations of the researcher come into play.

ROBERT: Jim, you're a physicist. One of your many books is *101 Things You Don't Know About Science.* Did you include parapsychology in your list?

JIM: No—that book was a tour of the frontiers of science at the end of the twentieth century.

ROBERT: Why didn't you include parapsychology?

JIM: One of the criteria I used for including an issue was that there had to be some reasonable expectation that the issue would be resolved in the foreseeable future. Parapsychology has been around, as has been said, for over a century. I don't see a resolution coming anytime soon, so I didn't include it.

ROBERT: Dean, take us through the categories of parapsychology. People know what mental telepathy is, but there's more.

DEAN: There are four classic categories that are studied as part of parapsychology. One is telepathy, as you said. The common understanding that telepathy means "the reading of minds" is not quite right, because that sounds as though thoughts were being perceived, and this virtually never happens. Telepathy means that there's some kind of mind-to-mind connection; it's often a feeling, the kind of emotion that seems to pass. The second category is clairvoyance, which is getting information from a distance, either in space or time. The third category is precognition, which can be considered a subset of clairvoyance, which is the acquisition of specific information through time.

ROBERT: So clairvoyance is defined as the occurrence of apprehending information directly, something that you couldn't know through the senses. Clairvoyance differs from telepathy in that clairvoyance perceives information directly from an object or about an event, whether past, present, or future, without the necessity of any other mind knowing about that object or event.

DEAN: Right. For example, the object or the event can be hidden, as in an envelope or at a distance, so that normal senses couldn't perceive it. Or it could be displaced in time, whether precognition [knowledge of the future] or retrocognition [knowledge of the past]. The fourth category is psychokinesis, popularly known as "mind over matter."

ROBERT: What's a classic "mind-over-matter" experiment?

DEAN: In the old days, gamblers would claim that they could toss the dice and make a certain number come up more often than chance should allow, and that initiated about forty or fifty years of research, doing exactly that experiment.

ROBERT: Might trips to casinos alleviate some of the financial pressure of funding parapsychological research?

DEAN: There are two questions here: first, is there any effect when gamblers "will" certain numbers to come up; and second, if there's an effect, what is its magnitude? It turns out that when we do the overall assessment, we discover that there's an effect, but its magnitude is less than one percent. That's not very big.

ROBERT: One percent is well below the lowest odds advantages of the house. Do we cancel the trip to Las Vegas?

DEAN: You'll continue to lose at the casinos, though maybe a little bit slower.

ROBERT: Charles, give us some sense of the classic experiments in parapsychology, and how the field developed originally as a science.

CHARLES: In Victorian days, people played what you might call telepathic parlor games. I might ask you to go off in another room, open a book, and read a certain passage, while back here the rest of our little group would try to write down our mental impression of whatever was in that passage. Let's say that on occasion some of us would get a few words that were the same as those in the book. This kind of experiment is very hard to evaluate; there are lots of words in a book passage. There were many informal, inconclusive experiments like this.

ROBERT: How were the first reasonably scientific experiments designed?

CHARLES: A more classic telepathy experiment would work something like this. Someone goes off to a different room and shuffles a stack of cards a dozen times to make sure it's thoroughly mixed. He or she would then, at predetermined time intervals—say, every sixty seconds—look at one card at a time. Meanwhile people back in the original room would write down their impression of the order of the cards. We could then evaluate, with statistical mathematics, whether the experiment produced results that were sufficiently above chance to justify the supposition that sometimes information was being transferred. I'd estimate that there are now several hundred experiments showing that this kind of telepathy experiment can produce results greater than chance. Now, it's a small effect, as Dean [Radin] said; it differs from chance by only a few percentage points. It's very rare to get a perfect score; getting a hundred-percent-correct result in such an experiment has happened maybe two or three times in the whole history of the field.

ROBERT: Given the huge number of experiments that have been conducted, one would expect, just from normal randomized statistical distribution, that every once in a while the results *would* be a hundred percent perfect. I'd equally expect that every now and then the results would be a complete bust—getting nothing right, zero percent.

CHARLES: Except that we have sophisticated sets of statistical tools that can differentiate between results that reflect statistical significance and random distribution. Of course, one can make the counterargument that the published results are only those experiments that happen to come out above chance, and that if you included all the actual experiments done but unpublished, then the total results would approximate chance. To test this claim, you can figure out how many unsuccessful, unpublished psi experiments would have to have been done. It turns out that for this counterargument to be true, then every man, woman, and child on the face of the earth would have to have been doing ten failed experiments a day for the last five thousand years. This shows the strength of the data. The evidence for the existence of telepathy or clairvoyance is overwhelming.

ROBERT: We're talking about a meta-analysis of parapsychological experiments—an analysis that pulls together a large number of independent experiments.

DEAN: Meta-analysis means the analysis of analyses, so rather than doing multiple trials in a single experiment, you look at the collected results of many experiments.

ROBERT: In the last thirty or forty years of parapsychological research, what's your strongest piece of evidence?

MARILYN: I don't think we can identify one particular experiment that makes the case for the field; we have to look at the aggregate. Research has taken different directions. There's the remote viewing work, where people are attempting to describe characteristics of geographical locations at a distance. A number of experiments have now been done using this kind of procedure—and have been replicated consistently—producing sufficient data to demonstrate that there's some kind of effect happening here.

ROBERT: You've conducted some of the interesting Ganzfeld experiments; this is a procedure where you reduce sensory input for subjects and then ask them to describe, say, a remote video clip. One of the favorite techniques is to tape sliced Ping-Pong balls over their eyes and feed white noise into their ears; then they're asked to imagine what somebody else is drawing, or something like that.

MARILYN: The Ganzfeld is a procedure that was initiated at the turn of the twentieth century, when introspective psychological experiments were popular. Sensory deprivation is a technique that induces imagery; in a way, it simulates the dream experience, and people start seeing images.

ROBERT: Is it like an altered state of consciousness?

CHARLES: Yes, sensory deprivation is conducive to inducing an altered state.

ROBERT: Has it been shown that altered states have a positive correlation with evidence for telepathy and clairvoyance?

CHARLES: There's a general literature to that effect, and I believe that it's probably true. If I say, use your ESP, that's a simple, rational thing to do—and it usually doesn't work. We don't know what part of the mind ESP comes from, but it doesn't seem to come from normal consciousness.

ROBERT: Barry, what does a skeptic make of all this?

BARRY: Unfortunately, the debate has gotten so technical that what we're now talking about are very, very small statistical effects. And when the effects are that small, and that difficult for skeptics like myself and my students to replicate, then we have to look to the possibility that there are interesting statistical anomalies and artifacts here, not real phenomena. A statistical effect, if you get one, means that it's unlikely for the event in question to have happened by chance alone. But even if there's something operating here, statistical significance alone can't tell you what that something is. Is it some paranormal phenomenon? Or is it sensory leakage? Is it fraud? Is it recording error? Or is it some kind of subtle artifact of the experiment that's well worth studying but is normal, in the sense that it doesn't violate our sense of the physical world. There are just so many possibilities other than paranormal explanations, and statistics alone will never tell us what's really going on. Statistics can only inform us that it's unlikely that there's nothing but chance operating there.

ROBERT: I have a sense that in recent times there's actually less research going on in parapsychology than there was a few decades ago. Innovative research interest, today, seems oriented more toward transpersonal and other kinds of holistic psychologies. Has the experimental side of parapsychology diminished in importance?

DEAN: I don't think the importance of parapsychological research has diminished at all. It may be that the total number of people actively doing experiments is probably somewhat lower.

ROBERT: Why is that?

DEAN: I think interest in parapsychology goes in cycles. There's something like a twenty-year funding cycle.

ROBERT: It has nothing to do with sunspots?

DEAN: Well, perhaps that, too—but I don't think so. It's quite interesting that fifty years ago the usual skeptical response was that parapsychological phenomena were just impossible, full stop. But something new has occurred in the last decade or so. Barry brought out that we're now dealing with technical issues of experimentation, where we're trying to figure out whether this anomaly is psi or something more commonplace. And that's a very dramatic change.

ROBERT: Are you suggesting a subtle admission by skeptics that experimental data of parapsychological phenomena are meeting the critical tests of good science, such as tightly controlled experimental design, replicability by independent scientists and labs, and statistical significance?

DEAN: It changes the playing field from "You guys are nuts, because this stuff couldn't possibly be real" to "Let's figure out whether these anomalies are what they appear to be—because, after all, they came from people's experiences, not from strange experiments in the lab—and if they're what they appear to be, we've captured psi."

ROBERT: What do your friends and colleagues in mainstream science think of your chosen profession?

DEAN: They hold a range of opinions, but in general here's what happens. Scientist friends or colleagues will come into my lab—some claiming they're skeptics, some not—and then they actually spend time running experiments and looking at the results. When they do these steps themselves, they usually change their opinion quite quickly. This opinion change is of two kinds. First, they realize that parapsychologists are as skeptical as they are. You have to be, because after years of scrutinizing these experiments, what we do now is quite good science. Second, they witness experiments that in some cases are really quite dramatic. Real anomalies emerge right before their eyes, and so my colleagues become really interested.

ROBERT: Jim, what would it take for you to move parapsychology from where you wouldn't even mention it in your books to recommending it for inclusion in mainstream scientific discussion?

JIM: In science, there's this process of first establishing that something happens—that there really is something going on that needs to be explained, and then you try to explain it; this is what you call experimental theory. My take on parapsychology is that I'm not convinced that there's something to be explained here.

ROBERT: What would convince you to change your opinion?

JIM: I could imagine carefully controlled experiments that produced anomalous data. I haven't seen Marilyn's [Schlitz] experiments; however, I've seen others that looked just as convincing initially, but then you get into these very technical discussions of the experimental design and the statistics. The issue often comes down to what sorts of things could produce these very small effects that people are measuring—things that wouldn't necessarily have anything to do with extrasensory perception but might be something in the design of the experiment or the way data was analyzed.

ROBERT: Charles, you've dealt with these issues for decades. Has the whole field of parapsychology devolved down to hypertechnicalities?

CHARLES: Meanwhile, back in the real world, real people are having real experiences that they believe are due to extrasensory perception. Surveys show that a majority of the population thinks they have had an ESP encounter personally. Of course, when you have people claiming

> *Meanwhile, back in the real world, real people are having real experiences that they believe are due to extrasensory perception.*

to have had a psychic experience, you ask yourself what it means. If you ask the people themselves, you get a large range of responses. Some go off the deep end, declaring, "I'm chosen by

God, because I'm so very special." Others try to make sense of what happened, but they run into skeptics who tell them that these experiences are impossible and anyone who thinks he's had such an experience is simply deluding himself. I don't think it's a particularly healthy response to invalidate people that way.

ROBERT: How would you respond to such a person describing an anomalous, seemingly psychic experience?

CHARLES: Some few of us look at the scientific literature on parapsychology and say, Well, we do have evidence for basic psi phenomena—like telepathy or precognition or something similar—so maybe this particular real-world instance was an actual occurrence. Psychic experiences are not just matters of academic interest. When people have a psychic experience, they quite often change their philosophy of life—or if they already have, say, spiritual values, these beliefs are then validated by the event. I'm not simply an experimental parapsychologist. I'm a transpersonal psychologist—which means that I'm interested in the personal, emotional applications of psychic experiences. I want us to have a good database on what happens in these experiences: What seems to be a real effect and what seems to be illusion? What kinds of people have them, and are they associated with mental illness? By the way, psi phenomena are not generally related to mental illness. Parapsychology can have practical relevance to real people's lives.

ROBERT: Charles, you wrote very personally that your initial interest in parapsychology related to an early conflict between science and religion. Do you think this tension, or longing, influenced your conclusions?

CHARLES: No. I have two guiding forces in my life. The first is that I hate to be fooled under any circumstances. And that makes me a very good scientist. I'm more critical of methodology in psi experiments than many scientists who take comparatively skeptical positions. My second guiding force is that I'd like there to be a bigger and more interesting universe, with meaning in it. So my way of dealing with my childhood conflict between science and religion was to become a scientifically rigorous researcher in parapsychology, just like the people who started the Society for Psychical Research in the nineteenth century. I applied the basic scientific method of observing data and testing theories to this area of unusual experiences, in order to see what's real and what's not—to ascertain what is, indeed, superstition and nonsense left over from earlier times.

ROBERT: How do you react to the increasing prominence and strength of the skeptical community?

CHARLES: I wish there were a genuinely skeptical community. I'm afraid that just about every skeptic I've ever met is what I call a pseudoskeptic. A real skeptic says, "I don't know about parapsychology and psi, and the explanations we have so far don't satisfy me. I want to look at the data." But the skeptics I've encountered claim to know already that there's nothing to it, and then they break all sorts of rules of scientific procedure to go about their debunking. Skepticism, as it is generally practiced, is neither legitimate science nor legitimate criticism.

ROBERT: Isn't it legitimate help when skeptics expose all the ridiculous claims that encrust serious parapsychology with absurdities?

CHARLES: That might have been true a hundred years ago, but the methodology in parapsychology has become so good, and parapsychologists are so thorough in their own criticism of one another's experiments, that the matter is pretty well handled.

ROBERT: But there are abundant common frauds, silly stories of ESP defying all credulity that circulate widely in the media. Furthermore, if the data are so robust, why do we have, right here, scientists on opposite sides? What is it about parapsychology that gives the field such weak acceptance?

MARILYN: I'm reminded of the joke that there are three stages in the skeptical acceptance of unorthodox ideas. First, the critics will say, "There's nothing in that data." Then, as you acquire more data, the second stage comes up: "Well, there might be something to it, but it's such a small effect that it's meaningless." And you acquire more data and show its relevance, and then the skeptical community says, "Of course, we knew it all along; so where have you been?"

ROBERT: Jim seems comfortably set in the first stage; Barry is, too, but he's also glancing at the second stage.

MARILYN: If we can give serious skeptics some education about the data, I think their stage could well change.

ROBERT: We'll arrange for Marilyn [Schlitz] to give Jim [Trefil] and Barry [Beyerstein] the results of her experiments. Then we'll get back together in the future—that's a promise.

MARILYN: I want to comment about the contribution of open-minded skeptics, because I

feel that they can make a great contribution to parapsychology. There's a lot of nonsense that dominates our culture. People are led down blind alleys and come to believe very strange things. General skepticism, therefore, is good for all of us. I agree with Dean [Radin] that para-

---

> *There's a lot of nonsense that dominates our culture. . . . General skepticism, therefore, is good for all of us.*

---

psychologists themselves are inherently skeptical, and I agree with Charles [Tart] that those of us collecting this data don't want to be fooled. But I've seen examples within the skeptical community where they are really helping us to refine our protocols and sharpen our critical skills.

ROBERT: That's a major contribution.

MARILYN: Yes, it is. There's a lot of room for healthy debate within the parapsychological community such that we can begin to move the field forward.

ROBERT: If there's genuine search for truth, parapsychologists and skeptical scientists make a great combination.

JIM: I've been involved in other areas of science where there's been a great deal of skepticism—for example, the skepticism greeting the theory that the dinosaurs were wiped out by the effects of an asteroid impact. I saw how the scientific community, driven by data, changed its mind and generally accepted this theory over a period of time. I just don't see that happening in parapsychology—it hasn't happened for a hundred years.

BARRY: I think Charles [Tart] is making a stereotype of what skeptics are. What he said doesn't jibe with the kind of skeptics that I know. It's not just that these supposed events are weird. We all accept quantum mechanics—which is totally counterintuitive—because it produces results. Quantum mechanics is replicable, it gives better explanations, and it makes predictions that turn out to be verified in experiments. There were many skeptical physicists; Albert Einstein himself went to his grave still figuring there was something wrong with it [see Chapter 25]. But quantum mechanics is not controversial anymore, because it has delivered the goods. And this is what parapsychology has yet to do. If it turns out that ESP or psi research does come up with something that tips the scales, then I don't know very many skeptics who would be any more skeptical about it than we are about quantum mechanics.

ROBERT: Dean, let's go on to something different. What is field consciousness? Give us some examples of how it may work.

DEAN: Field consciousness is a relatively new finding about what may happen when people get together in a group—say, as a choral group or a sports team—and they feel that something "just gels." Everyone is working together perfectly and there's a sense of coherence within the group. The same technology that we use to study mind-over-matter [psychokinetic] effects in the laboratory are applied to these situations to investigate whether there's something paranormal happening here.

ROBERT: Give us an example.

DEAN: Take an electronic random-number generator, which is like a coin flipper. The traditional experiments are one-to-one, with one generator and one person who tries to change the distribution, essentially, of heads and tails. The only difference, in field consciousness studies, is that you take this random-number generator and put it in the vicinity of a group that's doing something together, where there are moments of strong coherence—for example, during group meditation. The objective is to ascertain whether the act of coherence among a group is reflected as statistical anomalies in the random-number generator. There have been now something like seventy or eighty experiments of this kind in the past two years, and the grand accumulation of data suggests that something unusual does happen.

ROBERT: You've also used events on a grander scale, where very large populations are involved—such as when much of the world was tuned into the opening of the Olympics or the verdict in the O. J. Simpson trial—and come up with what you think is compelling data.

DEAN: This is the beginning of a new experimental area, but initial experiments suggest that something like a "mass-mind" effect might really exist—that when we have millions of minds thinking about the same thing, something happens.

ROBERT: Charles, give us some real-world examples of psychic phenomena.

CHARLES: During the Second World War, a friend of mine came home very tired from her defense job and fell sound asleep. Suddenly, in the middle of the night, she finds herself leaping out of bed and standing in the middle of the floor with a feeling of absolute horror. She has no idea what the absolute horror is about, and so she starts to feel silly after a while. She stands there for about thirty seconds, and then the house rumbles a little bit. She thinks maybe it's a minor earthquake, and she looks at the clock and goes back to bed. The next day she discovers that the Port Chicago Munitions Shipping Facility had blown up at the time she leaped out of bed, and the little rumble was the time it took the shock wave to go from Port Chicago to Berkeley. Was she responding to the horror of hundreds of people suddenly being killed and maimed? This is the kind of anomalous experience that happens to people in everyday life.

ROBERT: You've heard the following argument: Because every night so many people have so many nightmares about so many things, random coincidences like your friend's sudden waking timed with the munitions explosion must occur rather frequently. It's statistically mandated, though it's surely random. But when the random coincidence happens to one individual, it feels very special, even though it isn't. An analogy is winning the lottery—that's completely random, but to the winner it's very special.

CHARLES: The argument is a correct one, which is why we parapsychologists took all this psychic stuff into the laboratory almost a hundred years ago. We knew what coincidence was, and we had to rule it out conclusively.

ROBERT: Dean, do you have any amazing stories?

DEAN: Most of my amazing stories happen in the laboratory, for exactly the reason that Charles [Tart] just said. But the anecdotes are really compelling. I've had experiences like that

in my life, and you're absolutely right: it could be coincidence. So as a scientist I want to know whether, in principle, these coincidences could be some form of parapsychological phenomena.

ROBERT: The challenge is to investigate spontaneous, real-world psi phenomena in a controlled, scientific manner.

MARILYN: One parapsychologist did a study correlating the numbers of people who rode on trains on days when there were train wrecks with the numbers of people riding trains on average, safe days. Over the course of time, it looked as though there were significantly fewer passengers riding on the days of train wrecks. He also did some interesting work with business executives, assessing the incidence of psychic phenomena among people who were at top levels. The results indicated that high-level executives scored better than the average population on ESP, which suggests that these very successful people may be using certain kinds of psychic abilities in everyday life, in ordinary practice. Maybe they aren't labeling it psychic; certainly they don't consider it weird. But these successful executives may be, in fact, harnessing and employing psychic ability every day of their lives.

ROBERT: Dean, if a person is psychic but feels funny about admitting it, he may say he has a hunch or is just intuitive. That's our social protection. What are the standards of good science here? We normally talk about the replicability of evidence.

DEAN: Right. The gold standard of empirical science is whether an effect can be independently replicated by lots of people over a long period of time, and also whether conceptual replication can be shown—because, obviously, if you do exactly the same experiment and the experiment has a flaw in it, you just repeat the flaw. So in my book I focused on meta-analysis, combining many experiments in different classes of parapsychology to see whether replication exists, and comparing the results from parapsychology with those from other areas of science. The answer, very clearly, is yes, there is replication by many different people over long periods of time, and conceptual replication, in at least a few classes of parapsychological work.

BARRY: My trouble is that for the last twenty years I've been asking my psychology students to try replicating classic parapsychological experiments, without any positive results whatsoever. Since I have a random-number generator in my lab, other people from the community would come to ask my help in conducting ESP-type experiments. I've had psychics try to beat my random-number generator.

ROBERT: How have they done?

BARRY: Zip. Nothing. I just can't get any replication in these things.

MARILYN: To that I would argue that one can make the same kind of case for musical ability. To conclude that there's some genuine anomaly present, it doesn't necessarily have to be distributed evenly among the entire population.

BARRY: But I've done that. We've had people come in who claim to have psychic ability and they fall flat on their faces, too, just like my students.

DEAN: Are you claiming that you never get significant results?

BARRY: I'm saying [I get] nothing more than chance would predict.

DEAN: OK, but you're getting a distribution of results, some of which are positive and some negative.

BARRY: Individual trials and even individual persons may produce skewed results. If you run the random-number generator a hundred times, five of them, on average, will come out above chance. So the results match our statistical predictions for random behavior.

MARILYN: My experiments with Richard Wiseman—who is a member, recall, of the skeptical community—suggest that maybe there's something inherent in the experimenter's ability to elicit these kinds of phenomena.

BARRY: I like to take students who come to me because they want to prove me wrong. I give them the equipment, send them off and say, "OK, if it's bad vibes from me, fine—I'll be gone." Some of these students have actually refused to give me their data, because they were so embarrassed when nothing nonrandom happened.

DEAN: One of the problems here is that many scientists don't understand the meaning of statistics in the behavioral sciences. They're thinking of the type of precision you get in the physical sciences—which, of course, is substantially more precise than that in the behavioral sciences. Most conditions of human behavior are so variable that you need a much higher power of statistical analysis in order to pull out the significances.

ROBERT: This means more trials in the experiments and different mathematics in the analysis.

DEAN: Yes. If the underlying effect is very small, you need the right kind of statistics to come out with a significant result.

ROBERT: It makes me nervous when such a small effect is supporting a field that's challenging basic assumptions of the physical world.

DEAN: The effect is not so small. Sometimes the effects look small, but this is because the sum totals are the combined results of positive correlations and negative correlations canceling each other out.

ROBERT: A correlation of minus-one, which means a zero-percent relationship, is just as strong as a correlation of plus-one, which means a hundred-percent relationship.

CHARLES: If something is consistently wrong, it's just as useful as if something is consistently right. You just reverse the predictions.

BARRY: It's consistency that's the problem.

ROBERT: There are two opposing points here, both rather fun. On the one hand, it's conceivable that positive and negative correlations exist often in parapsychology, each representing massively significant psi; but since the positives and negatives are so entangled and can't be teased apart, they're constantly canceling each other out, so that the combined effect always appears minuscule. On the other hand, this argument does seem the perfect rationalization for little or nothing going on.

BARRY: Right; and [to a strict empiricist] it doesn't matter.

ROBERT: Jim, why are mainstream scientists reluctant to get involved, either as skeptics or participants, in this whole field?

JIM: It's about as risky as you can get.

MARILYN: So little money is allocated to parapsychology compared to any mainstream science.

ROBERT: Since the implications of parapsychology are so potentially momentous, why is a little risk such a deterrent to adventuresome scientists?

JIM: Let's look at this from the point of view of the scientist. The one bit of capital you have as a scientist is your research time, which is always limited. In building your career, you have to decide where you're going to spend your time and what the chances are of a payoff. When I look at parapsychology, I see a long history with

---

When I look at parapsychology, I see a long history with no payoff.

---

no payoff. I don't see any payoff upcoming. Speaking personally, I wouldn't do it. I have great admiration for people like Barry [Beyerstein] who get involved in the skeptical analyses, but frankly there's very little reward for such work in the scientific community. You don't get career-making points for skepticism.

ROBERT: Do you think that's good?

JIM: No, I don't think it's good, but it's a fact, OK? An individual scientist is much better off putting effort into normal research in a mainstream discipline than going off into a field like parapsychology, or even getting involved in opposing it, as a skeptic. There's just no payoff.

ROBERT: Charles, have you had a payoff?

CHARLES: Speaking as a parapsychologist, it's even more complicated than that. Not only don't you get any points for doing parapsychological research, you'll probably lose your university job if you do! This is especially true if you get positive results. This is historical fact; it's happened in many cases.

ROBERT: That sounds contrary to the ideals of scientific inquiry.

CHARLES: The academic world is not as open-minded as it's supposed to be, sad to say. But there's a deeper level that, as a psychologist, interests me greatly. It's only been a few hundred years since we burned people at the stake who we thought had strong psychic powers. Some of my own research shows that many people, under their conscious exteriors, harbor diffuse fears and emotional ambivalence about psychic results. Parapsychology is not a neutral topic—it affects people quite deeply.

ROBERT: Nobody will be burned at the stake today. We're going to take predictions. One hundred years from now, will parapsychology be recognized as a mainstream science?

DEAN: I think the answer is yes, but it won't be called parapsychology anymore. It'll be absorbed into mainstream science.

MARILYN: I would agree with Dean [Radin], and I think parapsychology is going to be applied to things like health care.

BARRY: I would actually like to agree, too, but I don't hold much hope that it will actually happen. If the data are there, then it's no longer "para" anything, it's part of physics or part of physiology, or both. If data come in a way that skeptics can accept, then parapsychology can fold its tent and become part of mainstream science.

ROBERT: But that's not going to happen?

BARRY: No, I'm not expecting that to happen.

JIM: I think we'll go along in the next century pretty much as we've gone along in the last century. There will be people who keep trying to establish parapsychology as a legitimate field of science, and it just won't happen.

CHARLES: I'm between the optimists and the pessimists. I think we'll have reasonable practical applications in which psychic abilities can help. Even more important, we'll be looking at the implications of psychic phenomena for our transpersonal or spiritual nature. That's what will be really important.

ROBERT: CONCLUDING COMMENT

About one fact there is no dispute. Paranormal phenomena have persisted in virtually every culture, and the varieties of such puzzling events are endless. How to explain it all? I think there are three possibilities. *One,* the paranormal does not exist and all the perplexing reports can be dismissed as illusion, delusion, misguided hope, mistaken belief, laboratory error, or furtive fraud. *Two,* the paranormal does exist and science will ultimately solve all these puzzles, perhaps using the counterintuitive concepts of quantum theory or something similar. *Three,* the paranormal does exist, but science in its present form can never get at it. We will have to wait until one of these alternatives brings us closer to truth.

OUTTAKES

MARILYN: *I'm probably going to dream about this stuff tonight.*

ROBERT: *If it's about the lottery, we all share and share alike.*

CHAPTER 6

Can ESP Affect Your Life?

Can we heal psychically? Cure illness through prayer? Spy on our enemies by means of ESP? See in our mind's eye places we have never visited and know nothing about? Extrasensory perception—ESP—has long been the fodder of public fantasy and media exploitation. Countless books, movies, and TV shows captivate audiences with beguiling tales of psychic phenomena and unexplained events. As we watch, we wonder, "Wow, what if that's true?" There is also a less well-known side of ESP: serious research conducted by a few university laboratories and private foundations. But why so many critics and skeptics? Why isn't the data any stronger? Is ESP simply wishful thinking, sloppy science, clever conjuring, or outright fraud? Is the public just being duped? Most people believe that ESP is all around us; most scientists assume that ESP does not—cannot—exist. If ESP is real, then it should be big news. Five scientists with experience in the field offer their varying views.

PARTICIPANTS

Dr. Barry Beyerstein of Simon Fraser University is a member of the Executive Council of the Committee for the Scientific Investigation of Claims of the Paranormal (CSICOP). Barry claims that experimental results in ESP investigations support neither the hope nor the hype.

Dr. Dean Radin, an experimental psychologist who has conducted extensive research programs investigating psi phenomena, has been president of the Parapsychological Association three times. Dean says he is skeptical of skeptics.

Dr. Marilyn Schlitz, a leading investigator in parapsychology and ESP, is research director of the Institute of Noetic Sciences. Marilyn offers evidence from her own investigations of telepathy and psychic healing.

Dr. Charles Tart, the author of numerous books on parapsychology and the nature of consciousness, is a core faculty member of the Institute of Transpersonal Psychology. Charles seeks to combine careful science with spiritual understanding.

Dr. James Trefil, a professor of physics at George Mason University, is the author of numerous science books, such as *101 Things You Don't Know About Science and No One Else Does Either.* Jim applies common sense where it is often missing.

ROBERT: Marilyn, as a parapsychologist, you focus on the practical implications of paranormal phenomena. What are some of the ways in which ESP can affect our lives?

MARILYN: It may be a little premature to think about the actual application of parapsychological phenomena, since we're still in the research-gathering stage. But some possible applications include healing. One idea is that the belief system or intention of the healer may influence a patient. Such healing can occur even at a distance and even when patients don't know that "good thoughts" are being sent to them.

ROBERT: This is not just psychosomatic medicine, where the mind influences the body hormonally?

MARILYN: I think it's a step beyond the notion of a placebo kind of effect. It would be some kind of distant intentionality effect on physical systems.

ROBERT: Define "distant intentionality."

MARILYN: It's the idea that one person's thoughts may be able to influence another person's physiology at a distance, without any normal sensory communication between the two. This type of claim is quite common; many healers

in many different cultures believe they can heal people at a distance.

ROBERT: What are other areas where ESP may have practical value?

MARILYN: Crime detection, certainly; many police departments use psychics on a regular basis. Detectives will try anything to solve a case, and sometimes a psychic can help them come up with a novel explanation.

ROBERT: Barry, as a skeptic, do you think that the only way ESP affects our lives is by wasting our time and taking our money?

BARRY: I don't put experimental parapsychologists in the same category as psychics who pester police departments and do waste their time. I have personal knowledge of one such case, and I've read about others, and I think that there's more noise in the system, really, where the police are concerned. But first we have to establish whether ESP exists. And even if it does, parapsychologists will admit that the effect is so tiny that it probably wouldn't have any practical effect in the real world.

ROBERT: But if there's a tiny effect, doesn't that significantly change our worldview?

BARRY: Absolutely. If ESP is there and can't be explained by prosaic means, then it does change

---

. . . as skeptics we say that extraordinary claims demand extraordinary evidence.

---

our worldview in significant ways. That's why as skeptics we say that extraordinary claims demand extraordinary evidence. The existence of paranormal phenomena would be such a fundamental change in the scientific worldview that we have to make sure of the evidence before we take that leap.

ROBERT: Charles, in your book *Body, Mind, Spirit,* you've considered the potential effect on our lives of learning to use ESP. Do you believe that everyone has these abilities, and can we develop them?

CHARLES: If I say everyone has psychic abilities, that's a matter of belief, because of course not everyone has been tested. But I see no reason not to assume that ESP is a fundamental human talent. It does need to be developed. As Barry [Beyerstein] mentioned, if we do have it, ESP is usually a very small-scale phenomenon. That's why I wrote a book called *Learning to Use ESP.*

ROBERT: But can you learn to use ESP? Can you show developmental increase of ability over time with any kind of training?

CHARLES: My best guess is that we can, but there hasn't been enough research on this. Our fundamental need is to get ESP ability up to where you can demonstrably use it at will.

ROBERT: But have you seen experiments in which there's an increasing level of psychic performance?

CHARLES: Yes.

ROBERT: Are these experiments replicable?

CHARLES: Very few people have even tried to replicate them under proper conditions. That's why I say that the human ability to increase ESP skills is my best guess at this point, but I'm not going to come out and say it's been proved yet.

ROBERT: Jim, in your many books, such as *The Dark Side of the Universe* and *Are We Unique?,* you scan the frontiers of science. Do you see ESP on the frontiers?

JIM: Not really—I see it as something that's been around. If the effects are there, as everyone has said, they're very small. But not even the small effects have been demonstrated to the satisfaction of the mainstream scientific community.

MARILYN: I'd like to address this question: Several people have mentioned the smallness of the effect. But it's been well established in conventional medicine, for example, that the use of aspirin can prevent second heart attacks. The size of the effect in that study was very small, too, across a very large sample size, but they actually stopped the study prematurely, because they were depriving the control group of a viable treatment.

BARRY: Sure, but there's a big difference. We understand what aspirin does; there's a perfectly reasonable hypothesis arising from the molecular function of aspirin and how it affects the body.

ROBERT: Do you have to understand the molecular mechanism to recognize an experimental result?

BARRY: No, but in this particular case we have a theory, and the result was a predictable outcome of the theory. It turns out to be a small effect, so you do need a large sample size to achieve statistical significance.

ROBERT: But isn't Marilyn [Schlitz] saying that small effects don't necessarily mean small importance?

MARILYN: Just because ESP effects may be small doesn't mean we can dismiss them. The same is true of many treatments given in conventional medicine. The goal, really, is to begin to harness all these things in such a way that they have better applicability.

ROBERT: Dean, in your book *The Conscious Universe,* you go after the skeptics pretty hard. Do you feel threatened by them?

DEAN: I'm skeptical about skeptics. Skepticism is truly a double-edged sword. It's usually imagined hacking away at things that you wish to debunk. Many ESP cases are easy to debunk, because they're just people fooling themselves.

I'm skeptical about skeptics.

But you also need to cut in the other direction and take a very careful look at the skeptical tactics and rhetoric that are used to try to explain something away. I did so in my book, and I discovered that in many cases of parapsychological phenomena, skeptical arguments are flawed.

ROBERT: Let's take a practical example. [Looking away] I have this feeling right now that Marilyn [Schlitz] is staring at me. We all have that feeling on occasion, such as when we stop at a red light and feel compelled to check whether the driver in the car next to us is looking at us. Is this just common psychology, or might there be some ESP lurking here?

DEAN: The only way to know for sure is to bring it into the laboratory.

ROBERT: Have you done that?

DEAN: I've tested staring in the lab; so has Marilyn. You can use conventional, well-understood, double-blind, randomized, controlled techniques to see whether or not people can actually tell when they're being stared at—or whether their physiology changes as the result of being stared at.

ROBERT: And?

DEAN: The result of some twenty studies shows that people, in general, are more aroused when they're being stared at than when they're not. But the arousal is unconscious, and we detect it by looking at autonomic measures.

MARILYN: In real-world situations, are people just experiencing enhanced peripheral vision, not consciously aware that they're seeing something out of the corner of their eye? The question can be answered only by going into a lab and reducing all conventional sensory inputs. Only then can we begin to look for some added x-factor that may increase our ability to detect someone looking at us. We've conducted two formal experiments, which we replicated twice. In all cases, we found a significant difference between the staring periods and the control periods.

ROBERT: What parameters do you check?

DEAN: We look at the EEG, the electrical activity of the cerebral cortex.

ROBERT: Alpha waves—the slow, rhythmic, electrical undulations characteristic of the resting brain?

DEAN: Right.

ROBERT: So if I'm in a relaxed state, showing alpha waves, and someone is staring at me, what happens?

DEAN: Whenever your attention shifts, it desynchronizes your alpha waves, which means that these nice slow waves disappear. If this happens at the same time as the person is doing the staring, then that's an interesting indicator.

ROBERT: Marilyn, were you staring at me before?

MARILYN: I'm looking at you always, mate.

BARRY: She wasn't before you said it. She looked at you when you said it.

ROBERT: Charles, are there any common personality characteristics for high ESP incidents?

CHARLES: No, I don't think so. There's been a fair amount of study on the personality correlates of people who score a little higher and a little lower. And they come out barely significant, but not very practical. One difference that's especially interesting, even if the effect is small, is between people who believe in ESP versus people who don't believe—something you find out before you test them for ESP.

ROBERT: You call them the sheep and the goats.

CHARLES: Right. The sheep are the believers; the goats are the nonbelievers. First, you categorize the believers and the nonbelievers, and then you give them what is essentially a multiple-choice test. When you score the results separately for the two groups, the believers—the sheep—tend to score significantly above chance,

---

> *The sheep are the believers; the goats are the nonbelievers.*

---

just as they were told to, and the goats often score significantly below chance. Now think about this for a minute. If I had a deck of ordinary playing cards, and asked you to guess red or black, we know you would get about fifty percent by chance. Even without statistics, if you got all fifty-two right, that would be extraordinary. How about if you got zero right? That would be just as extraordinary statistically. The goats score significantly below chance, and they feel good about it! They say, "See, there's no such thing as ESP; here I got a lousy score on the test, and that proves I'm right." But the only way someone can score significantly below chance is to use ESP unconsciously so that they know what the right card is and don't guess it.

ROBERT: That sounds like after-the-fact rationalization, what we call *a posteriori* reasoning. What happens when you average the sheep and the goats all together?

CHARLES: But you don't average them together. You make the distinction ahead of time; that's the point. As a psychologist, I find this disparity fascinating. I've studied many ways in which we distort our perceptions of reality to support our belief systems, and here are people pulling off a small miracle in order to prove that there are no such things as miracles. It's great!

ROBERT: Dean, do you find any common characteristics of high ESP incidents, other than the sheep-goat effect?

DEAN: Marilyn [Schlitz] has begun investigating the relationship between ESP and the nature of creativity. Among people who describe themselves as creative, there seems to be a high correlation with ESP. In telepathy tests among artists, writers, dancers, and musicians, creativity was a tested correlate, and it turned out that in these tests musicians had an effect size two to three times higher than the average person.

MARILYN: We did a study at the Juilliard School in which we asked whether people—music, dance, and drama students—could detect images of a video clip being played in another room. All these student groups scored significantly higher than the general population, though the musicians scored the best. This study was then replicated in a Ph.D. thesis at the University of Edinburgh.

ROBERT: Please describe a typical response—how was the study set up?

MARILYN: A person in one room would be watching a video clip from the musical *The Wiz,* a parody of *The Wizard of Oz.* Someone in another room would be under sensory isolation with Ping-Pong balls over the eyes and white noise fed into the ears, and knowing nothing at all about the video clip, they would describe a hot-air balloon, a black female nightclub performer, a lion, a wizard, a dog, the color yellow.

What was playing on the video at that very moment, in the other room, was a scene of Diana Ross as Dorothy, with the scarecrow, the wizard, the tin man, and the lion, all walking across the Brooklyn Bridge with the cityscape of New York in the background.

ROBERT: But how many times did this kind of direct hit *not* occur?

MARILYN: Well, what we did then was to show that same video clip, with three decoys, to the recipient, who was asked to identify which one most closely matched their described imagery. We did this in a number of experimental trials, in such a way that you could use statistics to identify how likely the response was on the basis of chance alone. If the recipients were just guessing, we would expect that about a quarter of the time they would get it right; in fact, we found that fifty percent of the time they were able to correctly identify the target clip.

ROBERT: But how robust is that data?

MARILYN: Qualitatively, there were very striking matches between the recipients' experience and the content of the actual target. Subjects were in this dreamlike state [induced by sensory isolation] as they described their imagery—

ROBERT: So they were in a dreamlike state? Charles, do you find more incidents of ESP during dreamlike states?

CHARLES: If you look at what happens in people's ordinary experience, yes—a great deal comes from dreams or similar states of reverie. Experimental work conducted some years ago at the Maimonides Medical Center in New York monitored people sleeping in the laboratory who were woken up during periods of dreaming, while a sender in another room was trying to tele-pathically influence those dreams. Overall the results were quite significant, and some of the individual results were striking. We may talk about average effects being small, but occasionally we find extremely good psychic descriptions.

ROBERT: Barry, what is the Committee for the Scientific Investigation of Claims of the Paranormal—or, to those who love her, CSI-COP? Why do you go after these hardworking parapsychologists and make their lives so difficult?

BARRY: It's not a witch-hunt. CSICOP is a group of people with expertise in a wide variety of scientific, philosophical, and other academic disciplines who simply ask for the evidence and the analysis. Those whom we criticize obviously think we're unfair. We think we're only doing our job. We're simply making sure that the evidence measures up, by our standards.

ROBERT: Let's focus on healing, an area of Marilyn's personal interest. Where do you look for transpersonal effects in the healing process? We've all heard stories of the power of therapeutic touch, such as the laying on of hands. Certainly many diverse religious groups invoke the power of prayer.

MARILYN: First of all, I must say that the skeptical community has been very helpful in these areas. There have been cases where skeptics have simulated a psychic surgeon doing an "operation" without any instruments—separating the skin, pulling out some kind of organ. Frequently these psychic surgeons are using some kind of false thumb filled with blood and tissues of animals, in some kind of a heavy dramatic ritual. In and of itself, this may not be wrong, because the shaman or the psychic sur-geon is trying to harness the patient's own belief system and this is their way of doing so.

ROBERT: But there's nothing psychic or paranormal going on?

MARILYN: I can't speak of all cases, but there are instances in which the psychic surgery is a fraud—which is a term I hate to use, because it implies evil intent. Certainly there's nothing paranormal involved. On the other hand, we have interesting data when we come into the laboratory and look at the effects of distant prayer, intercessory prayer, on patient populations. There was a very nice study of coronary care patients, all of whom were getting conventional medical intervention. These patients were split into two groups. One was prayed for—at a distance—and one was not prayed for, without either group knowing what was happening. The people who were prayed for had far better, statistically meaningful medical outcomes, relative to the control group.

ROBERT: Pardon my naïveté, but how do you direct your prayer to one group rather than another?

MARILYN: That's one of the challenges. And there are others: Exactly what do we mean by prayer? And what do you do about the fact that some people in the control group are being prayed for by their families?

ROBERT: What do you tell the healers? Pray for the patients in Room 302 but not in Room 308?

MARILYN: The healers aren't told anything about the control group; they just focus on the active group. At any rate, the experimental results seem supportive of an effect. In another project, we worked with patients with advanced

AIDS. Again, we split them at random into two groups; each person knew he was participating in a study that involved distant prayer, but no one knew which group he was in. And again, the medical outcomes for the prayed-for group were statistically better than for the group that wasn't prayed for.

JIM: I have a long experience of hearing such accounts, and when they're described they always sound like this, but when you start getting under the hood, the devil is in the details. You get down there and find that there are sub-

---

. . . when you start getting under the hood, the devil is in the details.

---

tleties in the way these experiments were designed, or in the statistical analysis, that make them much less powerful.

ROBERT: I'd be a little concerned about giving people a false sense of security: if they thought that the power of prayer was going to replace normal medical treatment, it could have deleterious consequences.

MARILYN: You're absolutely right. In studies conducted at Duke Medical Center, all the patients got conventional allopathic medical treatment. Prayer was just used as a booster.

ROBERT: Can you pray for this show?

MARILYN: I am intending highly for this show's success, trust me. In the Duke study, the group who received the distant prayer—the distant intentionality—apparently were differen-

tially benefited. The problem is that we don't know how to define the internal states or make them operational. Is the healer-sender praying? Intending? Meditating? Are there stronger effects in one kind of conscious state than in another? These are empirical questions; they can be tested down the road.

ROBERT: Dean, there was a time when the Central Intelligence Agency was involved in psychic research for intelligence reasons. Can you tell us about that?

DEAN: Before 1995 I couldn't have; the work was classified until then. But, yes, there's something like a twenty-year history of CIA funding, with two objectives: one, to find out whether the rumors about psychic experiments being done in Russia or China were true and, if so, were they a national security threat; and two, if ESP is real, then how do we improve its utilization for intelligence gathering and how do we find people who can do it? On the threat assessment side, the answer was that we didn't have much to worry about—not because there wasn't anything to ESP, but because no one knew anything more about ESP than we did.

ROBERT: Can ESP be useful for national security?

DEAN: The answer appears to be yes, but probably no more so than in a few exceptional cases of psychic detective work. For example, there might be a spy satellite picture of something that the National Security Council couldn't identify but was concerned about. A psychic would be asked to describe it.

ROBERT: How would the psychics locate the target? Would they be given longitude and latitude?

DEAN: We don't know how they locate it. They're just told that there's an important target and they're supposed to provide information about it. Then they do whatever they do—draw a sketch or describe it verbally. Obviously the intelligence community doesn't rely on psychics, because that would be just stupid. Instead, they take all of the human intelligence and the satellite intelligence and see if the psychic information fits in.

ROBERT: Some people might think that if the CIA was funding experiments in ESP, then there really is nothing to it.

DEAN: I have more faith in our government than that.

CHARLES: There was a rumor going around years ago that the Russians were using telepathic bombardment to make our national leaders act stupidly, but we showed that we didn't need any help on that score.

ROBERT: There was a world chess championship in which Viktor Korchnoi blamed his loss on the Russians' having planted a psychic in the audience to affect him.

CHARLES: Seriously, I've seen the same data Dean has. I was a consultant on the CIA projects. Sometimes the remote viewing worked extremely well. Of course you'd never use it as a sole source of intelligence, but at times it could make a wonderful supplemental source. Now, there is a concern here we need to address. Though many of us think that ESP is real and sometimes works strongly, that doesn't mean you should start basing your life decisions on apparent psychic information. You have to use your intelligence. Even Mohammed said, "Trust in God, but tie up your camel."

DEAN: That admonition goes for any application of psychic phenomena, whether currently in use or just being speculated about. At this point, ESP should be called in only when there's no other form of information, or healing, or whatever, available—when you have nothing to lose by trying it. I have high confidence that what we see in the lab is evidence of some kind of ESP—some kind of psychic perception that, in principle at least, can have some benefit.

ROBERT: Dean [Radin], Marilyn [Schlitz], Charles [Tart], you're all sheep, in that you believe in the existence of paranormal phenomena. Have any of you ever tested positive for ESP?

CHARLES: I've occasionally been tested positive. But I don't usually say that I believe. I do say that I've assessed the scientific evidence and have reached a conclusion on that basis.

MARILYN: I follow Charles.

DEAN: I feel the same way. My belief is based on empiricism. I always run myself on my own experiments, and sometimes I do pretty well.

ROBERT: And other times?

DEAN: And other times I don't. But statistically, over time, probably in the positive direction.

ROBERT: Barry, what do you make of this?

BARRY: I've done the same thing. I have some devices in my laboratory, off in one corner, where I've tested myself many, many times. I also run my students through, every time I teach a large course. And I have people visit my lab because they think they have psychic ability, and I run them on the machine. So far, the laws of chance are not in any great danger, as far as my experience is concerned.

ROBERT: At best, ESP seems to be a very weak phenomenon. What mechanisms could generate such a weak phenomenon?

DEAN: It's not clear that ESP is so weak. When we consider experimental psychology in general, which is essentially what this research is, we always find that effects in the laboratory are much weaker than they are in the real world. Why? Because we force a control. We put constraints on the experimental design in order to be able to make a scientific assessment. So I'm not disturbed by the fact that we get relatively small effects in the lab. It actually bolsters my expectation that once in a while some of the spectacular things that people say have happened in their lives might be real. Occurrences in the real world are always much richer than what we see in the lab.

ROBERT: One can imagine mechanisms for telepathy, such as strange brain emanations or quantum mechanical effects. Even clairvoyance, where one is apprehending information at a distance, could be subject to fields of some sort. But how in the world could precognition work? By what conceivable mechanisms can we know the future? It seems so contrary to everything we understand.

CHARLES: I think that's very exciting. It reminds us that we haven't been at science very long—that we don't know much about the universe. I have a conservative approach to science; I believe that data comes first. If your theory doesn't fit the data, that just means your theory is inadequate. You don't throw away data because your theories can't handle them. The

data for ESP are overwhelming, in my estimation. There are thousands of studies out there now. It happens, even though I don't understand why.

ROBERT: Dean, why are psychic experiences so compelling for the people who claim to have them?

DEAN: That's an interesting question, because we often think we're dealing only with the very small phenomena we see in the laboratory. But there's something called the luminosity of the experience—it's a sense of transcendence. The psychic effect is bigger than you are, and it's so compelling that it changes people's perceptions and drives them to wonder why. This has persisted for thousands of years.

BARRY: Well, my explanation for that is that people could well think they had a psychic experience and be mistaken, but the mere fact that they believed it would cause a tremendous emotional reaction.

ROBERT: Don't we find these transcendent feelings rather common in epileptic seizures?

BARRY: Epileptic seizures, drug effects, certain kinds of migraine headaches—there are all kinds of things that can produce illusions or hallucinations of transcendence. Direct electrical stimulation of the brain [in the temporal lobe] exposed for neurosurgery can induce transcendent experiences. So can magnetic fields. Transcendent experiences are triggered by activating specific circuits in the brain's limbic system.

ROBERT: Charles, as a transpersonal psychologist, what do you think are the clinical implications of ESP experiences?

CHARLES: We're very culture-bound in the way we look at ESP experiences. In certain societies, if you started hearing voices, you might go to the wise people, who would say, "You have the talent to become a shaman; we'll train you." If you start hearing voices in our society, our wise people—psychiatrists—will give you the conventional explanation that, basically, you're crazy. Our healers will say, "Take this drug and the voices will go away." If our society has got it right—if hearing voices is always imaginary and pathological—then treating such a person for insanity is appropriate.

ROBERT: Hearing voices is a neurological condition.

CHARLES: It might be a neurological condition, right. Or it might be that this person has some kind of telepathic ability working and once in a while hears someone else's thoughts.

ROBERT: How could you distinguish between the two? How could you ever prove your telepathic hypothesis?

CHARLES: You could test it. At the very least, you could allow the possibility that the voices are ESP. But suppose you *are* telepathic, what are you going to do with it? Are you going to let your ego swell up because this voice tells you you're wonderful? Are you going to do crazy things because you get bad advice from the voices? We still have a clinical responsibility to help people deal in a sane, mature way with this phenomenon. But it's important not to invalidate it to begin with. I've talked to many people who had what seemed to be garden-variety psychic experiences, but because they thought ESP was impossible they assumed they were crazy—and they suffered needlessly for lack of an adequate framework.

ROBERT: You've been one of the leaders in studying altered states of consciousness and how they may relate to ESP or different world-views. But since altered states are illusions, how can they possibly help us understand reality?

CHARLES: Altered states are illusions? How do you know that what we're doing now isn't an illusion? You're starting out with a value judgment. As a scientist, I want to know the data. If a person comes to me in a certain state of consciousness, I want to assess how that consciousness functions, what it's good for, what it's bad for. We can't have just one state, somehow superior to all others. Some altered states of consciousness are better for some things. For instance, being in love is an altered state of consciousness. Not a terribly good state for balancing your checkbook, but for interpersonal relationships there's a lot to be said for it.

ROBERT: Are people in love more receptive to ESP than people who aren't?

CHARLES: There's some suggestive evidence, but not much research, so I don't know.

ROBERT: Can you find enough people in love to construct a database?

CHARLES: We could find lots of people in love, but can we find enough parapsychologists who have the resources to test them? People shouldn't get the idea that parapsychology is a big research enterprise. It's minuscule.

ROBERT: Why is that?

CHARLES: One year I had a twenty-thousand-dollar grant, which made me one of the richest parapsychologists in the world. This is absolutely trivial by ordinary scientific standards. The people who run the funding agencies generally think there's no such thing as ESP, so they won't waste money giving out grants.

ROBERT: Sounds like a conspiracy.

CHARLES: No, I don't think it's a conspiracy so much as general cultural conditioning. You don't put your money into things you don't think are worthwhile.

DEAN: There's another reason as well. One of the reasons the government-funded ESP programs were top-secret for so many years had nothing to do with the objective itself but with what they called "the giggle factor." People in a position of authority are afraid of jeopardizing that position by saying, "Maybe I'll give a little funding to this area." It says a lot about the politics and sociology of how science is done. Charles is right: there are only about twenty to forty people around the world who are looking into parapsychology from a scientific point of view.

ROBERT: That's a very small number.

DEAN: It's an extremely small number. One of the nice things, though, is that we all know each other and what's going on in the field.

ROBERT: Do you have to use the Internet, or can you just, well, "communicate"?

DEAN: We use the best method available, which right now is the Internet.

MARILYN: What's exciting to me is that we have so many more questions than answers, even about something as fundamental as the brain. We can't debate the fact that we have a brain, but we know very little about how the

brain operates. Why should we exclude the possibility that people's experiences for centuries and centuries may have some legitimacy?

ROBERT: I'm not sure we know very little about how the brain operates.

BARRY: For centuries and centuries, people thought the world was flat, too. There are lots of things in the world that appear to be different from what they are.

MARILYN: That's just my point. There's data now being compiled implying a broader worldview, one in which consciousness is much more engaged in the universe than the materialist

---

. . . these data suggest that somehow our consciousnesses can reach out beyond our brains and touch the world.

---

model would predict. I think that we human beings are deeply embedded in the world. And these data suggest that somehow our consciousnesses can reach out beyond our brains and touch the world.

ROBERT: Marilyn, what data can you come up with in the next few years that would convince Jim [Trefil] and Barry [Beyerstein] that ESP research is worth pursuing seriously?

MARILYN: It has to do more with relationship building than with anything else. We need to develop enough trust and respect among smart and busy scientists so that they stop for a few moments and take seriously the data that currently exist. We don't need to collect more data; we need to communicate with each other. The data need to be shared among people with different disciplinary perspectives, who may begin to build the theoretical framework we're seeking.

ROBERT: If what you're saying is true, if your current evidence is as compelling as you think, you should want to spend millions of dollars promoting and developing it.

MARILYN: I'd be happy to spend millions of dollars on it. If there are any donors out there who want to contribute, we're ready.

ROBERT: But why doesn't this happen? Why no recognition, no appreciation? There's obviously no skeptics' conspiracy. I don't think Jim and Barry, for example, even met before today.

JIM: One thing that should be pointed out is that this isn't a complaint only about parapsychology. The entire federal funding system does very poorly in supporting high-risk research.

MARILYN: Right.

JIM: That's because the guy who's in charge of giving out the money wants to be able to say, at the end of the year, "I had *x* number of papers published; this is what I spent, and this is what I got for it." Supporting high-risk research means taking a big gamble—not just ESP but any high-risk science. For example, SETI, the search for extraterrestrial intelligence, has been in and out of funding for decades for the very same reason.

DEAN: Another reason it's been very difficult to get funding is because people in positions to make those decisions have only the popular conception of what it is I do. When they hear the terms "parapsychology" or "ESP," they im-

mediately turn off and won't even read the materials. But on virtually every occasion when I've had a chance to sit down with someone in my lab, run the experiments, and explain how they're analyzed, the person goes away thinking that this research is at least interesting and probably deserves some funding.

ROBERT: So, what happens now?

DEAN: Parapsychologists have to go out and meet people, educating physicists about what we do.

ROBERT: You need politics in ESP, just as you do in other avenues of life.

DEAN: You have to be a good salesman in any area of science.

ROBERT: OK, we fast-forward for a prediction. One hundred years from now, will ESP have any accepted applications?

MARILYN: No question, yes.

CHARLES: In healing, definitely.

JIM: I doubt it very much.

BARRY: There will be people who believe it as firmly then as now, and the effects will be as small and trivial then as now.

DEAN: I have trouble predicting next Tuesday, but if I had to guess I would say, yes, there will be real applications of ESP.

ROBERT: CONCLUDING COMMENT

I don't think we've convinced anyone not to visit fortune-tellers or call up the psychics, but perhaps we've cast a critical eye on those who would convert your hope into their dollars. ESP and psychic phenomena can make great entertainment; we think, "What if?" So enjoy the stories, but give your eye a critical glint; learn to distinguish science fact from media fiction. Although I reject the vast majority of ESP claims, I cannot discard them all. And while I strongly support skeptics disabusing the public of psychic fantasies, I also support serious parapsychologists continuing their investigations. I follow their research and enjoy their thinking. "Don't give in!" I cheer from the sidelines. "Pursue the dream!" The issue is vital—because if ESP does exist, if we ever admit the presence of anything nonphysical, our view of the world changes. Time and space dissolve and we redefine the human condition. But separate what you know from what you hope to get closer to truth.

OUTTAKES

ROBERT: *How long are the stares?*

MARILYN: *Thirty seconds.*

ROBERT: *You do thirty-second stares?*

MARILYN: *Right.*

DEAN: *I do sixty seconds.*

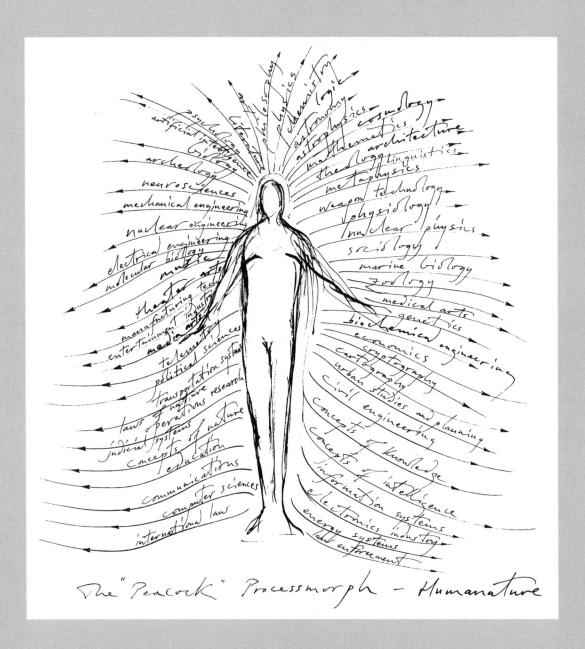

The "Peacock" Processmorph — Humanature

PART TWO

HEALTH & SEX

The Peacock Processmorph—Humanature. (Courtesy of Todd Siler.)

CHAPTER 7

Will Gene Therapy Change the Human Race?

Gene therapy is the remarkable treatment of disease by altering our DNA (deoxyribonucleic acid), the long, complex molecules that carry our genetic information and reside in the nuclei of all our cells. Gene therapy may sound like a normal medical advance. It is not. The restructuring of our genetic material is a revolution. But how far should we go? What are the subtle distinctions between genetic therapy and genetic enhancement—between curing old diseases and creating new bodies? You've heard of designer clothes? How about designer kids? Take your choice: Smart? Tall? Blue-eyed? Beautiful? Musical, mystical, ambitious, ambidextrous? Genetic engineering is power, with the capacity to cure or corrupt, heal or harm. But if we intervene and adjust human genes, do we impact and alter human evolution? We invited five world-renowned experts to examine a volatile medical future.

PARTICIPANTS

Dr. W. French Anderson, director of the Gene Therapy Laboratories at the University of Southern California, has been called "the father of gene therapy." French describes clinical protocols for the treatment of genetically based diseases.

Dr. Francisco Ayala, a geneticist and philosopher at the University of California at Irvine, is called the Renaissance man of evolutionary biology. Francisco has deep concerns about the long-range implications of gene therapy, about the potential for very great evil.

Dr. Sherwin (Shep) Nuland, a professor of surgery at Yale, is the author of two remarkable books, *How We Die* and *How We Live.* Shep worries about tampering with the essence of our humanness.

Dr. Gregory Stock, a biophysicist and MBA, is director of the Program on Medicine, Technology, and Society at the University of California, Los Angeles (UCLA). Greg envisions how germ-line engineering will radically change humanity.

Dr. Allan Tobin is director of the Brain Research Institute at the University of California, Los Angeles, and the scientific director of the Hereditary Disease Foundation. Allan explains how advanced technologies treat neurological diseases.

ROBERT: French, why is gene therapy particularly exciting now?

FRENCH: Over the next twenty to thirty years, gene therapy will probably revolutionize the practice of medicine. Since the basis of our bodies is in our genes, it's also the genes on which our whole health is based. Therefore it should be possible, once we decipher all the genes and understand what they do, to replace genes that are deficient or weak. For example, if people have a tendency to develop a certain kind of cancer, we'll supply them with a gene that protects them from that cancer.

ROBERT: Francisco, you're an evolutionary geneticist; in fact, you've used DNA as a kind of molecular clock to track evolution. Are you at all concerned that gene therapy might inadvertently interfere with the evolutionary process?

FRANCISCO: I'm concerned, of course, but I'm mostly concerned that gene therapy and gene enhancement may impact humans in other ways. The process of evolution is very slow, and in the scale of human evolution, gene therapy is going to have a very small impact. It's on a different scale.

ROBERT: But if you change genes in the human population pool artificially, couldn't that cause a rapid acceleration of evolution?

FRANCISCO: Gene therapy is a slow process. Take a typical genetically based disease, such as cystic fibrosis or muscular dystrophy. The frequency of these genes in the general population is on the order of a few percent. So assume that a disease-causing gene exists in the population at a one-percent level, and you cure everybody who's born with the disease by correcting the gene; it would take you a hundred generations, or some twenty-five hundred years to do that—to go through that one percent of the population. There's very little impact on the gene pool at large, because disease-causing genes have already been kept at a very low frequency, through natural selection.

ROBERT: We're going to get back to this issue. Allan, you're director of UCLA's Brain Research Institute, which, in the spirit of full disclosure, is where I received my doctorate three decades ago. You've been interested in how cell biology and molecular genetics can be used to create new therapies for disorders of the brain.

ALLAN: We're investigating the use of gene therapies to modify somatic cells—that is, the cells of body tissues and organs [as opposed to the germ cells, or gametes—the reproductive cells, sperms and eggs]. I've had a long-standing interest in Huntington's chorea, a degenerative disease of the brain, genetic in origin, which causes a loss of coordination and a dancing-like movement. We're looking into ways in which gene therapy can be used to understand and modify the process of neurodegeneration in that and other such diseases—Alzheimer's, Parkinson's disease, epilepsy.

ROBERT: Greg, you focus on genetic engineering, and you're a futurist. What do you see on the horizon for gene therapy?

GREG: When we start to do more profound genetic manipulations and enhancements, it's going to have very, very dramatic effects on human evolution. This slow process that Francisco [Ayala] was talking about is being supplanted. Technology is rapidly reshaping the world, at a pace orders of magnitude faster than anything in the past. These technologies are becoming so powerful that we can redirect them back upon ourselves.

ROBERT: Are you worried about that?

GREG: No, I'm not worried about it.

ROBERT: I'm worried.

GREG: That's not surprising. Genetic engineering is going to change life as we know it, and this can be very disturbing at a number of levels. Other technological developments are also going to have a marked impact on us, such as artificial intelligence and the way telecommunications knits us all together. Human life is going to change dramatically in the short-term future, I believe.

ROBERT: Shep, you teach bioethics [at Yale]. What concerns do you have as you look at the human condition, as it might be affected by the dramatic changes in gene therapy?

SHEP: I'm always skeptical of words like "revolutionary" and "dramatic." It hasn't happened yet, I'm not sure it's going to happen, and perhaps I can be a little bit of a dissenting voice here. But if genetic engineering goes as predicted, and in such a way as to "change life as we know it," the question obviously is, Do we want to change life as we know it? Have these 3.6 billion years of evolution since the first life appeared on earth meant anything? And is there a guiding biological purpose? If so, do we really want to play with it?

ROBERT: A fundamental question.

SHEP: The fundamental question really is, What is humanness? Is it our spiritual sense? Is it our sense of mystery? Is it our ability to love, to be altruistic in ways that animals can't be? Do we really want to run the risk of changing this?

The fundamental question really is, What is humanness?

Do we know the consequences of what we're doing? It seems to me that a technology that's potentially revolutionary—that can change the world—should demonstrate first that unambiguous benefits will come from it, before we start applying it.

ROBERT: We'll get back to fundamental questions. For now, let's stick to individual people with specific problems. French [Anderson], take a real-world situation, where I come to you as a patient with a disease that may be treatable by gene therapy. I don't know anything about the procedure, but my physician has recommended your experimental protocols. What would you be telling me in that first office visit?

FRENCH: The first thing I emphasize is that gene therapy is an experimental procedure and there are no fully successful gene therapy treatments yet. Certainly in future years there will be successful treatments. But there are over three hundred approved clinical protocols for gene therapy. As a possible patient in this experimental program, you would need to understand and sign an informed consent. That's a document that ensures that you understand what your disease is, or what your child's disease is, what the procedure is, what the risks of that procedure are, what the possible benefits are, and what the likelihood is that there will be any benefit at all.

ROBERT: What diseases might I have?

FRENCH: At present, about seventy percent of the clinical protocols are for one form of cancer or another: brain cancer, breast cancer, colon cancer.

ROBERT: These would usually be at advanced stages of the disease, where the risks of your procedure are less relevant?

FRENCH: At the present time, yes. Probably the most successful gene therapy currently— aside from therapies for some rare genetic diseases—is for heart disease. A physician at St. Elizabeth's Medical Center in Boston, Jeffrey Isner, has succeeded in injecting, directly into the hearts of patients who are bedridden, normal genes for a factor that causes the growth of blood vessels, and a number of these patients are now back to leading a perfectly normal life. The procedure—if I were Jeff Isner and you were referred to me as a cardiac patient— involves the same process of informed consent,

going over the risks, the potential benefits, and so forth.

ROBERT: What's the clinical procedure?

FRENCH: There are dozens of ways in which gene therapy is carried out. If it's an attempt to treat cystic fibrosis, the fluid carrying the replacement genes could be put in a bronchoscope and actually dripped into the lungs. In the brain tumor protocols, we inject a "suicide gene" directly into the tumor, which causes the cancerous cells to die. In many cases, we take cells, such as blood cells, out of the patient's body, insert the replacement genes into these cells, and then return the genetically engineered cells to his body.

ROBERT: How are the new genes inserted into the cells?

FRENCH: We use what we call vectors, which are molecules that carry the genes into the cells. The usual vectors are special viruses, but sometimes it's simply the DNA itself.*

ROBERT: Allan, are these gene therapies really much different from traditional medical procedures?

ALLAN: These therapies simply multiply a patient's existing cells. When French talks about injecting DNA into a diseased heart to stimulate

---

*A number of people have died during gene therapy trials, but they have been terminally ill cancer patients. In late 1999, the first true gene therapy death occurred after a patient with a non-life-threatening liver disease was given a genetically engineered adenovirus—a virus similar to those that cause colds. Adenovirus may be abandoned in favor of other delivery systems.

the growth of blood vessels or into a brain to stop a tumor from growing—or, what intrigues me, into an epileptic patient's brain cells to quiet their excessive neural noise—these procedures are not so different from other medical and surgical procedures. They're not going to have any impact on evolution. They're not going to be revolutionary in the sense that Shep [Nuland] worries about.

ROBERT: I'm not sure that's right, because we have to envision the technological extensions of these first early efforts—we'll explore this further. To continue: What's the Human Genome Project—a massive effort and an example of "big science"—which is expected to form the foundation of future gene therapies?

ALLAN: The Human Genome Project is a nationwide effort to determine the sequence of all three billion nucleotides, the building blocks of DNA located in the nucleus of every cell in our bodies. That is, the double helix of DNA in each cell carries two complete copies of these genetic instructions, and each set of instructions is composed of three billion nucleotides. But only about five percent of those three billion nucleotides are actually genes—sequences that code for specific proteins, which are the business end of a cell. It's estimated that there are about a hundred [to a hundred and forty] thousand genes in human DNA.

GREG: It's not just the sequencing that's important in the Human Genome Project, but also understanding all the polymorphisms, or variants, that exist—what makes you different from me—and being able to identify which clusters of those genes are associated with various human traits, by means of genomics, which uses computers to analyze all this complex data. By coupling this genetic understanding with new

technologies, like DNA chips, we'll be able to generate a genetic profile of an individual very cheaply and very quickly. DNA chips aren't science fiction; they're analogous to computer chips and they'll identify various polymorphisms on perhaps some hundred thousand genes eventually. When you start getting this kind of information, then it becomes feasible to imagine the alteration of genes at a more fundamental level—for instance, in the first cell of the embryo.

ROBERT: We've now entered into the brave new world of human germ-line engineering. Please explain.

GREG: Germ-line engineering involves the germinal cell, which is to animals as a seed is to plants—the original source of germination. There's an important difference between germ-line genetic engineering and the somatic-cell genetic engineering that French [Anderson] is doing. Gene therapy with somatic cells is intervention—just like any other medical procedure—in the existing cells of the adult. Germ-line engineering is qualitatively, radically different. Here you go back and alter the genes in the first cell, the *first* cell, of the early embryo. As a result, you're changing all the genes [in the body that will develop from that embryo and that will be passed on to subsequent generations], making very profound changes that are essentially the beginnings of human design. This kind of procedure will have enormous impact.

ROBERT: Francisco, this impact gets bigger than one percent? This guy is scaring me.

FRANCISCO: OK, now I *am* worried. I'm much more worried right now than when we started. Listening to Greg [Stock], I understand that he goes beyond curing the disease somatically, for an individual. He wants to correct the genes in the germ line, so that future generations will not have the disease. This can protect the descendants of the people who've been cured of cardiac disease—but who decides what human beings should be? Who has the wisdom for that?

ROBERT: Can germ-line engineering be stopped? When has technology not been applied? Look at nuclear weapons—

GREG: That's not a good example.

FRANCISCO: It's a very good example, because the efforts to design new human beings, in my book, are as destructive as atomic bombs. And it's easier to stop atomic bombs.

ROBERT: To build nuclear weapons, you need a large infrastructure. But to do germ-line engineering, all you need is a small laboratory. It will be like making bootleg liquor during Prohibition.

GREG: There's a major difference between using atomic weapons and doing genetic engineering. As long as decisions are made by the individual who's being treated—or by parents who are trying to do the best for their children—then innocent others are not at risk in the same way they would be with atomic weapons. An accident by some madman with atomic weapons can destroy vast numbers of human beings. The only way that germ-line genetic engineering—or any kind of genetic engineering—can be used broadly enough to have significant impact is if it's wholeheartedly embraced by masses of people, because they see it as being for their benefit.

ALLAN: You're assuming a nontotalitarian society in everything you've said. You're talking

about free choice as if it were a given. The history of the twentieth century says otherwise.

GREG: Any technology can be perverted by a totalitarian regime. But totalitarian regimes have at their disposal all sorts of low-tech technologies to perpetrate evils. If you look at what Hitler did with eugenics, you'll see that he did evil on a much greater scale with other technologies.

FRANCISCO: I have to say that the proposal you're making has the potential for very great evil. There are so many problems in creating human beings. Who makes the choices as to what we are going to select for? Do we get taller

---

I have to say that the proposal you're making has the potential for very great evil.

---

people, or more people with blue eyes? What about selecting for those who can make the most money?

ROBERT: Or ambidextrous people, who can pitch or fish, write or draw, with either hand?

FRANCISCO: When I raise this question, many people tell me that they would select for greater intelligence. Well, I'm not sure of that. I don't think the problems that humankind faces today will be solved by having more people of greater intelligence. In fact, the definitions of intelligence or high IQ may change in future environments. I'd rather have people who are more morally responsible or more sensitive to other people's needs.

ROBERT: Those genes will be harder to find.

SHEP: But Francisco, we've already been told what will happen. Did you listen to that list of supposed enhancements that Robert referred to in his introduction? Every one of them was not just a positive attribute but an egotistical positive attribute. I keep thinking of the year that my daughter was about to go off to a secondary school. The headmaster sent us each a form that included the question, "Is your child a leader?" And I wrote down, "No, but she's a great follower." The answer I got back said, "Dear Dr. Nuland: This is wonderful. We have 399 leaders in the class and one follower." What's the free choice? Who will get these genetic enhancements? Think about the differences in medical care we already have in this world. When we start adding genetic enhancement, we'll magnify that problem.

ALLAN: While genomics, gene therapy, and germ-line manipulation are important to discuss, I think that some of the human qualities we're talking about are unlikely to result from genetic determination. I find it curious that society has embraced the idea that things like mysticism or morality or ambidextrousness might be genetically based rather than cultural. To hear professors proclaim that their cleverness is genetically determined—present company excepted, of course—reminds me of Max Weber's argument about Calvinism: that somehow, by proving we're among the elect—proving we have good genes—is what justifies us.

ROBERT: No one here claims that genetics completely determines morality or mysticism or other such human qualities—though ambidextrousness probably does have a greater genetic component. I would think that genetics provides a predisposition—a bell-curve distribu-

tion of proclivities—over which the more powerful influences of family, culture, and society are layered. French, does this discussion concern you? The rest of us are up in the balcony kibitzing, commenting, and complaining; you're the one in the lab and the clinic helping people.

FRENCH: I first started to raise these issues about thirty years ago, when that kind of concern was considered weird—like worrying about property values on Mars. Why fret about such things? But our growing ability to practice not just gene therapy, which is good, but also gene enhancement, which is fraught with complexities, is what we're really talking about.

ROBERT: The line between practicing gene therapy and practicing gene enhancement is a thin one.

FRENCH: It won't be possible to change human beings in the next ten, fifteen, or twenty years—but fifty or a hundred years from now is quite another matter. My very strong feeling is that the only way to prevent the misuse of this

---

. . . the only way to prevent the misuse of this technology is public education, . . .

---

technology is public education, an aroused population that understands the potential problems and won't allow the subtle encroachment of doing this-or-that little enhancement.

ROBERT: Where would you draw the line?

FRENCH: We can't dictate what our society might want to do a hundred years from now.

That society might want to take genes like we take vitamins, but that would be their business. Our duty is to go into the era of genetic engineering in as responsible a way as possible, and that is to use genetic engineering strictly for the treatment of serious disease and for no other reason. Now, what's a serious disease? What's a minor disease? What's a cultural discomfort? We'll have to deal with this spectrum of issues. But everyone can agree that there are serious diseases that cause significant suffering and premature death, and treating these diseases is the only way, I believe, that genetic engineering should be used, until we develop the higher degree of the wisdom this society needs.

FRANCISCO: French, I agree with your limiting genetic engineering to the treatment of severe diseases. But would you allow *germ-line* genetic engineering to eliminate these diseases from subsequent generations?

FRENCH: That's a very good question.

ROBERT: Somatic genetic engineering changes just the genes of the individual, while germ-line genetic engineering changes the genes of all future generations. Somatic gene therapy cures the person without affecting the offspring. Germ-line gene therapy alters the future forever.

FRANCISCO: We don't know what will happen a hundred years from now, so perhaps we shouldn't make these choices now.

ROBERT: Has that ever happened? Has technology ever stood still because of possible moral problems in the future?

FRANCISCO: Oh, yes—and I hope it will in this case. I do think we can control this.

GREG: First of all, germ-line engineering would have to become safe and reliable, which it isn't yet. No responsible person would speak about doing these things today. But let's assume that genes do matter—that there are meaningful human traits that can be altered by altering the genes. Enormous interventions are going to happen. Look at what parents do for their kids—sending them to computer camp and so forth. If you could insert an extra gene, or a cluster of genes, on an artificial chromosome safely and reliably into your child, and you could thereby virtually guarantee increasing your child's IQ by ten points, do you think parents would not select that?

FRANCISCO: They would; this is what worries me. At a simpler level [of social engineering], this is what's happening in China. Boys are preferred over girls, so right now among children under the age of ten there are twenty percent more boys than girls. What will happen twenty years from now, when all those boys are looking for girls to marry? We don't have the wisdom to anticipate what future societies are going to want even within the range of a single generation. We could create a catastrophe!

GREG: Absolutely. We don't have the wisdom to foresee the implications of powerful technologies like genetic engineering. Therefore one approach is to use these technologies in a tentative way at first and make our mistakes while there are still small numbers of people involved. We should try to learn from these mistakes and gain wisdom in the process. The other approach is to think that we can figure it all out in advance—but we can never figure it all out in advance. And when the technologies become very powerful, there will always be the risk that some exuberant country is going to apply them on a broad scale and create huge problems for the world.

SHEP: Have we finally reached the point in the evolving history of science where the implications for society are so enormous that society as a whole, and not science in isolation, should be determining the directions and applications of research? Perhaps it's time that scientists by themselves should no longer be allowed to make such independent judgments.

FRENCH: I absolutely agree with that. Just look at the advances—we call them advances—over the last several years in human biology: cloning, the Human Genome Project, human genetic engineering, in-utero gene therapy. The implications for society are profound. Scientists are human beings, and human beings have their weaknesses. The only way for society to protect itself from perfectly well-meaning scientists is through institutional review boards and regulatory committees. We have to prevent the kinds of misuse that could unintentionally result from a not-well-thought-out implementation of these technologies.

ROBERT: Would you make it illegal for scientists to do proscribed research?

FRENCH: No. "Illegal" implies a law, and legislating is the worst thing you can do, because then you drive the outlawed technology underground and to other countries. Sunlight is what's needed. Public exposure. Encourage scientists to speak publicly about what they're doing. I've certainly done this many times. Let all the people look at the implications, like those of us on this panel, and point out the issues.

FRANCISCO: Let me put it in a different light. Although I do agree with you, the way I understood Shep's question was much more general. The last thing I want in this world is a society in which anyone dictates to scientists what kind of research they should be doing. Most of the major discoveries in the basic sciences would not have been mandated by committees. Consider the invention of the transistor, the laser, the discovery of the structure of DNA. Basic science has to go on its own. It's applied science that has to be regulated.

ROBERT: Is such a distinction clear?

GREG: Yes. These technologies did not become controversial because someone set out to do questionable things; certainly that's not the case with human germ-line engineering. The technologies developed for very good reasons, such as medical and pharmaceutical applications. It's easy to talk about society taking control, but who actually makes the decisions? I agree that it's the applications we have to regulate, not the basic research.

ROBERT: If you speak with scientists privately, you may get a less gracious view. Many scientists feel that they should be the ones making the broader decisions for all sectors of society, not the other way around.

ALLAN: As educators as well as scientists, we have a responsibility to bring these debates not only to our students in the universities but also into the public domain. It's important that there be adequate coverage in the media—in programs like this one, for example—so that a larger segment of society gets involved. We need the informed, thoughtful opinions of a broader public.

SHEP: You're talking about an informed society. I'm talking about a deterministic society. I'm going to disagree with Francisco [Ayala], since I think that times have changed. The enormity of these implications means that we've gone beyond the old sciences—that something has to change dramatically. Maybe we should revolutionize the directions of research.

ROBERT: How?

GREG: Exactly. "How?" is indeed the operative question. And I think that it's precisely because the possibilities are so profound that these technologies are inherently unregulatable. They emerge from a highly complex process that

---

The development of technology has a dynamic of its own; . . .

---

cannot be controlled. The development of technology has a dynamic of its own; we can guide it a little, but that's all.

SHEP: I'm not going to agree with that. There are institutional review boards. There was the presidential committee that decided there should be a five-year moratorium on attempting to clone a human being. These are the beginnings of society's input, and the mere fact that we don't know how to clone a human being at this moment doesn't mean that we'll never be able to.

ALLAN: But the cloning of human beings is an application, not fundamental research that opens up the potential for cloning human beings. The borderline is fuzzy.

FRANCISCO: The kind of basic science that most of us do cannot be directed, because it springs from individual creativity. My work depends on my creative imagination and no one else's.

ROBERT: If you as a scientist think your research is important, and others decide that you should stop, you're probably going to figure out some way to circumvent the edict.

FRANCISCO: In basic science, yes.

ALLAN: Society goes though a selection process by making financial decisions about what areas of research they think need attention and therefore funding. As scientists, we have a responsibility to make sure that the public is aware of these issues.

SHEP: Historically, scientific advance has been energized by creative imagination.

ROBERT: Historically, the most revolutionary discoveries have been made without major funding.

ALLAN: That's certainly not true of the Human Genome Project, and I'm not sure that it's generally true. The development of the laser by Bell Labs wasn't done in someone's home shop, though perhaps Bell's management didn't appreciate its significance. It *is* true that major discoveries have not been predictable.

FRANCISCO: One should distinguish between not funding research and trying to direct it. The process works best when funding is provided while facilitating the creative initiative of scientists.

ALLAN: It works for basic research. But what about, say, fertility research? That's a problem. Much fertility research has been driven underground [such as on embryonic stem cells], as French said, because of the ban on government support. So here's a field where both the science and the application are almost completely unregulated. Millions of dollars are being spent on increasing the population, at a time when the population explosion is a serious worldwide problem.

GREG: Who are you to tell people who are infertile that they can't spend money to try and have a child, just because you think that globally there's some problem with overpopulation?

ALLAN: We have a fundamental issue here between liberals and conservatives about what's more important, equality or freedom? For a couple to spend millions of dollars—literally, in

---

We have a fundamental issue here between liberals and conservatives about what's more important, equality or freedom?

---

some cases—to have a child seems to me as questionable as if they were spending the same amount of money on their own private jet plane. It's the same issue for society.

SHEP: Scientists are now starting to make money out of some of these applications and are even taking ownership in research factories. We have to put this new factor into the equation.

ROBERT: Let's make predictions. Looking back a hundred years from now, will we think that gene therapy has been positive or negative for human history?

FRENCH: I sincerely hope and believe that gene therapy will be a positive benefit for humanity, but we certainly have to be cautious about its gross misuse.

SHEP: What we're going to find is that the benefits of gene therapy are limited, that they will be used in conjunction with other therapies. The great revolution that's predicted and worried about won't happen. Even the narcissism of our society will prevent it from happening.

GREG: There will be limited applications of gene therapy that will be very powerful, and it will be viewed as just another arm of medicine. But people will be even more worried than they are now about the larger implications of these technologies.

ALLAN: Society will look back at gene therapy as really powerful and clever medicine developed by scientists in the 1980s and 1990s, starting with French [Anderson]. But I'm afraid that a hundred years from now people will ask, "Why did our ancestors spend so much money doing these foolish things while they allowed the environment to degrade, while they permitted the quality of life to decline, and while they tolerated society becoming a less friendly and less enriching place?" The enrichment of IQ is not going to come from gene therapy; it's going to come only from the richness of personal experience.

FRANCISCO: I'm much in agreement with most of what has been said. Gene therapy, on the whole, will be seen as a beneficial component of human life, because it will cure diseases in much more efficient, effective, and benevolent ways than we cure them now. Like French, I encourage the therapeutic application, not the attempt to produce better human beings. Genetic manipulation has risks that we cannot even comprehend.

ROBERT: CONCLUDING COMMENT

Gene therapy is not just remarkable—it is revolutionary. Numerous diseases will be cured when defective genes are replaced or repaired. Nothing in medicine will be as powerful or beneficial. The treatments could even be economi-.cal, reducing health care costs for all of society. But the ultimate impact of gene therapy may go beyond healing and beyond financial efficiencies—far beyond. Somatic genetic engineering alters only the genes of the individual, while germ-line genetic engineering—the deliberate modification of the initial embryonic cell— alters the genes of future generations. Somatic gene therapy cures the individual without affecting his or her offspring. Germ-line gene therapy has the potential to alter the human species permanently. Reworking the genetic structure of our human cells may reset the evolutionary future of our human race. Human

germ-line engineering will soon be easy, cheap, and safe enough to be widely available, even if illegal. Medical ethicists may speculate and postulate, but the long-term transformation is unpredictable, unknowable, and unstoppable. Appreciating the ramifications of such change— and the alert monitoring of every advance— keeps us closer to truth.

OUTTAKES

SHEP: *Unbelievably important.*

FRENCH: *The public must understand the misconceptions.*

GREG: *These types of programs keep people aware.*

FRANCISCO: *With respect to IQ, if you modify the environment sufficiently, it may not be those with the highest IQ who come out on top.*

ROBERT: *Shyness is not one of your genes.*

CHAPTER 8

Can You Really Extend Your Life?

How long will you live? Think you'll make it to ninety? A hundred? A hundred and twenty? With all the talk about increased longevity, it's time to learn the facts, fads, and fallacies that characterize the study of aging. There are lots of exciting developments and lots of phony promises. Long life is humanity's ancient and perennial goal. Prophets promised it; explorers searched for it. We all want ourselves and our loved ones to stay alive and well, vigorous and vibrant, as long as possible. We toast, "To Life." The real trick is to live younger and not just longer. Wouldn't you rather disembark at ninety, having lived most of your senior years as hale as a forty-year-old, than slog on to a hundred, wheezing, hobbling, and in a perpetual fog? Lotions, potions, diets, drugs—they are everywhere and offer a dizzying array of choices. How do you attain true longevity amid the clamor of conflicting claims? What exactly is the biology of aging—and the best, most sensible ways to slow its pace? Our five panelists, experts in gerontology and human fitness, give their prescriptions for a long life.

PARTICIPANTS

Dr. W. French Anderson, director of the University of Southern California's Gene Therapy Laboratories, is the current national champion in karate for his age group. French talks about his personal fitness agenda.

Dr. Arthur De Vany, a former professional athlete, is a professor of economics at the University of California at Irvine. Art, who is in great shape, is the originator of the radical Evolutionary Fitness Plan.

Dr. Sherwin (Shep) Nuland, a surgeon who teaches medical ethics at Yale, is the best-selling author of *How We Die.* Shep expresses his concerns about extending human life.

Dr. Gregory Stock, a biophysicist, is director of the Program on Medicine, Technology, and Society at the University of California, Los Angeles. Greg envisions a future in which we adjust our own biology to live well past our present maximum life span.

Dr. Roy Walford, a professor of pathology at the University of California, Los Angeles, and the physician on the Biosphere 2 team, is the author of *The 120-Year Diet.* Roy believes that the chief factor affecting longevity is diet, especially calorie restriction.

ROBERT: Roy, you're one of the leading authorities on the biology of aging. Your most recent book is *The Anti-Aging Plan.* Give us an overview of the primary factors in aging and what we can do to retard the inevitable. What should I be doing to live as long as I can?

ROY: You should eat a diet low in calories but high in nutrients. There's evidence for the life-extending effectiveness of that [regimen]. Then you have to exercise and maybe take some supplements. These are the best measures we know of, at the moment.

ROBERT: French, in addition to being the father of gene therapy, you're a national champion in various martial arts. Does exercise aid longevity?

FRENCH: We need to distinguish between two factors that determine the length of your life. First, you can die prematurely—from some disease such as cancer, heart disease, or pneumonia. Second, if you don't die from a disease, how long can you live and what will the quality of that life be? Exercise is a critical part both of extending life and improving its quality. And I'm a bit of a maverick, because I feel that diet has much less of a role than most people think—including, it seems, everyone else on this panel.

More important, in my opinion, is being active, both mentally and physically.

ROBERT: Suppose somebody hits you with a karate chop?

FRENCH: Then it wouldn't make any difference whether I was in the habit of eating hamburgers and pizzas or salads.

ROBERT: Shep, as a surgeon and author of two best-selling books on the workings of the human body, do you see any danger in interrupting the natural order by our increasing obsession with life extension?

SHEP: This term "life extension" is a little ambiguous. We have to differentiate between "life expectancy," which is what each of us would like to increase personally, and "life span," which is the natural, species-specific number of years.

ROBERT: There is a theoretical maximum life span for each species.

SHEP: Yes, but what concerns me is DNA research on telomeres.

ROBERT: What are telomeres?

FRENCH: Telomeres are little bunches of DNA at both ends of our chromosomes. The telomeres [in our somatic cells] decrease in size over time, as the cells keep dividing [and thus play a key role in cellular aging]. There's an enzyme called telomerase that not only prevents this decrease but can also make the telomeres longer. Cells [in the laboratory], exposed to increased telomerase, will divide seventy-five times instead of the usual fifty. And so people are starting to have these wonderful fantasies that we can use this procedure throughout the entire body, for all of our cells, and thereby increase our normal [maximum] life span—which, for our species, is about a hundred and twenty years. This prospect concerns me, too.

ROBERT: Shep, why does it concern you?

SHEP: Think about our planet and the implications of extended life—ecological turbulence, social turbulence, economic turbulence.

ROBERT: I'll get dizzy.

SHEP: Well, get dizzy! I, too, like the fantasy of continued life, whether it's the maintenance of physical life or the religious idea of life after death, which has been with us since we were

---

I can't imagine a greater form of tampering with biological laws than trying to increase life spans.

---

primitive. There are reasons that all animals and plants die at a given time. I can't imagine a greater form of tampering with biological laws than trying to increase life spans.

ROBERT: Art, you're a mathematical economist who takes longevity and fitness very seriously. Tell us about your theory of evolutionary fitness.

ART: I try to imagine the environment in which the human genome and human metabolism developed. I see an evolutionary environment of hunters and gatherers living with abundant, highly nutritious, low-caloric plant food, and low fats. I see our ancestors engaging in activities that promote those hormones that retard chronically elevated insulin levels; high insulin is facilitated by too little exercise and a diet that's too high in simple carbohydrates. I don't think there's a theoretical limit to life. I see aging more as a cascade—as a breakdown of coordination among all the billions of cooperative cells within the human body. The loss of the proper response to glucose, due to high insulin, is one of the primary leading indicators—as an economist would say—of the cascade that leads to aging and deterioration.

ROBERT: Greg, you're the author of a book called *Metaman,* which creatively merges humans and machines into what you call a global superorganism. How does life extension affect this superorganism?

GREG: The superorganism I speak of is really human endeavor—society as a whole, knitted together by technology. These linkages accelerate our ability to apply new technologies to transform ourselves, and an obvious target is aging: not just preventing people from dying prematurely—that is, extending life expectancy—but extending the maximum human life span. As we unravel our own biology to the point where we can begin to alter and adjust it, we will extend the human life span beyond a hundred and twenty years, which is the possible limit now. Our challenge is to last in a healthy state until this transfor-

> *As we unravel our own biology . . . we will extend the human life span beyond a hundred and twenty years, . . .*

mation becomes possible—I'd say in a generation or so.

ROBERT: Roy, describe the biology of aging.

ROY: Let me start by talking about the survival curve. The entire population is at a hundred-percent survival rate at the time of birth, and the rate eventually dribbles off to zero out at about a hundred and ten years, minus an occasional outlier. This is the maximum life span; when everyone has died, the survival curve hits zero. The fifty-percent point on the curve is the average life expectancy.

ROBERT: Average life expectancy differs from country to country, but there is a species-specific maximum for life span.

ROY: Both can be extended in animals by caloric restriction. You can extend the whole survival curve, including the animals' maximum life span. If this were applied to humans, it would extend the human life span curve out to a hundred and forty or a hundred and fifty years old.

ROBERT: Let's get back to me. What do I have to eat to extend my survival probability curve?

ROY: A low-calorie, high-quality diet is what

> *You could call it starvation on a healthy diet.*

works with animals. You could call it starvation on a healthy diet.

ROBERT: It doesn't sound like fun, but it may be worth it. Are there dangers in extrapolating from animals to humans?

ROY: At the moment, there are three monkey colonies in the United States living on calorie-restricted diets. Our close relatives are showing the same extensive health-enhancing physiological changes. One colony is showing a decreased incidence of diabetes, which is a good indication of retarded aging in a monkey population. And preliminary studies of humans show that a low-calorie diet induces the same sort of physiological changes as it does in rodents and monkeys.

ROBERT: Tell us about Biosphere 2.

ROY: Biosphere 2 was a big [3.15 acres] glass bubble in southern Arizona, in which eight people lived totally enclosed and sealed for two years [beginning in September 1991]. I was the physician inside. By accident—since there was an El Niño occurrence and that limited the light coming through the glass, and since there were more insect pests in the agriculture section than we had anticipated—we couldn't produce enough food in terms of calories. But the quality of the food was very good. So I recognized this situation as a so-called experiment of nature, which we could take advantage of. I told all the inhabitants that we'd be hungry but we'd also be very healthy. And so we all elected not to import food, in order to preserve the integrity of the experiment.

ROBERT: In addition to restricting calories, do you recommend making any changes in proportions of fats, carbohydrates, or proteins? For example, do you add supplements or any special types of foods?

ROY: You have to plan the low-calorie diet so that you're not deficient in any vitamins, minerals, or other essentials. If you just eat less of the normal bad American diet, you soon get into vitamin deficiencies that will certainly not extend your life span. So the low-calorie diet has to be nutrient-dense. There's pretty strong evidence now accumulated that this will work in humans.

GREG: It takes an enormous amount of self-control to essentially starve yourself in a controlled fashion. I can imagine the primates in those colonies wailing, "Oh, my God! I've been selected for the restriction diet, and to make things worse I'm going to live twenty-five-percent longer." I think the ideal—and there's a lot of research directed toward that—is to understand the biology of what's really causing the longer life span promoted by the caloric restriction, and to emulate that in some way pharmaceutically or genetically.

ROY: Calorie restriction is not something that everyone can do. But some can. There's an Internet calorie-restriction group of about three hundred people now in operation. It's possible.

FRENCH: "Restricted" means what? What's the recommended calorie intake per day?

ROY: It depends on the individual, but something like fifteen hundred to sixteen hundred calories.

ROBERT: For what body weight?

ROY: You can't quite do it like that. You have to be ten to twenty percent below what's called your set point, which is defined as your normal weight if you were continuing to eat normally. You can also calibrate it by body temperature. People on a real calorie restriction diet have a body temperature lower by one-and-a-half degrees.

ROBERT: French, are you being converted? Might you give up some of your dinner?

FRENCH: No, although I absolutely agree with Roy [Walford]'s basic point. Also Art [De Vany]'s, that human beings are part of nature. And if one does what are really very logical things, in terms of not overeating and so on, better health will result.

ROBERT: But calorie restriction is different from not overeating.

FRENCH: Exactly. At times, I do naturally what Roy is advocating, which is basically not eating for days.

ROBERT: Is that just because you're working too hard?

FRENCH: It's for a number of reasons, but I like to keep the system a little bit stressed; I

I think all this nutritional advice is less important than simply leading a very active, physical existence.

---

think it's healthy. My concern is that there are so many nutritionists who claim so many things— eat less of this or more of that, take these or those supplements. I think all this nutritional advice is less important than simply leading a very active, physical existence.

SHEP: If human beings are part of nature, as two of my colleagues here say, why do we want to increase our species' natural life span? Considering the delicate balance of the ecology of this planet, why do we want to take one species and increase the number of its elderly, with whom we are already having massive problems? It's not as if we were increasing the number of people thirty-five to fifty—the most productive members of our society. Or, as I like to think, sixty-five; the age of optimum productivity gets older every year. Why are we spending so much time, money, and societal and scientific resources attempting to destroy our ecology and our social system? What's the great benefit of living longer?

ROBERT: This is the classic trade-off between individual interests and collective needs.

ROY: There are three illusions common to arguments against longevity. First, the problem of population explosion. The real population problem is an excess of births: If too many children were to be born, this would lead to an exponential population increase, whereas if everybody just stopped dying, the increase would be linear. If, starting in prehistoric times, nobody ever died but each person had only one child, the linear increase would now have produced about half a billion people on earth. But because of overbirthing, we have the population escalating enormously. So I don't think that's enough of an argument against life extension. The second illusion is that humankind has

always had to find a reason to make death acceptable, which has plagued gerontology since the beginning. Religion tells us that you don't really die, you go to some other place. There have been all sorts of such rationalization of death, and extended life being bad for the ecology is just the latest example. The third illusion is that if you extend the human life span, you're only extending old age. But we move the entire survival curve out, not just its right-hand edge—so that the centenarians of tomorrow are going to resemble the forty- or fifty-years-olds of today.

ROBERT: That's the hope.

ROY: It's the reality. If you extend the human survival curve by fundamentally retarding the aging process, you extend all age groups.

GREG: I agree with Roy. If you really feel that we shouldn't extend the human life span, then the expenditures that should be stopped are those for the treatment of age-related diseases. Society spends enormous resources on cancer, heart disease, Alzheimer's—all of the maladies that come toward the end of life. If we can get at the fundamental biology of aging, then we would delay these diseases. People want to live longer; there's no question about that. What we really want is for people who can live longer to also live younger. Otherwise we should have a life expectancy of forty-five, as it was at the turn of the century. Is that what you think it should be?

SHEP: Well, another concern of mine is, What will happen to young people when older people remain productive into their seventies and beyond? Traditionally in our society, younger people have replaced older people who were dropping out of the job market. This limit on opportunities for young people is just one of the problems we face. Because the birthrate doesn't seem likely to change.

GREG: The birthrates have changed in the developed world.

SHEP: The developed world represents a relatively small part of the world's population. Isn't this another example of a kind of imperialism that works fine for the West but doesn't work elsewhere in the world?

GREG: We seem to apply advanced medicine to the developed world without a great deal of compunction.

SHEP: That doesn't mean it's good.

ROBERT: There's a natural tension between what will be good for ourselves personally and what will be good for society communally. Humans have faced this tension from the moment when we started to think; it's not going to go away.

ROY: It depends on how you look at the current structure of society, which is stratified like this: When you're a child, you go through a learning period, then there's a period of work, then a period of leisure or retirement. With a longer-lived society, you alter this stratification; people learn throughout life, people work throughout life, and there's no particular retirement, since you have leisure throughout life. That's a different social structure. This is where we're headed, and it obviates the objection of not making room for the young.

ROBERT: Shep, your book *How We Die* states that "death with dignity" is more wish than reality, and that death in fact is undignified and

harsh. Do you think longevity research can ease the process of death, which we all face?

SHEP: I'd like to think that research on life expectancy will compress the curve of suffering before death. We're already beginning to see improvements in quality of life, such that instead of dying slowly of some degenerative disease over five or six years, people are going along quite well and then dropping off over a relatively short period of time. This is the kind of longevity research that, with finite resources, I'd like to encourage.

ROBERT: Recall the words of that famous longevity philosopher, Norma Desmond, the aging movie star of *Sunset Boulevard*. She said there was nothing wrong with being fifty unless you were trying to act twenty.

SHEP: What's interesting to me is that at the beginning of our discussion, Robert chose age ninety—he said something like "Gee, I'd rather die at ninety." But why not seventy, which is a much more realistic age for most of us to die?

ROBERT: Twenty years ago I would have said seventy, but I'm now fifty-five. Let's move on to some of the fads and fallacies that we see in aging research. There seems to be more strange stuff circulating about longevity than even about religion.

ROY: The main reason we see so many fads is that you can make a good argument for a number of things that ought to influence aging, like vitamin E. If you read the vitamin E literature, it looks as though vitamin E should have an effect on aging, but when you actually give it to animals and run a test, it doesn't.

ROBERT: Do you take vitamins?

ROY: I take a general multivitamin, but it's not a big part of my program.

ART: I take antioxidants, such as E and C, which I do think are far more effective. And I take B-complex.

ROBERT: I take vitamins, not because I believe they're all that effective but because other people say they are. I'd feel bad psychologically if I didn't take vitamins, and this negative placebo effect might make me sick.

GREG: The real reason there are so many fads is because human beings so deeply crave a longer, healthier life—and therefore there's money to be made in the field. This is why, when we unravel our biology sufficiently, we'll almost certainly intervene and retard aging, regardless of the larger social issues. Longevity is just too compelling a temptation.

ART: Fads develop because people want quick, easy solutions to problems. In truth, longevity

---

In truth, longevity relates to how you live your life on a day-to-day basis.

---

relates to how you live your life on a day-to-day basis. It has nothing to do with some magic pill.

ROBERT: What about some of the new chemicals, such as DHEA, melatonin, and the like?

ROY: They haven't been shown, convincingly, to increase maximum life span in animal experiments, which is really the only indicator as to whether fundamental aging has been retarded.

ROBERT: Many people are ingesting these chemicals.

ROY: Some people argue that such-and-such ought to work, or might work, and this persuades other people to take it. But animal experiments should be conducted first, and generally they aren't.

ROBERT: French, out on the medical frontier, do you see aging becoming a target for your gene therapy bullets?

FRENCH: Unfortunately, the answer is yes. There's a lot of money to be made if you can develop a gene technique that switches off aging—and in fact we've located genes that do relate to aging, in fruit flies and other organisms. I say "unfortunately" because we know so little about the human body—or about animal bodies, for that matter. New feedback mechanisms, new regulators, and other new factors are being found all the time. So we have no idea what would happen if we tried to put a gene into a cell to interfere with something as fundamental as the aging clock. After all, nature has set the survival time. In my opinion, anti-aging genetic engineering would be a tremendously dangerous thing, but do I think somebody will do it? Yes.

ROBERT: What are some of the specific benefits of exercise, particularly for retarding aging?

SHEP: Exercise slows osteoporosis and can actually increase bone density. Here's how it works: the build-up of muscle increases stress on the bones, and the bones respond by building themselves up. That's very easily measured radiographically. Exercise also causes cholesterol to drop. Longevity seems to be increased. An interesting by-product is that anaerobic exercise—heavy weight lifting—burns about six to seven times as many calories as does aerobic exercise, the reason being that weight lifting breaks down muscle fibers and in the rebuilding of these fibers a lot of calories are expended.

ROBERT: So the effect of that kind of exercise lasts long beyond the actual workout?

SHEP: Exactly. You're out of the gym for forty-eight hours and you're still burning up those calories. And if you got sore—got a charley horse—from working too hard in the gym, that's a good sign. The most important factor as far as aging is concerned is that if you keep exercising heavily until, let's say, you're forty-five or fifty and then stop, that's not nearly as beneficial as beginning to exercise when you're sixty and continuing it. So for all people of my age—sixty-five—get thee to a gym and start an exercise program, which is what I did. I just started last year. My cholesterol has dropped, and, to interest all of you, my testosterone has increased significantly.

ROBERT: Let's talk about testosterone. What about patches worn by men in their sixties and seventies to increase testosterone?

ROY: Again, there's no evidence that testosterone increases either maximum survival or retards basic aging. Whether an increase makes you feel better, I don't know.

ROBERT: There could be health dangers hidden in superficial appearances. Bodybuilders take steroids, and although they look the picture of health, underneath they're deteriorating.

ROY: Absolutely. You have to distinguish between supplements, like vitamins E and C, which in normal amounts don't do harm, and

synthetic hormonelike chemicals that can cause a great deal of harm.

ROBERT: Are there dangers in taking multiple supplements whose interactions have not been studied?

ROY: It depends on the supplements. You should be much more careful about taking, for example, growth hormone. It's quite different from, say, vitamin C, in terms of potential harm compared to potential benefit.

ROBERT: What's interesting about the benefits of weight lifting for osteoporosis is that for a long time resistance training was almost ridiculed. It may make you look better, we were told, but it doesn't have any health benefits. And then, relatively recently, opinions changed.

ART: I've known this for many years. If you look at our ancestral activity patterns, you can see that we had lots of languid periods of rest interspersed with a few short bursts of very-high-intensity efforts. When you engage in bodybuilding or high-threshold kinds of activities—sprinting up a hill as opposed to taking a walk, say—you release lactic acid, which in turn releases beneficial hormones.

ROBERT: You advocate a great deal of variety in exercise, less aerobics, and many periods of rest. Is there danger of too much exercise?

ART: Absolutely. We mistakenly apply an industrial model to what's really a self-organized natural system. Variety is crucial. Repetitive stress breaks down all bodily tissues and is a fundamental cause of the premature aging of connective tissue. Heavy aerobicizers are producing excess levels of free radicals, which are aggressive groups of ionized atoms that damage cells. Boston Marathon participants have a high rate of brain cancer. Lots of joggers die of heart fibrillation. I had a colleague last year who died of it, in one of his ten-kilometer races; he had some scar tissue in his heart, which can break down the coordination waves. An aerobicizer or jogger restrains the chaos in the heartbeat, which is natural to an adaptive heart.

ROBERT: The human body is a complex system in which simple solutions are usually wrong and occasionally dangerous. Aerobic exercise is good for the heart and the circulatory system, but it can have ill effects when it's overdone.

GREG: So what do you do?

ART: I know what to do. I know what really works. I'm sixty-one and I have seven percent body fat.

ROBERT: You're just lucky because you picked good parents.

ART: My dad died at seventy-one of congestive heart failure; all his arteries were clogged up. I believe in variety and intensity of exercise, along with a moderately low-calorie diet of the kind that Roy emphasizes. Although with my basal metabolism and muscle mass, "low calorie" for me is something like thirty-five-hundred calories a day. Americans in general overeat and underexert. And what they do eat is all-too-simple carbohydrates; the pasta that most people eat is a bowl of sugar briefly deferred, low in nutrition and high in calories. The body can't metabolize that kind of load.

ROBERT: How many hours a week does everyone here exercise? I do about five to six.

ART: I do about an hour and a half.

GREG: About two.

ROY: About four.

SHEP: About five.

FRENCH: When I'm in training for national competition, which I'm now in, it's a lot of hours a week. But then I'll go for a week or two without doing anything. Actually, most of what I do is play.

ROBERT: We're ready for a prediction. A hundred years from now, what is the average life expectancy in America?

ROY: I'll still be here. . . . Many people alive today—at least, the children—will live through the next century and on into the following one. The average life expectancy will be a hundred and fifty years.

GREG: I recently convened a group of leading researchers in the biology of aging, and they were of the opinion that a hundred and fifty or more was a very realistic possibility.

ART: That doesn't square with the rapid rise of adult-onset diabetes and the surge of multiple sclerosis and a variety of other diseases. I don't have a number. It's always a distribution, and statistical fallacies arise because you have a finite sample. Frankly, I'm not interested—I probably won't be here. But I'm going to be as healthy as I can for the rest of my life.

FRENCH: I'm not sure that I can separate what I think from what I hope, but my feeling is that there won't be a major increase in life span. Nature will continue to dictate how long our cells survive. My number for average life expectancy would be a hundred and twenty, but

I suspect that Roy's survival curve will be such that human beings will be much healthier, much more active, much more productive for much longer—and then we'll suddenly crash. We'll go on for a hundred and twenty years, and then on the last day collapse.

SHEP: What we'll see is a compression of morbidity and suffering, with the recognition that even nerve cells can change if we work with them. Osteoporosis will decrease, if we exercise. We'll see vigorous people of a hundred and a hundred and ten, and they'll all be dead at a hundred and twenty, notwithstanding everything we've heard.

ROBERT: CONCLUDING COMMENT

Despite differences of opinion, there seems to be a commonsense prescription for longevity and long life. Eat a healthy, balanced diet of whole grains, fresh fruits and vegetables, some nuts; limit calories and animal fats. If you take vitamins, stick to the basics, like E and C. Exercise regularly, including aerobic and weight lifting; sleep well; be serene. Avoid injury, tobacco, excess alcohol, and stress—and keep fire detectors in your home. You can keep an eye out for all those "magic pills," but don't obsess and don't experiment with the latest fad. Moderation, though not a very original prescription, is often the right course. What's your report card? Here's mine: good on the diet, excellent on the exercise, but lousy on the stress—there is just too much pressure doing these health shows. But suppose you do live to be a hundred and twenty? How much more junk can you stuff into your closets? It's been said that millions seek immortality who don't know what to do on a rainy afternoon. But if rainy afternoons are not a problem for you, longevity is an attractive prospect. It takes common sense to bring us closer to truth.

OUTTAKES

SHEP: *So you extend your life, but all your friends and relatives are dead.*

ART: *I work out for half an hour, and then I get the heck out of the gym.*

CHAPTER 9

Does Sex Have a Future?

Sex occupies a good part of our psyche, engaging our thoughts and influencing our behavior. It has been around forever, baffling and unchanging. Sex is still baffling, but suddenly it is changing. Artificial insemination, even cloning, for reproduction? Virtual sex for recreation? Erotic adventures on the Internet? Sex is diversifying into a brave new world of biochemical procreation and electronic stimulation. But all software and no hardware? All pleasure and no intimacy? Is something missing here? Sex already pervades modern life, transforming our values and, for worse or for better, disrupting our morals. Now what happens when technology multiplies our sexual options and accelerates our moral shifts? What is the link between sensual pleasure and personal intimacy? And what is the impact on personal relationships and social cohesion? Where is sex going? To assess its future, we need to understand its nature. Our experts share with us their diverse views on human sexuality.

PARTICIPANTS

Dr. Paul Abramson is a professor of psychology at the University of California, Los Angeles, where he teaches courses on human sexuality, including one entitled "Sex and the Law." The co-author of *Sexual Nature/Sexual Culture,* Paul discusses the nature of sexual pleasure and why it's so important in evolutionary terms; he also gives his theory of cybersex.

Dr. Vern Bullough, a professor of history at California State University, Northridge, has written or edited over fifty books on sexuality, including *Human Sexuality: An Encyclopedia.* Vern focuses on the historical and cultural contexts of sexual practices.

Joyce Penner, R.N., a clinical nurse, and her husband, **Dr. Clifford Penner,** a clinical psychologist, are sex therapists working in the Christian community. Joyce and Cliff have co-written many books on the importance and pleasures of sex within marriage, including *Men and Sex.*

Dr. Gregory Stock, the director of the Program on Medicine, Technology, and Society at the University of California, Los Angeles, is the author of *The Book of Questions: Love and Sex.* Greg sees sex as growing in importance and as increasingly separated from procreation.

ROBERT: Paul, you're an expert witness in prominent legal cases involving sex. What kinds of sex-related lawsuits affect public policy?

PAUL: The colloquial phrase is "sexpert" witness. I'm concerned with the regulation of all expressions of sexuality: in our behavior, our speech, and even our fantasies—such as how they're played out on the Internet. And also with how society protects people from sexual harm—abuse, rape, harassment, and so on. All these behaviors are highly regulated, and all are in the legal domain. In your introduction, you said that sex pervades everything in our lives. One thing it doesn't pervade is the U.S. Constitution, and there's real debate about whether sex is a fundamental right and about the extent to which our freedoms of speech and press extend to sexual issues. Many of the cases center on constitutional rights of sexual expression, behavior, and privacy—like sexual expression on the Internet, where we now need global definitions; gay marriage; abortion as a privacy right; and how best to protect people from sexual harm.

ROBERT: These legal interpretations will affect our self-image as sexual beings.

PAUL: The laws that govern and regulate our sexuality are going to influence the way we talk about it, the way we express it, the way we cohabit, the way we associate, and so on. So I see the future of sex closely tied to the manner in which sex is legally regulated and the extent to which we have constitutional guarantees for expressing it.

ROBERT: Vern, as a medical historian, you've specialized in sex research and written numerous books such as *Sexual Attitudes: Myths and Realities.* Give us a historical overview of sexual understandings and misunderstandings.

VERN: Well, we know that sex existed back then, because we're all here, but in the past there was mostly tremendous misunderstanding—ranging from what causes pregnancy to what kind of sex is permissible, and the like. Cultures differ, and time periods differ. At some times, for example, masturbation has been acceptable, and at other times it hasn't. Sometimes there was very little talk about premarital sex, other times there was a great deal. How much sex a person could have was subject to debate. Judaism has been generally positive about sex, whereas Christianity has been hostile—it's what I would call a sex-negative culture. For much of its history, Christianity argued in essence that the best sex was no sex. Cultures vary tremendously. All you can say about sex in the past is that it was there, and everything we do today was done then.

ROBERT: Cliff, you and Joyce are sex therapists in the Christian tradition, which historically has avoided open discussions about sex. What has been the reaction of the Christian community to your very open and honest approach to sex? One of your books is *52 Ways to Have Fun, Fantastic Sex: A Guidebook for Married Couples.* Fifty-two? You're not limiting sex to once a week, are you?

CLIFF: Absolutely not! Have sex as many times a week as you like. The response to our message has been wide open, and it grows out of great need. We're applied people—we don't do much theory. We're out there working with people who are struggling with their sexual lives. In the Christian community, particularly, there's a widely felt need for therapy, because there are so many people having difficulties with their marriages. They see all the trouble there is in relationships, and they're eager to get any kind of help. So we get a very warm response. But regarding what Vern Bullough was saying—that traditional Christianity has had a hostile attitude toward sex—we've tried to come out with the exact opposite message: That people need to celebrate their sexuality.

ROBERT: Do you hear complaints that you deal too frankly with sex?

CLIFF: We get some complaints, but we go where we're invited, and they welcome us. When people are upset about what we say about sex, it often relates to something in their own past.

ROBERT: Greg, you look to the future. At the horizon, what do you see for sex?

GREG: There are going to be powerful forces impinging on sex, with the potential for changing it. The impacts are going to be enormous. First, sex and reproduction will be further separated. Second, sex is a very strong drive and it will increasingly pervade everything we do—in terms of advertising, the multiplication of social expressions, and so on. Sex has become dominant on the Internet in a very short period of time, and cybersex can provide immediate gratification of various sorts, even if it's only in a limited way. And then we'll have pharmaceuticals that create arousal—Viagra-like drugs. The abortion debate will become muted, as procedures like the RU486 pill make the decision to abort very personal and hence very difficult to regulate. The abortion issue will give way to debates on reproductive technologies—cloning, genetic engineering, things of that sort. So sex is going to become a lot more complicated.

ROBERT: How will these complications affect personal relationships?

GREG: The biggest impact on personal relationships will be this separation between reproduction and sex, which will continue to grow.

The biggest impact on personal relationships will be this separation between reproduction and sex, . . .

And then there's our ability to manipulate reproduction, using pharmaceuticals and other techniques.

ROBERT: Paul, let's explore the nature of fantasy, which is very much involved with sexuality. In a high-tech world, what happens to fantasy when we're surrounded with all these overt expressions of sexuality?

PAUL: The capacity for fantasy is shrinking.

ROBERT: That's the opposite of what some might expect—they'd think that with all these high-tech sexual exposures, fantasy would be greater.

PAUL: But all these innovations are substitutes for fantasy. If you look at all the media for simulated sex—photography, the VCR revolution, Dial-a-Porn phone sex, virtual sex on the Internet—they're all ways of co-opting the internal fantasy life, and they're primarily adjuncts to male masturbation. These are basically high-tech ways of masturbating. Instead of "stroke films" we have "stroke bytes."

ROBERT: Joyce, as a female, can you give us another perspective? Or are male-female differences an illusion?

JOYCE: Women do provide a different perspective. We bring the complexity, the unpredictableness, the ever-changingness to relationships.

Men want to figure women out, to get it down to a formula, and you can't do that. Women are too complex.

Men want to figure women out, to get it down to a formula, and you can't do that. Women are too complex.

ROBERT: If women are complex, does that mean you think that men are simple?

JOYCE: Yes, regarding sexuality. Men and women provide different dimensions of the whole picture. In the Christian community, we need to counteract the idea that the woman's role in sex is just to satisfy the man—the idea that she isn't a sexual person, doesn't have sexual needs. Ultimately that idea doesn't work: It isn't fulfilling for him, and it isn't fulfilling for her.

ROBERT: With the Internet and various new technologies expanding expressions of sexuality, do you find that your patients' fantasy lives are changing?

JOYCE: All of us are designed with the capacity for imagination and imagery, and fantasy can enhance the sexual relationship between a husband and wife. But when these self-generated thoughts are replaced with simplistic external images, we become distracted from the relationship.

PAUL: Females regulate sex—not only in our own species but among other primates as well. Females are the gatekeepers. It reminds me of the old joke about women having a sixth sense about whether a man is going to have sex that night or not.

JOYCE: Yes, we are. Anthropologists have written about this. Gatekeepers are a necessary role.

ROBERT: Paul, one of the things you talk about in your book *With Pleasure: Thoughts on the Nature of Human Sexuality* is how the concept of restraint underlies our historical understanding of sex.

PAUL: Yes. Just as there are evolutionary foundations for pleasure, there are evolutionary foundations for restraint. If you look broadly at primates, there's a lot of competition for sex, and competitive sex is often coupled with aggression. Well, you can segue from that to the current problems of human sexuality—sexually transmitted diseases, unwanted pregnancies, and so forth. Sex has its risks, and the value of restraint is that it weighs the negatives and the positives, balancing the side effects with the open and intimate expression of sex.

ROBERT: Joyce, do you see the concept of restraint as broader than what Paul describes—that is, is there more to it than the evolutionary sense of avoiding disease?

JOYCE: When you're talking about restraint in terms of boundaries, guidelines, limitations—they're necessary ultimately for sexual satisfaction. In a sense, the restraints provide fulfillment. They protect us from danger and harm and the misuse of sex. So much pleasure can be derived from sex, which is really a purpose of sex, but when it's misused it can also cause harm and pain and deprive us of that pleasure. And so, yes, the boundaries and restraints are necessary.

GREG: With sex and sexuality in our face all the time now, it becomes increasingly difficult to encourage restraint. People are shocked at the explosion of pornography on the Internet. Well, it's because that's what people want on the Internet.

PAUL: I don't think that's what people want. That's what men want.

VERN: Paul has hit on it. In the past, sex has been defined mostly in male terms. And what we're beginning to do now is define sex also in female terms, which are really quite different. And if we're talking about restraints, society is based upon limitations. Say you're married—the

question is, What limits are there? Can you go out and have two hundred different sexual contacts? What kind of limits do we impose? Sex is

---

In the past, sex has been defined mostly in male terms.

---

more than a physical exercise—it's also a way of becoming very intimate, very understanding, very appreciative. That aspect of it never really comes across, unless you talk to real people.

GREG: But once you decouple sex and reproduction, it becomes a different game—and that's what we're just beginning to deal with.

VERN: We need to talk about technology, which is so radically changing sex. The contraceptive pill is the obvious example, but what I'm fascinated by is how people can live their fantasies in different ways. Transsexuals, for instance. Technology has made it possible to change one's sex, legally and anatomically. And hormones have made this change more realistic than it was in the past. We've always had people changing their sexual anatomy—such as eunuchs, who were castrated—but they didn't adopt the role of the other sex, because they lacked the hormones.

GREG: It's now possible for these communities of sexual minorities to link up and form subcultures, which has been difficult to do in the past.

ROBERT: People with nonmainstream feelings aren't isolated anymore. They get more cohesive within their own groups, but the groups grow farther apart from one another.

PAUL: The psychological notion of fantasy is really about a narrative, an imaginary narrative that enhances or explores something. But the issue Vern [Bullough] brought up has more to do with a deep psychological substructure, in terms of gender. For transsexuals, it's not about fantasizing being of the opposite sex, but actually feeling at a very deep, intimate level that they belong to the opposite sex and just by a quirk of nature ended up with the wrong genital equipment.

VERN: I don't accept that my use of transsexual feelings is more reality than fantasy. Consider cross-dressing. Many people have always wanted to know what living as a member of the other sex is like, and so they live that fantasy. In our society, that's now possible. There are a tremendous variety of these groups. They're on the Internet, they hold conventions, they exchange information on such things as how to achieve a better passing ability, and so on.

GREG: In terms of role playing, it becomes very easy on the Internet to masquerade as a person of the other sex, or another age.

JOYCE: You can be whatever you want to be.

ROBERT: Is that good or bad?

GREG: Good or bad, this is one of the places where you can explore your fantasies and your curiosities. And it seems to me that this is the kind of sexual behavior we'll have to be increasingly dealing with.

ROBERT: What does the nature of fantasy teach us about the nature of sex?

PAUL: Well, two things: It shows the extent to which we—particularly males—are obsessed with whatever enhances, solidifies, and makes our fantasy life more real. And it shows the

extent to which we're willing to forgo intimacy for the opportunity to indulge in fantasy. Look at how we drive these enormous economic machines, the sex industries—X-rated videos, phone sex, Internet sex. It also speaks to what's missing in the relational aspects of sex.

ROBERT: Certainly any new technology welcomes sexuality as a primary economic driving force. Everyone talks about how silly and annoying cybersex is, but so many people are doing it.

PAUL: I think the whole story's economic, and I use the model of Dial-a-Porn. When the telephone companies were first deregulating and started offering various kinds of information providers, the first ones were Dial-a-Joke, Dial-a-Prayer, and Dial-a-Porn. You can guess which was the most lucrative. Dial-a-Porn became a cash cow for the telephone companies. The VCR revolution was driven in part by X-rated movies.

VERN: And the economy of the San Fernando Valley is driven in part by that.

GREG: Isn't it a little like sugar? We all have the drive toward sweetness. It's great when you can have that fruit you're seeking, but when you have easy access to all sorts of French pastries, it becomes a problem. We have to deal with an omnipresence of sexual supply.

PAUL: The question is, Are you motivated to get something or to avoid something else?

Maybe our craze for fantasy reveals a fear of intimacy.

Maybe our craze for fantasy reveals a fear of intimacy. The challenges associated with intimacy are often difficult, and it becomes easy to seek a substitute.

JOYCE: Some research suggests that couples who watch pornography together experience more excitement in that particular sexual event, but over time they lose the thrill, and ultimately they get less and less turned on by each other.

ROBERT: Do you ever use pornography in your therapy for married couples?

JOYCE: No. Externalizing fantasy, rather than internalizing and sharing the fantasy in the relationship, can be a stimulus in the short term but an inhibitor in the long term.

ROBERT: For example, virtual sex on the Internet can be addictive.

CLIFF: Right. We deal all the time with patients who suffer from that sort of addiction. In fact, we've seen couples where there's almost no real sex going on at all, because the man is getting all his gratification from the Internet. The couple usually comes to therapy when he gets busted by her, and he has to face up to the fact that he's getting all of his sex virtually and she's getting none at all. Men tend to be always looking for something new—that's one of the sexual differences between men and women.

PAUL: It's not only new sex but quick sex. Women are looking for something deeper.

VERN: It used to be that men had to sneak out with prostitutes or go to a girlie show.

CLIFF: The difference now is that instant sexual gratification is readily available in almost everyone's home. A man no longer has to head down to the other part of town.

GREG: That's a big difference—if you can log on in twenty seconds and remain completely private.

JOYCE: That's right.

PAUL: But this isn't really the future of sex. It's the evolution of male masturbation, and it's a limited domain. There will be more and more technological enhancements for making these fantasies seem more and more real, but ultimately they'll always miss the driving force in a relationship, the psychological connections.

ROBERT: So what are you saying? That cybersex is bad, but it's inevitable?

JOYCE: It's inevitable but it's unfulfilling.

GREG: It's separate from sex, in a sense.

PAUL: It's one aspect of nonreproductive sex, but, again, it's all about male masturbation masquerading as the future of sex. I think the primary use of cybersex is for male masturbation.

GREG: Well, that seems very dismissive of the potency of this new medium and its cultural impact.

PAUL: But I think it's indicative of the lack of intimacy in modern relationships. Greg [Stock] is commenting that the reason men choose this form of sexual expression reveals deep social and psychological issues, and I don't want to be dismissive of those.

JOYCE: Cybersex promises to satisfy. And it doesn't require anything from a man. Everything he wants is there. And the women complain. It disrupts relationships.

CLIFF: Well, we have female patients who are hooked on Internet chat rooms.

JOYCE: They're hooked on relationships.

CLIFF: So for women, it's more the relational use of the Internet than the pornographic that counts.

GREG: The challenge is that if our sex drives can be gratified so easily, uniformly, around the clock, then it alters the ways in which those drives are contributing to the building of relationships.

JOYCE: But ultimately cybersex doesn't satisfy the longing of each of us to overcome our separateness and our isolation.

VERN: The difficulty is that that longing has existed all throughout the past, and you have to remember that most people didn't have that kind of companionship, for the most part—certainly not the women. In fact, it took money to be married, and a lot of people never did marry.

GREG: What happens as reproduction is increasingly decoupled from sex? How does that impact the nature of sex in relationships—and for that matter in encounters with people we're less intimate with?

ROBERT: Take the thought question to the extreme and assume that reproduction has nothing to do with sex anymore. What then happens to sex?

VERN: It changes the whole outlook of society. In fact, this is already happening to some extent. The whole fight of gays for equality is in essence a legal separation of reproduction from sex and marriage.

JOYCE: What's interesting for us is dealing with unconsummated marriages, in which the couple has not been able to have sexual intercourse, for physical or sometimes psychological reasons. Yet they're often achieving full sexual satisfaction, so they don't come for sexual therapy until they want to have children. We see sex as having three functions: procreation, pleasure, and unity or intimacy. These couples fulfill the last two but they can't reproduce.

PAUL: Isn't it problematic to frame human sexuality in procreative ways? Most human sexual expression throughout life is nonreproductive. From sexual exploration in early childhood to postmenopausal intercourse, our bodies are designed, in some ways, for enjoying nonreproductive sexual pleasure.

JOYCE: That's right. And this is different from most of the rest of the animal kingdom.

PAUL: The clitoris has no reproductive function.

JOYCE: In fact we use that to teach women that they're sexual persons with sexual needs, that they were designed for pleasure, that they aren't just the receptacle of male sexual aggression. We teach women that sex is something within all of us, because the clitoris has no other purpose in the body.

VERN: There can be real difficulties with technology. Fertility clinics are an illustration of this: These are places where, in a sense, sex becomes a duty and you forget what marriage is about. You rush down to the clinic at some technologically determined moment, and you go in and masturbate—and here masturbation is justified, perhaps even by the church. And suppose the artificial insemination doesn't work. You become afraid to have sex in between, and you just wait until next month's visit.

CLIFF: When sex is simply for procreation, it really moves us apart, doesn't it?

VERN: Yes, it does.

JOYCE: And then the couple ends up in our office a year or two later, after they've had their baby. We often see couples who've lost their sexual relationship after going through infertility struggles, because the whole essence of why couples get together is interrupted by that process.

ROBERT: Trying to regulate sexual behavior distorts it. Whenever sex becomes goal-oriented rather than pleasure-oriented, problems arise. Whether sex is programmed for natural procreation, artificial insemination, or even buttressing one's self-image, something is lost.

GREG: But part of the reason is that in-vitro fertilization and these other kinds of reproductive technologies are still so primitive and so difficult and so horribly intrusive. As they improve, that onus will be reduced.

JOYCE: Goal-oriented sex loses its power—often quite quickly. It's a shame that in our culture we're conditioned to achieve our goals quickly. Speed is one way we define success—this is certainly true for men and increasingly for women. And yet with sex, it's just the opposite. What may be great in the rest of life doesn't work in bed. So take your time, slow down, enjoy the pleasure, don't go for the goal, don't raise the bar, just enjoy the moment. That's when it works best.

ROBERT: In terms of speed and sensitivity, then, sexuality is very different from almost everything else happening in society.

GREG: In a sense, sex compares with eating; the more intimate it is, the more enjoyable.

CLIFF: Yes, instead of gobbling down our food and being done with it. If we really want to savor a meal, we spend two or three hours at it.

JOYCE: If we put too much in our stomachs and feed ourselves with technology, will we be as satisfied?

PAUL: I think there's a generational difference in this. Teenagers and young adults now—women, in particular—are making much more explicit demands regarding their own sexuality, in terms of partner choices, sexual fulfillment, orgasm, and so on. They grew up in a different era—they're sexually knowledgeable and their expectations are higher. They're very much in touch with their sexual needs, and willing to explore those needs and to demand satisfaction. The real risks of sex are unwanted pregnancies and sexually transmitted diseases. So to me the future of sex is condoms . . . sounds like "Plastics," from *The Graduate,* doesn't it? We need better condom technologies. The condoms we use today are not much different from what they were in the seventeenth century. They're not user-friendly. They diminish sexual enjoyment. We need something like a contraceptive lubricant that goes on smoothly, facilitates the conductivity of heat, enhances the actual act of sex. Then we'll see a great explosion of sexuality, even within the context of relationships. This kind of technology will drive the relationship of the couple, not the masturbation of the male.

GREG: So if you eliminate sexually transmitted diseases and decouple reproduction, then won't sex be used much more broadly than in a monogamous relationship?

PAUL: Definitely.

ROBERT: Do you agree with that, Joyce?

JOYCE: Women open up sexually when they feel loved and cared for and have an emotional connection, and so they will demand a relationship.

PAUL: There may be a period of exploration. As adults, we do prefer relationships. But without the risk of sexually transmitted diseases, without the risk of unwanted pregnancy, the teenage years and the early twenties will look different.

VERN: Even with Viagra and other sex-enhancing drugs, sex becomes less important to many people than the intimacy involved. You recognize that the relationship is more important than the orgasm. The best examples are some of the gay couples I've studied who have been living together for a long time. They have no sex whatsoever—they might be having it on the side, but they don't have it with each other. But they're very close, very intimate with each other. What holds them together? It may be the cat or the house they own together, or not knowing what to do with the garden if the other one's gone.

ROBERT: Paul, what can we learn about human sexuality from observing primates?

PAUL: Bonobos, sometimes known as pigmy chimps, are considered our closest relatives. Their sexual behavior is diverse, and it mirrors the diversity of human sexuality.

VERN: Any telephone sex?

PAUL: Check out the sexual positions. They can use the missionary position, which kills the idea that this was the position forced upon us by—

ROBERT: Maybe the bonobos were watching missionaries.

PAUL: What we learn from the bonobos is the extent to which the concept of "natural" extends beyond reproductive sex. They have oral sex; they have intergenerational sex; they have sex on the run; they have sex for recreational purposes. Their most frequent sexual expression is female-female genital rubbing. They use nonreproductive sex for conflict resolution, for bonding, and so forth. Bonobo sex has a primary social function. It's a full-bodied sexuality—quite different from that of chimpanzees, who have a limited sexuality tied to a specific estrus period. The bonobos act as if they'd read the *Kama Sutra* and *The Joy of Sex.*

ROBERT: Cliff, do you see human sexuality as going beyond the animal model?

CLIFF: Oh, it absolutely has to, because unless we're able to make that deeper personal connection, that soul connection, sex doesn't have that meaning we're all looking for.

JOYCE: And we're having sex far more than just to reproduce.

PAUL: From an evolutionary perspective, the reason sex feels so good is that it's the incentive to get us to copulate often so that more offspring are produced. But the significant characteristic of human sexuality is that it's not specific to procreative sex. It's like an evolutionary loophole: Human sex drives can be satisfied by nonreproductive sexual behaviors. So you get this incentive to engage in sex, which in most other animals would be tailored only to reproductive behaviors, but in humans it's not.

CLIFF: Human males are ultimately satisfied the most when they're in a relationship with a partner who is deeply satisfied. And when that happens, there's something more going on than just having an orgasm.

ROBERT: What does that tell you about the nature of sex?

CLIFF: That it's terribly complicated. Unless sex is able to happen between two people, it's not going to deeply satisfy the soul.

GREG: Talking about the soul connection, there are many couples who have very little sex and yet have that same intensity of relationship.

PAUL: Sexual diversity would help mitigate one of humanity's major problems, overpopulation. Oral sex, for example, is a contraceptive activity, because it doesn't result in new births. Religious texts that authorize sex only for reproductive purposes exacerbate overpopulation in ways that were never meant to be. The use of nonreproductive forms of sex limits population growth, because you achieve sexual fulfillment in nonreproductive ways.

JOYCE: We've done a good job of fulfilling the command to be fruitful and multiply.

VERN: A little too good.

JOYCE: What we need to do is fulfill the command that a husband and wife ought to leave father and mother and "become one"—be totally open and unashamed of each other and enjoy sexual pleasure together.

CLIFF: If you look at the Song of Solomon in the Bible, it's just full of pleasure. So it's hard to accept the argument that the Judeo-Christian religion, at least originally, was against sexual pleasure.

ROBERT: Later interpretations distorted the original intent.

VERN: The traditional hostility of the religious community toward masturbation, for example, simply because it was not procreative, has been very great.

PAUL: As I understand it, that hostility can be traced to the sin of Onan, in the Book of Genesis, where Onan's brother died and by custom he was supposed to impregnate his brother's wife. And Onan said, "Sure, I'm ready for that, but I'm just not going to impregnate her," and he spilled his seed on the ground instead.

CLIFF: That was the withdrawal method of birth control, not masturbation.

PAUL: But the spilling of the seed on the ground came to refer to masturbation, and became known as onanism.

JOYCE: It's a misuse of scripture.

PAUL: If you look at the crusade of Anthony Comstock in the late nineteenth century—that was an anti-obscenity movement but it was also anti-masturbation.

VERN: Actually, it's even worse, because Comstock regarded contraceptive information as the greatest sin—the greatest evil. The Comstock laws practically prevented any dissemination of contraceptive information in the United States.

CLIFF: We're talking years ago. You're not saying that the religious community is still putting up those boundaries today?

PAUL: No, no, not at all. And I understand you're working—

JOYCE: We hope we've broken those down.

PAUL: But we're thinking in terms of Saint Augustine and Thomas Aquinas—and more recently the Vatican's edict on condoms. So there are clearly pointed examples that still exist.

VERN: All you need to do is listen to some of the TV preachers to know that they're still not accepting nonreproductive sex.

ROBERT: Well, they may not be accepting it on television.

GREG: Reproductive issues and overpopulation will probably be dealt with technically rather than through alterations of our sexual behavior.

PAUL: Or dealt with legally. Constraints could be placed on the number of children you can have.

ROBERT: Cliff, how does your theology influence your approach to sex?

CLIFF: The basic belief is that we are created to be in a relationship, and we envision sex to be

---

Sex is living out our humanness in its ultimate form.

---

the highest expression of that relationship and that intimacy. Sex is living out our humanness in its ultimate form.

ROBERT: But sex has also been classified by various religious groups as among the worst of the sins. Is that changing?

CLIFF: Well, I think it depends on whom you have it with.

VERN: And who's doing the talking within the religious community. There's no agreement in the religious community on the joys of sex.

ROBERT: But is there a change?

JOYCE: There's definitely a change.

ROBERT: And both of you are helping make that change?

CLIFF: We hope so.

ROBERT: Good. We want a prediction. A hundred years from now, what will have happened to sex?

PAUL: Better condoms.

VERN: The biggest change in sex will be the changing attitudes of women. The key to what sex can be is what women make it to be. In the past, we've thought of sex in male terms, and maybe by the year 2100 we'll be talking about it from a female point of view.

JOYCE: Vern took my point. Yes. Intimacy is necessary for both men and women. But women will be the ones who require sex to be something more than just technical, more than just physical.

CLIFF: Men will get beyond just the momentary gratification. They'll become more complex in their sexuality, so that they will have moved in the direction of women.

GREG: There's great diversity of opinion here, and that's what we're going to see more of in the future—all sorts of coupling, linking, and using technology, using pharmaceuticals. And I think that sexually transmitted diseases will not be an issue. Sex will be much more diverse and much more recreational—separated from reproduction, and in fact separated from relationships in some ways.

ROBERT: CONCLUDING COMMENT

I'm not sure it's progress, but eventually we will make better babies by cloning our genetic material, and we will feel more intense sexual pleasure when stimulated chemically or electrically. These new products will be advertised as "cleaner" and "risk-free" and marketed with no danger of disease or emotional trauma—that will be the sales pitch, but the goods may be damaged. Sex is a primary descriptor of the human psyche. It occupies significant ground on our mental map, more than what is needed for procreation or even pleasure. As the search for intimacy intensifies in an age of depersonalizing technology, it may well be the intimacy of

sexuality that provides the greatest fulfillment. But while technology may heighten physical satisfaction, it may also make true intimacy harder to achieve. How humans deal with their sexuality helps define what it means to be human, and that, at least, won't change in the future, as sex continues to bring us closer to truth.

OUTTAKES

GREG: *We didn't talk enough about manipulating both sexual desire and sexual performance pharmaceutically.*

VERN: *Something else we didn't get to, that I think will be different in a hundred years, is that we'll probably better understand male and female hormones, and when we get those managed, that's really going to change—*

PAUL: *You see, I think just the opposite. Pleasure is the simple and exquisite way of regulating human sexuality. In other animals, sexuality is regulated through estrus, hormonally. We've evolved to a place where our sexuality is determined by the physical and psychological consequences of pleasurable acts, which we engage in because they feel good.*

CHAPTER 10

Who Needs Sex Therapy?

HHow's your sex life? Would you like to make it better? Can we even agree on what "better sex" means? Talking about sex used to be off limits; now there's surely more talk, more obsession, but possibly less pleasure and fulfillment. Can sex therapy help? Who is in need of sex therapy? Not too long ago, sex therapists were dealing with odd problems of few people. Today, sex therapists work with normal problems of many people. But what is a "normal" problem when it comes to sex? And what sort of measures do professional sex therapists recommend? There seems to be surprising consensus.

PARTICIPANTS

Dr. Paul Abramson, a leading authority on human sexuality at the University of California, Los Angeles, is the author of *With Pleasure: Thoughts on Human Sexuality.* Paul describes male-female roles in the context of evolution; he also deals with sexual trauma.

Dr. Vern Bullough, a professor of medical history at California State University, Northridge, has written many books about sex, including *Sexual Attitudes: Myths and Realities.* Vern critiques the poor practices of unprofessional sex therapists and points out that historically love and sex have been separate matters.

Dr. Sherwin (Shep) Nuland, author of *How We Die* and *How We Live,* teaches medical history and bioethics at Yale. Shep believes that our sexuality is central to our humanity, and he describes aesthetic, altruistic, and psychoanalytic aspects of love and sex.

Dr. Clifford Penner and his wife, **Joyce Penner, R.N.,** are sex therapists and marriage counselors with a long-standing practice in the Christian community. Cliff and Joyce emphasize that intimacy and communication are fundamental to a successful sexual relationship and that there are profound differences between male and female sexuality. They also describe how sexual counseling works, and why women should take the lead in bed.

ROBERT: Joyce, as a sex therapist, and as co-author with Cliff of such books as *What Every Wife Wants Her Husband to Know About Sex,* can you describe some of the common problems your clients face?

JOYCE: The problems we're treating are becoming more complex, because nowadays more self-help books have become available.

ROBERT: Now that people can solve the simple problems themselves, they save the tough ones for you.

JOYCE: Yes. Most commonly we deal with the lack of sexual desire—surprisingly widespread in both men and women, though it's more characteristic of women than men.

ROBERT: Lack of sexual desire seems paradoxical in our sexually open society.

JOYCE: And then pain for women, pain that interrupts the pleasure—

ROBERT: Physical pain?

JOYCE: Yes, physical pain. Often caused by destructive relationship patterns that manifest themselves in the sexual relationship. The most common example of such a destructive pattern is the one set up by an insecure, sexually demanding male.

ROBERT: Paul, you're one of the leading scientists in sexual research. This is not a silly question: Why is sex so pleasurable?

PAUL: From an evolutionary perspective, sex is a simple but exquisite mechanism for motivating human beings to engage in those behaviors likely to lead to conception. The propagation of the species is the ancient biological force behind sex.

ROBERT: Cliff, with the increasing openness of sex in society, are the sexual problems that you encounter changing?

CLIFF: Many more people now believe that they should find deeper fulfillment in sex. They are seeking more exquisite satisfaction. And so problems arise, I would say, when realizations don't meet expectations.

ROBERT: Shep, as a medical doctor, you have a chapter on the act of love in your best-selling book *How We Live.* How important are sexual function and dysfunction in normal human relationships?

SHEP: Sexual function is the primary center of everything we are as human beings. Sexuality is the core of our personality; its powers focus our ability to love, to enjoy a heightened sense of our surroundings. It's moonlight, it's roses, it's poetry. If this sounds too Freudian, I won't retract a word of it. Sexuality empowers us to express everything that is within us. And that's one reason we often think of sex as a release.

ROBERT: Modern scholars criticize Freud for precisely your grand view—eloquently expressed—that sex is pandemic in its power over human thought and behavior. Do you agree with this Freudian maximal position of sexual influence and control?

SHEP: I think sex is the sum total of what we are as biological, sentient creatures. What we must come to consider is sexuality as an aesthetic. What we must come to appreciate is the true romance in sex. What we must come to understand is the altruism in sexual love. And it's this grander notion of the aesthetics of sex that can be lost in our need to understand the mechanics of sex. True sexual fulfillment means satisfying another person as well as satisfying oneself.

ROBERT: Vern, you've written or edited dozens of books about sex, such as *How I Got into Sex*—the personal stories of people who make their living dealing in one way or another with sex. As a keen, longtime observer of the sexual scene, can you tell us about some of the common mistakes that sex therapists make?

VERN: It's dangerous to generalize about sex therapists. They vary tremendously; there are good ones and there are bad ones, and the difficulty is that you don't know which is which. Choosing a sex therapist can be like stepping into the water and finding out that it's scalding hot, but you're already in deep and already getting burned. Unfortunately, many practicing sex therapists pay little attention to current research. They just don't follow the literature; they wing it.

ROBERT: Sex therapy is a field that lends itself to intuitive practitioners setting themselves up as armchair experts, even though they're not professionally trained and can't comprehend the latest research. Sexuality is something that most people think they instinctively understand—common sense alone can supposedly provide an effective prescription. But in the highly complex world of human sexuality, instincts and common sense may point in the wrong direction. Worse, some sex therapists are like partisan fanatics, propounding their own peculiar views, which often do more harm than good. No one thinks of "winging it" where nuclear physics or neurosurgery are concerned, but there's little reluctance to spout untrained advice in sex therapy—just as in diet and nutrition, to pick another favorite field of intuitive practitioners.

VERN: Yes, that's all true. The difficulty with sex therapy is that there are no professional standards regarding specific training. Where do you go to become a qualified sex therapist? Many come into the profession through clinical psychology—but you can be a marriage and family counselor, or you can be a used-car salesman, or you can be any number of things [that don't require certification]. All you need do is put up a sign and instantly you're a sex therapist.

ROBERT: Let's get back to pleasure. Does an emphasis on pure pleasure, which is becoming more prevalent in sexual discourse, decrease personal intimacy?

JOYCE: I don't think so. Pleasure can lead to intimacy just as easily as intimacy can lead to pleasure. If pleasure is just satisfying a physical need, if personal enjoyment is expressed only as physical gratification, then pleasure can counteract intimacy. But if pleasure means two people enjoying each other's bodies, delighting in each other, and feeling good sensations of being together and sharing that moment, physically and emotionally, then pleasure can actually enhance intimacy.

ROBERT: Since sex in society has become so readily available—for example, on the Internet—doesn't it become more difficult to generate pleasure through intimacy rather than pleasure through isolation? Certainly, pleasure through intimacy takes more work than typing "www.xxx.com."

JOYCE: As we noted in the last program [Chapter 9], this is true particularly for men. When men go to the Internet to get a quick fix, so to speak, rather than going to their wives to have those moments of intimacy and connection, which is much more meaningful to women, then there's a progressive deterioration of the relationship. The sad irony is that such men don't end up happy, either, even though at the moment it feels good.

ROBERT: Paul, you've investigated sexual trauma in its many forms and variations. Do you see any change in recent years?

PAUL: Sexual trauma and sexual victimization have always been pervasive, but two kinds of changes have emerged in recent years. First, society has taken these matters more seriously; we now give the victims more credence. In the past, credence was a problem, because sexual abuse was often perpetrated by people in positions of considerable authority—husbands, fathers, police officers, priests, and so on. Second, society is much more sympathetic to the victim, because sexual victimization is so pervasive, touching all social and economic circles. Today there's a great deal more support and sympathy available in a social structure designed to deal with sexual trauma—the therapeutic community, the forensic community, the criminal justice system. Many district attorneys' offices have sexual-abuse units, which target such crimes.

ROBERT: Let's go to the counseling situation itself. Cliff, Joyce, you obviously work together as a therapy team. Perhaps the fundamental operating principle that informs your counseling techniques is that there are marked differences between male and female sexuality. What are these differences, and how do they affect your counseling?

JOYCE: Who should begin?

ROBERT: I'm not going to decide; I don't want trouble.

JOYCE: One of the clear differences between male and female sexuality is pace. We deal with

---

One of the clear differences between male and female sexuality is pace.

---

this all the time. Normally, we teach the man how to slow down and learn to enjoy the scenery as he takes his trip.

ROBERT: How much time do you need?

PAUL: That's a particularly male kind of thing to say.

JOYCE: Go for the goal—just go a little slower.

ROBERT: Go a little slower and you'll get there a little faster?

CLIFF: A man gets his greatest pleasure from experiencing the joy of a woman's response. There's nothing that turns on a man more than a turned-on woman. And when a male experiences a female turn-on, when a woman is really able to get with her own sexuality, when a male can take in a woman's sexuality, then they both end up satisfied.

JOYCE: But all too often the man doesn't know any of this. He comes into sexual therapy complaining about the woman and her lack of responsiveness, not realizing that his satisfaction can come out of getting with her and allowing her to express herself sexually. If a man is more focused on "She never meets my needs" than he is on "How can I meet her needs?," he's the one who needs therapy the most. When such a man comes to our office, and many do, we encourage him to realize that getting with his mate and her complex sexuality—relating to her emotional needs and to everything that's going on with her—will be the key to opening her up sexually. And once she does open up, then she wants to be with him sexually and even takes the initiative by inviting him—and he's excited, because he feels affirmed and desired, and they both end up fulfilled and happy. It's a win-win situation.

ROBERT: Paul, if there are these differences between males and females, what do you think is the underlying cause?

PAUL: When you have such pronounced differences and you see them so consistently, you have to start asking whether these reflect some real fundamental differences between men and women. One idea that has been floating around recently is that these male-female differences represent true reproductive strategies across the genders. The old adage "Mother's baby; Father's maybe," conveys a biological truth. The woman is always sure of her maternity, so that female sexual strategy should be restrictive and protective. But because the man never can really be

sure of his paternity, the male sexual strategy should be more permissive. If these fundamental differences are true, then sexual therapeutic solutions have to take them into account. So maybe fast-paced sex is all right at times because it reflects a male perspective. Good sex therapy has to negotiate solutions to reflect both male and female patterns of sexual behavior.

ROBERT: Joyce, you've asked a rather provocative question in your books: Who should lead in bed?

JOYCE: The woman.

CLIFF: We always emphasize that it's the woman who should lead. Female leadership in sexual activity goes against what traditionally has been taught. But because women are so much more complex—because so much more

---

Female leadership in sexual activity goes against what traditionally has been taught.

---

has to happen for women in the sexual experience—when the woman can lead sexually from within herself and the man can follow that lead, then they usually both end up being more satisfied.

VERN: I think what you both are emphasizing—and this is the sign of a good therapist—

CLIFF: Thank you, Vern.

ROBERT: I want to hear what Vern says before we endorse it. I may not agree with him.

VERN: —is that good therapists should always develop a whole series of data before they try to offer any therapy. They offer therapies to help their clients, not to change their clients. The key is to listen to the patient, going beneath the superficial. When the husband says, "Well, she never responds to me," it's vital to find out what he really means by that. Until you do, you can't really be a good therapist.

ROBERT: Good sex therapists should not seek to change patients to their own sense of perfection.

SHEP: Joyce, how do you deal with the fact that many husbands are threatened by the thought of allowing their wives to take the lead in sex? That many men feel, whether for cultural or other reasons, that they should be the ones to take the lead?

JOYCE: Men should be the authority; they should know how to turn their wives on, so that their wives will then initiate sex.

SHEP: But how do you change such ingrained perceptions? How do you get men to do that?

JOYCE: First of all, as Vern just said, a therapist has to really understand the man, getting with him, finding out where he's coming from. Does he feel a lot of anxiety because he's unable to satisfy his wife? Ultimately, even though he's pointing the finger at her, he's really saying, "I'm inadequate—

CLIFF: "—I'm failing—"

JOYCE: "—I'm failing—I'm not satisfying her." That's when we can take the pressure off him and say, "Hey, she's going to keep changing every minute. There's no way you're ever going to figure her out. You know, it's as if she had an itch someplace on her back where you can't

reach it and she has to tell you exactly how to scratch it. You're not going to know where the itch is and when it's there."

PAUL: Maybe I'm a nonconformist, but I like the idea of fast women, women who like to take the lead in sex. I think the way these things play themselves out in relationships depends on how we're embedded into specific roles. And I suspect that you'll find generational differences here. I don't think that the issue of masculine control, masculine initiative, and so on comes up very much with teenagers and young adults today. Gender parity in sexual relations is common now.

JOYCE: Not in bed. Not in bed.

ROBERT: Joyce, are you perpetuating a stereotype?

JOYCE: I don't think so. Gender differences are a big dilemma for most of the couples I see, and in our practice we work mainly with couples in their twenties.

VERN: One of the primary challenges in therapy is to facilitate communication about sex between the man and the woman. Often, communication difficulty is a male problem, but one of the big hurdles is getting the female to tell the male what satisfies her and what makes her happy.

JOYCE: I'll say it again: The female must take more responsibility in sex, absolutely!

VERN: Facilitating communication is the key, and that's what a good therapist should do.

PAUL: I think that if sexual relations are modeled strictly on male and female roles, then one would expect homosexual relationships to be void of these sorts of dysfunctions. But we know that gay relationships, lesbian relationships, have their own dynamics that interfere with fulfilling sexual expression. These relationships play themselves out in ways that aren't specific to gender roles.

ROBERT: Paul, do I sense that you're a little troubled by the specificity that Joyce and Cliff are suggesting, in terms of male and female typecasting?

PAUL: We may be referring to different population samples; the Penners may have a more limited sample of individuals who come to them for counseling.

CLIFF: There's no question. We're talking about the people we see in our office.

ROBERT: Joyce, Cliff, about how many couples have you counseled in your career?

JOYCE: Large numbers. Cliff?

CLIFF: I'd say between a thousand and two thousand.

JOYCE: In addition, about three weekends each month, we teach sex seminars for audiences of up to five hundred people.

ROBERT: It's real data, but it's still a relatively small sample, compared to the general population. More significantly, it's obviously not a random sample.*

---

*The first sampling bias is "couples seeking professional sex therapy," and the second sampling bias is "couples within the evangelical Christian community." Such biases mitigate taking the results as a generalized reflection of the entire population. On the other hand, the Penner's substantial number of clients seem significant for portraying "couples in the evangelical Christian community who seek sex counseling."

VERN: I'll raise a delicate question for Joyce and Cliff: Have you ever counseled gay couples and lesbian couples?

CLIFF: Most of our clients are married, mainly because we work in the Christian community. And so I would agree; our sample is biased.

PAUL: The concern I was raising is that we shouldn't truncate the application of sexual therapy to the very limited domain of married

---

There is a rainbow of diversity in the way people couple and express their sexuality.

---

couples or individuals on that track. Sexuality is embraced by everyone. There is a rainbow of diversity in the way people couple and express their sexuality.

JOYCE: People are sexual persons from birth—they don't become sexual persons when they marry. But in our sexual therapy practice, we particularly work with heterosexuals.

CLIFF: And we'd say that we work with the general masses. We don't work with groups on the edges. That's just how our practice is.

ROBERT: Joyce, let's talk about a specific counseling situation. A couple comes to you and they say they're having some problems. What's your procedure? Do you interview the wife? Does Cliff interview the husband? Do both of you work with both of them in a group? How do you counsel?

JOYCE: We usually begin by going through a three-hour process. In the first hour, I meet with the woman and Cliff meets with the man.

CLIFF: In the second hour, we reverse roles. I have an hour with the woman, while Joyce has an hour with the man.

JOYCE: And then the two of us meet with the two of them.

ROBERT: All on the same day?

CLIFF: All on the same day, and our goal during that time is to make a very thorough assessment, mainly because we see people who have already been seeking help from other places. We try to define, as narrowly as we can, specifically what the issues are. And very often these issues turn out to be quite different from what our clients first report.

ROBERT: What's an example?

CLIFF: An example would be a sexually insecure male who comes in saying that his wife is not responsive to him, that she lacks sexual desire. What's really going on, in fact, is that he gets much of his affirmation as a person from her response to him as a sexual being.

ROBERT: So a superficial sexual denial becomes a deep personal insult?

JOYCE: Right. Another scenario might occur on the honeymoon. Husband and wife are both excited about starting their marriage and—usually—their sexual relationship. Often she's eager for sex, expecting that they'll have sex once or twice a day. And so they do have sex, and the sex is good, but perhaps one time when he approaches her she isn't ready. And so his inse-

curity rises instantly and his self-assessed value as a person tumbles.

ROBERT: Insecurity is the only thing that rises, right?

JOYCE: Yes, that's right, insecurity is the only thing that rises. And now he starts getting anxious about whether she's ever going to be interested in him sexually again. So he starts evaluating her, watching her, making comments. This kind of behavior can go on for a year or so before they come into to our office, both of them complaining about her lack of sexual desire—because now it's no longer coming spontaneously, from inside. Instead, she's feeling on trial—observed and evaluated.

CLIFF: And she's trying to respond to him, but can't.

ROBERT: Both thought that she was the cause of their problems, when in fact it was his actions that stunted her sexual desire.

PAUL: It reminds me of the scene in *Annie Hall* where Woody Allen is talking to his male psychiatrist and says, "You know, we never have sex—only two or three times a week." And then you see Diane Keaton complaining to her female psychiatrist, "We have sex all the time, two or three times a week."

CLIFF: So the data may be the same, but the perception can be very different.

JOYCE: That's the one question a therapist always asks in counseling couples—"How often are you having sex?"—and you compare their answers. Then you ask, "How often do you think your spouse would want to have sex?"—and again you compare their answers. These comparisons are often very interesting and instructive.

ROBERT: What about all the increasing technology enhancing or openly offering sex—from Internet cybersex to chemical enhancers like Viagra? Are these sexual technologies affecting your practice?

CLIFF: That's a complex issue. For example, Viagra can greatly reduce the length of time it takes to treat impotence. We can concentrate on the emotional and relational aspects, because the physical side is resolved in about seventy percent of the men.

ROBERT: But Viagra can also alter the psychosexual status quo. Some older men may suddenly desire a higher level of sexual activity, and such demands may be uncomfortably intense for their spouses. Other men may feel intimidated by the new pressures to perform. Likewise, Internet cybersex can be addicting and distracting to some people while stimulating and reinvigorating to others.

VERN: Many men take Viagra thinking it's going to cure all their sexual problems, because suddenly they're able to perform physically. But their wives, or their companions, are not prepared for this.

JOYCE: That's right. She's complaining, "I thought it was over!"

CLIFF: She thought his sexual demands were history, part of their past, and now, all of a sudden, he's back pressuring her about sex again.

SHEP: Where is love in all of this? You're Christian therapists, and in the Judeo-Christian tradi-

tion we say, "Cast your bread upon the waters, and it will return ere many a day." It seems to me that the lesson you're giving us is that the essence of sex is mutuality, and that it's love that enables sex to engender fulfillment. So, why don't we talk more about love? Let's go back to your clients on their honeymoon. Here are two

Where is love in all of this?

people who have just gotten married, for God's sake! They must be desperately in love. We should ideally—as I am sure you do—appeal to exactly that. Love in some ways is self-generating, self-replicating—at least, temporarily—although it needs constant refurbishment. Love is the essence of everything we feel for another person, and we express it, or try to express it, with sexuality, which, as counselors and therapists, you help us to do.

JOYCE: Sometimes, when a couple starts having sexual problems, the first question that arises in their minds is "Did I marry the wrong person?"

CLIFF: Or "Am I not in love?" This is a very common question—one of the questions they come into counseling to answer.

ROBERT: Is such fundamental insecurity common in sexual dysfunction? When something goes wrong in the bedroom, husbands and wives question their love?

CLIFF: That's right.

JOYCE: And we really have to help them sort this out.

SHEP: In your experience, do people realize that sex in the evening is a reflection of what has happened during the course of the day? Or do they think of sex as a kind of event, on a timetable? "Here I am—it's Thursday." Too often it's—

JOYCE: It's the male-female difference again. The woman says, "You came home from work, or we came home from work, we put the kids to bed, we had dinner, you went and watched TV, you didn't have any interest in me at all, we got into bed, you flipped off the remote control, you slapped your hand over me, and now you're ready for sex? Now you're interested in me?"

PAUL: But that's a plain failure of communication and intimacy.

JOYCE: Yes, that's right.

ROBERT: I don't know anybody who hasn't experienced that.

PAUL: What counts is how we partition our time.

JOYCE: How you stay connected.

PAUL: And also the impact of children on one's sex life.

ROBERT: Someone once said that the frequency of sex is inversely proportional to the number of diapers.

JOYCE: Yes, and that "Sex makes children, but children don't make sex."

PAUL: I thought you were going to say, "Insanity's inherited—you get it from your kids."

ROBERT: To what extent is love necessary for sex? For enhancing a long-term relationship, we should want love and sex to be intimately intertwined. But is our tradition of connecting sex and love a universal requirement? Each one of these words—sex, love, intimacy, pleasure—maintains its own separate existence. There's no perfect correlation between any of these terms, but I think what you're all saying is that the more correlated they are, the stronger the total satisfaction.

SHEP: What sort of pleasure are we looking for? Sometimes we talk in terms of this involuntary, mechanical reflex, this wonderful tickling sensation, this orgasm. But of course the ultimate pleasure is the pleasure of love. The pleasure of experiencing another human being and giving to that human being that which is entirely you. And if people thought more in terms of this kind of other-person-centered love and less in terms of the self-centered, mechanistic kind of sexual pleasure, which is only part of a larger pleasure, we might do a lot better.

CLIFF: You're talking about the sex beyond the orgasm, aren't you?

SHEP: I'm talking about a larger view of sexuality, but I would like to ask Vern [Bullough], What's the relationship between sex and love, historically?

VERN: They're not very closely related. In many societies, marriages were arranged, and it might become love afterward. Marriages were arranged for various reasons—economic, say, or political. Romantic love is a rather late invention. It begins in the fourteenth and fifteenth centuries, but it doesn't really become a major factor until the nineteenth and twentieth centuries. So, love and sex are something we are trying to wed, so to speak, because love and sex were traditionally separate. Historically, you

---

Romantic love is a rather late invention.

---

usually got married because you intended to reproduce.

SHEP: I would argue that love and sex are linked both biologically and culturally, and that in previous ages we didn't recognize that.

JOYCE: That's a good way of putting it.

PAUL: But what's the biological basis of love?

SHEP: You should read my book [*How We Live*]. Love is an expression of psychological harmony, symmetry, and unity, which I think the human organism requires in order to fight off the sense of chaotic disaster and death that goes on within us and that we are on some level, whether consciously or not, aware of.

ROBERT: I'd like to discuss sexual behavior from a different angle. Vern, let's talk about sex and old age. Give us your take on this sensitive subject. Most people can't imagine their parents having sex, much less their grandparents. I hope it's a fallacy that men reach their sexual prime at nineteen.

VERN: Even if we peak at a young age, we can coast along at a high plateau for many years.

JOYCE: The older you get, the more creative you become.

ROBERT: The more creative you have to become.

VERN: As a sexually active male past seventy, I can give personal testimony that sex does exist and is a very important part of life. But, again, it depends on communication. Older couples for whom sex is no longer important have lost something valuable. If the wife says, "Thank God, I'm past the menopause, and sex is over," that's a real problem in the marriage—not a problem of sex per se, but of the marriage.

JOYCE: It's a problem for the older women personally, too, because she hasn't yet accepted her sexuality and her sexual needs.

VERN: Well, the older man still feels a great desire—witness the popularity of Viagra. Previously it was all the plastic penile inserts, and so forth. Wives would sometimes tell me, "He didn't ask me before he went and got that piece of plastic. I didn't care about all that—I'd like something else."

ROBERT: What about sexual addiction? We hear about it at all levels of society. Is sexual addiction a real illness or a clever excuse?

CLIFF: Whether we call it an addiction or not, there are people who are hooked in their behaviors—compelled to look for sexual gratification outside their normal relationship. Sex controls them; they don't control sex. This is what makes the behavior look like an addiction.

PAUL: "Sexual addiction" is probably more a misnomer than a legitimate illness, because true addictions presume a physiological dependence, for which we have no evidence in the case of sex. What we're basically dealing with is compulsive sexuality, which is detrimental to individuals and destructive to their relationships.

ROBERT: In any medical procedures, there are misdiagnoses. What happens when patients are misdiagnosed in sexual counseling? What are some examples?

JOYCE: Early in our practice, before there was general awareness of sexual addiction, compulsion, or abuse, we missed some of these diagnoses.

CLIFF: Yes, we missed many cases of abuse. We didn't understand why a woman reacted as she did, because we were not taking the abuse in her past seriously. Now we do.

JOYCE: As another example, because of what we now understand physiologically about hormonal regulation, we're now treating conditions we didn't treat previously. We're working much more with the medical profession than we were in the past. New information changes the sexual therapy process.

SHEP: Is sexual abuse a one-way street? Or is there some mutuality here? Does the abused person have a need to be abused? Do they somehow, on an almost conscious level, find each other?

CLIFF: Well, what we're talking about is a situation in which a five-year-old, say, is abused by an adult.

SHEP: Oh, about children—that's something completely different. I was referring to something like chronic sexual dissatisfaction, in which one of the partners is obviously very much at fault and therefore the other partner, in a sense, is being abused. Is there any mutuality there?

CLIFF: There's always this relational issue to consider, absolutely. Often the abuser came from a situation of abuse and is now reliving it, hoping to make things come out all right.

ROBERT: How often do you face sexual abuse within marriages?

JOYCE: That's hard to define. Are the behaviors simply perceived as abuse, or are they actually abuse? It's often difficult to determine, because an action can feel like abuse to the wife—particularly if she was abused as a child—in situations where the husband may not have been abusive at all. His actions may constitute normal sexual behavior patterns, but because of her past abuse, what he's doing feels like abuse. The solution largely depends on the man in this case. He has to change his behavior, even though it's not truly abusive, until she heals; because as long as she perceives what he's doing as abuse, it is abuse. And it won't work.

PAUL: Abuse is not limited to the sexual arena. Complaints about abuse are really more often about psychological abuse—domination and intimidation and issues like that are typical goals of abusers.

JOYCE: That's right.

SHEP: So, once again, it's the relationship that's the important thing.

VERN: Understanding the relationship is the key to good sex therapy.

JOYCE: One of the key points in our book *What Every Wife Wants Her Husband to Know About Sex* is, How do you negotiate? Good negotiations between husbands and wives about sexual matters sustain a robust relationship.

ROBERT: I have a question for the Penners. Cliff, Joyce, you are a sex therapist couple. So I assume that many of your patients would like to know, but are too polite to ask, whether you guys ever have problems when your bedroom doors are closed?

CLIFF: That's private [*with a smile*].

ROBERT: I promise not to tell.

JOYCE: Sure we do; everyone has problems. Fortunately, we function very well together and have for over thirty-five years. Sex has been a vital part of our lives, personally as well as professionally. Sex is important for me, and I appreciate Cliff for following my lead in the bedroom, allowing me to express myself. We have fun with our sexuality, and we negotiate our differences.

CLIFF: I was just going to say the same thing.

ROBERT: Allow me to get a little more personal—I'll be your sex therapist for a moment. Joyce, what percentage of the time do you take the lead in initiating sex?

JOYCE: I would say—

CLIFF: Joyce, what do you think?

ROBERT: No checking; no communications. Cliff, Joyce, write down your numbers: "What percentage of the time does Joyce initiate sex?" No peeking.

JOYCE: I wrote seventy percent.

CLIFF: I wrote seventy-five percent.

ROBERT: That's pretty close; I'm impressed.

CLIFF: One of the reasons our relationship works well is that Joyce has a higher sexual drive than I do. At least she seems to express it more frequently. Joyce has a greater need for sex than I do, and that has been true all along.

JOYCE: I was fortunate to have grown up extremely naïve; I was never taught a thing about sex. I then went to nursing school where I was taught a very clinical, very positive approach to sexuality. I have always been a good student; I took down every note; I studied sex avidly.

CLIFF: And then she lived it out for the last thirty-five years.

ROBERT: Joyce, are you faster than he is?

CLIFF: Sexually, or just . . .

ROBERT: You may interpret my questions as you like.

JOYCE: Sex is not a race.

ROBERT: Joyce, when you initiate sex—seventy percent of the time as the whole world now knows—do the sexual behaviors differ from when Cliff initiates sex? Or are your sexual patterns pretty much the same no matter who makes the first move?

JOYCE: There is a difference.

ROBERT: So, what is it? Don't worry; we're still private here.

JOYCE: I think that when sex starts with me, it has more intensity.

CLIFF: I agree. And when sex starts with me, it is more about meeting my needs—but Joyce is not really there and it is not quite as good.

JOYCE: But I can get there.

CLIFF: Yeah.

JOYCE: And I do.

ROBERT: We're ready for a prediction. In a hundred years, will there be a greater or lesser need for sex therapy?

JOYCE: I'd say "greater." And not just behavioral sex therapy, but intimacy training as well.

ROBERT: That's a good business decision for a sex therapist. But do you really believe it?

JOYCE: In a hundred years, I don't think it will matter to us.

CLIFF: Because our sexual world is getting more complicated, people are going to need more help in a greater variety of areas. And one topic we haven't dealt with here is the whole issue of commitment. It's a key issue in building relationships. Maintaining commitment is a struggle in society these days, and unless we get that worked out, we're in for trouble.

PAUL: Like rock 'n' roll, sex therapy is here to stay. The kinds of societal pressures that disrupt couples and attenuate their ability to stay close and communicate will increase, so there's going to be a continuing need for sex therapy.

VERN: I don't think there will be a need for sex therapy in a hundred years, but I do think there will be a need for therapy to encourage intimacy and conversation. I hope we'll have learned all the techniques of sex by that time, so we shouldn't call it sex therapy anymore—we should call it intimacy therapy.

JOYCE: We hope that encouraging intimacy would always be a part of sex therapy.

VERN: Then I think it shouldn't be called sex therapy.

JOYCE: You're right—"intimacy therapy" might be a better term.

SHEP: I'd call it estrangement therapy. As our society grows more mechanistic and distancing, what we'll need is therapy to strengthen relationships, out of which will grow appropriate expressions of sexuality.

JOYCE: This is what the best sex therapy is already more concerned with.

ROBERT: CONCLUDING COMMENT

We all agree that seeking sexual fulfillment is a natural need of human beings. We all believe that sex therapy can play a useful role in improving the sex lives of normal people. Where some may disagree is in the nature of the therapies. Is pleasure the crowning achievement? Or does intimacy take top honors? Must there be a higher purpose? Pleasure is important, to be sure, but as we have seen, it may diminish without intimacy. Delving a little deeper into controversy, how do we compare male and female sexuality? Do the genders respond similarly? Or are there fundamental sexual differences between men and women? A failure to appreciate some of these differences, it seems, may lead to frustration, even irritation. Much as we may hate to admit it, we all probably need some lessons. Optimal sexual fulfillment doesn't come quite so naturally. But its achievement is surely worth it. Admissions like these are what bring us closer to truth.

OUTTAKES

VERN: *Maybe we should put sex therapy in the schools.*

PAUL: *That might turn kids off right away.*

JOYCE: *That's a new form of contraception— force them to take sex ed.*

PAUL: *They'll be clamoring for driver's ed.*

Defying Gravity

PART THREE

CREATIVITY & THINKING

Minds Defying Gravity. (Courtesy of Todd Siler.)

CHAPTER 11

What's Creativity and Who's Creative?

Are you creative? Would you like to be? Why? Don't creative people just get into trouble? Creativity is the expression of originality—it's exciting but also demanding, consuming, frustrating, and addictive; it's inspiring but also fickle, erratic, tricky, and risky. Creativity can be found anywhere, at home or work as easily as in art or science. It can erupt suddenly or emerge slowly. Creativity means being both different and better. Being different without being better is often pointless or just odd; being better without being different is just evolution, not revolution. For an act to be deemed creative, there must be an accepted style or method against which it can be judged original. The accepted style or method is the benchmark, and creativity often begins by rejecting or at least questioning it. An activity may seem creative up front, according to intent, but not creative in hindsight, according to results. The burden of proof is with the creators to demonstrate that their innovation is an improvement over what's gone before. Creativity comes in many flavors, and it is well represented in the diverse group we gathered. Three of our guests have run large, creative organizations; two are foremost teachers of creativity. All are personally creative. No two are alike in what they do; all are remarkably alike in how they think about what they do.

PARTICIPANTS

Stephen J. Cannell is one of the most prolific producers and writers of network television series in Hollywood. He is also a best-selling novelist, author of such thrillers as *The Devil's Workshop* and *Riding the Snake*. But what kind of English grades did Stephen get in high school?

Dr. Mihaly (Mike) Csikszentmihalyi was for many years a professor of psychology at the University of Chicago; he is now at the Claremont Graduate University, in

California. The author of various books on creativity, including *Flow: The Psychology of Optimal Experience* and *Creativity: Flow and the Psychology of Discovery and Invention,* Mike describes some common characteristics of creative people.

Dr. Robert Freeman, a pianist and music historian, is Dean of the School of Fine Arts at the University of Texas, Austin, and has been chief executive of the Eastman School of Music and the New England Conservatory of Music. Was Mozart more creative than Beethoven? Bob explores different styles of creativity.

Dr. John Kao, trained as a psychiatrist and active as an entrepreneur, has taught business creativity at Harvard Business School and Stanford University Graduate School of Business. John gives us some practical insights into the creative process.

Ray Kurzweil is an inventor, entrepreneur, and executive who has founded and managed four high-technology companies. He is also the author of two important books on the future of computers: *The Age of Spiritual Machines* and *The Age of Intelligent Machines.* Ray talks about sleep, risk, and group creativity.

ROBERT: Stephen, you've created or co-created forty television series, including *The Rockford Files* and *The A-Team*—an American record. How does it feel in your gut when you create a new show?

STEPHEN: For me it's always, Will I like it? I start with one premise: I want to be able to go home, look at that show, and be proud of it. And I always ask myself, "Would I be willing, three years hence, to come in and write a script over the weekend?"

ROBERT: Are you proud of all your shows?

STEPHEN: No. Obviously I've made mistakes along the way. I made shows that only my parents watched. But they all started off trying to be the best thing I ever did.

ROBERT: How did you feel when a show you really liked was canceled?

STEPHEN: I'm pretty good about cancellations. I do my best. I try not to worry about things I can't control—and I certainly can't control network thinking—

ROBERT: You can't control this show, either.

STEPHEN: That's right—I've known you long enough to know that. If a show gets canceled, I try to learn from the cancellation. I look at it and ask myself, "Did I do anything wrong? Was I stubborn, was I pigheaded? Could I have made the show better? Could I have affected its longevity in some important way?" And once I've gone through that—usually in two or three days—I can move on.

ROBERT: Mike, your book *Flow* is considered a classic in the study of creativity. What is flow, and what is its relationship to creativity?

MIKE: By flow, I mean a state that people feel when they're totally involved in whatever they're doing—when they're completely focused on the activity at hand. I started by studying artists, musicians, chess players, and athletes, and I found that despite the great variety of things they're doing, when they're really involved their inner states are the same. They describe their feelings in the same way. And the relationship to creativity is that this thorough involvement is always present when they're working in a creative medium. Flow may not result in creativity, but it has to be there.

ROBERT: Are there cross-cultural differences, or is the flow of creativity a universally consistent human trait?

MIKE: It seems universal. The creative output may differ from culture to culture, but the creative state is described very similarly in Korea, India, China, Japan.

ROBERT: Bob, tell us about some of the great composers. Their styles are very different, but is there a root similarity in their creativity?

BOB: Beethoven left us large numbers of individual sketch books, single pages, notebooks, continuity drafts—obviously, he worked on a fair number of pieces at the same time. And he worked with great pain. Mozart, on the other hand, was well known for hardly leaving any marks behind. He could go for a walk, come back, and write a whole string quartet.

ROBERT: Was creativity harder for Beethoven than it was for Mozart?

BOB: Looks as though it was harder. Brahms composed more like Beethoven, except that he went to the trouble of destroying all his tracks afterward, so it's very hard to get at the sketches.

ROBERT: John, as an author and jazz pianist as well as a psychiatrist, what can you tell us about the process of creativity?

JOHN: Well, I think it's important to recognize that the popular image of Archimedes jumping out of the bathtub, or of someone with a lightbulb popping up over his head, is just a part of an overall grammar, you might say, or of a series of events that constitutes the creative process. If you look at creativity as moving from the existing to the preferred, there's a whole lot of preparation prior to that lightbulb and a whole lot of work that needs to follow on after that. And the lightbulb doesn't appear over the head of only one person, necessarily, although the process clearly can occur between the ears of a creative person—which in some respects, we all are. Creativity also pops up in the space between people, and also within organizations—within society, if you will.

ROBERT: If ever there were lightbulbs popping up over someone's head, he's sitting right next to you. Ray, you're a successful entrepreneur, a remarkably prolific inventor—speech recognition devices, computer music keyboards, reading machines for the blind. It's an incredible list. Compare for us the process of creativity when you create new companies with the process that goes in writing your books.

RAY: I'll mention one similarity and one difference. The similarity is that creativity involves a sort of fantasy or daydreaming. When I start a technology, I try to imagine I'm at a conference four years from now, demonstrating how this thing works, and I just go with that fantasy. I find that I'm describing how it must have been—the problems we must have solved—and I work backward from there. The creative process of writing a book is similar: I have something I'm trying to accomplish, and I fantasize about how I will accomplish it. So I start daydreaming—and, really, a lot of creativity is done while you're sleeping. I like to think about a problem before I go to sleep—just frame what I know about it. Then, in the morning, somehow, some of the answer is there.

ROBERT: I went to bed last night thinking about the questions I was going to ask you.

RAY: The difference is that with technology you have to catch the wave. You can't be a little bit too early or a little bit too late—neither one works. You've got to be right on the wave of what's currently feasible. In writing, you can be more imaginative and have a much broader canvas to work with. For example, my latest book is about the twenty-first century, so you don't need to be concerned just with what's feasible today.

ROBERT: Mike, I need some help. Analyze me. I've been in a creative mode, working on this show, but I have to tell you I'm continuously grumpy. But paradoxically, even though I'm so grumpy, I've never been quite so happy. Am I just nuts?

MIKE: I don't think jolliness is necessarily a sign of how you feel inside. When Beethoven was struggling with his compositions, he probably felt like you did; he was grumpy, too. But inside he may have felt so consumed by what he was working on that those were the greatest days of his life.

ROBERT: Stephen, are you grumpy when you're writing a novel?

STEPHEN: No, no; I have so much fun doing it. For me, writing is a release of something I

really enjoy doing. I look forward to it. I love what Ray [Kurzweil] was just saying, about our sleeping hours producing results. Sometimes I'll end a chapter and I'll think, Boy, I've written myself into a hole here. And the next morning I'll get up and I'll go "Whew!"

RAY: But it's a struggle. It's not an easy process. It's the hardest work you can do, and you're constantly faced with problems to solve. As John [Kao] mentioned, the lightbulb is a very small part of it. There's the whole process of continuous improvement. I try to sketch out the first draft of a book very quickly, in one month—at least an outline of it. Then I progressively improve it. You're constantly framing problems that you need to solve and trying to find solutions.

STEPHEN: My outline is the framework, the architecture, of the novel. I know what the first act is, I know what my complication is at the top of Act Two, I know what my second-act curtain is. Some people say books shouldn't be written in three acts. I think any good story has to be told in three acts—just as a piece of music has to have its structure. And so I work that structure out; the process is very cerebral. Then I write a sixty- or seventy-page narrative, which breaks it into chapters. And once I've got that done, then I can enjoy the writing process, because I won't deviate too much from this framework. Sometimes I find mistakes that I've made in the structure, but basically the books write pretty easily from there.

JOHN: As a follow-on to what Stephen [Cannell] is saying, you can write books in several different ways. Some involve structure and having a plan, and some are about the play and the joy and the discovery. And I think that says something about the creative process, too: it's not just one way of thinking, it's multiple. In a sense, intelligence is made up of diverse ways of thinking that come together. There's the tension in setting up a goal, which may be a part of this process—a picture of the future, with all the uncertainty attached to trying something, failing, experimenting and failing. To be certain of your goal and at the same time uncertain how to achieve it can be very difficult.

BOB: I have a question for Stephen [Cannell]. When you sit down to write a book, you're trying to write something which is good, which is moving, and which satisfies your standards of excellence. In that way, I could compare you to Mozart—to the way he thought about what he was doing.

STEPHEN: Mozart and I are frequently compared.

BOB: To what degree would it complicate things for you—this is what Beethoven's principal preoccupation was—to write something that would be a masterwork for the ages? Do you have any sort of historical self-consciousness?

STEPHEN: I would reject that as a concept. When you put that kind of pressure on yourself—to write something so monumental that it will live thousands of years after you—by nature you just dry up your creative process.

BOB: It's not a necessary part of creativity?

STEPHEN: I'll give you an example. Shakespeare—who we'll all agree was one of the greatest English playwrights ever—was writing those plays to pay his rent. In his own mind, his sonnets were his truly great literature. He'd go down to the Globe and write those plays for the masses, and yet they'll live forever. I try and

come up with an idea that I think is going to be exciting and interesting and pleases me intellectually. And there may be some humor in it that I'll enjoy. But I try not to burden myself with the notion that it has to be brilliant, because that will dry me up.

ROBERT: Mike, you started out studying happiness and got into creativity as a result. What's the relationship between happiness and creativity? Are happy people creative? Are creative people happy?

MIKE: It depends. Creative people are often creative in order to escape unhappiness. Many people, especially in the arts and literature, are

---

Creative people are often creative in order to escape unhappiness.

---

trying to produce a world in which they feel comfortable—someplace more harmonious, more ordered, more livable than the actual world in which they live. And when they're immersed in their own world, they feel happy.

RAY: There's another aspect of creativity. We've been talking about great individual contributors, but when you're creating technology it's necessarily a group process, because technology today is so complex that it has to be interdisciplinary. In my companies, for example, experts in speech, speech recognition, signal processing, computers, and linguistics all need to work together. And they're all essentially speaking their own languages, even about the same concepts. So we will spend months establishing our common language—which is actually a useful thing to do, because if anybody ever overhears our conversations they'll have no idea what we're talking about. I have a technique to get people to think outside the box: I'll give a signal-processing problem to the linguists, and vice versa, and let them apply the disciplines in which they've grown up to a completely different problem. The result is often an approach that the experts in the original field would never have thought of. Group process gives creativity a new dimension.

ROBERT: John, have you worked with high-technology companies?

JOHN: Several times. What Ray [Kurzweil] says is very true—that in order to move people out of a literal definition of what's interesting to pursue, it's important to be like the curator of the set of group experiences. You bring together people with very different points of view, you blend together disciplines, to produce new perspectives.

ROBERT: You're saying that the organizational creative process is different in some respects from the individual creative process. Let's compare, say, Stephen Cannell and Mozart, as one class, with technology companies like Ray [Kurzweil]'s.

JOHN: I would argue that everyone at this table is probably a good example of this kind of arbitrage between different kinds of work, or between different ways of seeing things. Even as one person in one career, we've all practiced both individual and group creativity. Our lives, in a sense, are a creative improvisation around themes, adding novelty when what we're doing gets boring, augmenting our portfolios. And in a high-tech company, it's often similar. You start off with some significant initial moves, assemble the founding team. But in order to inject the

kind of energy and the additional perspective you need, you have to be a great manager—like a great chef mixing the right ingredients. You have to manage the tensions, find the sweet spot all the time.

RAY: I think there's a relationship between group process and Mike [Csikszentmihalyi]'s concept of flow. Flow is hard enough to achieve for an individual, because our daily needs and problems distract us from connecting in that profound way with the creative task at hand. But it's even harder to achieve flow in a group, because political issues often arise within the group, and people aren't all communicating. To really achieve that kind of flow in a group, everybody has to be firmly connected to the project—to the point that when ideas arise from the group, you don't necessarily know exactly whose idea it was. Groups form because they can accomplish things that individuals never can. There's a blending of perspectives.

BOB: Absolutely. We all start out as fairly narrow disciplinary specialists. And nothing worthwhile can be achieved except through the intelligence that emerges from a bunch of different specialists working together. And that's not an easy process.

ROBERT: But isn't there a danger, in today's world, of ceding too much creative responsibility to the group at the expense of the individual? Isn't there something to be said for loners—people sitting three or four standard deviations off the chart, messing around and shaking up the world?

STEPHEN: I think we can spark each other. In television we work with staffs of writers, and it's fascinating to watch what happens. It's what you guys were just saying: You have to give up your sense of self to the group. You have to say, OK, we're all here to make a story for Bob to write. I always characterize ideas as little pink things running around on the floor—we can either stomp 'em to death or we can nurture them. Somebody might throw out a stupid idea, but instead of saying, "Oh, that's dumb!" you can say, "Well, . . ." and play with it for a little while. Then something develops: Other people add their ideas to it; someone says, "That's kind of cool," and the process builds like that. The next thing you know, you've built something, among all of you, that no one of you alone would ever have thought of. Bob will then take the ideas and write the script, because, as a staff of writers, we're creating the ideas for him to write. And he'll give it his stamp, adding his own creative flavor.

JOHN: It's "Yes, and" versus "Yes, but"—which is what you get in great jazz, where talented people work together. When you're playing in a jazz

---

When you're playing in a jazz group, if somebody offers you an idea you've got to go with it, and add to it.

---

group, if somebody offers you an idea you've got to go with it, and add to it. You don't exercise judgment on the front end or you'll never get to something truly sweet.

BOB: The alternative is Richard Wagner, who's going to write the words and the music, conduct the work, and be the dramatic director—all by himself.

ROBERT: So occasionally individuals still have the freedom to go against the whole world—

though less so today, where high technology is concerned.

MIKE: Oh, yes. Creative people often work both ways, bringing this kind of division inside their own practice. For the first four hours of the day, let's say, they're alone with the doors closed, working by themselves. Then they open the doors and start interacting and getting as much information and as many different points of view as possible.

BOB: You still need a prime mover. There's a group process, but generally you need one person who has the vision, who can provide the leadership and move the thing forward. This

---

. . . you need one person who has the vision, who can provide the leadership . . .

---

person has to have the intelligence and the understanding to make use of contributions from a broad array of other kinds of people.

ROBERT: Stephen, I want to get inside your head, since I—

STEPHEN: You'll be the first.

ROBERT: —since I didn't get the chance with Mozart. You love being a writer. Ever since we've known each other, I always see a sparkle in your eye whenever we talk about writing. It's never about success, it's never about money, it's always about writing. You've written five novels since you started, at age fifty. Five best-sellers. You've written four hundred episodes of network television. Remarkably, you're dyslexic. I want you to tell us what that means.

STEPHEN: I have fairly classic dyslexia. I mirror-read. I'm a very slow reader; I read about two hundred words a minute. I have sequencing difficulties, which makes computer work very hard

---

I have fairly classic dyslexia. I mirror-read . . . I flunked three grades before I got out of high school.

---

for me. Every time I turn my computer on, I have to reread the instructions—I can't remember the sequence of events. I have recall difficulties.

ROBERT: In high school and college, what kind of grades did you get in English?

STEPHEN: Terrible. Terrible. As a matter of fact, I flunked three grades before I got out of high school. I went back to the twentieth reunion of my high school class in Pasadena. By that time, I'd won a few Emmys and had a fairly high-profile career—

ROBERT: I love this story.

STEPHEN: There was this guy sort of circling me. It was my old teacher, who'd given me F's throughout high school. At the end of the evening, he finally came up to me and said, "So, you, ah, really make your living writing?" But what he'd been looking at back then was my spelling—and spelling isn't writing. I can compose a sentence and say it to you, or I can compose it and put it down on paper.

ROBERT: But to look at it on paper—

STEPHEN: The words are totally misspelled, just phonetically spelled. I've ruined the spelling of my twenty-year associate, who inputs all my stuff for me. She can't spell anything anymore; she was great when she started.

ROBERT: This is so fascinating! Doesn't Stephen demonstrate an enormous disconnect between creativity and what we normally think of as standardized-test, SAT [Scholastic Aptitude Test] intelligence?

MIKE: How many in this group have similar backgrounds? I was very bad in high school.

ROBERT: Unfortunately, I wasn't. Sorry. I feel out of place, embarrassed—as if I'm not creative because I got decent grades.

BOB: I was pretty good in high school, because I knew that if I didn't work hard I'd lose my scholarship. What it would have been like otherwise, I don't know.

ROBERT: Einstein received poor grades in mathematics.

STEPHEN: Dyslexia often comes with a capacity for abstract thought. People who are very good with abstract thought have been dyslexic—Einstein and Edison, two of our greatest inventors, were dyslexic.

MIKE: Practically all of the hundred people I interviewed in my study of very creative individuals—ninety out of a hundred—had pretty bad things to say about their formal education. They usually had one or two teachers who made a big difference in their lives and whom they remembered fondly. But the structured, mass-produced instruction that their schools generally provided was something they just couldn't take.

JOHN: What we're circling around is the issue of who gets to decide what's valuable. You said it in your introduction, Robert: There has to be something of value created; it's not enough just to come up with something new. Otherwise, throwing paint against the wall would be creative, and that's surely not very valuable. But the question is, Who decides? This is especially hard when it comes to social situations or organizations. There are plenty of people who look at a new idea, or at somebody who's a creative troublemaker, and say, "That's not particularly good." When does the perspective change, so that that new idea has its day in the sun?

RAY: The world is changing. We're entering an era in which the creation of new knowledge really constitutes the wealth and power of a nation's organizations and individuals. It's no longer just about being disciplined in manufacturing or intelligent in some rote way. Economics is really about creating new knowledge. That's why the United States is as successful as it is, and why there are economic problems elsewhere. We have a culture of risk taking; people seek new frontiers, and we reward that. We have entrepreneurial institutions—such as venture capital and incentive stock options—all designed to create new knowledge and value. The Internet is giving tremendous empowerment to the arts; those millions of Web pages need pictures and music, and that's where wealth is being created today.

ROBERT: How important is risk in creativity? The willingness to accept failure?

RAY: An important part of creativity is failure and one's attitude toward it. My view of failure is

that it's just success deferred. But not everybody feels that way. If you're afraid of failing, if that's

---

My view of failure is that it's just success deferred.

---

a devastating experience, then you can't be creative. You have to see disappointment as part of the inner process of getting to where you need to go.

STEPHEN: I really like that—failure as success deferred. That's a great line.

JOHN: It's inherent in learning. We never did anything perfectly the first time through. We didn't ride a bike the first time we got on it; we had to fail in order to learn. Look at designers: They take an idea and make a model, which by definition is going to be destroyed—preferably as quickly as possible. So you go from version 1.0 to version 2.0.

STEPHEN: I think it's important to have target fixation when you're creating, and not think about failure, not think about criticism, not think about rewards, not think about anything but what you're trying to do. Just focus on your target and screen the rest of that stuff out.

RAY: That's another difference between a book and a technology. With a book, you finally do launch it and it's out there. Whereas with technology, if version 1.0 doesn't work—well, fine, you can upgrade to version 1.1 and version 2.0.

ROBERT: Mike, do many of the people you've studied fear failure?

MIKE: You can't ever achieve much if you fear failure—because, as everybody here says, that's how you learn. You have to have the confidence that you can do it yourself. As people say, you have to obsolete yourself before others obsolete you—which means that you're always trying to get better and better in order to beat the competition.

ROBERT: When I consider the creative process, ego is a two-edged blade. One edge is an outsized anxiety about your public image: "How am I going to look in front of my colleagues and friends? I've been successful before, and if I fail now, my image suffers, my standing goes down." The other is a manic, sometimes offensive, outsized confidence. Both these attitudes are primitive, but the latter is more productive than the former.

STEPHEN: I think ego is a motor. It's really an important motor, especially for creative people. Your ego is what pushes you out on stage after failure. It's that little voice in the back of your head that says, "Yeah, I screwed that one up, but what about the next one?" When I joined the Writers Guild, all the new members were convened in a theater, and they asked us, "What do you think the biggest motivation for writers is?" And some people thought it was money, and others mentioned the creative satisfaction, and this guy said, "No, it's ego. That's what gets people to sit down in front of that keyboard."

MIKE: But I think it's important to realize that the creative ego is different from the normal ego.

STEPHEN: Well, it's not a boastful ego.

MIKE: You're so identified with what you're doing that you cannot let it fail, because it reflects on you. It's the activity itself—the writing or the painting or the music—that has become so much a part of you that you have to make it succeed, and through it make yourself succeed.

BOB: There are different kinds of egos. Going back to Mozart for a moment—he succeeded musically and artistically every time he put pen to paper. But in a larger sense, he didn't succeed at all—with respect to Salieri. The whole point of *Amadeus* was that the outcome was Salieri's fault, but Mozart just couldn't handle Salieri. If he'd been able to handle Salieri, he'd have lived twenty years longer, and who knows what works he would have composed?

STEPHEN: What I'm saying is that since failure does hover over every creative project, there's some part of you that wants not to enter into it, because you're liable to fail. What gets you over that hump is your ego, which says, "Yeah, but what if it turns out to be the best thing I ever did?"

RAY: I'd express the goal of creativity a little differently. The real satisfaction in creating either music or a book or a technology is the impact that it has on other people. Seeing a technology change people's lives, or a book change people's ideas, is deeply satisfying. Now, maybe that's an ego drive, but it's more than just saying, "OK, I accomplished this." It's experiencing other people's input.

ROBERT: You can almost say the reverse: That is, creative people do get lots of input—but ultimately you have to do what you yourself feel good about. If you compromise, you're often not going to be as effective. I can't tell you how many contradictory opinions I've had on producing this *Closer to Truth* series—from topics and guests to set and structure—and when I violate the principle of listening to one's own gut, I usually make the wrong decision.

RAY: But Stephen [Cannell], doesn't your definition of "the best thing you ever did" reflect how your work affects other people?

STEPHEN: Well . . . probably a difference between the two of us in the way we approach the creative process is that I never look beyond the goal, the finishing of it. I don't say, "This is going to have a tremendous effect on humankind."

RAY: But you've internalized your audience. If no one ever reacted to your books or your TV shows, it wouldn't be as satisfying.

STEPHEN: But where television series are concerned—aside from the ratings, which are sometimes devastating to read—you don't have the response you'd get in a theater, where people are laughing or crying at the lines. [Writing for television], you're sitting there with your wife, asking, "Well, what did you think?"

RAY: Then you internalize what people will say when they come to you afterward and tell you how it's affected them?

STEPHEN: To some degree, but not as much as you might think, or as I might like.

ROBERT: We need a prediction from everyone. Fast-forward a hundred years. Where is creativity making its greatest contribution to society?

STEPHEN: Because I'm a writer, I would hope it's in literature. Literature is about thought, and society should be about thought.

RAY: We'll have expanded our intelligence and creativity by merging with nonbiological intelligence, and we'll be creating new types of entities that we can't imagine today, such as virtual-reality environments. But we'll still have elements that are based on our foundation of music and art, and various forms of culture will be the primary expressions of knowledge.

JOHN: In a hundred years, we'll have better tools to take our innate creativity and collaborate with one another in more effective ways, and we'll realize our ideas much more immediately.

BOB: The creative teacher—whether it was someone alive in 1800, 1900, this year, or a hundred years from now—is going to be someone who sees in each of his or her students what makes them different and can enable them to see their own futures.

MIKE: Technological creativity is certainly going to continue and flourish, but I'm not sure that will be formal creativity's most important contribution in the future. Humanity needs a creativity that can help us find our place in this evolving cosmos, so that we can respect one another, live together peacefully, and not destroy one another in order to feel good about ourselves.

ROBERT: CONCLUDING COMMENT

What is creativity? It's certainly not standardized-test intelligence. Stephen Cannell, all by himself, is proof of that. How do you solve a problem creatively? It's often a mistake to get too smart too quickly. Expert opinion fouls up the creative engine; conventional wisdom is creative death. So develop your own ideas yourself, alone, without external information and before seeking the opinion of others. Your naïveté will be more ally than enemy on the creativity battlefield. Brood. Cogitate. Meditate. Agonize. Uncertainty, ambiguity, and doubt are all friends of the creative process. Experience tension, frustration, stress. Stimulating creativity means multiplying your options, generating alternative, contrasting, conflicting solutions. Lose yourself. Feel the flow. But remember what psychologist Abraham Maslow said: Creativity might be as much found in a first-rate chicken soup as in a third-rate painting. Suffer with humor to get closer to truth.

OUTTAKES

ROBERT: *This chair is too high for me. I'm a midget; they try to make me look taller, but comfort is more important than appearance.*

STEPHEN: *I seemed the stupidest kid in school.*

RAY: *We should have dealt more with failure and mistakes.*

STEPHEN: *I never try to be perfect; I just try to entertain myself.*

CHAPTER 12

How Does Creativity Work at Work?

Today's global marketplace is dynamic and hypercompetitive. Organizations must innovate constantly, producing unending lines of better goods and services. Business creativity is now a necessity, not a luxury. Can your company survive without creativity? What about you personally? Do you have original ideas that work? Your career could depend on it. But why are creativity and innovation important? And what's the difference between creativity and innovation? Creativity forms something from nothing, while innovation shapes that something into ever-more-practical products and services. Creativity by itself can be aimless, shooting off in all directions, some of them useless; while innovation by itself can be sterile, producing nothing fundamentally novel. So how can organizations be structured and managed to be both creative and innovative? And what can we do to bring imagination and productivity to our jobs? If the creative process can be focused and replicated, it can help to build companies and promote careers. We assembled a group of creative professionals—three have been chief executives of creative organizations—to answer these questions.

PARTICIPANTS

Stephen J. Cannell has written some four hundred episodes for network television, as well as five best-selling novels. As the founder, owner, and chief executive of one of Hollywood's largest independent television studios, Steve takes us behind the scenes in a business filled with creative egos.

Dr. Mihaly (Mike) Csikszentmihalyi, a professor of psychology at Claremont Graduate School, is the author of leading books on creativity. Mike holds that a company's success depends not as much on coming up with a lot of original ideas as on selecting and realizing the best of them.

Dr. Robert Freeman is the former chief executive of the New England Conservatory of Music and the Eastman School of Music, and the current Dean of the School of Fine Arts at the University of Texas, Austin. Bob tells us what it's like to manage an organization overflowing with creative artists.

Dr. John Kao, a psychiatrist and entrepreneur, is the author of *Jamming: The Art and Discipline of Business Creativity.* John helps companies to foster creativity and sees the successful ones as "idea factories."

Ray Kurzweil, who has founded four high-technology companies based on his pioneering work in computer science, believes that technical diversity and group creativity are essential in a high-tech company. Ray is the author of *The Age of Spiritual Machines.*

ROBERT: Ray, you've started, built, and managed a series of companies based on revolutionary, computer-based systems for new processes, such as speech recognition, and new products, such as musical keyboards. How do you encourage and inspire your employees to be creative?

RAY: Take speech recognition, where the technology is interdisciplinary, requiring experts in signal processing, speech science, linguistics, and half a dozen other disciplines. These people really needed to think as a group, so the first thing we did was to get them all together to understand these different disciplines. An interesting technique—as I noted in the last show [see Chapter 11]—we gave problems from one field to people from another and let them apply their own tools and traditions to a problem they'd never dealt with before. That way, they really did think "out of the box," and they came up with very creative ideas.

ROBERT: Does the boss have to be reasonably familiar with each of those disciplines?

RAY: You do need one person who knows what's feasible: Technology has to be feasible but

ahead of the edge. It's important to catch the wave at the right time. You have to aim at something that's going to be an advance when the product comes out—which might be two years later. So you really have to think about where the technology will be.

ROBERT: John, in your book, *Jamming,* you use your experience as a jazz musician to point up the similarities between that kind of spontaneous creativity and creativity in the workplace. You're also the chief executive of a company called The Idea Factory. What's an idea factory?

JOHN: In a general sense, an idea factory is any organization whose central competitive strengths are creativity, originality, flexibility, and foresight—the ability to see into the future. All businesses want and need creativity, but going from platitudes and slogans to actual practice—which means dealing with people, budgets, opportunities, technology—is very difficult to do. So an idea factory is actually a place, a setting, where creativity can happen every day.

ROBERT: Is creativity more easily generated in a high-tech company than in, say, a distribution company?

JOHN: The only kinds of companies that don't need creativity these days are companies that don't need to change—don't need to keep an eye on rapidly shifting environments. I'd say that would be no companies.

ROBERT: Bob, what's it like running an organization of musical artists, all of whom think they're something special?

BOB: Each of those creative artists is going to have a fairly narrow area of professional disciplinary focus. The bassoon teacher is going to want to make bassoon reeds, the historical musicologist is going to want to deal with watermarks and manuscripts from J. S. Bach, and the piano teacher is going to want to play Chopin études. If you put out on the table $75,000 to $100,000 a year, out of an operating budget of $20 million, and say that you will allocate these discretionary funds to projects in which those colleagues work together, you'll get a rush toward the center and some pretty creative ideas.

ROBERT: What's an example of that?

BOB: Oh, a project concerned with the future relationship of supply and demand for classically trained musicians. As soon as you get musicians thinking about that, they'll come to the conclusion that the supply of pianists is already far ahead of the demand. But that's the case only if you plan on sending out the five best pianists from New York to give concerts all over the country. If you can put each of twenty thousand pianists in a different small town in America and get them to develop the musical life in those communities to a pretty high level, you get a wholly different variable.

ROBERT: Steve, you built your private company, Stephen J. Cannell Productions, into the largest independent television studio in Hollywood. You produced a thousand hours of network television, shows like *Wise Guy* and *Silk Stalkings*. As a writer yourself, what's it like managing other writers?

STEPHEN: It's an interesting dilemma, because as a writer I have tremendous pride of authorship—which you have to have. And yet as an executive running a company with fifteen hundred employees, many of whom are creative people, you have to do a whole other thing—

> *Just because my name's on the building doesn't mean I'm the smartest guy in the building. If I have a bad idea, I want you to tell me.*

you have to be a referee. You need to learn how to keep people working together. You have a lot of high-octane people who can get sideways with one another, and in order to keep everything moving forward, you have to subjugate yourself. I always say to people when I come in, "Just because my name's on the building doesn't mean I'm the smartest guy in the building. If I have a bad idea, I want you to tell me."

ROBERT: Do they?

STEPHEN: Oh, boy! If they don't, if I feel they're just slathering Vaseline on me, I pull people aside and say, "Hey, you know what? You're not doing me any good." I need to know when I'm not thinking straight, because I make creative mistakes just like anybody else in the business. In a creative environment, the best idea wins, not the idea that comes from the guy with the biggest title. Everyone should feel part of the process. If the assistant film editor's idea is used in the cutting room, she says to herself, "God, I told them to cut there. I made a contribution, and that's great!" In a creative company, all of a sudden you have this kind of collective heartbeat; people get really excited, and that excitement feeds on itself. Of course, you have to work hard to keep the politicians out of the mix. I have actually let people go who I thought were really talented because they were playing politics—because they were interested in fomenting anxiety in order to promote themselves. In a creative environment, you have to eliminate politics.

ROBERT: Mike, you've interviewed and analyzed hundreds of creative people from all walks of life. This is the real world, raw data that forms the substrate of your books like *Creativity: Flow and the Psychology of Discovery and Invention*. From what you've heard about Ray [Kurzweil]'s technology companies, Bob [Freeman]'s music schools, and Stephen [Cannell]'s television studio, what do you think of these guys?

MIKE: When we think about creativity in organizations, we usually focus on how to generate more and more new ideas from as many people as possible. But that's not where the real issue is. There are lots of good ideas out there. The problem with implementing creativity is how to select, encourage, and realize the good ideas. That's where we don't do a very good job. I think everyone here knows how to do that, but in many organizations they don't. Some CEOs will even hire psychologists to get workers to think "out of the box," and although they may increase the number of new ideas, they still don't know how to select the good ones. We

have to concentrate more on implementation than on origination.

RAY: The key issue in a group process is defining what you're trying to create. In my companies, we spend a lot of time defining very precisely what it is we're trying to accomplish, and then we take each aspect and break it down in more detail, and we keep doing that until that definition actually becomes the creative output itself.

ROBERT: John, when you work with companies, how do you deal with the selection process that Mike [Csikszentmihalyi]'s talking about?

JOHN: It's fundamental. People often associate creativity in organizations with the big lightbulb, but just in order to prime the pump, companies and all kinds of organizations need to take note of the little possibilities, the small ideas, the pieces of information that don't quite fit with the existing way of thinking. And once an idea gets onto the table, that's just the beginning of the journey. Most companies are a Darwinian jungle, where ideas get killed or stabbed in the back or somehow manage to survive despite the political environment—and that's what constitutes the selection process.

ROBERT: But is that bad?

JOHN: It depends. If you're talking about organizational creativity as a process that requires investment and involves important resources, like people's careers and intellectual property, you have to be more intentional—you can't just let 'er rip. This is not to say that you need to plan every aspect of how you proceed, but you do have to have a process for developing ideas, funding them, and stewarding them to the point where they have value.

STEPHEN: Well, that's one of the points that Ray [Kurzweil] made right at the beginning—that somebody needs to be the quarterback. It's one thing to foster the ideas and get everybody thinking in the same direction, but if the team starts to wander off, you have to get it back on track.

RAY: And the ideas are not the key thing. As Mike [Csikszentmihalyi] pointed out, there are lots of ideas out there. When we dissect a goal into its parts, we find that there are hundreds of ideas for each of these little subproblems. The question is, How do you select the ideas and put them all together? We try to solve the problem very quickly, which means that we might come up with a first step that doesn't work—but then we analyze that step and determine why it doesn't work. It's an iterative process of getting closer and closer to the goal.

BOB: There needs to be a forum for discussing the ideas.

ROBERT: Mike, if you were doing a book on organizational creativity and Ray [Kurzweil],

---

There needs to be a forum for discussing the ideas.

Stephen [Cannell], Bob [Freeman], and John [Kao] were among your interviewees, what questions would you ask them?

MIKE: On what basis do you promote people in your company? And what are you looking for among your chief people?

ROBERT: How important is promotion in creative management? Bob, how does promotion work in the worlds of music and academe?

BOB: One of the fascinating things about American universities, including music schools, is the process whereby young men and women of age thirty or so, who have just finished doctoral degrees, are taken into the machinery of the selection process leading to tenure and by age forty have made valuable contributions. This has a lot to do with how that process is managed and what the incentives are. What one is always doing in the academic world is looking for teachers who, by age forty, have a good enough national reputation to attract good students and good enough teaching skills to make those students improve and prosper.

STEPHEN: The promotion process is critical to a creative company, and it differs from that in, say, brokerage houses or accounting firms. When you decide to put someone in charge of other people you may have to make a choice between creative talent and management skill. Some people who have tremendous creative ability may not have any management skills and never will—and vice versa. I've put writers in charge of television shows who I didn't think were necessarily my best writers, but they were best at getting the show going, making the whole thing run, and fostering a feeling of creativity.

ROBERT: How did you handle the writers you thought were the best but who weren't given the promotions?

STEPHEN: Well, what I try to do with those people is work with them—because you can teach management skills to people. For instance, one thing I sometimes find with creative people is that they behave badly because they're insecure. A writer may scream at his secretary, say, to show how important he is, but what he's really doing is waving a flag over his head that says, "I'm not secure, so I need to build up my own importance by humiliating someone who can't defend herself." So what I'll do is pull that person in and say, "Here's what you're doing, guy. You've just raised a flag, and I can read that flag."

RAY: Managerial promotion is not the only thing that's important. Being put in charge of a group of people is not the only way to get recognition. In our technology companies, creative individuals are really the most important contributors, not necessarily the manager of an R&D [research and development] department.

ROBERT: How do you reward those people?

RAY: By creating a culture in which they understand that their ability to create knowledge, even if they're working all by themselves, is at least as important as being a manager.

JOHN: There are many ways to reward people which fundamentally reflect what you value. There are companies that will reward people with more free time or money from a slush fund to pursue personal interests.

ROBERT: It's more important than even a personal bonus?

JOHN: It might be a lot more important than cash. Let's look at what motivates creative people—and Mike [Csikszentmihalyi] can certainly help us with that. Often creative people are best motivated by being part of a community in which they can do their best work with people whom they regard as being their peers at the top of their game.

STEPHEN: My brother-in-law says that when people come in for employment interviews at his architectural firm, more and more frequently the first question they ask is "How much free time will I have?" This is a very strange question, because when I was starting out, that was the last thing I was worried about. I wanted to get employed; I wanted to make my mark; I wanted to climb the ladder; I didn't worry about my vacation time.

MIKE: Well, time is the ultimate resource, so now in some sense it's a symbol of power. But I think that what all you gentlemen are saying is very important, and not often implemented in organizations. You're not just throwing money or power at people below you, but you're paying attention to them and to what they're trying to

> *. . . time is the ultimate resource, so now in some sense it's a symbol of power.*

do. You're trying to find the best match between them and the needs of the organization. I don't think you can achieve creative results in organizations simply by rewarding people financially or with power; you have to pay attention to people and treat them with respect.

RAY: We try not to let rank and ego issues get in the way. We try to create a group enthusiasm—to create a flow, if you will. When this works well, ideas come out of a session and nobody knows who actually came up with them. The group is working as one mind, internalizing the problems and coming up with solutions.

ROBERT: As society becomes more knowledge-based, creative organizations, however diverse in content and customers, are becoming more similar to one another in process and structure. Bob produces knowledge in music schools, Ray in technology companies, Stephen in the entertainment business, John in facilitating new ventures. It's the creative output that makes such similarity of style so fascinating.

RAY: Increasingly, knowledge production is really where it's at. We've created a trillion dollars of new market capitalization in Silicon Valley alone over the last ten years and it's all new knowledge. That's how wealth is being created in the world today. And it's not just computers and software; it's art and music and writing and all kinds, all forms, of knowledge. One reason we're successful in this country is that we have the culture and the institutions to encourage that.

JOHN: The importance of creativity today reflects a fundamental shift in the nature of the economy. In the old days, wealth was created by standardization. In the industrial era, you manufactured something, you sought long production runs to get economies of scale, you were really efficient—you could get a Model-T any color you wanted as long as it was black. And there was a whole set of assumptions about how to manage. Organizations had a typical hierarchical structure to make sure things ran smoothly. That system worked well when the industrial environment was relatively stable, but now it's fundamentally unstable—and so we need fewer economies of scale and more economies of discovery. This means that the approach to organizational structure and management has to shift as well.

RAY: And these shifts are happening faster, because technological change is accelerating—and it's going to continue to get faster.

ROBERT: Let's look at the dark side. What are some of the things organizations do that inhibit creativity?

RAY: If you have a lot of hierarchy, it causes problems by cutting down communication. I've moved away from hierarchical organizations; I've flattened them. I try to recognize everybody's skills and find ways that the group can work together and give people satisfaction.

ROBERT: All of you, I'm sure, have made mistakes. Ray, in retrospect, what have you done that inhibited creativity?

RAY: Throwing too many people at a project.

ROBERT: Bob, I bet it's easy to aggravate musicians. Have you ever done that?

BOB: I'm sure I have, undoubtedly every day, though without intending to. I hope it won't be irrelevant here to draw a contrast between symphony orchestras and string quartets. A symphony orchestra is a very hierarchical organization that gets its artistic direction from a strong leader who's standing on a box with a stick in his hand and who brooks no discussion or enjoys no collaboration on anything. If he says, "It's now too loud," it is indeed now too loud. In a string quartet, the four players who are members of that organization have to interact with one another to achieve creative results. I'm not going to name this famous European string quartet, but it uses no [sheet] music and has played together for thirty years. The one woman member, who plays second violin, has been married at one time or another to each of the three others. How you get creative results with that kind of collaboration Mike [Csikszentmihalyi] may know, but I don't.

ROBERT: Stephen, are you going to try that system?

STEPHEN: No, I wouldn't try that system. We have in filmmaking what is called the auteur theory, which means that the director has a vision and his vision is omnipotent. This is very similar to Bob [Freeman]'s orchestra model, where the conductor is the absolute boss. I've always fought against the auteur theory, because it doesn't bring the best creativity to the table. You have writers, you have actors, you have directors, and the idea that only one person on a set can have a vision is, I think, wrong. Everybody should have a vision of what he or she has to do, and it's the director's task to mold those visions and keep everything moving in the right direction. A really good director would be willing to see something unexpected that an actor is doing, adjust his own vision, and change the way he directs the scene. I don't think the auteur theory is healthy for filmmaking.

ROBERT: Sounds like you're a perfect boss. Tell me a mistake that you've made.

STEPHEN: Oh, I make 'em all the time.

ROBERT: Tell us one; I won't tell anyone.

STEPHEN: Well, OK. I once blew up at a network in a meeting—

ROBERT: But they deserved it.

STEPHEN: No, actually I just lost it. I allowed myself to vent in the wrong circumstances. It

was my fault, and I left the meeting knowing I had made a horrible error—and when I make a mistake like that I'm affecting not only my own career but the careers of all the other people who are working with me on these projects. And I didn't work for that network again for about nine years.

ROBERT: You bring up an important distinction, because you're a creative person running a large creative organization—as are Ray [Kurzweil] and Bob [Freeman]. How can the same human being be personally creative and at the same time be managing the creativity of others?

STEPHEN: You have to become a little schizophrenic. You have to compartmentalize. There's some part of you that has to be a manager and has to say, "OK, I'm not fronting for this project; I'm not the writer here."

ROBERT: Ray, you're an inventor and you run companies. Isn't that a managerial conflict of interest?

RAY: I try to collaborate. My own creative process is to frame a problem at night, think about it, and then go to sleep—and in the morning there's often some creative ideas to work

---

My own creative process is to frame a problem at night, think about it, and then go to sleep . . .

---

with. But then to get everybody involved in the creative process, we try to recognize everybody's contribution—which is really their reward, along with the thrill of having the technology affect people's lives.

ROBERT: Mike, do you see a conflict when a manager is both personally creative and trying to manage the creativity of others?

MIKE: It could happen, but there's a lot of creativity in management itself. If you can enjoy orchestrating talent and skill, being a manager of creativity can be very satisfying.

ROBERT: John, when you work with companies, what are some keys to engender creativity?

JOHN: That's about a ten-hour subject, but I'll comment on a couple of things. One is to look explicitly at the environment within which creative work might occur—I mean both the physical and emotional environments. On the physical side, it's no accident that in Hollywood and in the recording industry the workspace is generally free of the "Dilbert" kind of cubicles, and there are special conference rooms for brainstorming sessions. Big ideas need a big space. The emotional environment is about how

---

Big ideas need a big space.

---

the person managing the process makes people brave enough to step forward with their ideas. It also has to do with what the company believes in, because organizations need a north star in order to fix a purpose for creativity. Creativity in and of itself, as we've mentioned, is just new stuff, so a company needs to link creativity to a larger vision of the future. It needs to have what you might call strategic foresight, so that creative work is organized and focused.

ROBERT: Stephen, as a north star, how do you make decisions in your company?

STEPHEN: I'm very intuitive. I was actually asked this question in a magazine interview. I said that if I don't have an answer, I try to solicit the best opinions in my company, but then I make a gut shot at it. The reporter said that I was the first executive to acknowledge relying on intuition in decision making. The other people he'd interviewed all said that they made decisions empirically. They would collect information, they would make graphs, they would use efficiency scales and equations and whatever to figure out the bottom line, and then they would make a decision based on that.

ROBERT: Those other guys may be making decisions just as intuitively as you do, but they could have been embarrassed to say so, because it's socially unacceptable to make decisions based on intuition.

STEPHEN: Well, that's what this reporter said. He said that intuition is considered a feminine trait, and most of those guys wouldn't admit to it. Of course, I will.

ROBERT: Intuition and analysis each have their role; the best decision makers use both.

STEPHEN: You know me. I don't need to claim to use empirical studies to support my decisions just to justify getting paid a lot of money.

ROBERT: Ray, how do you see creativity in rapidly changing technologies?

RAY: Creative groups are dynamic and shifting and aren't necessarily long lasting. With the Web, we can create virtual companies very quickly and have work groups that aren't geographically in the same place. With increasing bandwidth, we can tap math talent in Russia, programming talent in India, and musical talent in China. Creative groups can be formed around the world.

ROBERT: The Web is amazing. Last night I was searching for John [Kao]'s résumé on my paper-strewn desk when I realized that it would be easier to download it again from his Web site five hundred miles away. Took about eight seconds.

RAY: There's a fantastic network of knowledge that's at our fingertips, and it's becoming more compelling. I feel very plugged in.

ROBERT: Does the integration of technology enhance creativity? Some say that technology enhances control and thus stifles creativity.

RAY: Many solutions to problems are out there; people just have to discover them. With all this knowledge at our fingertips, and with powerful tools to find it, we can attack more complex and demanding tasks.

JOHN: This notion of a group memory is very important. Companies often don't know what they know. Technology enables the representation and sharing of knowledge in ways that haven't been possible before. We're just at the beginning of an exciting era.

ROBERT: Let's fast-forward into that era a hundred years. How will creativity impact business?

MIKE: I've been studying many traditional manufacturing firms, and it's incredible how creative they now have to become to survive. They have to change every few years. Previously, they could wait twenty years or so before they had to make their products obsolete, but now it has to be done almost immediately.

BOB: Education in the next century will embody something that the Scandinavians already understand: We're training people for careers that aren't going to end at age sixty-five or seventy but go on until eighty or ninety. Thus the importance of continuing education—the opportunity to bring men and women, perhaps in their mid-forties, back to school either to improve skills that aren't up to current standards or to help them begin new careers.

RAY: A hundred years from now, society will be profoundly different, and people will be profoundly different. We're not going to have unmet material needs. The whole point of society will be to focus on innovation, the creation of new knowledge. And as a species, we will have vastly expanded intellectual skills, because of a merger between our biological brains and the very powerful new technologies we're creating. We're already putting [very simple] implants in our brains, and that will be routine a hundred years from now. We'll be a lot smarter, and the goal will be creating new knowledge.

JOHN: Companies will be measured by a new kind of ROI, return on *innovation*. There will be chief innovation officers, who will be responsible for these innovation processes, which will move ideas forward in very explicit ways. People will look at the management of ideas then as routinely as they look at the management of money now.

ROBERT: Stephen, you'll still be writing novels a hundred years from today?

STEPHEN: I'm counting on it; I'll be in a crypt somewhere typing away. I think we're looking at such a huge technological revolution that flexibility and creativity will be essential. There will be many new delivery systems, many more ways to get ideas to the consumer. You'll need to be much more flexible to take advantage of this increasingly innovative world we're in.

ROBERT: CONCLUDING COMMENT

Creativity and innovation mark the economic frontier of contemporary commerce. Finding new and better products to sell, services to offer, and ways to work are all essential for survival in highly competitive environments. With increasingly rapid change, the need to anticipate change is critical. Creativity in business involves surprise, breakthrough, leaps of logic, sudden shifts in modus operandi. But creativity has to be directed or it may well spin out of control. Modern organizations require both creative management and the management of the creativity—that is, executives who cook up novel ideas themselves and executives who can direct the creativity of others. Creativity is required in all sectors—business, the professions, not-for-profit, academic, government. Creativity works its magic across the organization, from overall strategy to specific research and development, from finance to production, distribution to customer service. Creativity, in short, propels the country's business and catapults its citizens' careers. What drives the best people in the best organizations? An almost obsessive need to change, even to shock. Creative individuals are rolling dynamos; they are intense, gutsy, spirited, strange. It's personalities like these that push us closer to truth.

OUTTAKES

ROBERT: *This may not have been our most controversial subject, but it's an important one. Knowledge-producing organizations are the new wealth of the new world.*

STEPHEN: *I just hope to continue writing one novel a year.*

CHAPTER 13

Can You Learn to Be Creative?

Most of us want to be more creative, but the plethora of advice is enough to drive you crazy. There are literally thousands of books and self-help programs that promise to teach you all the special secrets of creativity. So let's begin with three commonly held myths, first among them that creativity is a rare form of genius. Not true—everyone can learn to be more imaginative. Second, that creativity matters only in the arts and sciences. Again, not true—fresh ideas can invigorate any area of human endeavor. Third, that creativity is a talent and thus effortless. False—intense energy and strong motivation are needed to generate original ideas. How do creative people create? And what can the most creative people—writers, artists, scientists, entrepreneurs—teach us? Can we apply in our lives what they practice in theirs? Can creativity be learned? Are there any techniques for generating originality in projects and ideas? Our contributors, all of them prolific and creative people from diverse fields, share some of their secrets with us.

PARTICIPANTS

Dr. Gregory Benford, an astrophysicist at the University of California, Irvine, has written more than thirty books of science fiction. Greg talks about how to break the creative logjam and make the writing process fun.

Dr. Mihaly (Mike) Csikszentmihalyi, the author of *Flow: The Psychology of Optimum Experiences,* is a leading authority on creativity. Mike emphasizes the openness and the curiosity of creative people and how we can all share in the creative experience.

Dr. Rhoda Janzen, a poet and instructor of English literature at the University of California, Los Angeles, has twice been the poet laureate of California. Rhoda describes her creative process, analyzes one of her poems, and talks about how she encourages creativity in her students.

Dr. John Kao, a noted teacher, entrepreneur, and the author of *Jamming: The Art and Discipline of Business Creativity,* is an expert on corporate creativity and management. Trained as a psychiatrist, John discusses the training necessary to develop personal creativity.

Dr. Todd Siler, an internationally known artist, author, and entrepreneur, is the first visual artist to receive a doctorate from the Massachusetts Institute of Technology. Todd believes that you don't have to be a genius to think like one.

ROBERT: John, you're a creative machine—entrepreneur, jazz pianist, author, movie producer [John was a production executive on *Sex, Lies and Videotape,* which won the Palme d'Or (First Prize) at the 1989 Cannes Film Festival]. Is creativity a talent that only comes naturally, or can you teach it?

JOHN: The answer to both questions is yes. I think we all have tremendous creative abilities. And yes, creativity can be taught. Maybe not in

. . . yes, creativity can be taught.

the sense of finding one set of rules that works for everyone, but by looking for patterns, for different aspects of creative skills.

ROBERT: Rhoda, you've published over a hundred and fifty poems. Describe the creative process when you write poetry. What's the root of your own personal creativity?

RHODA: Well, creativity for me, as it manifests itself in my poetry, is a process that's almost like a trance. I just sit down when I have that idea,

and I begin to write. I've learned how to intellectualize it, to rationalize it, to speak about my poetry in an academic way. But the process itself—that first act—is just sitting down and letting myself go.

ROBERT: We're going to ask Mike [Csikszentmihalyi] to analyze you later. Greg, you're an astrophysicist and science fiction writer of such books as *If the Stars Are Gods,* in which beings are collected like songs—quite a creative concept. But what do you do when you're stuck, when the page is blank, when your creativity is cramped, when the ideas just aren't flowing?

GREG: Then I go for a walk, or I go for a swim. One thing I've learned is, don't make it hard. The surest way to block yourself is to make writing a disagreeable experience, so that your unconscious remembers next time that it doesn't want to go there.

ROBERT: Does that happen often?

GREG: No, because for me it's always fun. If it's not fun, I don't do it.

ROBERT: Todd, your science-based paintings are collected by major museums around the world. And you have a company that teaches creativity in schools and businesses, based on your book *Think Like a Genius.* Can anyone think like a genius?

TODD: You don't have to be one to think like one. Look at that enormous treasure chest you have—the three-pound complex we call a brain, which encompasses such a vast range of thought and feeling and experience. The first rule to tap your potential is just to be open. And to embark on that inner search for yourself.

ROBERT: You have to be willing to work at it?

TODD: Yes. Most people are more creative than they give themselves credit for. There's a beautiful thought by Goethe, who said that if children were allowed to develop naturally from the day of their birth, they'd all be pure geniuses. I absolutely believe that.

ROBERT: Mike, in your book *Creativity: Flow and the Psychology of Discovery and Invention,* you profile many of the world's most innovative people in the arts, sciences, and public leadership. What makes these folks tick? What's at their core that generates such creativity?

MIKE: Oh, they're quite different from one another in many ways, but one thing they have in common is their tremendous curiosity, which leads to a kind of unfettered openness in experiencing the world. There are people eighty, ninety years of age who are like children of six or seven; they're still open and curious about the world.

ROBERT: There's hope for us.

MIKE: I think so. The more childlike we become, the better.

ROBERT: I'm in good shape, then. Are these principles applicable to normal people who want to be more creative in their daily lives—as opposed to the superstars you deal with?

MIKE: The important thing is not to confound success—recognition—with the creative experience. We can all experience creativity, but unfortunately not all of us can be recognized as artists. Recognition comes only to a few people,

---

The important thing is not to confound success—recognition—with the creative experience.

---

although that would change if society paid attention to more disciplines and domains. But if we're talking about the experience itself—then, yes, we can all live much more creatively.

ROBERT: Greg, I want to put you in a hypothetical situation. Imagine you're lecturing on creativity to two diverse groups, both of which you're quite familiar with. During the day, you're teaching physics graduate students. At night, you're conducting a workshop for young science fiction writers. Your assignment is to engender creativity. Are you going to use a different approach with each group?

GREG: No, I think I'd start with the simplest thing, which is analogical thinking. I'd teach them to ask, "How is this thing like that thing, and how is it not?" To look for comparisons where you wouldn't think any basis for comparison existed, and go on from there—see if something comes out of the woodwork. Creativity is really just a process of trying to make a connection that you didn't see before. But you have to be open to it.

ROBERT: But physics students have been trained to do structured problem sets in, say, differential equations, while the science fiction writers may be free-form thinkers. Does that make a difference?

GREG: Well, with the physics students, you might ask, as Einstein did, "How is going up in an elevator like standing on the earth? Are they the same experience?" That's the equivalence principle, which was a giant step toward understanding gravity. Nobody had ever thought of it before, but these two experiences are the same. It's just that simple.

JOHN: Greg is in a good position to consider your hypothetical example of bringing two groups together and seeing what crosses boundaries. New ideas often come from the collision of different perspectives—from almost forcing the square peg into the round hole.

ROBERT: Greg is the personification of collision.

TODD: One of the best things you can do to spark the creative process—whether in scientists or writers or whomever—is to get people to approach problems from unique angles. Getting rid of the normal categories we all put things into also helps.

JOHN: And the categories can be demographic. In our company, our information-systems guy is sixteen years old, and so he's also our token teenager. We make sure to have a blend of different kinds of people—different ages as well as different disciplines.

ROBERT: Rhoda, you've won awards for innovation in teaching. What do you do to generate creativity in your students?

RHODA: I agree with what's being said about bringing different groups, different demographics, into dialogue. At UCLA we're fortunate to have one of the most diverse student bodies in the country. In my classrooms, I deliberately invite dialogue between different cultures, different ethnic groups, different racial groups, and we begin to challenge assumptions—the act of going into dialogue pushes us and expands our boundaries. But by the same token it's also important to ignore categories. For instance, if I'm trying to emphasize creativity in a classroom, I might say, "Let's look at this mid-nineteenth-century novel and find some commonalities with this late-twentieth-century film"—so not only are we crossing the boundaries of art, we're putting these oppositional forces into contact.

ROBERT: John, what are the primary mistakes that people make when they're trying to be creative? What forces inhibit creativity?

JOHN: Part of it is the voice of judgment. "I'm not doing work that's good enough" or "I'm not creative, it's not part of my job." Another big mistake is to assume that there's a right way to practice creativity—that there's an objective set of principles that you have to study. Obviously there are certain principles, in a general sense, but one writer I know in Hollywood works only between four and five o'clock in the afternoon. Others work ten hours a day—

ROBERT: With both hands—

JOHN: —and probably both feet as well. Creativity is variable, in terms of the specific style, and people need to understand that they are free to develop their own style.

ROBERT: Mike, what are some mistakes that you've seen among the hundreds of creative people you've interviewed?

MIKE: Most of those people were lucky enough to have survived all their mistakes, so they don't make as many as they used to. But I agree with John [Kao] that many people feel constrained—they feel they're not entitled to try something different. They think their lives have been set for them from the beginning, and that they shouldn't explore other interests. This can lead to a routinization of thinking as well as living, which then spoils their chances to be someone else.

ROBERT: Todd, tell us about your school programs and how they engender creativity in young children.

TODD: We have an art and science program that integrates the inventions and languages and ways of looking at the world that the arts and sciences employ. We use a range of tools that I find useful for people who don't describe ideas well in words but can model them.

ROBERT: Physical, tangible models?

TODD: Right. For instance, we ask groups of people from diverse backgrounds and of different ages and interests, "What's your ideal learning environment? But don't tell me, show me." And we supply them with a range of ordinary materials, with which they build these fabulous multidimensional symbolic models that represent their ideas, visions, and viewpoints.

ROBERT: So you have them use model building to express abstract ideas. What other questions might you ask?

TODD: What does learning mean to them? How do they like to be taught? What are the kinds of things they want to learn? And how do they want to apply what they learn? Today what's happening in schools is that children are becoming brilliant test takers, if that, and then they dump the information, literally, at the door. Ask them three weeks later, "What is it that you studied? How are you applying it to your life?"—and many of them are clueless. Our program increases the meaning and the usefulness of the information they're learning, so that they can apply it to their lives, interests, and passions. This model building allows them to do that. They can use their own intelligences and learning styles to build something that makes their thought processes tangible.

ROBERT: People actually build these abstract sculptures.

TODD: Yes. They're not making art or science or engineering per se. We ask them literally to give form to their thoughts: "Show me!" It's a sophisticated show-and-tell. Using various common materials, they draw, cut, paste, and build

> *There's also a fifth dimension, which is the symbolism expressed.*

multiform objects inspired by mental connection-making techniques. These objects look three-dimensional, but they're more, because they have parts that move [and change over the fourth dimension of time]. There's also a fifth dimension, which is the symbolism expressed. The signs, stories, and symbols cross intellectual barriers.

JOHN: I'm reminded of the process that designers go through.

TODD: Prototyping.

JOHN: Designers have to move right away into something concrete, because if they stay stuck in the conceptual, their conversations will be pyrotechnic but useless in the final analysis. So how do you move quickly from concept to some kind of an embodiment? In business, people often think of creativity primarily as moving from generic concept to specific concept. Todd seems to have created some kind of language for making thoughts concrete, enabling people to communicate.

TODD: Yes. It's a form of prototyping, because you're actually bestowing form. But it's not as restrictive; it's much more free-form. And it's nonthreatening—there's no prerequisite of having to be an artist or a scientist, a poet or a thinker, or anything. You take the most common materials and give form to thought. It's the symbolic embodiment of thought.

JOHN: That's important, because people are often stuck in the notion that they have to find *the* right answer—say, when they're making a decision about their future—as opposed to figuring out something that's good enough for now, until you transcend that with a new understanding.

RHODA: And once you've got your embodiment, once you've built your model, you're going to change it. Constant change is one of the wonderful things about the creative process.

Constant change is one of the wonderful things about the creative process.

It takes the sting and the pain out of thinking, "Oh, I've got to create something fabulous!"

TODD: Nothing's fixed. It's all changeable; it's all modifiable—the point is the growth. It's like part of the evolutionary process. Since you allow free interpretations, it's going to be morphing and doing all kinds of things.

MIKE: One of the problems of the creative process is that people think they'll get to the end of it and that's it. But in the creative process, you learn from each step of the way, and with each step something changes, and you don't know what the end will be.

ROBERT: Finality is often a fallacy in creativity. Mike [Csikszentmihalyi], you often refer to Viktor Frankl, the Austrian psychotherapist and concentration camp survivor, who wrote *Man's Search for Meaning*. Is there a relationship between creativity and a search for meaning?

MIKE: All creative people, whether they're scientists or artists, are really trying to understand how the universe is put together, why it's there, what it's doing.

ROBERT: If we had the answers, we wouldn't be doing this series.

MIKE: That's right. And that quest keeps going on. New questions arise all the time, and the search gets more and more interesting.

ROBERT: To make the universe even more interesting, we're going to ask Rhoda to read one of her poems for us.

RHODA: I'd be happy to read a poem. It's called "Seniors Witness Portent." It's set in urban Los Angeles, and it's based on something that happens virtually every day—an event I witnessed one day when I was out with a friend.

> I was driving with my friend the optimist
> who despite her optimism had that afternoon
> noticed at Ralphs that on her shopping list
> she had scribbled ground belief. The moon,
>
> starlike, air-kissed the Hollywood jacaranda.
> The unhappy geriatrics withheld applause,
> sitting on what they wished was a verandah,
> not the bald cement abutment that it was.
>
> They were motionless after a matzo supper,
> watching as on a stage a curse-hungry teen,
> whose face was tossed like a crumpled wrapper
> into our headlights and our panic of adrenaline:
>
> he seized a bicycle and sheered it at our car.
> It was one of L.A.'s casual cruelties, the faces
> as from a hole punch, dispensable and sure,
> the earth that roils with unnamed psychosis
>
> just under the urban blanket we have tucked
> around its bulk, the faultfinding and the path
> seismic—oh, it's been coming, it's been sicced
> on us, the six-toed night-blooming behemoth.

ROBERT: Rhoda, I'm going to put you into a difficult situation. I want you to be the teacher in your English class, and you're going to analyze this poem, written by some woman you've never met. How would you dissect it? What's the core of its creativity? Why did it win prizes?

RHODA: Well, before I would ask my students why it's a successful poem, I'd just look at it in terms of what's happening. What is this poem about? I'd probably ask my students to tell me

what's going on at the literal level. You know, there are so many negative stereotypes attached to poetry. Students think it's about *love* and fancy emotions and anguish and so forth. And poems don't have to be about that. So I would ask my students, "Look, what do we know about the speaker? Who is this friend that the speaker is driving with? What do we know about their relationship? Literally, what's happening in the poem? Can you describe to me this incident of violence, and the intentionality behind it?" And then, once we've established what's actually going on, I might try to move the discussion into why these comparisons are being made. I think it all goes back to what we mentioned earlier—connections and discursiveness. How and why are we bringing together things that don't seem to have much in common? For instance, in this poem, why has the poet compared seismic activity to a gesture of adolescent rage? What do those two things have in common? I would take it from there and invite my students to participate in this sort of unfolding analysis.

ROBERT: Greg, in your science fiction, do you do similar things? Do you bring conflicting ideas together?

GREG: Oh, sure. The best way I know to generate a story is to smack people together, basically. The big problem I usually have is not starting a novel but stopping a novel. I just finished a novel and then realized there was something more I wanted to do with it. So I called up my editor, and she said, "Can't you leave those people alone?" And the answer is no. The problem is that my characters keep on doing things, because they engender their own lives. And it's really hard for me to put them down.

ROBERT: Give us an example.

GREG: Well, there's this character who dies and then reappears.

ROBERT: Not a problem for you.

GREG: Appears in a different form. And it was a big surprise to me to have this person coming back, as it would be in real life. But being a science fiction novelist, I could do it technically. But I didn't know what was going to happen until I initially turned the page and found out at about the same time the reader will. I really like that, although it's kind of tough. It's not sailing smoothly on the lake of serene consciousness—it's more like whitewater rapids all the time. And that's why I turn to writing very eagerly, and in a sense to find out what happens next. And this is the way I hope people read my books—wondering what's going to happen.

RHODA: Do you ever feel out of control in your artistic process?

GREG: There's always an element of being out of control. Skiing is like that. There's *some* sense of control—one thing I finally learned from my high school English teacher was to outline. I outline more and more, but it's just to put a frame around the story.

ROBERT: Todd has been out of control ever since I met him twenty years ago at MIT.

TODD: I love listening to this. When I finish reading a novel, I'm really involved with the characters and I tend to create continuing virtual stories with them. They go on living in our imaginations, and we do things with them even after they've stopped at the end of the book.

GREG: Now you understand the disease of unendingitis.

ROBERT: Rhoda, are students afraid to be creative because they don't want to look silly?

RHODA: Frequently they *are* afraid to be creative, and it's one of the things I fight against in the classroom. Students need to be comfortable. They need to feel confident in their own skills. I want a student to be able to make connections between things. I want to be able to ask them, "Look, what's the connection between a Faulkner novel and a Drew Barrymore film?" And if they feel comfortable coming up with that commonality, they'll be able to develop a fruitful analysis.

ROBERT: What is the connection?

RHODA: Well, that's up to the students. And I don't necessarily want them to end up with Drew Barrymore, but until they feel comfortable and have faith in their own connections—in their own ideas; the ideas that they originate—then they won't feel comfortable going on to further analysis.

MIKE: In general, when very creative people are engaged in a voyage of discovery, they don't know what the end product will be. It's a scary thing. And you have to learn to control that fear, and be like Ulysses.

JOHN: Creativity is intangible. You sit in a room and you think, until ideas become concrete in some way. You may have no navigational aids to tell you where you are. So an important part of the process is to develop trust in yourself. It's almost a way of having a dialogue with yourself, as if you were your own patron, or your own best friend, or your own nurturer, encouraging yourself to step forward, be brave, change the frame, alter your work habits, try new things with no guarantee of success.

ROBERT: Where have you done that in your own life?

JOHN: When I was involved in academic teaching, I wanted to empathize with my students. So for several months before classes started, I would study something that I knew nothing about—like learning to play a new musical instrument or reading about some obscure period in history—just because I wanted, in some respects, to give myself permission to start with a blank piece of paper and get back into a beginner's mind. These kinds of experiments, this internal theater of maneuvers, might seem a bit nutty—whether it's setting up your workspace, or pretending you're an investigative reporter in your hometown, or putting on someone else's head and trying to see the world through a different set of lenses. But they might get you the metaphoric pot of gold.

ROBERT: That's how I thought about this show—at least, the nutty part.

JOHN: There you go. Thank goodness.

TODD: You have to have the courage to experiment. You leave behind your fears. That's the hardest part—getting people to suspend that fear, that self-judgment. Getting them to say, "Gee, what would this connection be like? What's behind it? What could it mean?" And having the confidence to undertake the kind of independent thinking that we often don't cultivate. We all subscribe to more of a herd mentality. We all agree on ways of looking at the world, instead of allowing ourselves to experiment—not in the structured way that science experiments but in a very loose way, where you welcome serendipity and surprise.

ROBERT: How does the integration process work in all this—where you need a period of time just to sit and let it stew?

GREG: We've been talking about work. I want to talk about not working. I favor creative laziness. Every night, I fix in my mind the things I'm struggling with, and I go to sleep. In the morning, lying face down, before any signs of life, I just go to the mailbox [in my mind] and see if anything has arrived. I just let it happen for five or ten minutes. It may appear as though I'm being lazy—and in fact I am—but I'm trying

---

I favor creative laziness.

---

to get the unconscious to do the work that I don't have the time to do. And it's like a gift every time it arrives. I think this works about a third of the time—that is, every three days or so, I get something in the mail. Sometimes it's just junk mail—you know, "YOU MAY HAVE WON A MILLION DOLLARS!"—but at least it's something.

MIKE: Most creative people have these routines that help them break away from linear, rational attempts to solve problems by the usual means. Your mind is able to make connections you would never have made no matter how hard you tried. But you have to have the skills. I talked to a musician, for instance, who says that he looks at his hand with awe and wonderment as it composes. Of course, he could look at his hand for twenty years, and if he didn't have that skill, it wouldn't do anything. So, you have to have the skill, and then this creative laziness will let you look at it from points of view you never had before.

TODD: There's a complement to creative laziness, which is the other extreme. Some people actually increase their creative vigor by working—creatively working and multitasking lots of different things. And while other people are dropping dead just looking at them, they're revitalizing themselves. You'd think that somebody who finishes a project that would kill most mortals would want to rest. But in fact it's the creative fever that—

ROBERT: —energizes them.

TODD: Energizes them. It's unbelievable. It's a fast burn all the time. Feels great.

ROBERT: Excellence in all fields can be produced by contradictory styles. Gary Kasparov and Anatoly Karpov are great chess players, though each has a radically different approach—one is an aggressive attacker, the other's a plodding defender—yet both are world champions. It's the ability to do what you do extraordinarily well.

MIKE: And finding your own way of doing it.

ROBERT: John, what can we learn from these three creative people: a poet [Rhoda Janzen], a writer [Greg Benford], and an artist [Todd Siler]? What in the richness of their experiences can help normal people in everyday life?

JOHN: Let's put on the hat of an anthropologist and simply study them in their native habitat, to see what kind of work processes they employ. When do they work, where do they work? Greg [Benford] was talking about being willing to go for a swim if he felt he was getting a little stale. What's the work setting? What does it look like? What's on the desk? Is it solitary? It is interactive? We begin to build case studies of how the creative process works.

ROBERT: Mike, how would you study these creative people we're holding captive here?

MIKE: Just to follow on from what John [Kao] was saying, I think what we learn from them is that they've taken control of their own lives—maybe willy-nilly, maybe under pressure—and developed a way of personalizing their own activity and experience. They're not pushed around, they don't follow an externally imposed pattern; instead, they try to figure out how they can express what they know in the best possible way.

ROBERT: How about their methodology?

MIKE: Each one probably has a different way of working. You can look at when they get up in the morning, when they eat, when they sleep, and so on—and you'll come up with an average that doesn't mean anything. The only thing they have in common is that each has discovered how to manage the creative process for himself or herself in the best possible way.

ROBERT: Creativity is the combination of general principles and individual variability.

JOHN: But they all probably have a fascinating creative biography—how their interest began, how it evolved, whatever reversals they may have had. And what their learning process has been, throughout. If we could find some overall time dimension as well, that would be fascinating.

ROBERT: Let's contemplate a time dimension here and look forward a hundred years. Will creativity be a subject we learn in school, like English and history?

JOHN: It already is, in some countries and in some communities. What's going to be different a hundred years from now is that we'll all have access to a rich array of technology-based tools, and perhaps other kinds of methods, for amplifying our creativity.

MIKE: What probably will be different is that we'll be less and less obliged to follow certain patterns that are foisted on us, either by backward technology or backward social arrangements. And this freedom could make us a fantastically creative society.

RHODA: I hope so. I hope that the boundaries between disciplines will be down, or at least flexible, and that art will be enriched by responses and accomplishments from other fields.

GREG: I think we may be able to access creativity technologically. Literally get some sense—because we know how the brain works—of what it feels like to be creative. And that would be something new for human prospects.

TODD: I think our world culture will eventually be struck on the road to Damascus and realize that creativity is the growth engine of learning, the way to discovery, to invention, to civility. To humanity. And we'll get wise to that, and we'll study it and respect it, and this will allow us to flourish. Period.

ROBERT: CONCLUDING COMMENT

Although the fields in which creativity is applied are radically different, the processes whereby creativity is generated are remarkably similar. Learning to be creative really works—but it takes work. How do you solve a problem creatively? The first key to creative problem solving is to generate numerous alternative solutions that are sufficiently different from one another. Don't fear conflict, even confusion, among these competing ideas. Be willing to be wrong. Allow insight and inspiration to wash over you. But don't evaluate possible solutions too quickly; analysis—even accurate analysis—stifles creativity. Develop your entire set of creative solutions first; then, and only then, appraise them. But then you had better be rigorous and merciless in your analysis. Woolly brained, poorly structured, creative solutions can be worse than no solution at all. So test them all; eradicate the weak ones. Kill off your own babies! Never be satisfied; always monitor results; constantly reassess everything. That's how you learn to be creative, as the right processes move us closer to truth.

OUTTAKES

JOHN: *I felt kind of like I was at a banquet. It was really rich.*

GREG: *I always feel stupid when I talk about how I create.*

RHODA: *I didn't get the chance to—*

ROBERT: *You'll get another shot at us [in Chapter 16].*

CHAPTER 14

How Did We Think in the Last Millennium?

W hat will the new millennium bring? To forecast the future, we should process the past. The last thousand years have been astonishing in their extremes. Humanity was wondrously transformed—from knights on horseback to kids on computers—but the price paid was very high. So much collective suffering; so much individual agony. If how we think helps to define how we live, then it should be useful to look at the thought processes that led to the triumphs, as well as the ravages, of civilization. Our future may depend on our ability to think, and perhaps think differently than we have in the past. So let's attempt to understand the nature of thinking itself—rational versus creative thinking; deductive versus inductive thinking; logic versus perception; analysis versus synthesis; game theory, heuristics, algorithms, the "expert systems" of artificial intelligence. What does each contribute to our intellectual and material advancement, and how do they further (or inhibit) our personal, social, and political relations? If we can think more clearly, shouldn't we be able to live more happily? Understanding thinking—its categories and applications—is the specialty of our panel. What's particularly interesting is how the diversity of their fields affects the direction of their thinking.

PARTICIPANTS

Edward de Bono, author of over fifty books, including *Lateral Thinking: Creativity Step by Step* and *De Bono's Thinking Course,* is an international authority in both creative thinking and the direct teaching of thinking. Edward calls for design, synthesis, and creativity in human thinking.

Dr. Edward Feigenbaum, a professor of computer science at Stanford, is often called the father of expert systems, which are software programs that incorporate the best human thinking. Ed explains how artificial intelligence can assist our thinking.

Graham T. T. Molitor, a prolific author about the future, is vice president and legal counsel of the World Future Society. Graham believes that our brains will ultimately be enhanced through advances in genetics and neuroscience.

Dr. Sherwin (Shep) Nuland, a surgeon and medical ethicist at Yale University School of Medicine, is the author of *How We Die,* a poetic book describing the end of the human lifecycle. Shep sees human beings as mostly irrational by nature.

Dr. Brian Skyrms, a professor of philosophy and social science at the University of California, Irvine, is the author of *Evolution of the Social Contract.* Brian examines the nature and tools of thinking.

ROBERT: Edward, you've taught creativity and thinking to schools and corporations throughout the world. What are your notions about how we handled these matters over the last millennium? Why such extremes?

EDWARD DE BONO: On the whole, our thinking has been rather disastrous. The three Greeks—Socrates, Plato, Aristotle—really wrecked Western thinking, which has been concerned only with truth, analysis, judgment, argument. This type of thinking has led to persecutions, wars, discrimination, pogroms. What we've left out is "What

---

On the whole, our thinking has been rather disastrous.

---

can be?" thinking. "What can be?" thinking is design, creativity, synthesis—putting things together to achieve something new. We've had a very limited thinking system—a system excellent in itself, but only as the front left wheel of a motor car is excellent. By itself, it's inadequate.

ROBERT: Ed, how can so-called expert systems help us understand human thinking?

ED FEIGENBAUM: Expert systems are part of a field in computer science called artificial intelligence, wherein scientists and engineers are attempting to create models of human thinking, primarily the models of thinking that Edward [de Bono] was just calling "the front left wheel" of the automobile—namely, logical thinking. Expert systems are attempts to model the knowledge and the expertise of first-class human professionals [for example, physicians], who are practicing their professions at very high levels of performance. This relates to the ultimate goal of artificial intelligence: to generate programs that are extremely intelligent—that is, beyond human capability.

ROBERT: Brian, as a philosopher you've explored the concepts of decision making and rational choice. What is a "social contract" and how can it help us understand the collective thinking of the last millennium?

BRIAN: The social contract is a metaphor for a kind of tacit agreement, or deal, that people make in order to form a society and live together in it. A lot of philosophers try to justify ethical rules by saying that they would be part of an ideal social contract. But we can also think about how the actual social contract of real institutions arises from evolutionary and learning processes. That's the sort of thing I'm interested in.

ROBERT: Shep, you're a surgeon who has written two extraordinary, sensitive books, *How We Die* and *How We Live*. Do you see a shift in human thinking as we enter a new millennium?

SHEP: Not essentially. To me, human thinking is unfortunately irrational. We retreat to magical thinking at every opportunity. As much as I applaud attempts to make thought processes coherent and complete—to put four wheels on

---

. . . human thinking is unfortunately irrational. We retreat to magical thinking at every opportunity.

---

that automobile—I think ultimately we're dealing with a flawed creature and a flawed way of putting information and memories together.

ROBERT: Can't we improve our thinking?

SHEP: We certainly can improve it. That's what this is all about.

ROBERT: Good, we'll give it a shot. Graham, as a futurist, you usually look forward. But start by looking backward.

GRAHAM: The last thousand years had some extraordinary benchmarks. We came out of the

depths of the Dark Ages and we launched this world of ours into the era of the Enlightenment. We spawned great scientists and inventors, like Leonardo Da Vinci—many of the things he conceived became reality. Then in the last two hundred years came the development of mechanization, mass production, electricity, nuclear energy—all of these powerful mechanisms that drive society and provide the foundations of our economy and the basis of our livelihoods.

ROBERT: But in what direction are these mechanisms taking us? Let's explore the nature of thinking by comparing those left and right front wheels—rational thinking and what we might call postrational thinking. Let's start with rational thinking. Brian, talk about some of its components, such as deductive and inductive thinking.

BRIAN: Deductive thinking, or deductive logic, is the kind of logic used in pure mathematics—that is, how we think about mathematical objects and their relations to one another. You don't have to know anything about the real world to understand deductive thinking.

ROBERT: It's like tenth-grade geometry, where we used axioms and rules of logic to develop proofs of theorems.

BRIAN: That's part of it, of course. But if you want to look at the real world and try to confirm your scientific theories or your medical diagnoses or what you think is the truth of a legal case, then you have to use inductive logic and inductive thinking. Inductive thinking deals with evidence.

ROBERT: It starts with data, the messy stuff in the world around us, and then we develop theories to explain that data, always testing the theories by doing experiments and making predictions.

BRIAN: In the real world, you cannot know the

In the real world, you cannot know the truth of any theory with the absolute certainty of formal logic.

truth of any theory with the absolute certainty of formal logic.

ROBERT: Ed, in the work you've done in artificial intelligence, there are two concepts you use which I'd like you to define for us: heuristics and algorithms.

ED FEIGENBAUM: Well, first I should say that I see thinking as a discovery process, not a deductive process—discovery in a very large space of possibilities. Heuristics are those pieces of knowledge—tricks and rules of thumb—that allow us to prune that space of possibilities in order to get to acceptable solutions in a reasonable amount of time. These acceptable solutions aren't necessarily optimal, aren't necessarily the best, but they're good enough. Herbert Simon, one of the pioneers of artificial intelligence, coined the word "satisficing" to distinguish the process from optimizing. Now that's where algorithms come in. Algorithms are structured pieces of mathematical and logical thinking that computer scientists and mathematicians use that lead you step by step to an answer that is guaranteed to be the correct answer, but it could take a very long time to get there. Heuristics are shortcuts; you could call them elements of the

art of good guessing, the knowledge that goes into pruning that big space of possibilities. It's what expert chess players know that novice chess players don't.

ROBERT: Chess is a wonderful field for analyzing algorithms and heuristics. You might think that since there are only sixty-four squares and thirty-two pieces, a supercomputer could consider all the moves in a normal game. But if this supercomputer were required to consider all the legal moves in a forty-move game of chess before making its first move, the universe would burn out before that first move could be made.

ED FEIGENBAUM: That's right. The total number of possibilities at the opening of a chess game is 1 followed by 120 zeros. It's impossible to calculate, so chess players use all kinds of heuristics. Here's one, for example: In the opening of a chess game, don't move the pawns at the edges of the board; focus on control of the center.

ROBERT: Edward, let's check the right wheel of your mental motor car—the other side of logic, analysis, and judgment.

EDWARD DE BONO: Something like ninety percent of all errors in thinking are errors of perception—this is indicated by work done by David Perkins at the Harvard Graduate School of Education—yet culturally we focus on logic. But logic can't even begin to be applied until there are concepts with which the logic can work, and these concepts are rooted in perception. Historically, we focused on logic because we assumed that the perceptions were given and obvious, but only in some cases is this true.

ROBERT: What is your perception of "perception"?

EDWARD DE BONO: Perception is a different system from logic. Perception works as a self-organizing information system. Logic works in what I call a passive surface system. And the differences are huge. I'll give you a practical example of the differences. Imagine the bottom of a diamond mine in South Africa, with illiterate workers who have never been to school in their lives, who come from seven different tribes, and so on. They used to have two hundred and ten major fights, disputes, grievances every month. So we started teaching them how to think. Those two hundred and ten fights a month dropped to just four. It made a huge difference to their lives: productivity is up, absenteeism is down, safety is up. One can teach thinking very directly. I'm involved in schools in many countries now, doing just that.

ROBERT: What's the theory underlying lateral thinking?

EDWARD DE BONO: Lateral thinking tells you that if you look at self-organizing information systems—how we think—they form patterns that are asymmetric, meaning that from the end of the pattern you can see all the way back to the beginning, but from the beginning of the pattern you cannot see all the way forward to the end. Lateral thinking is [a way to deal with this asymmetry], and it's based on the process of provocation—and we've coined a new word, "po," which means "provocative operation." For instance, in the case of river pollution, you put in a provocation by stipulating that factories should use their own pollution. It sounds illogical, but from that comes an idea which is now the law in many countries—that if you build a factory on a river, your water input has to be downstream from your own output, so that you're the first to get your pollution.

ROBERT: Provocations are intermediate steps for creating new ideas; they are deliberately unsettling and disturb the current equilibrium.

EDWARD DE BONO: Provocations allow us to jump from one equilibrium to another. Once you're there, you see in hindsight that such new ideas are of course obvious. There are various techniques of lateral thinking—provocations is one, random input is another; they're all based on asymmetric patterns in self-organizing systems.

ROBERT: How do hypotheses figure in your system of thinking?

EDWARD DE BONO: We can talk about testing hypotheses, but where do the hypotheses come from? Hypotheses are creative possibilities, and progress always comes from creating new possibilities. Indeed, Chinese culture, which was way ahead of the West a thousand years ago, came to a dead end because they never developed the possibilities of hypotheses.

ROBERT: How do you break out of the normal, or traditional, way of thinking?

EDWARD DE BONO: You need to look at thinking as the operation of a self-organizing system. There are various tools, such as attention-directing tools. Let's give an example. One of the simplest tools we use in school is called the PMI—Plus, Minus, Interesting. I asked a class of thirty kids, "Would it be a good idea if you were paid to come to school every week?" Thirty out of thirty said, "Great we'd love it; we can buy candy, chewing gum, comics." I didn't argue with them; I didn't ask, "What about this, what about that?" Instead, we introduced the PMI, and they thought about my question in terms of plus points, minus points, and interesting points. At the end of the session, twenty-nine out of thirty had changed their minds. On their own, they had conducted a little perceptual scan; there was a bigger picture to see, and as a result their perceptions changed and their decision changed. Emotions changed, too, and that's key. If you change perception, you change emotions. Logic will never change emotions; perceptions will.

ROBERT: Brian, let's talk about game theory. This is a relatively new area of thinking that is often used in behavioral science.

BRIAN: Game theory is a misnomer. It's really the theory of strategic interaction. It was called game theory because games like chess are special examples of strategic interaction. But of course there are many such examples: war, international politics, coalition formation, oligarchies controlling prices, and so forth. These are all situations where what's good for me depends on what the other guys do. And what's good for them depends on what I do. You can't optimize your position without worrying about how the other guys are optimizing their positions.

ROBERT: So this kind of thinking doesn't occur in isolation; you have to be concerned about what the other person is thinking.

BRIAN: You have to model the other person's thinking, you have to model his thinking about your thinking, and so on. It can get very complicated.

ROBERT: But this is closer to the real world?

BRIAN: This is closer to the real world. The question is, How many levels up do you have to model before you can get a sufficiently good answer? Game theory is a kind of deep dynamic analysis that explains how people grope their way to a solution, so that when they are finally

at a solution point, each is happy with what the other thinks, and with what the other thinks you think, and with what each is doing. These strategic interaction problems are solved not only by people but also by animals in all kinds of interactive systems.

EDWARD DE BONO: But there's an underlying point here, which is if you set out a strategy of "win-lose"—that is, I'll win because I'll make you lose—then your strategic thinking will follow that design. But if you set out a strategy of "win-win"—in other words, how can we both benefit?—your whole thinking structure will be different. It all depends on the underlying assumption.

BRIAN: Win-win is not always easy, because there may be different ways to win-win. If we want to coordinate something—say, if I want to meet you someplace, but we haven't decided where—win-win is when we both get to the same place. But I still have to worry about going to the place that you think I'm going to, and the same is true for you.

EDWARD DE BONO: Sure. But I meant that underlying game theory was the notion that one person wins and one person loses.

BRIAN: That was in the 1940s, when game theory was originally devised.* But now, mod-

---

*Game theory is a new branch of mathematics that was conceived by John von Neumann, a mathematician, and Oskar Morgenstern, an economist, to solve problems in economics (e.g., optimum pricing strategies). Since then, game theory has been applied in politics (e.g., coalition building), military planning (e.g., strikes and counterstrikes), business (e.g., product positioning or plant locations)—situations in which there are a number of decision-making players who have similar, opposed, or mixed interests.

ern game theory deals mostly with situations of win-win or partial conflict and partial cooperation.

ROBERT: Graham, how much of the future is dependent upon ways of thinking? Wouldn't different mechanisms of thinking lead to different futures?

GRAHAM: Well, yes. But I think that the key to assessing the long-range future is recognizing that there are a thousand tiny threads that tie the tapestry of tomorrow together, and one must look back carefully to see what the precedents and benchmarks are. I take a little different approach to thinking. One gross measure has it that we use only approximately one to three percent of our brains. We may use no more than ten percent—which means that we can move up the

---

> *. . . there are a thousand tiny threads that tie the tapestry of tomorrow together, . . .*

---

scale, so that we can use, say, as much as ninety-seven percent of our brain capacity. Will we do that? I think the answer is yes. I go back and look at the crude surrogate for intellect—which is basically average brain size, the cubic-centimeter measurement. For the first [hominids], it was about 500 cubic centimeters, and it's about three times that today. By the year 3000, with advances in genetics, my feeling is that the size of the human brain will increase drastically, up to as much as 2000 cubic centimeters.

ROBERT: That three-percent brain utilization idea sounds to me like a popular misconception.

And I question the wisdom, if not the ultimate technology, of brain enlargement.

SHEP: Wait. Why should brain size increase, if we're only using three to ten percent? Wouldn't cultural evolution simply mean that we'll begin using ten to fifteen to twenty percent, and therefore there's no evolutionary need for brain size to increase?

EDWARD DE BONO: The pinheads will be happy.

SHEP: Furthermore, the last significant evolutionary change in human brain size occurred 25,000 to 40,000 years ago, and in spite of the enormity of the input that humanity has been subjected to, our brain size hasn't changed one bit since.

ED FEIGENBAUM: Graham [Molitor]'s argument completely ignores the growth of artificial intelligence. When computers are doing a great deal of our thinking, there will be no evolutionary pressures to increase our biological brains' capacity.

GRAHAM: Well, I'll go a step further. Right now, we can augment our visual and auditory capabilities through implants. There will be a lot more of that—and I agree with you a hundred percent that this is another technological trend.

EDWARD DE BONO: You can simulate a brain with only five neurons on a computer; that brain is capable of fifty billion thoughts. Five neurons, fifty billion thoughts. We've got a hundred billion neurons. So brain size, I think, is irrelevant. It's how we use what we've got that counts.

GRAHAM: Well, I said it was a crude surrogate. There's also the long-standing conundrum about whether genetics or environment is the controlling factor [in intelligence]—I say that both are.

ROBERT: I agree with that. But are you saying that evolution will not proceed in its normal way—that through genetic enhancements we'll be able to increase brain size?

GRAHAM: Well, the historical data tell us that we now have a brain roughly three times the size of our hominid predecessors. But several other things have to happen here. You have to increase the bone structure to support a larger head. You have to increase the size of the pelvis to allow the head to pass through the birth canal.

ROBERT: But I don't think that brain size has much relationship to what we do with our brains. If we need amplification or artificial intelligence, it's right there. What we're doing with our current brain size has not been all that good.

EDWARD DE BONO: We need better software for our brains.

ED FEIGENBAUM: Exactly. As Robert mentioned earlier, there has been an enormous transformation in the past millennium, but not any in brain size or function; that is, there has been no change in the hardware—what we call the wetware. What has changed has been the introduction of an enormous number of new knowledge artifacts into our collective culture—artifacts that we store and use and build upon, such as new concepts, new vocabulary, new technologies, and so on.

EDWARD DE BONO: Here's an example of what I mean by better software. Our normal argument mode is a primitive and often barbaric method of thinking and should be supplanted by parallel thinking. Parallel processing in

humans, not machines. One large corporation, using a framework I designed for parallel thinking, reduced discussion time on a national project from twenty days to two. Two days! Huge increases in productivity, just from using better thinking software.

ROBERT: What about the role of emotions and feeling in the thinking process? Aren't we leaving these out?

SHEP: Emotion—that brings me back to the notion of perception. It seems to me that perception, as Edward [de Bono] is describing it, is really the interpretation of observations; and the way we perceive comes from our background, the memories we have, our emotional state, the stake we have in observing something one way or another. The result is that the same observation will be interpreted, or perceived, in many, many different ways. For example, the Greeks noted that people with cancer became depressed, so they were certain that depression was the cause of cancer. Although [coincidentally] they may turn out to be partially right, this was a mistake in interpreting observation, which is a mistake in perception. How do we solve the problem of what people bring to the perception in the first place?

EDWARD DE BONO: That's the point; you're right. Perception is the aggregate of experience, emotions, momentary attitudes, and the like. We can develop methods of changing perceptions—for example, by encouraging different ways of looking at the same situation.

ROBERT: Are there dangers of programming thinking so carefully?

EDWARD DE BONO: No, no. These are just tools that open up a broader scan, and as a result your emotions change. So I agree that perceptions are the result of upbringing, background, chemical levels at the moment, but they're not immutable.

SHEP: The historical progress of science has been made on the basis of changed perceptions of the same observations or data.

EDWARD DE BONO: A hypothesis is a perceptual change. And it's sad that even in leading universities where I've been—Oxford, Cambridge, Harvard, London—so little time is spent on generating hypotheses. A senior executive in the CNRS—the Centre National de la Recherche Scientifique, in Paris—once said to me, "I want you to help my scientists generate hypotheses. They've been told that science is the analysis of data, and deductive conclusions. But without hypotheses, you can't get anywhere."

ROBERT: You're talking about inductive thinking.

EDWARD DE BONO: It's more. It's what you bring to the data. The analysis of data won't produce new ideas. The brain can see only what it is prepared to see. It's your hypothesis, your speculation, that says, "Let's look at this situation from this viewpoint; now what do we see?"

BRIAN: Hypothesis guides induction, but inductive logic doesn't give you the hypothesis.

ROBERT: Inductive logic evaluates the hypothesis.

EDWARD DE BONO: Exactly.

ROBERT: Ed, are you a closet reductionist? Do you believe that thinking is completely knowable?

ED FEIGENBAUM: I'm not in the closet. I'm an out-front reductionist. Edward [de Bono] has said that thinking is software. I would say that thinking is software plus knowledge, running on an information-processing device. This

---

. . . thinking is software plus knowledge, . . .

---

device is the brain, and it can be understood, or known, at various levels. It's known at psychological levels; it's known at neurophysiological levels; it's known at molecular levels. It's complex, and although it's not completely known, it's completely knowable. There is no magic in our heads.

EDWARD DE BONO: I agree with that entirely. But one of the difficulties is that the universe changes. If you're looking at a passive information universe, the things you can know are very different from the things you can know if you're looking at a self-organizing information universe. Now, we know a lot about self-organizing systems. For instance, we know that provocation is a necessity, otherwise you get bogged down at a local equilibrium and you can never get more global.

ROBERT: If you have a self-organizing system with high complexity and emergent properties, it may be impossible to provide predictable explanatory mechanisms below the observable level, no matter how much analysis you do.

EDWARD DE BONO: You can analyze the behavior; you might be able to predict consequences, but you may not be able to predict exactly.

BRIAN: There are still dynamics that you can study. And there is still no magic.

ROBERT: We can't logically exclude the possibility that there may be other things that exist in the nature of reality that affect human thinking. There are religious views, spiritual views, other nonreductive theories of mind that deny that thinking can ever be totally reduced to computer programs. Do you believe that human-level thinking can be totally reducible to computer programs?

EDWARD DE BONO: No. Not computer programs, because computers don't work that way yet.

ROBERT: Yet? But ultimately, will they? This is the key question.

EDWARD DE BONO: Yes, sure.

SHEP: The discredited vitalist philosophers believed that no biological function was ultimately knowable. We now believe that all biological function is ultimately knowable. Human thought, just like human biology, is all ultimately explainable. I'm the ultimate reductionist.

BRIAN: The physical system is all that exists. The question is whether we can ever actually write down the state of the physical system in complete detail, and then write down the equations that govern it—so that we can predict what you'll be thinking five minutes from now. It's not at all clear that that will ever happen.

EDWARD DE BONO: I agree. I'd make an analogy to the relationship between the dancer and the dance. The dancer is the biological system, the dance is the performance. You can't necessarily predict the dance from the nature of the dancer, but the dance is dependent directly and solely on the dancer. Similarly, you can't necessarily predict thinking from the nature of the biological system, but thinking is dependent directly and solely on the biological system.

SHEP: Otto Loewi, who discovered acetylcholine, the chemical transmitter that excites muscle cells [and enables neurons to communicate in the brain], is supposed to have said, during a concert by the Guarneri String Quartet, that "there must be more to this than just a little acetylcholine." But that doesn't make the function unknowable at all. But speaking of transphysical things, let me ask Graham [Molitor] a question. Since all thought is value-tinged, and we're talking about methods of thinking, is there a role for philosophy, for theology, in examining the values of our society as we develop new methods of thinking?

GRAHAM: Well, philosophy and theology are regulatory mechanisms for controlling what is abroad in society. They are key, and they're responsible for major jumps—what scientists like to call paradigm shifts—in our values and our lifestyle. The most recent of these shifts occurred during the Renaissance, and we're in the middle of another one, which is mainly driven by computer science and artificial intelligence—all these things we've been talking about. If you think you're the ultimate reductionist, I'm probably the penultimate. We'll crack the genetic code, we'll understand how to encode life, and I see the same kind of principles applied to neural technology, to enhancing the brain. It will take a long time, but it will come.

ROBERT: I'll bring it back to the "perceptions" with which we started. Those of us schooled in science naturally come at the question of the contemporary relevance of philosophy or theology from a different perspective than do philosophers or theologians—or most ordinary people for that matter. We have to ask ourselves, Is our scientific method of thinking the sole system for accessing truth? Is our way the only way to view the world, examine reality, and understand thinking?

EDWARD DE BONO: Let's go back to the moral point. In England there's a school that accepts kids who are too violent to be taught in ordinary schools. When this school started teaching them broad perceptual thinking, the level of violence dropped to one-eighth of what it had been previously.

ROBERT: Let's take a prediction. One hundred years from now, what will have happened to thinking?

EDWARD DE BONO: Every school in the world will be teaching my thinking methods. Kids will be much more productive, much more tolerant of one another, much more able to create value for themselves and for society.

BRIAN: We'll have better theories about some things. We'll have new tools that we can use. Look at the computing power you have on your desk right now, just running a word processor. You can analyze dynamic systems that nobody could analyze twenty years ago. Assisted thinking will lead to better and better predictions of complex systems.

SHEP: I think there'll be increasing recognition of the basic irrationality of human thought processes, and of the necessity for the kinds of changes that we've been talking about here.

GRAHAM: No matter how much we talk about the subjective or theoretical dimensions of existence, the basic sciences are what drive society. And by the year 2100 certainly, and probably before, the life sciences—particularly genetic engineering—will dominate society. It's the opening of a new era—with Dolly [the cloned sheep] and the complete description of the human genome being the major benchmarks—in which humankind will control its own evolution.

ED FEIGENBAUM: Not only will we have very powerful artifacts in the form of computers, and pattern-recognition machines to handle perception, but the construction of those machines will lead to a science of thought that is every bit as rigorous and useful for prediction as what we have now in chemistry and physics.

ROBERT: CONCLUDING COMMENT

So how do we assess the last millennium? Often the smarter we got, it seems, the stupider we acted. Rational, linear thought produced the most efficient social advancement but also the most destructive human debasement. This is what happens when value-free analysis serves the capricious whims of conventional human nature. You get amplification: Good gets better but bad gets worse. Genocide has frequently occurred alongside the most advanced science, several of the worst examples in our own twentieth century. So if we continue to be arrogant, bigoted, greedy, and jingoistic, then rational thinking will continue to generate maximal trauma. Rational thinking makes good technology, but our cognitive processes must grow in order for humanity to prosper. Human thinking must change. We need novel, original ideas that can enable us to leap beyond the traditional boundaries of inquiry and establish new standards of value creation. We need synergy and harmony between rational and postrational thinking, the left and right wheels of our mental motor car working together. Our thinking must become creative and holistic as well as analytic and diagnostic. Try this combination of both kinds of thinking in your personal life, and your decision making will undoubtedly improve. It is the best thinking that brings us closer to truth.

CHAPTER 15

How Does Technology Transform Thinking?

Iget cranky when there's a ten-second delay in downloading a Web site. A few years ago, I was thrilled to receive a same-day letter by fax, and a few years before that, snail mail that arrived within the week was just fine. It's not time that's accelerating; it's our thinking. Technology has produced multitudes of machines with alluring functions, features, and options—machines that benefit our lives. But what is the real impact of technology? Don't let the superficial glitz of flashy gadgets and light-speed information deceive you. Acquiring knowledge and making decisions—both for individuals and institutions—has been altered forever. The real impact of technology is not on the design of electronic apparatus but on human cognition; the true transformation is in the way we think. How do advances in technology affect our modes of thought? How is thinking changing, and how do we adapt to those changes? We invited five accomplished thinkers to reflect on the deeper consequences of technology.

PARTICIPANTS

Dr. Francis (Frank) Fukuyama, a professor of public policy at George Mason University, is an international authority on social and political thought. Frank discusses how trust works in a high-technology society and what happens to decision making under pressure of time.

Dr. Bart Kosko, a professor of electrical engineering at the University of Southern California, is the author of *The Fuzzy Future*. Bart explains how the uncertainties of fuzzy logic and the process of pattern recognition can help our thinking.

Dr. George Kozmetsky, cofounder of Teledyne and an early investor in Dell Computers, was awarded the National Medal of Technology by President Clinton, for building business incubators where young companies can grow. George discusses how technology creates wealth and prosperity.

Dr. Marvin Minsky, the longtime director of the Massachusetts Institute of Technology's Artificial Intelligence Laboratory, is the author of The *Society of Mind.* Marvin talks about some of the social consequences of burgeoning technology and shows how artificial intelligence can explain and improve human thinking.

Dr. Bruce Murray, a professor of planetary science and geology at the California Institute of Technology and a former director of the National Aeronautics and Space Administration's Jet Propulsion Laboratory, is president of the Planetary Society, in Pasadena, California, which fosters public interest and participation in space exploration. Bruce reflects on the relationship between communications technology and human development.

ROBERT: George, for fifty years you've participated in the technology revolution. You've been president of the Institute of Management Sciences, and you've assisted in developing over a hundred technology-based companies, including Dell. For fifteen years, you were dean of the Graduate School of Business of the University of Texas at Austin. Give us an overview of the progress of technology and how it affects our thinking.

GEORGE: When our current technology started coming in, we could stop using paper-and-pencil methods. We could formulate complex equations, which is the scientific way, and solve them electronically. We believed that we'd

---

. . . our horizons were expanding faster than we could collect data, . . .

---

get more time to think, but what we discovered was that technology just made it easier to find things—we could replace an hour of searching with fifteen minutes of reading. But then we found that our horizons were expanding faster than we could collect data, and so we realized that we needed to get into artificial intelligence and other techniques.

ROBERT: Speaking of artificial intelligence, Marvin, you are professor of media sciences and arts at MIT and a pioneer, of course, in artificial intelligence. Your book, *The Society of Mind,* combines insights from developmental child psychology and computer systems. What's the basic theory behind the book?

MARVIN: Well, it's to try to figure out how the mind works without the traditional belief that somewhere inside the mind there's a "self" in control and commanding everything. So the question is, How do you get mindlike behavior from the brain? The brain is really made of about four hundred different computers. They do different things, they don't agree on everything—so how do you get reasonable, common-sense behavior out of such a system?

ROBERT: And the concept of a "society" means that all of these brain systems are working together?

MARVIN: Right. It's not like human society, where a person does pretty well independently.

ROBERT: And how has the impact of technology affected human thinking?

MARVIN: I don't know that technology has changed thinking very much yet, but we're just at the threshold. Computers only got going around 1950. We still don't know how to program them to do commonsense kinds of things, just technical things. But that's going to happen, sometime in the near or far future. Then our thinking will change.

ROBERT: Frank, you're the author of an acclaimed book, *Trust: The Social Virtues and the Creation of Prosperity*. What do you mean by trust?

FRANK: Trust is basic to any human activity, which is almost always social, involving the cooperation of two or more people. Trust is simply the ability of people to interact with one another in the expectation that they're going to be honest, they're going to reciprocate, they're going to make good on their commitments.

ROBERT: And how is trust affected in a society dominated by technology?

FRANK: It doesn't become less important. In a way, it becomes more important. Take something like the Internet. You can deal with anybody anywhere in the world—that's the potential—but can you trust them? The real core of the problem in creating E-commerce or socializing over the Net is, How do people come to share values, not just bytes and bits?

ROBERT: Bart, your books on fuzzy thinking sanction contradiction, endorse ambiguity, and demand that we get comfortable with uncertainty. What is fuzzy logic, and how does it affect our thinking?

BART: Fuzzy logic or fuzzy thinking is trying to see things in shades of gray as we reason. For example, when does life begin? At conception? In the first trimester? When does a teenager become an adult? Is it exactly on the first second of the eighteenth birthday? The law says it is,

---

. . . fuzzy thinking is trying to see things in shades of gray . . .

---

but such precision isn't real or practical. So fuzzy logic has been trying to capture the grayness of inherent uncertainty in our reasoning and thinking processes. Capture it in mathematics, and then endow that structure in computers to make them a bit smarter.

ROBERT: Bruce, how can the concept of space exploration help human beings think about themselves in new ways?

BRUCE: Well, it already has. The seminal effect of the first images of Earth taken from orbit and from the moon, back in the sixties, revolutionized our global self-perspective and led to the environmental movement. Similarly, when *Voyager* took pictures of the earth as a pale blue dot embedded in the vastness of the solar system, it had the secondary effect of reminding people that the universe doesn't revolve around the earth, doesn't even revolve around the star we call the sun. And so space has already changed our frame of reference, to say nothing of what may lie ahead.

ROBERT: Was the environmental movement actually triggered by those pictures of Earth?

BRUCE: Yes, that really happened, and that's why it spread so rapidly—because the catalyst was those images, spread by television, which was our medium of global communication at that point.

ROBERT: Let's broadly look at how technology affects thinking, because some say that it's nothing less than a shift in worldview. George [Kozmetsky] was talking about how something that used to take an hour now takes fifteen minutes. What does that do to the way we make decisions, the way we reflect or meditate?

MARVIN: Again, I have mixed feelings about questions like that, because I think we still think in pretty much the same way. Our brains haven't been changed, but the tools that we have are immensely better. If somebody asks me a question of fact, I can usually either fail or succeed in finding the answer from the Web pretty fast. As for computing, we can solve problems numerically and analytically—

ROBERT: Aren't there pressures to be less reflective and make decisions faster, because facts are coming at us faster and are more readily at our disposal, and people expect faster answers?

MARVIN: Well, there are a lot of problems like that. Sometimes we're under pressure to decide faster; sometimes, with the great leverage of technology, a decision can affect more people and in a shorter time. One of the most dangerous things is the rapid communication in political affairs: you might have a TV network asking, "What does the public think?" and five minutes later they'll say that seventy percent of the American people think such-and-such, and so forth.

ROBERT: And maybe it was thirty percent just two days earlier.

MARVIN: That's right. And if you wait a week, maybe it'll settle down. But very few of these media people are aware that such sampling is unstable and very dangerous—opinions can spread like an epidemic. The general populace seems to think that if a lot of people believe something, then they should, too. It's called a flip-flop, and in computers it leads to the destruction of information rather than the increasing of it.

ROBERT: Bart, do you find that your own decision-making processes have been speeding up?

BART: Well, to some degree—which is a typical answer of a fuzzy theorist. In the early days of radio, we could hear a story; later we could see it on television; now we can experience it with interactive, multimedia effects on the Internet and perhaps in theaters in the future. I'd like to advance a thesis, though. How does technology, in the broadest terms, increase our ability to recognize more and more complex patterns? Bruce mentioned a good example— we finally saw Earth as a small blue sphere. In the 1940s, science fiction movies cast the earth as gray. As recently as the American Revolution, say, weather was still a mystery. Benjamin Franklin was one of the first to work out the concept of weather fronts—something we take for granted when we look at that nightly weather map. Our perspective takes on ever larger scales, going back into geological time;

with each step of technology, we recognize more patterns, process more patterns, make more connections, in an ever richer way.

ROBERT: Frank, let's explore the impact of technology—from how you write your books to how institutions make decisions.

FRANK: For me, technology makes things easier. If I had to deal with typists, with gathering information, and the other kinds of headaches that you have in writing a book, it would not be possible to publish what I do. I think there are certain institutions and situations where the impact of technology is even greater. For example, in foreign policy, there's no question that officials are under pressure to make decisions faster. That's the big impact of worldwide telecommunications—the CNN effect, which has been talked about in the media. When vast audiences see immediate images of refugees, or a captured soldier being dragged through the streets of a foreign city, it forces policy makers to react immediately, which they wouldn't have had to do in an earlier generation. And it seems to me that speed doesn't necessarily improve the quality of their decisions. On the other hand, you have this huge impact in terms of sympathy. You see somebody starving to death in Africa— if you'd seen it in newsprint, it would have been an abstraction. But when you see these same images on television, it becomes something that's much harder to push aside.

ROBERT: How do you assess instant telecommunications? Do you worry about the manipulation of public opinion?

FRANK: Overall, the immediacy is probably a good thing, but it can certainly be mismanaged. As Marvin [Minsky] was saying, poll numbers going up can lead to instantaneous decisions—

you've got to do something—when a more reflective kind of thought process would have allowed you to think of possible counterproductive results, things that you hadn't thought about before. So I think this is something that needs management.

BART: It certainly doesn't make for a stable state of mind. Doubt is very hard for us to cope with. We like rounding things off in a binary, yes-or-no way—with them or against them— particularly in response to graphic images on TV. Or in polls. It's hard living with uncertainty, but the world's full of it.

ROBERT: So you're teaching us how to put up with doubt and uncertainty?

BART: I usually find myself saying that there's nothing uncertain about uncertainty if you're very certain you don't know something. Or you're not sure. And you learn to live with it.

GEORGE: Let me put the issue in political terms. I remember worrying, when we were first developing information technology, that in a democracy people could vote out of their kitchens, right? Push a button—give your opinion on any issue you like. We've been seeing some of that—for example, initiatives in California. We're reacting so quickly! And boy, have we created a new uncertainty that we'd better be afraid of! I'd rather have the old uncertainty, where I knew it was uncertain and I'd have to think about it.

BRUCE: It's always helpful to view problems not just over the last year or two but over the last century or many centuries. There's been what I like to term a symbiotic relationship between human development and communications technology. Go back to Gutenberg and the invention of the printing press. That was the first major way for propaganda or new ideas to be circulated to the masses. And that led to the development of a whole set of religious and cultural transformations. More recently, there was radio, especially battery-powered portables with earphones, which revolutionized the Middle

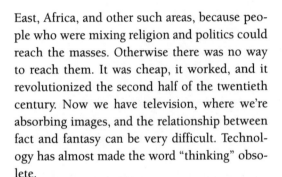

Technology has almost made the word "thinking" obsolete.

East, Africa, and other such areas, because people who were mixing religion and politics could reach the masses. Otherwise there was no way to reach them. It was cheap, it worked, and it revolutionized the second half of the twentieth century. Now we have television, where we're absorbing images, and the relationship between fact and fantasy can be very difficult. Technology has almost made the word "thinking" obsolete.

ROBERT: This can be dangerous. The potential for mass manipulation is frightening.

BRUCE: We're reacting. We're dealing with tremendous sensory inputs and producing outputs in shorter and shorter time frames.

ROBERT: You may get a hundred E-mails a day, and you have to react to them.

BRUCE: But that's good, because I have to react to the content. What's very bad is seeing images, or hearing sounds or the opinions of celebrities, which I don't evaluate. There I'm just reacting—

ROBERT: —emotionally, not analytically.

BRUCE: This is not some academic exercise in logical thinking. What really happens to people when they're bombarded with this kind of input? That's the big, scary question.

ROBERT: Let's talk about interdisciplinary thinking, a critical characteristic of technology. George, you've pioneered getting academia, business, and government to work together.

GEORGE: You need a focus to all this. When I started out, I came up with the question: "How do you generate wealth and prosperity and share it at home and abroad?" And I wondered, Gosh, is it possible to get the three sectors to work together? The academic sector working with the business sector, and both working with the government sector? And I found that if you have a crisis, it's easier to do. But how do you do it without a crisis? I'd like some ideas on that.

ROBERT: Tell us about your pioneering work with business incubators, where numerous new companies have been "hatched," often in association with universities or government labs.

GEORGE: Most innovations are bottom-up, not top-down. You have to have laboratories to do that. But how do you convert innovations into wealth and prosperity? I said, "Hell, I'm just going to have real companies try it and see what happens." But then I found that that wasn't enough by itself. We needed a physical place where these newly born companies could be housed [i.e., incubated] and get all the administrative and business services easily and efficiently, so they could concentrate on their new products or services. And we know that venture capital doesn't do much for start-up companies—people with venture capital like to invest when you're a long way downstream. So I started a capital network—just simply matching investors with entrepreneurs, like a TV dating game.

ROBERT: Had any successful marriages?

GEORGE: We've now learned how to place about $150 million to $200 million a year.

FRANK: There are many forces in the modern academy that are pushing in the opposite direction. The complexity of technology and the volume of it result in this disciplinary specialization that exerts a kind of tyrannical influence over the way people are trained. You'll never find anyone more intimidated than a young professor without tenure, because his or her discipline exerts this absolute control over any kind of thinking outside the box. There are a lot of institutional obstacles to interdisciplinary thinking.

ROBERT: Marvin, do you see institutional pressures against interdisciplinary thinking?

MARVIN: I'm not sure there are any good generalizations to make. There are so many different kinds of personalities in young professors. Some may be intimidated—they want security and they get what they want. But some aren't.

ROBERT: Have you ever felt intimidated?

MARVIN: I don't care much what other people think about me. So it's hard to intimidate me, unless you're Richard Feynman—

ROBERT: And he's dead.

MARVIN: Well, it doesn't matter that he's dead. I have a very good copy of him, and if I say

something too speculative, I can hear him say, "Well, what would be the experiment for that?" I think young academics need attachments—peers, people who imprint them, self ideals. We all have imprints from a bunch of people. Sometimes, when I'm writing, I hear the voice of another dead scientist, [artificial intelligence pioneer] Warren McCullough, and he says, "Oh, that's very nice" or "that's pretentious." What I'm afraid of is, given the advance of the media, who are the internal mentors built into the minds of our citizens? It's ninety-eight percent sports idiots, actresses, actors. Why are actors heroes? Because they're good liars. That's what it takes to be an actor.

ROBERT: Not to mention hosts.

MARVIN: Well, I actually like some of the hosts. But we have this strange celebrity thing, and instead of children being attached to and getting values from the right people, they get it from people who have the gift of pretending to be charismatic. Celebrities are celebrities because they somehow make people trust them. They have to get you to trust them when they're playing a role.

BART: You could even become president, if you play your cards right.

MARVIN: That particular president [once-actor Ronald Reagan] was a pretty smart one. He did all of those things.

ROBERT: Before technology, you couldn't have chosen him.

BRUCE: But before technology was your high priest, somebody else was—and I don't know whether we're still in the same frying pan or a different one. You have to be careful not to take a two- to five-year period and extrapolate it to the past or the future. I grew up at the end of World War Two. I was too young to serve, but I was old enough to understand what Buchenwald meant, what Hitler meant—the atom bomb was a real thing to me. You go another generation and all that's gone—that's history in the history books; none of that experience is there. Like my father's experience in the Great Depression—he never got over it; it colored his whole view of things. Vietnam was personally threatening to young people who feared they would get drafted, and it did lead to some intellectual development. Then you have Ronald Reagan saying, "Self-centered consumerism is good." That was the new ethic and it worked, producing the "Now Generation." So, with all these trends going on, we have to be careful when we generalize, because we're all very strongly imprinted by the culture—the things that were going on—when we were thirteen years old.

ROBERT: Frank, as an undergraduate you majored in classics; your doctorate is in political science. Does this give you a different perspective on technology from that of a scientist or engineer?

FRANK: Well, your perspective, in a way, is that the whole technological mindset, and modern natural science, is something that was deliberately chosen by human societies four hundred or five hundred years ago, but it's not the only way of approaching social organization and the pursuit of a good life. Science and technology is the way we've chosen, but it's not a necessary one. I think a lot of people assume that technology *has* to exist, that technological progress is inevitable and basically a good thing, and they

don't go back and examine the premises of this attempt to conquer nature—whether conquering nature is really doable, and whether it will provide the kind of meaning that people think it will.

ROBERT: What about technology's impact cross-culturally? You've compared different cultures—for example, Asian and American.

FRANK: Technology is homogenizing everybody, for better or worse. Technology produces modern economic societies, enhanced production possibilities—that's really what you mean

---

Technology is homogenizing everybody, for better or worse.

---

when you say that liberal democracy and markets are the only way to go. For the kind of technological world we live in, where information is critical for technological advancement, you have to have political democracy and decentralized economic decision making—and there are few cultures that can stand up against that.

ROBERT: Marvin, I'm fascinated by the power that people have. I often go to a Web site created by a person, not a company, because that one person has better insight. How do you see technology empowering people?

MARVIN: We could call it the popular-power paradox, because with this capability of setting up a great Web site, one person can make a huge difference. But then the next thing is, "Well, everybody can make a huge difference," and so they all somehow cancel one another out.

ROBERT: Frank, isn't that the essence of markets, where everything is competing and the best emerge?

FRANK: That's right: The best have to emerge at the end, but you also need filters and some way of picking the winners and allowing them to emerge.

ROBERT: Does education fulfill this role in a high-tech society?

FRANK: That's one of the real transformations that has come about. You cannot survive in a high-tech society without a much more substantial education, and education really changes the way people interact. There's much less regimentation in a university department than in an old-style factory, where everyone had less than a high school education. This is a major change.

ROBERT: George, you've pioneered educational transformation.

GEORGE: Yes. The first thing we found out in California and Texas is that forty to sixty percent of today's high school students can't apply for a job that's technology-based. Which led us to the conclusion that in the twenty-first century, knowledge that creates understanding will be called "education" and knowledge that creates value will be called "training." It doesn't make any sense to me to force everyone to get a college degree.

BART: We have a high level of scientific illiteracy in this country. There's the notorious poll data showing that over half of American adults don't even know that the earth takes a year to go around the sun.

GEORGE: When is education going to come up with some fresh ideas? There's no good theory in education today—certainly not in [grades] K [Kindergarten] through 12—about how to teach science and mathematics. Or the understanding of technology. Are we to do it with science fiction, which is not taught yet?

BRUCE: That gets into another dimension—critical thinking, critical evaluation. As the amount of stuff that the media bombards us with grows, most of it driven by commercial or political considerations, the need for the individual to be able to filter and assess and make critical comparison also grows. So maybe the word "education" will become obsolete. Training is extremely important, because the jobs are not manual labor anymore—you're not born with the ability to fill those jobs. You have to know how things work, but most important is the ability to think critically about the information you're exposed to.

ROBERT: Bart, regarding critical thinking, what happens to religion in a high-tech society?

BART: Science has often hoped that religion would go away. It certainly hasn't. It's a very adaptive belief system, and I'm sure it will adapt to the times, even when we evolve into different types of information creatures. I think religion will be just as virulent as ever. It tends to be the basis of large conflicts around the world, and as countries splinter into ever-finer groups and communicate on the Internet, that [sectarianism] will only increase.

MARVIN: Bruce [Murray] has put his finger on it, because one thing we need in order to understand things well is critical thinking. If somebody tells you something, you ask, "Well, what's the evidence for that?" In most religions, the idea is that, well, there are certain questions we can't decide in any such way, and so it's important to have faith. And if you're very good at having faith, it means you're not very good at critical thinking. Some people seem to be able to tolerate both, but in general I think if people put emphasis on believing a set of rules that come from an authority figure, then we're in terrible danger. Does the structure of the authority you're not allowed to question undermine understanding and progress?

ROBERT: You think faith and critical thinking are mutually exclusive?

MARVIN: I do. Some people say that faith and critical thought are concerned with such different subjects that they're not incompatible. But I don't think so.

FRANK: As offensive as faith-based thought may be to scientists, it seems to me that it's extremely important, and it's not likely to disappear. It's the basis for civil society—

MARVIN: It's not the only basis.

FRANK: It socialized physics [i.e., provided the initial social structure in which physics could develop], it's what creates community, and I think one of the reasons people have returned to religion is precisely that they're lonely, and that religion gives them a way of—

MARVIN: You don't see a downside?

FRANK: Of course there's a downside.

MARVIN: What about the religious wars, and the ethnic divisions, and so forth?

FRANK: We haven't fought any religious wars in the United States in a long time.

BRUCE: During the last thirty to forty years—during the time of this extraordinary technological revolution all over the whole world—the fundamentalist elements in Islam, Christianity, and Judaism have all been on the rise. Now why is that?

ROBERT: Isn't that fascinating?

BRUCE: It's fascinating, but it's also significant. That's real information, being fed back by real human societies. And the answer is that there's a need for belief systems and explanations that the populace is not receiving from the technological revolution.

MARVIN: But I think we see some of the needs. One is that people don't know how to think critically.

BRUCE: But critical thinking is not going to help you with death.

MARVIN: Oh, yes it is. Bart [Kosko] said you can learn to live with doubt, and you don't need someone to tell you, "Here's the answer." That's the kind of critical thinking we lack.

BRUCE: But people aren't little automatons with no emotions. When you deal with death, or obviously bad things that have no rational explanation, there has to be a context for real human beings to deal with it.

MARVIN: Well, I disagree. I think death has a rational explanation. If it weren't for religion in the two thousand years during which science didn't develop, we wouldn't have death. We would have longevity. You could live as long as you want. The belief in the afterlife is why we don't live forever. The fundamental paradox is that religion has deprived us of our immortality.

BRUCE: I wish we could settle this question empirically.

MARVIN: I think there will be some big biological advances, and one of them will be longevity. Nobody knows why we die when we do. We live twice as long as the chimpanzees, which are the mammals most similar to us, and they live twice as long as most other mammals. So we've already extended our life spans. It may be that it takes only five or ten genes to make people live a hundred years, two hundred years, four hundred years. Nobody knows. And I'll bet you'll find out pretty soon—within the next century. So, some people who are alive now may live three hundred years.

ROBERT: Marvin, you're working on a new book, *The Emotion Machine*—I read a little of the first chapter, on love. How do you understand love, perhaps the strongest human emotion, in an increasingly technological age?

MARVIN: Well, people don't like the idea of understanding emotions, because there are all sorts of surprises. That particular chapter starts by describing a person who comes in and says, "I've fallen in love with a wonderful person— incredibly beautiful, unbelievably sensitive! I'd do anything for that person!" And then I translate that emotion and it turns out that all those sentences aren't positive things about the other person but negative things about you. You say "incredible," "unbelievable"—meaning no rational person would believe this. "I'd do any-

thing for that person" means "I've decided that none of my own goals are worthwhile." So then you have to ask, What is the nature of this emotion and how does it work? And it seems to me as though a switch is thrown and you're a different computing machine, you're a different thinking machine, and you're using different resources and ways to represent the world. You're seeing things differently. My picture is that there are a couple of hundred systems in

---

. . . people don't like the idea of understanding emotions, . . .

---

your brain, and for each of one of them you might have five different ways of seeing things, five ways of representing knowledge, and five ways of saying what's good, changing your goals. And emotions are big switches that evolved over five hundred million years.

ROBERT: But do you see something as human as love changing because of technology?

MARVIN: I think that when we understand these things, we might be able to make other kinds of choices. And of course somebody will ask, "Well, what's the right choice?" And I don't know—

ROBERT: I'd be scared if you did.

MARVIN: No, but I like the idea of having more options rather than less. There are all sorts of ways that humankind could end up forever locked in some particular way of looking at things, but none of them seem very good. That's why we need progress and understanding.

There must be something better than all the things humans have done so far.

ROBERT: Let's look ahead a hundred years and ask a summary prediction question. What kinds of changes will technology make in human thinking?

GEORGE: I think human thinking is going to make changes in technology.

FRANK: Oh, we'll probably be smarter in a lot of ways. Just as we're taller and healthier and live longer. Technology will directly affect our thinking, getting right into human cognition and emotions.

BART: We'll be smarter because we'll have implanted computers into our brains, and later we'll replace our brains with chips—and then we'll have the irony of thinking fuzzy thoughts in a discrete, digital medium.

ROBERT: That may be "smarter" for you.

BRUCE: I'll give an outrageous answer. I think the term "we" may mean something different, because we are going to be connected in so many ways, to so many other people, both past and present, that the question will have to be answered in a very different way. My guess, not prediction, is that the coming century will be the one in which we transform as a social organism through communication, interactive as well as passive, into a different kind of species.

MARVIN: I think you're all correct. I agree with everybody. But what Bart says is very important. When we learn how parts of our brains work, maybe you could stick in a million little electrodes as a little module—the way you buy memory for your home computer.

ROBERT: But love will still be there?

MARVIN: Ah, love will still be there, but you can decide whom you'll be in love with, instead of letting it decide for you. When you like things, you never know whether you're choosing what you like or some little tiny machine in your head is doing it.

ROBERT: A rather depressing, mechanistic world you propose there.

MARVIN: But now we're just kicked around by things we don't understand.

ROBERT: CONCLUDING COMMENT

Few people get what's really going on here. The change in mental process is nothing less than a shift in worldview. Technology is radically transforming our thinking in at least three new ways: (1) information is freely available, and therefore interdisciplinary ideas and cross-cultural communication are widely accessible; (2) time is compressed, and therefore reflection is condensed and decision making is compacted; (3) individuals are empowered, and therefore private choice and reach are strengthened and one person can have the presence of an institution. So what kind of new thinking is technology engendering? Notice what happens. With an increasing number of diverse ideas circulating freely and widely, and with people more empowered but with less time to assess value, and with vast communications amplifying opinions, this new thinking is at once creative and innovative, volatile and turbulent. We have to face such complexity to keep closer to truth.

OUTTAKES

MARVIN: *I don't think I've ever said that before.*

BART: *He always says something funny.*

ROBERT: *That one [Concluding Comment] was hard to read.*

BART: *I was reading it to myself, and I stumbled four times.*

ROBERT: *If I had more time, I'd have made it shorter.*

BART: *Well! He [Robert]'s already got the ending written, so that's how he's trying to steer the conversation.*

CHAPTER 16

Why Do We Make Music and Art?

T hink of your favorite painting, your favorite poem, your favorite piece of music. How do these works of art make you feel? What do they reveal about you? In museums and music halls across the country, appreciation of the arts is enjoying a renaissance. The opening of a Picasso or Van Gogh exhibit, for instance, produces crowds customarily seen at rock concerts or sporting events. What is it about music and art that causes this excitement? We seem suspended, transported, connected, expanded—as if subsumed by something larger. A piece of music or a painting or a poem may lift our hearts, or fill us with ecstasy, or bring us to the brink of despair, or do absolutely nothing to us. What relationship is there between these human emotions and our analytical, rational selves? And what about the social import of art? Does art reflect our culture, or does art help to create our culture? From earliest times, in virtually every society on earth, an advanced aesthetic has marked the high point of civilization. Are these circumstances necessarily linked? We invited five very different artists to speculate about how music, poetry, painting, and other art forms release the human spirit and advance the human condition.

PARTICIPANTS

Todd Boyd, author of *Am I Black Enough For You?: Popular Culture from the 'Hood and Beyond,* teaches critical studies in the School of Cinema-Television at the University of Southern California. Todd talks about how rap music, hip-hop culture, jazz, and American movies have helped to create a global community.

Dr. Robert (Bob) Freeman, Dean of the School of Fine Arts at the University of Texas, Austin, is a leading music educator, historian, pianist, and public spokesman for music education. Bob discusses the importance of musical education and the powerful impact of music on all levels of society.

Dr. Rhoda Janzen has won numerous poetry prizes and received a teaching award for innovation at the University of California, Los Angeles. Rhoda describes art as a visceral experience, much needed in a cerebral world.

Ray Kurzweil, scientist, author, and entrepreneur, is the inventor of the first computer music keyboard. Ray believes that nonbiological entities will eventually contribute significantly to all forms of art and even create new ones.

Dr. Todd Siler is an artist whose science-based multimedia works are in major museums and numerous collections worldwide. Todd talks about art as immersion without boundaries and about the observer as an integral part of the work.

ROBERT: Bob, you became director of the Eastman School of Music at the young age of thirty-seven, as a tenured professor from MIT [Massachusetts Institute of Technology]; you've been chief executive of the New England Conservatory. You've traveled throughout the world of music. How can music so powerfully affect human emotion?

BOB: There is, of course, concert music, to which I've dedicated my life, but I'm going to tell you a story that doesn't have to do with music you hear in a concert hall. Bishop Matthew Clark of Rochester told this story, at the dedication of an organ in a Catholic church in his diocese. He spoke about the recent death of his mother. The bishop has three brothers—two of them priests—and four sisters. They were all gathered around the bedside of their eighty-nine-year-old mother, who was in great pain and dying of cancer. They'd given her the last rites, and they all prayed that she wouldn't linger. And their mother would not die. She remained in great pain. The more they prayed, the more nothing seemed to happen. And finally the oldest sister said, "Let's sing some of the songs she taught us when we were children." Holding hands around her bed, they began with "You Are My Sunshine." By the end of the first verse, her breathing had become more regular and relaxed, and by the end of the second verse she had died. These seven people, looking to the heavens, had just found out how powerful a force music can be. And the bishop said, "Don't misuse music."

ROBERT: Todd Boyd—we're honored to have two Todds with us today—you've been called one of the new public intellectuals on matters of race, class, and gender. How do music and art contribute to a common culture in America?

TODD BOYD: If you look closely back over the twentieth century, you'll find commonalities in music and other forms of culture that you may not find in social or political areas of life. A recent example would be rap music and hip-hop culture, which, interestingly enough, together constitute one of the few movements in our society that includes a broad cross-section of the people who make up the fabric of America. And if you go beyond America's shores, you'll find that this phenomenon has saturated the globe. That you can start from something as small as a song, or an album, and connect people throughout the world is strong testimony to what music and culture can do to create community at a higher level.

ROBERT: Ray, you've written two pathbreaking books—*The Age of Intelligent Machines* some years ago, and more recently, *The Age of Spiritual Machines: When Computers Exceed Human Intelligence.* Do you see computers moving in an artistic direction?

RAY: Computers today are better than people expect in terms of music and art. There's [University of California, Santa Cruz, professor of music] David Cope's Experiments in Musical Intelligence computer program [a program that generates new compositions in the styles of various composers, among them Bach, Mozart, Prokofiev, and Scott Joplin]. The British abstract artist Harold Cohen has developed a robotic painter named Aaron, which actually does pretty interesting work. Harold signs his own name to Aaron's drawings, but Aaron has not been programmed to complain. And I think there's a message there—that Aaron is really an expression of Harold Cohen's human intelligence, which he expresses through this program that in turn creates art. That's where we are today.

ROBERT: Will computers ever be able to create original works of music and art that will move human beings? Will they be proficient to the same degree as, say, Deep Blue, the computer that beat the world chess champion a few years ago?

RAY: Computers today are amplifying our human intelligence, providing new canvases, new tools. But computers—or, as I'd prefer to say, nonbiological forms of intelligence—are going to become more and more powerful. We're going to be able to replicate human intelligence by scanning it, understanding it, and reinstantiating it in new media. So we will meet entities in the twenty-first century that are very human and can express and respond appropriately to human emotion—which is really the ultimate expression of our intelligence. And music, art, and culture are perhaps the ultimate

> *Computers today are amplifying our human intelligence, providing new canvases, new tools.*

expression of our emotion. And I'd say that within thirty years or so nonbiological entities will have their own artistic reputations and will be creating paintings and music and other forms of art, too, such as virtual-reality environments.

ROBERT: I hope they don't replace Rhoda too quickly. Rhoda, you're a well-known poet who specializes in the nature of aesthetics. What is it about music and art that moves us so deeply, that gets inside us and ties our stomach in knots?

RHODA: Well, for every respondent it's different. I'm going to answer personally. I like listening to music, looking at art, and reading poetry so much because it gives me something that I don't get in the course of my regular life. My regular life is all about responding to analytical forms, using my mind, consciously engaging on

> *. . . when I'm listening to music or reading poetry, I'm being invited to respond at a visceral level, with my whole body.*

an intellectual level. But when I'm listening to music or reading poetry, I'm being invited to respond at a visceral level, with my whole body. And it creates a space for me that's completely unlike anything I experience elsewhere. It gives me an opportunity to step away from the didactic messages that we're surrounded with. I mean, we're bombarded with messages about morality, civility, culture, race, and so forth, and we're asked to think about those things. And they're important. But poetry and music and art give us more; they invite us to respond sensually and viscerally.

ROBERT: Todd Siler, you're an important artist whose starkly original works project strong emotions. You were the first visual artist to receive a doctorate from MIT, where, I should disclose, we met twenty years ago, when I was a research affiliate in brain science and you were in my class. What do you feel when you create? Do your emotions depend upon the medium?

TODD SILER: When I get involved in the installations and things I build that involve painting, drawing, video, and other kinds of media, I don't draw any boundaries between them. It's a complete immersion.

ROBERT: What's the relationship between the objects you create and the observers who see them?

TODD SILER: I like to break down that distinction; I want the observer to literally become part of my art. In fact, I may finish the work, but

---

> ### I want the observer to literally become part of my art.

---

it remains unfinished. It's completed by the constant interpretations and revisits that people have when they come to it, from all different disciplines, backgrounds, and experiences. My work tries to represent the nature of the thought process, as I studied it, experienced it. I'm not trying to paint thought, but I'm trying to paint the process of thought. So I love it when people begin to map their world onto my artwork. That's what completes it.

ROBERT: Does interaction with observers ever change your work?

TODD SILER: Very much so. All the time, I discover more things about a piece—when children approach it with openness, when colleagues approach it from a scholarly perspective. I welcome every kind of approach. Interaction is a way of journeying into the greatest mystery that we have—human thought—and not worrying whether it's going to be interpreted as you see it but rather inviting all kinds of interpretations.

ROBERT: Bob, you're a first-class pianist as well as a top administrator. What does performing feel like?

BOB: A successful performance depends upon a variety of elements. First is preparation. Are you fully in charge of what's going on? Do you know the material really well, so that you don't have to worry about it? Are you well rested? Your body can't do what your mind tells it to if you're not. Most important, many musicians suffer from terrible stage fright. The way to keep that from happening is to make sure that you're not playing for stakes that are too high: that if I don't play this piece really beautifully—

ROBERT: —I won't eat.

BOB: Well, "I won't eat" is the least of it. If you

can get rid of all extraneous matters and play directly to the audience—as though you're playing for a particular person in the third row,

---

. . . get rid of all extraneous matters and play directly to the audience . . .

---

say—it can be very successful. And enormously exhilarating.

RAY: There's an aspect of computer technology that gets to the heart of what computers can do today for the arts—which is to amplify our abilities and bring the tools to make art and music to more people. My father was a composer. He died in 1970, and in the 1960s, when he wanted to hear his multi-instrumental compositions, he had to raise money, bring a whole orchestra together, hand-write and mimeograph the scores. Finally, he'd hear his composition. And God forbid he didn't like it—then he'd have to start all over again, raise more money, and so forth. Now music students in any conservatory, or in their own apartments, can hear a multi-instrumental composition and change it as easily as you rewrite a letter on your word processor. And while they will still want to hear it performed by a real orchestra, they can create music as never before. Computers provide a whole new canvas for the arts. Also, synthesizers provide new sounds, which were impossible before.

BOB: Computers provide a whole new basis for musical literacy. You can [compose] without worrying about how many sharps there are in E major.

ROBERT: Ray's music keyboards have been one of the major forces expanding the range of music. Many people are very grateful for these new worlds that have opened to them.

RAY: That's the thrill of being an inventor—moving from equations on a blackboard to actually affecting people's lives. We get lots of feedback from musicians who, with this new technology, create forms of music that weren't feasible before.

ROBERT: Todd Boyd, you specialize in the critical analysis of motion pictures and popular culture. How significant is film as an art form?

TODD BOYD: Motion pictures certainly play a powerful role in all our lives—particularly with the advent of the VCR which transformed movies by bringing them into the American home. And just as with any other art form, there are a few classics—I often refer to [Francis Ford] Coppola's *The Godfather* and *Godfather II* as a kind of quintessential text of the latter half of the twentieth century. Those films, at some level, can speak to all of us. The particular story may not be exactly like everyone's, but you can find something there about family, about the struggle to integrate into mainstream America. You can study these films and take them apart; not only are they fascinating, they're fulfilling. I often set up a screening for myself on Sunday afternoons, when I have the time to watch all six hours of *The Godfather* and *Godfather II*, with a bottle of Bordeaux and a nice cigar, and take it all in at the sensory level.

ROBERT: *Godfather III* didn't have the same quality?

TODD BOYD: *Godfather III* came out seventeen years later and had a whole different scenario—but Coppola needed the money.

RHODA: Do you feel that the accessibility of film is putting other genres, like poetry and music, into the background?

TODD BOYD: I think so, because film is now so prevalent. When I was teaching in Stockholm, I was amazed how much knowledge the Swedish people had of America, even those who

---

Film definitely does overshadow other areas of culture . . .

---

hadn't traveled very much. The reason was that they had watched so many American films. So imagine the impact here in America. We have a common language now. Even if you aren't a moviegoer, it's in the popular dialogue. Film definitely does overshadow other areas of culture—music, poetry, what have you—because, at some level, film contains them all.

RAY: Film and TV have certainly empowered the arts, but what has really empowered the arts is the World Wide Web. I have artist friends who used to make four or five thousand dollars a year, and now they're doing extremely well. There's a tremendous explosion of demand for graphic arts on the Web. The same is true of music, film, video, writing, even poetry. We need content that's exciting and creates this sense of transcendence. There's a tremendous demand for content now.

ROBERT: Todd Siler, give us a sense of your art—I'm a great fan. What do you do? What do you see? What do you want to accomplish?

TODD SILER: My world is about the synthesis of different disciplines, and the only way I know

how to express it is by using lots of different media. Sometimes I wish I were a filmmaker, because they get to use all those good things—animation and so on. My journey began when I became fascinated with how the brain puts ideas and information together, and I approach my work from both the arts and the sciences, from both sets of inquiry. And my search, really, has been about helping people understand their own creative process—not in a didactic way, but experientially. You literally have to go in and feel the rapture, feel the pain, feel a range of emotions—and allow yourself to understand the process from your own perspective, not from mine. I consider my works just as creative catalysts to get people going. And often I have to invent new technologies to create these works—like one installation I did, for example, which was twelve feet high and a hundred feet long and involved many different kinds of printing processes.*

ROBERT: In some of your installations, you have people moving through, as if the people become part of the installation.

TODD SILER: Yes, absolutely. They're very much part of that mental and physical space. I try to break the distinction down, literally, by setting up conditions for a kind of magic, for people to catch themselves in their own reverie. Even a month later, they begin to understand that all the different elements of the creative process were at work there—from confusion to clarity, a full range of things. Everything, in a way, is meant to prompt viewers to examine their own experience. That's where my art comes back full circle.

---

*Todd Siler's art work appears on the back jacket of the book and on the opening page of each Part.

ROBERT: Is confusion a legitimate emotion you want to trigger in us mortals?

TODD SILER: Ah, no—but I think ambiguity is. There's enormous power in ambiguity. People try to edit it out of the creative process. I welcome it. I think there are moments when you need enormous chaos, and sometimes, in preparing for presentations, I absorb an overload of information and allow myself to literally fail—and then I find the order in the chaos, which enables the installation to live. This is part of the creative process and how it unfolds.

BOB: Doesn't a lot of that have to do with pattern recognition? Certainly it does in music, which unfolds in patterns. Isn't it important for kids to learn pattern recognition at an early age?

RAY: Pattern recognition is based on mastering chaos. Our earlier computers were based on structured rules, and that's why they were so formulaic and predictable and brittle. We're learning that we need to build machines in a different way to master self-organizing, complex, chaotic processing, which is really how the human brain works.

BOB: With respect to music, you can see what a poor job we're doing nationally with pattern recognition. Anytime you go to a restaurant where the staff sings "Happy Birthday" to the honoree of the day, almost none of the waiters and waitresses can hit the right notes—just going up an octave is practically impossible.

ROBERT: Certainly for me it is.

TODD SILER: I recently did a collaboration where, for the first time in my life, a musician completed my art by composing and performing a dedicated piece. The music and the textures and the layers were so integrated that I saw the seamlessness of all those different connections and relationships—I was so moved I was crying. That's the magic of emotion and ambiguity . . . all that.

ROBERT: What contributions do you think the arts make to human development?

TODD SILER: Billions of contributions, and that's not hyperbole. James Baldwin summed it up eloquently: The purpose of art is to lay bare the questions that have been concealed by the answers. And when you think of all the answers we give one another, imagine how many questions become hidden; so this is the arts' greatest contribution—to enable us to deepen the inquiry, to enrich the questions, to extend the inner journey we make in attempting to understand our own inner world and how it connects to other worlds.

BOB: Several years ago I had the privilege of chairing an international commission on the future of the principal music school in Finland, the Sibelius Academy. I learned at that time that in a country of five million people, with high rates of alcoholism and suicide and seventeen-percent unemployment, there were a hundred and fifty music schools. None of the musicians were unemployed, and why? Because the country cares deeply about music. This is the kind of society we're looking for; music and the arts bring Finland together.

TODD BOYD: I want to follow up on what Todd [Siler] said about art laying bare the questions but take it someplace a little different. I remember hearing Miles Davis talk about how he structured a trumpet solo after watching a Sugar Ray Robinson boxing match. Sugar Ray was known as a master of style—you know, he would walk into the ring wearing two robes, and he'd take off the outer robe and underneath would be this white silk robe. It was all about presentation and performance. But Miles focused specifically on how Sugar Ray, in the first round of a fight, would set traps for his opponent without springing them. And then he'd come back in the second round and spring one of those traps, and the fight, of course, would be over. And Miles took that idea and applied it to his solo, so at the beginning of the solo there are all these traps set, and in the second half of the solo, he's springing the trap. So you can flow between those two disparate forms and find that sort of inspiration. Art really does lay bare the questions, and the questions can become much more interesting than the answers sometimes.

RAY: What's so interesting is that Miles was doing a form of boxing and Sugar Ray a form of music. A fascinating exchange and synthesis.

ROBERT: It's the resonance of great talent. Rhoda, you've unified art forms with a wonderful poem about a piece of art.

RHODA: It fits very well into this discussion, in the sense that it's a piece of art that responds to another piece of art. To give you some background: I was in the J. Paul Getty Museum looking at an exhibit of twelfth-century sacramentaries. These are liturgical books, and they were displayed under glass, open. And in these books the first letter on each page was enlarged and beautifully decorated, with flowers, vines, animals; and sometimes the initial was inhabited by human figures. These initials were illustrative of the semantic; that is, they were in some way connected to the message on the page. And they were pictorializing and literaliz-

ing the language. And what promoted my poem was an inhabited "D"—a large capital D inhabited by a tiny male figure. It was a little man with one foot inside the D and one foot outside the D, just sort of taking a tentative step onto the page. And when I saw it, I knew this was poem material, this was going to be a poem for me. I was immediately struck by the possibilities implicit in the idea of language as symbolic shelter. I mean, the little man looked as if he were leaving a little D house. In this poem, the speaker is speaking to the little man who is leaving the D.

Like a decorous swimmer you test
the world outside your D. Is language
then so easy to bear? Your D shells

your narrow shoulders, poised for retreat
in case the sentence into which you
have maneuvered is tiresome or dangerous.

How do you design your view, with its *illu-
    minare*
so deucedly gold? That tendril of filigree
tickling your hat? A sacramentary denizen,

devotee of diffidence, must commence some
    praise
of Christ, your neighbor in the word. Or is
your interior too fretted with script,

damask drapes, damson drawing room?
You men of letters remind me it's time
to pay my calls, to entertain, to correspond

devoutly with those whose residence you recall.
Careful, *piccolino,* the nobleman with heavy
plume and shadowed chin would love to invite

you out, himself in. Then where would you
    be—
homeless? Damnified, or keeping house
with Lord of Arguments, who seeks, I hear,

a D for personal definition? What is
your mission, if you must depart? At least
look up. Your domestic D is half a world

of comfort and could attract difficulty. Perhaps you venture out simply to return to depth as some in recent centuries

shore pages in foam, the waves' declension
dreams, dreaming, dreamt, where no traveler
speaks our salt. Desiccate, unlettered land.

TODD SILER: That's beautiful; it's the same affect I try to engender in my art.

ROBERT: Ray, from your pioneering vision applying computer technology to generate music, what can we learn about the nature of human intelligence and its relationship to art?

RAY: The history of trying to emulate human intelligence through computers has been surprising. Even early computers were able to do mathematics problems that leading mathematicians had done, diagnose disease, and the like, but what has been very difficult, and what we still can't do, is master human emotion [replicate it in a computer], just to [give a computer the capacity to] understand a poem or respond to a piece of music [meaningfully]. We're really finding that the arts, which is a sort of transcendent expression of human emotion, represent the cutting edge of human intelligence. It will be the most difficult aspect of our intelligence to re-create [nonbiologically]. But in the process of trying to do that [i.e., develop profound artificial intelligence], we're learning some of the underlying elements and structure of art that are behind the inspiration.

ROBERT: And what does that process tell you about the human emotional response to art?

RAY: Well, it's clear that human emotion is the most subtle, most sublime, most complex, deepest aspect of human intelligence, and the hardest aspect to model fully in nonbiological systems.

ROBERT: Bob, let's get to education, because it enables appreciation of music and art. You've been a great proponent of bringing music education to everyone in America, not just to the elite. Why is this important?

BOB: It's important to musicians, for obvious reasons, but music education is important to humanity—not just America—because of the message music brings, which is a liberating one. All kinds of music can be for all kinds of people. There's a wonderful young string quartet from the Eastman School called the Ying Quartet, which spent two years in residence in a little town named Jessup, Iowa, and turned this town of corn and hog farmers into music lovers and string players. At their last concert in a gymnasium, a thousand people came—the population of Jessup is only two thousand. When the quartet members were invited to testify on Capitol Hill at the reauthorization hearing for the National Endowment for the Arts, twelve farmers came along, each at his own expense, to tell Congress what an important force this was for their town.

ROBERT: Todd Boyd, can music play a role in promoting racial harmony and bringing America together?

TODD BOYD: It certainly does that, though historically it has been quite divisive as well. Music has probably erected as many barriers as it has broken down. But in my mind the most significant American music is jazz, and this is a music that clearly emanates from an African-American cultural perspective. Jazz is high art at this point, and it's truly fascinating how for so many years it has been able to cut across boundaries in America and throughout the world. We're now seeing the same sort of thing with hip-hop, which is attracting very broad audiences. I was in Japan and happened upon a hip-hop club in which all the people were Japanese, none spoke any English, but they knew every word of Biggie Smalls' "Big Papa." And they could rap it just as if they'd lived in America all their lives. There's something about art—music, film, and other forms—that transcends social and national barriers, and when people encounter these things they tend to put aside some of the baggage they'd otherwise be carrying.

BOB: A big question with respect to the future of jazz is whether it should now be essentially a classical form, as invented in the 1920s and 1930s, or whether it should continue to grow.

TODD BOYD: I don't think jazz could ever be classical in the traditional sense, because the root of jazz, of course, is improvisation. And therefore it's constantly growing, constantly changing—and the minute you try to, say, put it under glass, then problems come about. That's what happened in the 1970s, and then in the 1980s there was a resurgence, when people realized that you couldn't treat jazz like a precious art object—you had to engage it for it to grow.

BOB: Like the rest of art, jazz must be growing, changing, and evolving.

TODD BOYD: Exactly.

BOB: At the New England Conservatory of Music, for the past twenty-five years, there's been an annual event called the Gospel Jubilee—lots of gospel music. The hall is packed with an audience largely, but not exclusively, African-American. At the last concert, on my left were an African-American from the conservatory and her boyfriend, and on my right were two Russian immigrants—ladies in their mid-eighties. And the Russian ladies asked me, "What is this music?" And I said, "Well, this expresses something of the way in which African-Americans learned to live with pain during the days of slavery. This music represents a way of moving forward despite lots of sadness, and it involves a kind of responsive procedure with the audience. If you want to get into it, why don't you start singing right off, 'Amen' and 'Hallelujah,' with everybody else?" They did, and at the end of the evening they said, "You know, this concert made us feel like real Americans for the first time."

TODD BOYD: The idea that gospel music would be the quintessential American experience for them speaks a lot about its power.

ROBERT: And the ability of music to unify a culture. Let's look forward a hundred years. Will music and art be more or less important in society?

BOB: It depends on how we proceed with the education of young musicians. If they believe that music is for everybody, and that everybody needs to be involved in it, whether or not they become Paganinis or Heifitzes in the long run, then we'll have a vibrant culture and music will serve as a force to unify us all. If not, it'll be just the way it is now.

ROBERT: We wouldn't want too many Paganinis.

TODD BOYD: Music and art, for me, are always organic. As long as there's the need and desire to create, there will always be art forms, and art will continue to be significant, because this is how people throughout history have expressed themselves. And that's the beauty of it—there's no way we can restrain this organic process as it takes place.

TODD SILER: The arts are going to be central to tapping and developing human potential. People are going to realize the enormous power of art to liberate and innovate the human spirit.

RHODA: We usually talk about the future in terms of our achievements in science, but I think we're going to have a resurgence in the fine arts in the coming decades. And I hope that that will continue, including the development of new art forms, such as the screenplay.

RAY: As the technologist on the panel, I think society is going to be very different a hundred years from now. We'll have overcome our material needs and we'll have literally expanded our minds by merging with very intelligent nonbiological entities. And what we're going to do is create art. Music will take on different forms. We'll have new art forms, like virtual-reality environments, and we're going to experience new forms of knowledge with our expanded mental faculties.

ROBERT: CONCLUDING COMMENT

Great music and art, as we feel the emotion and sense the insight, penetrates our psyches and marks us as human beings. But what is "great art"? The fact is that "greatness" has little to do with it: what counts is the enjoyment, the vision, the soaring of emotion. "Great" is not relevant, because it's almost impossible to decide what is great. Some say that great music or art must improve with age—that the marketplace of ideas, given sufficient time, will sift the diamonds from the dirt. But fads are common, and rediscovered works can speak with surprising freshness. So it's up to each generation, and history, to say what endures. Education in music and art should focus on appreciation as well as performance, and not on an academic analysis. Above all, that kind of education must be open to everyone; art and music are not to be limited to society's elite. An aesthetic education, widespread and well-structured, can become a powerful social equalizer. There's no better way to civilize and unify our society. But if you feel the emotion and sense the insight, if the piece lifts and ennobles the spirit, that's enough to make the case for now. Such exhilaration is already closer to truth.

OUTTAKES

RHODA: *If you write a poem, your life really does mean something.*

TODD SILER: *Art is something you brood about for hundreds of hours.*

ROBERT: *We'll do a show a hundred years from now, sit together, and see what we sing.*

RAY: *We won't have to be together in the same physical place.*

BOB: *Considering it's so late in the afternoon, I thought we were pretty good.*

PART FOUR

TECHNOLOGY & SOCIETY

Seeing States of Matter. (Courtesy of Todd Siler.)

CHAPTER 17

New Communities for the New Millennium?

The word "community" may sound pleasantly archaic, a remnant of an idyllic past. Community was where we put down roots, celebrating common heritage and shared beliefs. But today our roots are like radio waves, planted anywhere and beaming everywhere. And so the concept of community is changing. What is a community? It's more where your mind connects than where your body resides. We have ethnic communities with special customs, spiritual communities with special visions, scientific communities with special languages, and online communities where no one has ever heard a voice, much less seen a face. But ironically, in an age of instant information, community is more relevant than ever—and its expanded boundaries, greater diversity, and subtle powers may surprise you. New communities are more than your friendly neighborhood or favorite chat room. They have spread across the planet, erasing time, distance, and national borders. We asked five prominent thinkers to describe the communities of tomorrow. Each has enhanced the meaning of community, and they bring a rich variety of perspectives.

PARTICIPANTS

Bruce Chapman, a former director of the United States Census Bureau, is the founder and president of the Discovery Institute, a Seattle-based public policy center that promotes representative government, free markets, and individual liberties. Bruce talks about how shared obligations generate connectedness and why old neighborhoods are reviving.

Barbara Marx Hubbard, the author of *Conscious Evolution: Awakening the Power of Our Social Potential,* is an inventive futurist, citizen diplomat, and social architect. She envisions a global community in which people work together to construct an improved world.

Saru Jayaraman, a law student at Yale, is the national founder of WYSE (Women and Youth Supporting Each other), a group that empowers young inner-city girls. While an undergraduate at the University of California, Los Angeles, Saru was recognized as one of the top three students in the nation.

Dr. John McWhorter is a professor of linguistics at the University of California, Berkeley, where he is an outspoken social critic. John is the author of *The Word on the Street: Fact and Fable About American English,* and he discusses the power of language to define and differentiate communities.

Dr. Neil de Grasse Tyson, an astrophysicist at Princeton University, is the director of the Hayden Planetarium of the American Museum of Natural History, in New York. Neil offers a broader-than-usual definition of the scientific community.

ROBERT: Bruce, you've had a full career in public policy, from writer and publisher to member of Ronald Reagan's White House staff and diplomat. Now, as president of the Discovery Institute, you're involved with diverse communities. As you look to the future, how do you see this diversity playing out?

BRUCE: With the technological revolution that one of our fellows, George Gilder, has written so much about, we're going to see new forms of community developing. There will be many niche communities, but along with this fragmentation you're also going to see a return to the old kinds of communities and a sense of neighborhood—the place where your body resides, to use the term you used. And we're going to find people paying more attention to how to revive those kinds of communities.

ROBERT: You look at communities from regional to religious, cultural to civic.

BRUCE: Exactly. We're talking about relationships among people and the sense of obligation and connectedness that results.

ROBERT: Neil, as an astrophysicist, you deal with galactic communities, but tell us about the scientific community here on Earth.

NEIL: I like to think of the scientific community as not simply those who practice science but those who can appreciate science at its more fundamental levels. I'll give you a perfect example. It's sometimes said that the state lottery system is a tax on those who never did well in mathematics. A scientifically literate community consists of people who know what scientific issues are important and can think coherently and collectively about them. And in that sense, we create a scientific community that pervades society.

ROBERT: So the scientific community should be pandemic, embracing everyone?

NEIL: Of course, because it's not my science or your science. Science describes the nature of the world around us, and no one has a monopoly on it. Yes, there are a few people who know it better than others, but the same laws of physics apply to me as apply to you, and there's no reason why

I should hold all the reins. Science is for everyone.

ROBERT: John, I'm trying to figure out how many different communities you belong to. You're a professor at a major university, you're a linguist, a musician, a historian, an American, an African-American, a social commentator, a critic—forgive me if I've left anything out. Focus on how language can unify and differentiate communities.

JOHN: Language is ever-changing; it just has to be. And one of the indexes of a community—or a group of people intimately connected—is that it will have its own version of whatever the reigning language is. You can expect of a group of people who feel unified among themselves that they will have ways of speaking that are different from everyone else's. That's true not only in America but everywhere in the world. And so one index of a community's feeling of not being a part of the greater community is the extent to which their speech differs from that which is considered mainstream.

ROBERT: Does that create social fragmentation?

JOHN: Often it does, yes. You can think of linguistic differences—although in themselves fine, harmless, and often wonderful—as indexes of fragmentation. If people are speaking in a very different way, it most likely means that there's a social problem—or at best they're separate but peaceably coexisting.

ROBERT: Saru, you call yourself a nonviolent revolutionary. After you graduate with advanced degrees—in public policy from Harvard and in law from Yale—you plan to go into social activism. Tell us about WYSE, the organization

you created, and how it helps redefine a sense of community.

SARU: WYSE works with young women, age twelve to fourteen, in disadvantaged communities across the country and provides them with the resources, information, and support to help them make responsible decisions, create community change, and then go on and become leaders in their communities. WYSE gives young women the tools to think critically, deconstruct the images that are coming at them, and counter pressures from a variety of sources—peers, parents, school, society.

ROBERT: How do you teach young people to think critically? It's an unusual task.

SARU: It's all about teaching them to ask the right questions and getting them to express themselves, and also about giving them new lenses through which to view the world—lenses such as feminism, social power dynamics, classism, those kinds of things. But what I've seen increasingly with these young women—and with young people in general—is that because they don't feel part of a larger American community they've sometimes gone on to create their own alternative communities.

ROBERT: For this show, you'll promise to remain nonviolent?

SARU: I promise.

ROBERT: Barbara, tell us of your transformation from a mother of five into a pioneer of global consciousness.

BARBARA: My own movement in this direction came when the United States dropped the bomb on Japan. I had always thought we were making progress by knowing more, but now I suddenly saw that we could kill ourselves by knowing more. So I asked, What's good in all this power of science, technology, industry? Where are the positive images of the future in our new power? There weren't any. We had images of destruction and Armageddon—very mystical images, like the New Jerusalem. But where was the human race going? When I was twenty-one, my father took me to visit President Eisenhower, and I asked him, "Mr. President, what is the purpose of all our power that's good?" And I'll never forget his answer. He shook his head and said, "I have no idea." I decided to make a lifelong search for an image of the future based on real power that would be good. And this has led me to the view that something of huge importance is happening through evolution, through unconscious natural selection.

ROBERT: And now we're involved in the evolutionary process ourselves?

BARBARA: Yes, we're consciously involved. When humanity understood $E = mc^2$ from Einstein, we made a bomb. Now that humanity is beginning to understand our own genetic code, we can make monsters or we can cure diseases and extend our life span. So we have to become conscious and ethical about how we use our power. My work is to show people that if we use our power well, we can have an unlimited future.

ROBERT: How does conscious evolution—your hallmark—enrich the sense of community?

BARBARA: Very deeply. First, it gives all human beings, wherever they are, a sense that there's meaning to the struggle—that human existence isn't just a mistake, that the human race has great potential. Second, it means that every human being has a personal potential. So if you're frustrated and upset in your world, that's the universe evolving through you. I've conducted twenty-five conferences—called SYCON, for Synergistic Convergence—where a cross section of the human species was represented: young kids, welfare mothers, ambassadors, former criminals, Nobel Prize–winning scientists. We asked all of them, What do you want to create? What are your needs? What are your resources? And they had to listen to one another on such topics as education, the environment. We took down walls, searched for common goals, matched resources with needs. We used diversity to lead toward synergy.

BRUCE: I'm troubled by the use of the term "evolution" in describing the development of communities, because I think evolution itself is coming into a period of great redefinition and even challenge. People like Michael Behe and William Dembski in the so-called intelligent-design movement are challenging the whole concept of Darwinian evolution. As a result, we may think very differently about what it means to be part of a community. This is not a problem of science but of the applications of science. If our world is totally materialist, if we are only the products of evolution, then we think one way about what it means to be human—we come up with justifications for the consequences of our action. For example, we start to explain problems in law enforcement based on genetic disposition.

ROBERT: Are you criticizing such applications of science?

BRUCE: Yes. It robs us of part of our humanity, because it robs us of responsibility. But if the term "intelligent design" has meaning, we'll come up with attitudes different from those we had in the twentieth century.

ROBERT: Do you respect the capabilities of science?

BRUCE: I think we need a debate about it, a civil discussion. We ought to reflect on the applications of evolution to our politics and our social order.

NEIL: The social order wasn't perfect before Darwinian evolution.

BRUCE: Of course not.

NEIL: Why blame our social problems on evolution? Surely nations laid siege to other nations before Darwin was ever born.

BRUCE: It has nothing to do with that. It has to do with how we see the world in which we live today and whether or not it's a materialist world. Now, we're talking about new communities. Is evolution going to be guided, and is technology going to take over the process, as Ray Kurzweil [see Chapters 11, 12, and 16] says? Then we'd have a very different world than we would if the computer, as George Gilder says, is "the triumph of mind over matter."

ROBERT: Your litmus test seems to the ultimate nature of human beings, whether random accident of evolution or purposeful result of intelligent design.

BRUCE: The question has to do with how you see human beings, and whether or not there's a scientific basis—

JOHN: Now, Michael Behe's point is about God.

BRUCE: No, it's not, actually.

JOHN: Well, yes it is. The idea of Behe's book [*Darwin's Black Box: The Biochemical Challenge to Evolution*] is that Darwinian evolution is a nice idea but that some things [biochemical complexity] can be explained only as having been created by a higher power. I found it a very interesting book. But are you by any chance saying that one can't have proper ethics and communities without religion or God? I just want to see if that's your point.

BRUCE: I think you can have an ethical order without God—there are examples throughout history, such as the Stoics. But what the intelligent-design movement is really saying is that it looks like there is a design in the universe. And if that's the case, then an ethical order should be based on that idea, with very different consequences for how you regard people.

JOHN: A design by God?

BRUCE: It doesn't describe what the designer might be, just states the likelihood of a design.

BARBARA: I wanted to say that the sense in which I mean evolution—

BRUCE: I know. It's not the narrow definition of mechanistic Darwinian evolution.

BARBARA: I got it from Teilhard de Chardin—the idea that there is a process of creation leading to higher complexity and greater consciousness and freedom. Nobody knows precisely how that design got there, but I think there's certainly the presence of design.

BRUCE: That's a very good distinction. I'm glad you made it.

ROBERT: Let's get into the workings of the scientific community. Neil, how do scientists—astronomers, physicists, biologists—think? How does that community work together?

NEIL: Very differently from the rest of society. We're trained to be problem solvers. We're taught to trim the fat off the questions, get to the dewdrop essence of what matters, and focus our analysis on that. And as you get nearer, maybe there's more and more fat to be trimmed. So you narrow your questions, to bring yourself closer to truth of how the universe works—

ROBERT: —and to see holes in your own hypotheses.

NEIL: Exactly. We don't always know whether the questions we ask are the ones that will lead to the answers, but I can tell you that every question that was the right question led to an answer that was testable and created a deeper sense of world order. We can go way back to Copernicus, who put the sun back into the center of the solar system, producing an answer that completely changed how humans view themselves in the big picture. And so, in fact, Darwin wasn't the first; he was just part of this whole sequence that has, over time, redefined what it is to be human on this earth, in this solar system, in this galaxy, in this universe.

ROBERT: This is a rather idealized picture. Peel away at the onion. What really happens when scientists get together? What kinds of hierarchies, pecking orders, are there?

NEIL: You want the dirty laundry. Well, the laundry isn't as dirty as the stereotype suggests. Because ultimately it's your knowledge base, and your ability to figure out solutions to problems, that wins arguments. It's not how loud you

are, or how persuasive, or whether you won debating contests in your day, because in the end you answer to nature. Nature is the ultimate adjudicator of all that we do. So we are humble

---

. . . in the end you answer to nature.

---

in the presence of nature, which can send us back to the drawing board at any moment.

ROBERT: Is science useful in unifying humanity?

NEIL: Yes, because it's one universe. It's our universe. When I tell people about the galaxy, I say, "It's not my galaxy, it's our galaxy." And people want a sense of belonging. I can tell you that comets streaking through the sky have a chemical composition that's identical to what you've got in your body. To me, that's empowering. We are all star dust. So "community" is not just your own little neighborhood—with all deference to what communities were in the 1950s. "Community" is a sense of what your place is in the universe. I know it sounds pie-in-the-sky, but this is what flows through my veins every time I contemplate problems in astronomy.

SARU: But that feeling in part rests on whether you believe that you have an equal stake in the universe along with everybody else—that everybody is a part of the same universal community. You have to have some sense of belonging. And I just don't think that a large percentage of America feels that way.

NEIL: Look at the Hubble Space Telescope—beautiful pictures making the cover of *Time* magazine. It's mostly taxpayers' money paying for that. I see people gathering around, asking questions about what Hubble is seeing—

SARU: Which people, though?

JOHN: The people who don't gather around feel disincluded from society. But it doesn't have to be that way. The people you're talking about, Saru, could take delight in seeing pictures of, say, Mars, despite the inequities—

SARU: I'm sure.

JOHN: The fact that they don't is—

SARU: —education! If education were more equal—

BARBARA: It may be that some of them do. I'll never forget meeting with gang leaders in a community-based SYCON in Los Angeles. I walked in there, and the heads of the gangs asked me, "What's the difference between you

---

. . . I think the human species is aiming toward universal life together.

---

and the rest of the social workers?" They were scornful of me. And I said, "Well, my difference is that I think the human species is aiming toward universal life together. I think we're going to explore space, for instance." And a Mexican-American came up to me and said, "My people have always known that." And the black leaders loved the idea that there was something beyond the inner city. And I do

believe—it's in the biochemistry of our brains—that we are the universe awakening.

NEIL: It was that picture of Earth from space that changed how we thought of Earth. There were no national boundaries, just continents. Humanity shifted to another level, and we started seeing this delicate fragile planet, this spaceship Earth, moving through space.

SARU: That's true. I'm not saying that young people aren't interested in science and technology. If they were taught about these things, and provided with this information, they'd be deeply interested.

ROBERT: That's the challenge.

SARU: But I don't think it would move them any closer to a sense of commonality with those who oppress them, unless those who oppress them—the haves—admit that these young inner-city people are a part of the universe as well.

ROBERT: John, take us back to language and its relationship to culture.

JOHN: The development of a different form of the dominant language is part of the formation of a different culture. It goes along with it; it's something you'd expect. For example, in this country, even African-Americans who have several degrees, who have spent a lot of time with white people, who are a part of the general society, almost always—ninety-nine percent of the time—have what we don't call, but in fact is, a black accent. There is such a thing as sounding black. It's not a matter of slang, it's not a matter of sentence structure, it's just a matter of sound. You can generally tell on the radio—say, on National Public Radio—when someone is black.

And except in rare cases—like Neil and me—African-Americans do not sound like, for example, you, Robert. That's just a fact. And the reason is that there's always been a feeling among people in the black community, regardless of their socioeconomic level, of a certain separation, and other issues that we all know

The development of a different form of the dominant language is part of the formation of a different culture.

quite a bit about. So if there's a community feeling, then there's probably a community language. It's true in Bavaria; it's true in New Guinea. It's also true in scientific communities; scientists use a different form of language. So do chefs; so do mechanics. Language is an index of community.

ROBERT: Neil, scientific communities, African-American communities—I turn to you.

NEIL: I want to distinguish between word choice and language differences. Just because some jargon uses categories of words that aren't common, I don't think that's necessarily a different way of communicating. In the scientific community, language is introduced to provide a level of precision that everyday English does not allow, and often this language becomes stilted. In astrophysics, though, we have no such problems: big red stars, for example, are called red giants. The beginning of the universe? The Big Bang. Our language was never separatist, not deliberately. The universe is complicated enough; why complicate it more? We use com-

mon, ordinary language. Our vocabulary comes from the general public.

BRUCE: Neil, I couldn't read an astrophysics paper.

NEIL: No, but you could pick up the term "red giant." Other matters are complicated, but the term itself is clear.

ROBERT: But doesn't the fact that we have a scientific class create a new elite, so that knowledge becomes the great divide of society? It used to be money and class—now it's knowledge.

NEIL: It's unfortunate, but that's the reality, and it will continue. It's a battle between the knows and the know-nots.

BRUCE: Educators realize that this gap exists, and they're trying to do something about it in their curricula. We see a return to a basic core curriculum in science. They're saying to people like me, who are history or English majors, that we have to take a course in science—not necessarily a specific discipline but the history of science, say, or the philosophy of science. So that later on in life we'll be better customers for Neil's papers. You're not going to create a universal understanding of science, but you are going to expand that understanding greatly.

SARU: But there has to be an appreciation that there are different forms of knowledge—that even the know-nots have a form of knowledge that we, the elite, do not. Call it street knowledge, or some other term for cultural knowledge, but it needs to be respected and brought into the discourse. If the philosophy of science is being taught, then other forms of knowledge should be included as well.

BARBARA: I like the difference between IQ and EQ. We can be brilliant [i.e., a high intelligence quotient] but have a low emotional quotient. There are whole ranges of capacities that don't involve analytical, critical intellect. We need to broaden our definition of intelligence.

ROBERT: Saru, tell us about the communities where you work, and the alternative structures you've created.

SARU: One of the communities is ninety-five-percent Spanish-speaking Latina and Latino. Unfortunately, in California, language has been used to divide and oppress communities instead of bringing them together. And many people who feel marginalized have formed their own alternative communities—some of them identity communities and some gangs, some positive and some negative. Our point is to provide young people and marginalized groups with positive, constructive tools, so that they can create communities that then can work productively with other communities, as opposed to destroying themselves.

ROBERT: Bruce, how do you build an international community?

BRUCE: When you reach across an international border, as we do with the Cascadia Project [the development of common strategies in support of intermodal transportation, trade, tourism, environment, and technology] between the state of Washington and the province of British Columbia, you immediately run into problems, believe me. It's not like crossing a state border. You have to think about and treat people somewhat differently. For example, there's some anti-Americanism in Canada, and so when you relate to Canadians you need to take that into account. On the other hand, if we can't relate to

Canadians, how are we ever going to establish peace in the Balkans?

ROBERT: You've also been involved with the revitalization of local communities.

BRUCE: I think we're going to see renewed commitments to local communities. All these interesting new technologies are generating fragmented new communities. But at the same time they're creating a yearning for the old-fashioned community, a living place where you know your neighbors, where there's some sort of institution, such as a church, to bring people together. And this yearning has inspired a new sense of architecture. Fifty years ago, there was no such thing as a historic preservation movement; now it's the way we build cities. We try to

---

. . . we're going to see renewed commitments to local communities.

---

save and reuse what we have, and we've learned a lot more about the civic amenities—simple things, like street trees. And neighbors who have very little in common with one another cooperate on such projects. I look for a transformation of the suburbs into someplace more humane—a place that doesn't separate living from work, from shopping, from church. In the twenty-first century, this is going to happen, because people will demand it.

NEIL: But there's a limiting factor here. It's not like the 1950s, where you were a company man, you got your job and worked at it for fifteen years, you lived in the same house for fifteen years—so your neighbors and community had a foundation upon which to build. Now we're in a technologically driven economy, with timescales of three to five years before things are all changed around. We have people moving from one place to another, and this old-fashioned kind of community can no longer be where you drop your anchor. We have to be more imaginative about what we call community.

BRUCE: You actually can have both. You're going to have these various fragmented communities, but you're also going to have a revival of the smaller, physical communities—towns—because people are moving less today than they were ten or so years ago. Today there are more entrepreneurs, more people who are working for themselves [more people telecommuting], more people who can decide where they want to live, more people who can make volitional decisions on their own. It's not for everybody, but it is a trend.

SARU: The nonelites don't have as much volition as others do.

ROBERT: They will when you get finished with them.

SARU: I hope.

ROBERT: It's a good goal.

SARU: But Bruce is right in that there's been a movement toward developing local geographic communities, organized on the ground—for example, through church-based relationship building. And once relationships are built, then a fight for change against the power structure can begin. Such local communities have developed in Brooklyn and other places and have allowed the people living there to actually take the lead.

ROBERT (with a smile): When you're the power structure, I'm going to joust with you.

SARU: You won't be able to.

ROBERT: A final question: A hundred years from now, which kinds of communities will have become more important than they are today?

BARBARA: High-synergy, win-win communities, in which everyone can contribute his or her gifts—what I call cocreative communities.

JOHN: Certain Asian communities, particularly Chinese and Japanese, doing well commercially and spreading their influence in Asia—and also through their strong immigrant communities in this country.

BRUCE: Internet fragmentation will create many more niche communities, which will enrich us. We lose the power of some previous communities, such as newspaper readership, and so forth, but these niche communities will, ironically, complement a counterpart movement to strengthen old-style neighborhoods.

SARU: Identity-based communities are another wave of the future—communities of women, communities of people of color, gathering and building strength within themselves so that they can then go on and work together with other communities to build a larger community.

NEIL: I'm not going to say what I think it should be, but what I think it will be. It will be the ultimate revenge of the nerds. Society used to be divided between the haves and the have-nots. And it will soon become divided between those who know and those who know not.

ROBERT: The nerds and the nerd-nots.

NEIL: Bill Gates is the richest man in the world and he's the patron saint of the nerd community. In the revenge of the nerds, those who have embraced technology will be the lead community and in control.

ROBERT: CONCLUDING COMMENT

The concept of community is a good descriptor of how we cope with social change. If the traditional community was once the geographical place where we live physically, the new community is the psychological space where we live mentally, emotionally, and spiritually. Community integrates individual desire with collective need, balancing personal expression with social requirement. Today we have many kinds of communities—technology-empowered virtual groups, science-linked knowledge groups, self-reliant social-action groups, spiritual gatherings, local activism, regional cooperation, global awareness. It's fascinating to watch such diversity emerge. Global telecommunications allow us to live in many communities at the same time. A key, I think, is language. The power of words can unify or divide. Computer programmers from India, China, and Israel speak a similar language, much more so than do, say, politicians in Boston, Belfast, and Birmingham. The range of these new communities is staggering and promises to broaden individual opportunity and enrich humanity as a whole, though we should expect some splintering and conflict—and we will have to remain ever-vigilant against an accelerating specialization that can trigger social fragmentation. Our best hope for the future, it seems, is an increase in communities of shared interests and meaningful action—a new consciousness of a new connectedness. New communities can bring us closer together and, it is hoped, closer to truth.

OUTTAKES

BARBARA: *Boy, that took some doing.*

SARU: *Was that the whole show?*

ROBERT: *It goes fast. We had a lot of material we didn't get to.*

CHAPTER 18

Whatever Happened to Ethics and Civility?

Can you remain ethical when a devious rival is promoted ahead of you? Can you stay civil when a cursing driver cuts you off the road? Modern life means constant competition. We struggle at school for grades and admissions, battle at work for markets and money, and everywhere strive for status and recognition. In this pressure-cooker environment, obsessed by out-of-reach goals and hemmed in by potential adversaries, how can we expect high moral values, let alone courteous behavior, to survive? The decline in ethics and civility in the contemporary urban world has become more and more precipitate. We are all impoverished by the deterioration of morals and the erosion of respect. But can we fairly place the blame only on the frantic pace and ferocity of our day-to-day existence? What can each of us do to make ourselves and our common polity a little more civil, a little more ethical? We assembled some ethically minded experts who promised to be civil.

PARTICIPANTS

Bruce Chapman, a former United States Ambassador to the United Nations Organizations in Vienna, is president of the Discovery Institute, a Seattle-based think tank whose mission is "to make a positive vision of the future practical." Bruce believes that civil debate is the best way to solve social problems.

Barbara Marx Hubbard is a founder of the World Future Society and cofounder of the Foundation for Conscious Evolution, in Santa Barbara, California. She is also the author of many books, including *The Revelation: A Message of Hope for the New Millennium.* She takes a global perspective and views the human community as a whole.

Saru Jayaraman, a Yale law student, is the national founder of WYSE [Women and Youth Supporting Each other], an inner-city youth organization praised by President Clinton as "America at its best." Saru talks about the despair and anger of young inner-city girls and how that leads to what is often perceived as asocial behavior, and she explains the importance of teaching them critical thinking.

Dr. John McWhorter, a professor of linguistics at the University of California, Berkeley, specializes in Creole languages and the social dynamics of language; he has written extensively on the use of black English. John discusses the effects of language on social relationships and behaviors.

Dr. Richard Mouw is the president of Fuller Theological Seminary, in Pasadena, California, where he is a professor of Christian philosophy and ethics. He is the author of ten books, including *Uncommon Decency: Christian Civility in an Uncivil World.* Richard defines ethics and civility in an elegant and broadly Christian context.

ROBERT: Richard, what's the difference between ethics and civility, and why are they important today?

RICHARD: Ethics concerns issues of right and wrong, good and bad, virtue and vice. And civility is subsumed within that. The word "civility" comes from the Latin *civitas,* for city. To be civil is to know how to get along in the city—how to

---

Civility, . . . is public politeness, . . .

---

treat people who are different from you, who have different beliefs or ethnic backgrounds. Civility, then, is public politeness, toleration, all the kinds of things that are important to maintain good citizenship and facilitate interactions in the public square.

ROBERT: Barbara, I want you to forget for a moment your role as a global visionary. As a mother of five and grandmother of five, what do you teach your grandchildren about ethics and civility?

BARBARA: I think you teach mostly by example, so what I'm trying to give my grandchildren is an example of somebody who's doing her best to be ethical. And since one of my definitions of futurism is "expanded parenthood"—looking ahead for the whole human community—the same principle applies.

ROBERT: Is that practical in a modern, cutthroat economy?

BARBARA: It's the greatest practicality there is, because otherwise you're less than you can be. Real joy, real meaning, comes from that sense of connectedness with one another, however difficult [it may be to maintain].

ROBERT: Bruce, you've had a long career in government service, including serving as director of the Office of Planning and Evaluation in the Reagan White House. Why do you think civil discourse is so important in creating a positive future?

BRUCE: People really do have disputes—we see things differently, and we need to adjudicate those disputes. Paradoxically, the tendency to try to cover up our disputes and make everybody agree is what causes conflict in the long run. So honest debate conducted in a civil manner turns out to be the best social system.

ROBERT: Even if the two sides disagree violently?

BRUCE: It's still the way to get at the truth. And in the long run—paradoxically, as I say—it makes people happier with one another.

ROBERT: We'll see if it makes people happier here. John, as a linguist, how do you see language as a dynamic element of social change?

JOHN: There are many answers to that question, but one is that language labels things, and labels have a way of changing people's conceptions. Take the slogan "Save the Whales," which is probably a fixture by now in most of our minds. The fact of the matter is that only certain

---

. . . language has a way of bringing society into awareness.

---

groups of whales have ever actually been endangered, but the phrase has been useful in communicating an ecological perspective. To have said, "Save Certain Stocks of Whales" wouldn't have worked as well. So language has a way of bringing society into awareness.

ROBERT: What are the implications for civility?

JOHN: Language often operates on two levels. They're called, for better or worse, the high and the low. And most people in the world speak one of the two varieties, neither one superior to the other in God's or anyone else's eyes. But generally, in the ideal society, everybody would be able to meet in the middle, all on some generally accepted standard level, while preserving their own nonstandard, but not substandard, kind of speech. And those who can manipulate both the high level and the low level are best equipped to be civil in the broadest sense of the term.

ROBERT: Saru, what kinds of inequalities do young people face today, and how has this contributed to fraying the social fabric of America?

SARU: Young people are increasingly angry, realizing that they've been left out of this high-level discourse you're talking about. For example, many of our young women have been told by their teachers that they will never go to college, that they'll end up working at McDonald's. They're twelve to fourteen years old and they live in the inner cities of Los Angeles, say, or New Haven. So if they'll never be part of that race for status, they end up resorting to another race for another form of status. Many young women become pregnant, because they feel valued having a baby. They've told us that having a baby gives them status in school. It's very difficult for young people to maintain any form of civility when they're interacting with mainstream institutions, because they're very angry at being completely shut out.

ROBERT: You teach these young women critical thinking, thereby improving their self-image?

SARU: Absolutely. The media pressure young women in many potent ways—telling them how to look, how to think, how to act. There are always societal messages and images coming at them, telling them that they don't belong, that they don't look the way they should—and so their self-esteem is greatly diminished. We provide these young women with critical thinking in order to break down those messages and deconstruct those images, allowing them to take power for themselves. The result is a gain in self-esteem, enhanced interpersonal relationships, improved ethical behavior—all preparing them to take leadership in the world.

ROBERT: It's nice to be talking about civility when everyone's so agreeable. But what happens when there's severe controversy? Richard, what about the intense, sometimes brutal confrontation between the pro-choice and pro-life movements? How do you maintain civility in such a bloody conflict?

RICHARD: It's not easy—that needs to be said at the outset. The religious scholar Martin Marty, of the University of Chicago, puts it well. He points out that often people who are civil don't have strong convictions and people who have strong convictions aren't civil. The real challenge is to have convicted civility. We must learn how to engage in that high-level discourse, to treat other people as having value even when we seriously disagree with them. That's the challenge.

ROBERT: How do you do that?

RICHARD: As a Christian, it's important for me to cultivate self-criticism and humility in conducting a dialogue with other people—and I'm very conservative on many of these issues. It's awful when my kind of people enter into those debates in a self-righteous and judgmental

manner. We need to state our convictions honestly and listen to each other genuinely.

ROBERT: Bruce, you've had experience in civil debate.

BRUCE: [The way that the abortion question is usually dealt with] is a perfect example of what not to do. When you make it difficult to have civil debate, to have real discussion, on highly charged issues, you marginalize people, you push them out of the civil discourse arena and into the uncivil streets. They take it to the abortion clinic. People say, "I don't want to hear about that, I don't want to talk about that." Well, hearing and talking are a lot better than negative action. And so you come back to the proper role of politics, which is to teach young people how to take part in public discourse. We should reinstitute what we used to call civics—political education—to instruct people how to participate in civil society.

ROBERT: John, you've also been engaged in controversial issues, particularly black English in education. How do you engender civility in emotionally charged situations?

JOHN: Well, for one thing, it would help if more people accepted the fact that there are certain issues—abortion being one of them—where unfortunately there will always be fundamental disagreement over fundamental principles. A comfort with agreeing to disagree is something often sadly missing. We need to put ourselves in each other's heads, as I like to put it. For example, in the black English debate, it's often difficult for black advocates of using black English in schools to realize that a white person who questions the wisdom of this is not necessarily a racist. On the other hand, it's often difficult for white commentators to imagine that a black person who advocates black English in schools isn't some kind of woolly headed anti-constructive militant. So, trying to understand where others are coming from is important, though difficult.

ROBERT: Sounds like you've been criticized by both sides?

JOHN: Yes, I've been there, taken it from both sides.

ROBERT: Some would call that a compliment.

JOHN: I suppose, but the most important thing I've learned is that despite what happens, you have to try and rise above it. You can feel the burning in the pit of your stomach, but then you ought to be thinking, How am I going to look at this tomorrow?

ROBERT: Barbara, as someone who always sees high levels, tell us about conscious evolution and its implications for civility.

BARBARA: The human species now has so much power that if we don't become civil with one another we can destroy our whole life-support system. The danger of incivility has escalated. And the need to survive is driving us toward a global consciousness. We have to recognize the interdependence of the environment. For example, if there's a nuclear accident, it affects everybody. So it seems to me that the interconnections and complexification of the world are making ethics pragmatically necessary for survival, whereas in the past it might have been desirable but not essential.

ROBERT: You speak about ethical evolution.

BARBARA: My primary phrase is "conscious evolution"—becoming aware of our impact on nature. We understand the gene; we understand the brain; we can start making new life-forms.

. . . human consciousness is entering nature.

This means human consciousness is entering nature. And so ethical evolution will become the key to the future.

ROBERT: Bruce, let's talk politics. How has political reform affected general morality?

BRUCE: In a perverse way. Reform has backfired in my opinion. I used to be a big reformer. I believed that if we passed enough laws governing how people should behave, they would behave better. I've changed my mind. For one thing, I went back and read some of my college Aristotle and realized that virtue, in order to be virtue, has to be voluntary. It has to be something volitional on your part. If you're forced to be virtuous, especially in every little detail, you'll rebel against it. It's like paying your taxes; you have to do it, so paying your taxes isn't virtuous. Virtue entails choice. So as we take choices out of politics—as we put politicians under more and more strictures—then people of real virtue don't want to be involved. They stay away from politics. And what happens is just the opposite of what groups such as Common Cause and the like predicted. Instead of restoring trust in government, we've done the opposite—we've destroyed trust in government. The more laws we pass, the more investigations we've had.

ROBERT: Examples?

BRUCE: We have all these laws about what you may or may not do with gratuities. Someone whom we trust to declare war we don't trust to accept a lunch? This is ridiculous. And since no one wants to live a ridiculous life, good people—especially young people—stay away from politics. The founders of this country understood that the nature of man is fallen. So you set up a system where interests compete in a civilized fashion. Sure, you'll get some wrong decisions, but by and large it'll work, because people will be part of it.

SARU: "The nature of man"—that's part of the problem. There's no inclusion of women or other groups. People feel totally alienated from the political process, because it continues to be the same group, in their view, that rules in Washington and elsewhere. It's white men, typically, in office.

ROBERT: What's a solution?

SARU: Providing young women with the ability to feel like leaders themselves. We encourage young women to take action in their community, then to go on and get politically involved

---

it happens by allowing them to question authority, . . .

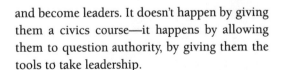

---

and become leaders. It doesn't happen by giving them a civics course—it happens by allowing them to question authority, by giving them the tools to take leadership.

ROBERT: If women had a larger role in leadership, would that make a difference?

SARU: It would depend. If they were the kind of women who encouraged other women to take leadership—then, yes. But if they were the kind who felt "Well, I've made it on my own, and everybody else should, too"—then, no. Young women need to feel that they're a part of the discourse, otherwise there's no point in talking about civility; because if the only way you can be virtuous is by having options, then there's no way that these young people can be truly virtuous, since right now the only options they have are forced.

ROBERT: John, are young university students frustrated because of the system?

JOHN: Yes, they are. This may be an unpopular thing to say, but I think that if one is an adolescent, any kind of adolescent, then it's natural to have a certain frustration with the system. There's a natural insecurity that adolescents presumably have had since the year one, and they need outlets to cope. Thirty years ago, some very good things happened on college campuses—events that made my own life possible. But now I think there's a kind of copycat reflex: On many campuses, every spring, there has to be an issue that you chain yourself to something about. And frankly, as sympathetic as I am to these students, often the issues nowadays are getting so small that I sense more hormones and life force than intellectual substance—

ROBERT: What's wrong with hormones and life force?

JOHN: I'm not sure there's anything inherently wrong with it—

SARU: There's nothing wrong with it. It's wonderful that young people are taking leadership and taking action. Let me tell you that the vast majority of people are in no way politically active or conscious and feel unable to act or voice their opinion—they're totally separate from public discourse.

RICHARD: But I wonder how much of that separation is grounded in deeper issues. The food-service people on campuses tell us that students don't dine, they graze—the dining hall is set up as a series of grazing stations. And that's an extension, really, of family life. The family meal is a wonderful workshop in civility, where we learn to hang in there with people with whom we're irritated and don't agree. And unless we have those earlier workshops in civility, I'm not sure that simply giving voice to people who haven't learned the basics of human interaction is going to do a lot of good.

JOHN: See, that's the problem with some of what's happening on campus. I agree that young people shouldn't just be led, that they need an active involvement in what's going on. But unfortunately, what often accompanies this is a lack of what we're calling civility—an inability to even make the pretense of listening to any other opinion. That, I think, is not healthy.

SARU: But can you please tell me how older people have provided proper role models? Young people don't feel that they've been listened to, either. And if their role models are spouting and not listening, how will they learn to listen and not spout?

BRUCE: It's interesting to see a kind of revolution on a generational basis against the baby boomers—the generation that was raised with the family meals and yet had the high divorce rates. We're seeing better behavior, sociologically, in the younger generation—particularly the millennials, the really young kids who will

come to maturity in the new millennium, because they have rebelled against the older generation and are moving toward more normative behaviors. This revolution is also taking place spiritually, with millions of college students transforming their campuses through groups like Inter-Varsity Fellowship and Campus Crusade. About fifteen years ago, the social scientist James Q. Wilson said that if we're going to change the culture, we have to start from the ground up. Well, to my amazement, this great transformation is happening with many young people. They're not going to have the number of abortions, they're going to have more stable families, and they're going to be more civil, because they are also going to be more ethical.

ROBERT: Saru, can you have civility without economic equality?

SARU: No, I don't think so, because young people know who the haves and the have-nots are. And as long as they don't feel part of the haves, it's very difficult for them to engage in what polite society would call ethical behavior—

ROBERT: Is that an excuse to be unethical?

SARU: I wouldn't necessarily call the kinds of behaviors that young people engage in unethical, but I think mainstream society would. And as long as there is that judgment, young people cannot feel included or positive about themselves. They lack self-esteem, which leads to an inability to take leadership.

BRUCE: Unless there is not just opportunity but some stakeholder's share in the economy, we'll have this increasing disparity between the haves and the have-nots. And it ends up in some sort of civil conflict. One of the reasons I'm a strong supporter of privatizing at least some of

Social Security is that people who change jobs often, who have what most people consider menial jobs, will nonetheless get a share, a stake, in the economy and its future. Otherwise we're going to have people who are expected to become highly skilled and high-tech, and if they don't make it they're just going to be left out.

JOHN: I agree with Saru that there are people who don't feel included in society, and that sense leads to unethical behavior. It's not just young people but a great many people; for example, many Latino communities and much of the African-American community. Mainstream culture is seen by them as something outside their ken, and therefore, quite naturally, something hostile and not to be emulated. And there's a great deal of unethical behavior. We could argue that it's not unethical if it's provoked by economic disparity, but that's not the point; that kind of behavior is going to keep happening, unless we work harder to bring rich and poor together, to bridge this disparity.

BARBARA: I think we have to be inventive about the very economic system that's causing inequality. For example, devise situations where you don't depend only on a job for your income. If people have skills, they can barter, so everybody has work, everybody gets to do something.

ROBERT: What about global capitalism?

BRUCE: The economist Richard Rahn, one of our senior fellows at the Discovery Institute, has written a book called *The End of Money and the Struggle for Financial Privacy,* in which he predicts that people will be able to move money around so fast that governments won't be able to keep track of it, and therefore the whole taxation system will come under question. What constitutes ethical behavior in the exchange of money and the paying of taxes may change radically in the next century.

RICHARD: I want to raise a question about Saru [Jayaraman]'s strong emphasis on the need to give youth a voice that they don't have. Most popular culture I see is very youth-oriented. The new TV shows focus on youth—turn on MTV and you see very angry expressions of a youth culture and what many of us in the mainstream culture would consider to be alternative lifestyles being displayed as perfectly acceptable and normal.

SARU: OK, but what kind of political power does that give young people—or what kind of economic power, for that matter? None. It provides them perhaps with some forms of expression, many of which, such as the violence you see depicted in the media, are self-destructive. But it provides them with no positive alternatives or no positive tools to really take leadership or feel included.

RICHARD: But when the whole market is geared toward youth culture, where are the issues?

SARU: You may see the market as reflecting what young people want. I see young people reflecting what the market is trying to sell them, which is violence, which is sexism, racism, body image.

RICHARD: The market didn't create baggy clothes. The market commodified baggy clothes.

JOHN: I will make the extreme statement that if you watch a lot of TV, and if you really follow the movies—not just the big hits—you will see just about every conceivable kind of young person in this society covered. Nice white people, bad white people, inner-city thugs, inner-city people getting along, middle-class black young people. You really see the whole thing. I think it's easy to forget how important youth are to our popular culture, because, Saru, you and I have grown up in a world where popular culture has been synonymous with youth. In the mid-1950s, you could turn on the TV and see Mary Martin and Noel Coward, both quite middle-aged, doing a TV special, singing songs that would be most uncool today.

SARU: But I'd like to know how that translates into any form of political or economic power. It's easy for us sitting here to say, "Oh, our culture reflects youth." But in what way are youth being included in the benefits of society?

ROBERT: What's the solution? What do you want to see happening?

SARU: I want young people to be able to deconstruct what they see in media and take action in their real lives, not in their media lives.

BRUCE: My wife is a high school counselor, and she deals with young people in the inner city every day. She sees the abortions, the murders, the problems of abuse, and so forth. She also sees that these people are not represented

---

What you see in the media is largely a commodified protest culture.

---

by the protest culture. What you see in the media is largely a commodified protest culture. The real revolution among young people is spir-

itual, religious. You never see that represented in the media, and you hardly ever hear people discussing it.

ROBERT: Well, one thing I see represented here are two women from different generations who have taken charge of their own lives and have become significant leaders themselves. Barbara [Marx Hubbard], you've pioneered a new way of thinking about the globe. Saru [Jayaraman], you've created an activist organization that gives young girls real opportunities. What have you as women brought to this new culture?

BARBARA: I cover the gap: I was born in 1929, I got married in 1951, I had five children—and I was a member of the so-called most boring generation. I went to Bryn Mawr, I had a good education, but I immediately got pregnant; Margaret Mead called it "mindless fecundity." I love my children deeply, but the fact is that in the 1950s there was no sense of identity as a woman beyond being a wife and mother. I got depressed, but then I read Betty Friedan's *The Feminine Mystique*. She noticed that many women suffered from "the problem with no name"—they wanted to be themselves as well as wives and mothers. I read the psychologist Abraham Maslow, who said that all self-actualizing people—productive and creative people—have vocations. And I realized that what was happening for me as a woman was that although I loved my children, my vocation was not motherhood. My vocation was out in the world. And as I began to find my vocation, I became a better mother. Now I'm in my second motherhood, because I'm back with my children and my grandchildren, but as somebody who has found her vocation.

ROBERT: Your vocation as a global visionary—

BARBARA: As a communicator. To see a positive future. As women have fewer children and live longer lives—like myself, I'm almost seventy and I still feel I'm at the beginning—there's an arousal. I call it the vocational arousal. We're being awakened from within.

ROBERT: Saru, you, too, have had this vocational arousal. How have you had the power to create a whole new institution?

SARU: Only from anger, really.

ROBERT: We'd be a great society if everybody were as productively angry as you are.

SARU: Well, growing up, even in junior high school, I realized how much inequality there was—particularly for girls—and how much pressure to conform. Our whole effort is to let young women know that they can be whoever they want to be—that they can take whatever role they want to take.

ROBERT: But you made your own opportunity.

SARU: I want to provide more young women with more opportunities.

BARBARA: That's leadership. Leadership means empowering others to become leaders. We have to face it, some people are pioneering souls— that's what I call them. Some people are drawn to the growing edge of things. It's beautiful that the image of women now is more open and far, far richer than it ever was when I was growing up.

SARU: I hope so.

ROBERT: A prediction, please. In a hundred years, will new technologies make the world more or less ethical and civil?

BRUCE: More, but also posing great dangers. It all comes back to our understanding of human nature—who and what human beings are.

RICHARD: Technology has the potential for creating new modes of community, but at the same time we're seeing a reaction against modernization, in the form of new tribalism and warfare.

SARU: I hope we'll be more ethical and civil. If we can provide young people with positive role models and sufficient change to feel included, yes.

BARBARA: If the evolutionary trend of greater complexity leading to greater consciousness and greater freedom continues—and it's a fifteen-billion-year trend—more and more people are going to experience themselves as part of the whole.

JOHN: Frankly, to the extent that the communications revolution supports global capitalism, we will see an increasing disparity between rich and poor, which means that civility will continue to be eroded, because economic disparity creates inevitable tension.

ROBERT: CONCLUDING COMMENT

Ethics and civility don't come easily in a socially diverse, competitively charged society. They take work. Even experts disagree about what can be done. For some professions—doctors, lawyers, the police—there are required rules of conduct, though we know they're frequently broken. For some communities, there are particular patterns of ethics that are absolutely wrong, such as experimental fraud in the scientific community and plagiarism among writers. But some rules are changing. Take E-mail; there's a new informality, brevity, rapidity—and less concern about spelling. I get E-mails from scholars making grade-school mistakes, and I no doubt zap back clunkers myself. Certainly there should be minimum standards for everyone. For example, people shouldn't shout at one another, except to prevent accidents. So, let's impose—don't laugh—a legal limitation on shouting, like the limitations on pollution. Hereafter you are allowed only two shouts per month. If you need more, we'll establish a Shouter's Market, where you can purchase the rights for additional shouting. Sure, it sounds like farce—but maybe it's closer to truth.

OUTTAKES

BARBARA: *That was fun.*

BRUCE: *In New York, you get a five-hundred-dollar fine for honking. And you know what? It encourages civility.*

CHAPTER 19

Will the Internet Change Humanity?

Exactly how many hours a week do you surf the Internet? Compare that number with what it was a year ago. Now project forward at the same growth rate, and within two years you'll never get off. If you're one of the millions who surf the Net, you've probably seen your online time increase dramatically. What happens when everybody is online? When access is immediate? When contact is constant? When individuals can usurp institutions? When gratification must be instant? On what's been called the information superhighway, distance disappears and destinations emerge within seconds. And it's fundamentally changing how we gather data, conduct business, exchange ideas. The original "internet"—known as the ARPAnet (the acronym refers to the United States Defense Department's Advanced Research Projects Agency)—was established to provide a secure and survivable communications network for organizations, mainly universities, engaged in defense-related research. The very first computer link-up transmission, in 1969, was from the University of California in Los Angeles to the Stanford Research Institute near San Francisco. In the next three decades, this small network grew into the Internet, which now comprises tens of millions of uses around the world and will eventually include just about everyone. This remarkable growth was energized by the advent of the World Wide Web, which made interlinked, hypertext, multimedia documents accessible and usable by common people. Hypertext radically transformed the way we think and work by freeing us from the traditional linear constraints of accessing information. Hypertext enabled highlighted words or phrases to be traced directly as we skip and jump from document to document, each of which has a unique address, all over the world. The Web was developed by Timothy Berners-Lee from 1988 to 1990 when he was at the European Laboratory for Particle Physics (CERN) near Geneva and wrote a trio of protocols—HTTP (hypertext transfer protocol), HTML (hypertext markup language), and what eventually became URLs (uniform resource locators), the domain name or Internet address so recognizable to all Web users today. But is the Internet changing what we are, while altering what we do? Some say the Internet is as revolutionary as the harnessing of electricity or the advent of the internal combustion engine. Others believe its impact will be far greater. Depending on which of these camps you're in, our topic is a thrilling or a frightening look at the future. What's really happening here? We asked our participants, all of whom are plugged in, to assess the Internet's impact on society and particularly on the development of the human race. Though they come from different fields—computer science, space science, public policy, engineering, business—all see the same remarkable transformation.

PARTICIPANTS

Dr. Francis (Frank) Fukuyama, a professor of public policy at George Mason University, is the author of several important books including *The End of History and the Last Man.* Frank sees the Internet accelerating the development of liberal democracy around the world.

Dr. George Geis, an adjunct professor at the Anderson School of Management at the University of California, Los Angeles, specializes in business strategies for the digital economy. George considers psychological as well as economic issues on the Internet and focuses on separating the wheat from the chaff.

Dr. Bart Kosko, a professor of engineering at the University of Southern California, is an expert on fuzzy logic and the author of *The Fuzzy Future.* Bart predicts that the Internet will help to erode professional monopolies and end governments as we know them.

Dr. Marvin Minsky, the Toshiba Professor of Media Arts and Sciences at the Massachusetts Institute of Technology, is a pioneer in artificial intelligence. He relishes the Internet and assesses its significance with several trenchant observations— watch out for Uncle Louie!

Dr. Bruce Murray, a professor of planetary science and geology at the California Institute of Technology, was the director of the Jet Propulsion Laboratory, the National Aeronautics and Space Administration's center for planetary and deep-space missions, from 1976 to 1982. Bruce believes that the Internet is a seminal— indeed, evolutionary—event in the history of humankind.

ROBERT: Marvin, you've explored the frontiers of machine intelligence and knowledge representation. You've seen the whole world of communications change. Give us a historical perspective for the Internet. Is it as significant as people think?

MARVIN: Certainly is. The Internet started in the late 1960s, when people began connecting terminals to computers remotely, and then, in the early 1970s, connecting them all around the country—that's when E-mail really got started. Then there were twenty years of rapid development—in the 1980s, something called USENET grew up, which was a precursor to the World Wide Web, where people could send messages to one another and they would be stored—and in the early 1990s the Web appeared, which has made it easier for everyone to use the Internet.

ROBERT: Was the sudden broad-based use of the Web a surprise?

MARVIN: It was quite a surprise to people who weren't already using the Internet. But by that time, E-mail was very well developed. I have three children, and probably a hundred students, and I've been in constant contact with them since the early 1970s through E-mail. So I've grown up in a world where I assume that if I want to talk to someone, I can.

ROBERT: We're just catching up with you?

MARVIN: You're just catching up.

ROBERT: Frank, your book *The End of History and the Last Man* is one of the most original and important works on international political economy. What is the end of history? Give us a short overview.

FRANK: First of all, it's history with a capital H, the progressive evolution of political and economic institutions. And in my view, progressive intellectuals used to believe that this evolution would culminate in some form of socialism. But I think it's quite evident that that's not going to happen, and that modern liberal democracy and market-oriented economic systems are basically it. In a way, it's the end of the line of development of modern postindustrial societies.

ROBERT: Why did your thesis cause such a firestorm?

FRANK: Well, people thought it cut off hope for progress in the future. And people are, I think justifiably, a little uncomfortable with liberal democracy and markets. If this is the end of the line, people want to know whether there's a Utopia beyond that.

ROBERT: How do you see the Internet, in this move toward liberal democracy and markets?

FRANK: It's very intimately connected to that. The newer information technologies are profoundly democratizing, because they don't reward economies of scale. They work best in decentralized, noncontrolled societies. They're anti-authoritarian, because authoritarians control societies by their ability to control access to information. So if people can get information on their own simply by dialing up a computer, then we have ways of getting around hierarchies. The Internet helps to spread power out rather than concentrating it.

ROBERT: Bruce, you think a great deal about the future. What are the implications of the Internet for the future of humankind?

BRUCE: Oh, I can answer that by noting that

you pose the question of how the Internet will change humanity. Two years ago I gave a talk to science fiction writers—the most avant-garde audience you can have. And I tentatively threw out the idea that the Internet *might* change humanity. Two years later, we take for granted that it will and now we want to know the details of how. The Internet is more than an end-of-the-century phenomenon. This is one of those transitions in human social structure [i.e., cultural evolution] that happens only once every few thousand years.

ROBERT: Bart, what's the impact of the Internet on the professions?

BART: I think it means the end of the professional monopolies, in law, medicine, education. It means that people all around the world, in the poor countries as well as the wealthy ones, will have access to information that they didn't have before. So, in a very real sense, lawyers and doctors and professors will be given a run for their money.

ROBERT: That sounds like good fun. George, how does the Internet differ from other media in the business world?

GEORGE: Other media, traditionally, have been one-dimensional, along a content-interaction grid. For example, newspapers are content-rich but interaction-poor. You can write a letter to the editor, but that's about it for interaction. The telephone is communications-rich but relatively content-poor—just the human voice. With the Internet, you have rich growth along both content and interaction dimensions. Given the growth of digital video and other types of multimedia broadband communications, what we're going to see is a closer and closer approximation to human experience.

ROBERT: Let's talk about key characteristics of the Internet.

MARVIN: Well, I haven't been in a library in thirty years. When I want to know something, I go on the Net. The other day I was lecturing on child development, and I raised the question of how children get attached to their mothers, and I said that it doesn't really happen until late in the first year of life—a child can't even recognize its mother until it's three months old or maybe more. And one of the students who'd been working with children said, "No, that's not true—children recognize their mothers just after birth." So, there was an argument, and I went home and I typed four keywords into a

---

. . . I haven't been in a library in thirty years.

---

search engine: infant, face, recognition, brain. I got a list of people, and I sent them E-mails. One of the more interesting responses came from a woman in France, a graduate student doing research on this subject, and she said, "Yes, infants seem to recognize the mother right away, but if you put a scarf over the mother's head and hide the hairline, then they don't." So the infant is not seeing facial features but something about the shape. That's the Internet.

ROBERT: How long did it take you to get that answer?

MARVIN: About an hour, because she was away.

ROBERT: Before the Internet, you probably wouldn't have gotten any of those answers at all, or at least it would have taken weeks.

MARVIN: Oh, the woman in France was doing a Ph.D. thesis, and it wouldn't have been published for a long time.

ROBERT: Bart, what do people mean when they say that the Internet is self-organizing?

BART: It has no central authority or commands, which I think many people find scary. And—related to Frank [Fukuyama]'s thesis about the rise of liberal democracies and the end of history—the Internet erodes and fuzzifies the jurisdictions of governments. Governments can pretty well define their boundaries in terms of land, but it's not at all clear who's in charge on the Internet. If you live in California and visit a Web site [that originates from], say, Tennessee or Germany, are you subject to laws that apply in that state or country? In some countries, like Burma, it's a crime to have an unlisted account on the Internet. But attempts to regulate the Internet—in China and elsewhere—have not been effective. Another example is Internet gambling. There have been many efforts to stamp it out, but that's simply had the effect of increasing encryption technology and spurring innovations. No one's in control, and that scares people.

ROBERT: What traits differentiate the Internet from other forms of communication?

BRUCE: I want to take issue with Frank's statement, because I don't think it goes far enough.

ROBERT: He's rarely accused of that.

BRUCE: In his view, these previous centralizing structures, such as Marxism, or religions before that, are collapsing or at least modifying, and the default is capitalism—which is avarice at the local and national level—and liberal democracy, which is in the eye of the beholder

but generally means that people can try doing whatever they want, to some extent. But I think that that system, too, is transitional—and the reason is linked to the Internet and the Web. If you look at the history of evolving technology—printing press, broadcast radio, broadcast TV—each one of these enormously affected culture. With the Internet as the emergent technology, other cultural structures will evolve—political, economic, religious—that will dominate the next century. And so we're in transition.

FRANK: In a sense, liberal democracy doesn't tell you what to think, and so all that is compatible within its framework. But I think it's correct to say that the one big technological change in communications is that broadcasting—that is, TV and radio—went only in one direction, from one source out to many recipients. But the self-organization features begin to appear when people can communicate in both directions.

BART: I hope we're not going to see the end of freedom.

BRUCE: You don't know. We haven't been there yet. We don't know what will happen, that's the point. There's never been a time in human existence, ever, like the present. There's never been a time when you could do what we have just described—that is, sit down and communicate with people all over the world in a very information-rich way. It's never happened.

BART: Will freedom increase or decrease in time?

BRUCE: Did freedom increase or decrease when previous [political-economic] structures changed? Sometimes it got worse; sometimes it got better. It depended. That's probably going to be true in the future.

BART: Right now, governments haven't figured out the Internet jurisdiction issue, but when they do, you'd expect a loss of freedom, not an increase.

ROBERT: Information currently on the Web amounts to roughly the total amount in the Library of Congress—twenty terabytes, which is twenty trillion bytes. George, what does this mean?

GEORGE: It goes to what Marvin [Minsky] was saying: There's so much content out there that it becomes extraordinarily important to assess the value of that content. Marvin may be able to judge whether or not the expertise he has access to in Europe makes a valuable contribution to his child development class, but others may not be quite so adept at assessing what they pick up. So the question of separating the wheat from the chaff, whether it be in commerce or science or health, becomes vital, as people try to evaluate what they see out on the Web.

ROBERT: There are new metrics for describing Internet communications, new ways of looking at how people collect information—the so-called laws of surfing: how many visits, or hits, per hour, how many pages per visit, time per visit, and so forth. If a Web site doesn't download in ten seconds, for instance, you go some-place else.

BRUCE: When you use the word "information" I think you have to be very careful. Information implies some processing. What people see on a Web site is basically data, and turning data into information depends, among other things, on what happens in their minds. Therein lies the big challenge. There's a lot of data out there—how do you convert it to information that's useful to you?

ROBERT: Let's move beyond accessibility. Marvin, how has the Internet amplified individual choice and the power of the person?

MARVIN: There are rather trivial things, like marketing. If you want to buy something, search engines can find the lowest price for a product. I don't know quite what this will do to normal business practices, but I use it, and things cost twenty to forty percent less.

ROBERT: But I bet you're buying more, though. I do—it gets me all the time.

MARVIN: Well, I don't have to pay for these things, because—

ROBERT: That's cheating. Come on.

MARVIN: I get these grants, and—

ROBERT: What about us normal people? I go on a Web site and I save a few dollars, but then I buy three times as much as I had planned.

MARVIN: Another way the Internet empowers people is in enabling them to keep in contact. This is going to be a very strange thing. Right now, we have a mobile society: We go to grade school and then we move on, somewhere else, and we learn to make new friends. Here I have Motorola's little gadget that enables me to send E-mail anywhere. What will happen in the future, when children have this access? So when you're seven years old, you make a dozen friends, and now even when they move away, you still have them. You can spend your whole life with your first friends. We may get a society of people who don't bother to form new friendships.

GEORGE: Even if we continue to make new friends, we may have a better connection to our past—which is especially important for personal integrity as people get older.

BART: The Internet also lowers transaction costs. If you have a brain tumor, in theory the surgeon could be in France operating a robotic device that cuts your brain while you stay in New York. Your access to skills and services will change dramatically.

ROBERT: Frank, how does the Internet break barriers between cultures, or between organizations, or within cultures and organizations?

FRANK: Well, it certainly accelerates the decline of sovereignty. As Bart said, communications don't respect international jurisdictions, and so governments can't regulate it. On the other hand, I have to take a little bit of exception and talk about the disadvantages. One of the problems of the Internet is that it encourages a kind of superficiality of human social interaction. A good example of this is your typical USENET group or chat room. You get these so-called flame wars, where people are simply uncivil to one another, and part of the reason is the impermanence of the association. It's not like the bricks-and-mortar kinds of human communities. The people of the Jamestown settlement and the pilgrims landing at Plymouth were stuck with one another; they couldn't get away. But anyone can get in and out of an Internet community whenever he or she wants, so it doesn't lend itself to the development of shared norms and values, the sorts of things that really bind the more traditional kind of human community together.

MARVIN: I disagree with that. I don't like civility. The trouble with insulting people in their presence is that they might hit you. And you can't express yourself very well. I've made many

friends on USENET newsgroups whom I've never met—and in many cases I don't hope to meet. These flame wars are wonderful: People tell you what they really think. Or maybe they lie—it doesn't matter. But I think you learn more per hour this way, by getting right to the heart of the matter. The polite people are a waste of time; they write all these words, and I usually turn to another screen when that happens.

ROBERT: What about Frank's shared norms and values of traditional human communities?

MARVIN: You're talking about people getting into their own culture, and I don't like cultures. I think cultures are a waste of the human mind. A person becomes a kind of robot because he's a Serb or he's a whatever-he-is. Everybody says we should respect these cultures, but why should we? I belong to some scientific cultures on the Net; these are my cultures, and we're very close, because we share ideas much more intimately than we could if we were meeting in person.

ROBERT: But your scientific cultures on the Net aren't any more legitimate than national cultures.

MARVIN: I don't know. When you meet people, you look at them, and their face or their posture or something may remind you of your Uncle Louie, or some person you don't like. So you're dominated by that stereotype. Face-to-face contact is almost impossible to penetrate. When you talk to people on the Net, though, what you're dominated by is their ideas.

BRUCE: I have some experience. For the last four or five years, I've been working on how to use the Web for the deliberative discourse on complex issues that affect a lot of people. And we've done a series of experiments. The approach is called HyperForum, which is the copyrighted brand name for it. The idea is to counterbalance the consequences of radio and TV talk shows, which tend to exploit the short term, and Internet chat rooms, which I think are terrible because they're based on instant interaction and posturing—

ROBERT: How does HyperForum work?

BRUCE: It's all non-real-time. There's lots of information, a structure, moderators. You type out what your position is, in a form that other people can read, and then they can comment. Everybody plays under his or her real name; there are no avatars, no pseudonyms, the bios are known and accessible. An authoritative

---

. . . there is a way to use the Web for truly thoughtful discourse.

---

facilitator is in control. Participation is often restricted to a certain group of people from a certain community, because people will not open up on a difficult subject if they think journalists or outsiders may be listening. Our demonstration topic is sustainability. So there is a way to use the Web for truly thoughtful discourse. But it's extremely difficult to have that kind of discourse in our real-time, shoot-from-the-hip society.

ROBERT: Are you saying that an unformed discourse is bad?

BRUCE: No, but in this series of experiments we've learned something very important—it's best done if you have a face-to-face meeting at the beginning. Then you go through these

extended Internet-based interactions, maybe for three months, following which you have a face-to-face outcome session. One of the conclusions I'm drawing from this empirical research is that it's the hybrid—the human interaction with the technology—that is so powerful. Technology does not and cannot replace human interaction.

ROBERT: Marvin disagrees.

BRUCE: I know. And I differ. I differ very much. I'm concerned that we're at risk when people have completely impersonal communication—especially when they don't even have to be themselves.

GEORGE: One of the challenges we face in the next decade is to figure out the form of the virtual identity versus real identity. For different personalities, different groups, the combination will come together in different ways. We know very little about how the virtual world and the real world will blend in creative combinations. The one thing we do know is that both worlds will remain very important. What I'm hearing now, for example, is people saying, "Wait a minute, let's drive commerce back to the real world. Let's not use the Internet to do all our shopping; let's use it to build a mirror of a community—a local community—so we can send the business back to local shops." So we're seeing mixes and creative blends of the virtual and the physical worlds.

BART: There's a downside that has to do with the issue of civility. You can really hurt people badly by defaming them on the Internet—and you can do it easily, in ways you couldn't otherwise. The accusation that Mr. X beats his wife can become very widespread, given the links you have. And if Marvin has a new book coming out and a graduate student sneaks a copy of the files and dumps them on the Internet, what happens to the proprietorship of Marvin's bits of information? These questions have not been settled.

MARVIN: But that's not a new problem. Stealing has always been a problem.

BART: Now it's amplified.

MARVIN: I'd like to challenge the idea of real identity versus Net identity, because I think when you're in the same room with a person there's no real identity. You're talking to that person in his role as a salesman, as a member of a religion, as a member of a culture, as a member of a profession, and—

ROBERT: Aren't those real attributes?

MARVIN: Well, I don't know what "real" means. The same applies when you talk to somebody via E-mail; you're communicating with a certain aspect of that person's personality. You could just as well say that the E-mail personality is the real personality and the [face-to-face] personality is just a tradition.

GEORGE: We have to use the words "virtual" and "real" with appropriate definitions, because "virtual" does convey certain real information and "real" does convey certain virtual information—

MARVIN: —and lacks others; the "real" personality is very incomplete.

ROBERT: How about privacy? Is it enhanced or compromised by the Internet?

GEORGE: There's great concern over that. In fact, many corporations now state that they won't deal with Web sites that don't have privacy

statements [i.e., written policies protecting the confidentiality of customer or visitor data]. So

---

> *. . . we're seeing this continual tug of war between individual privacy and access to information.*

---

we're seeing this continual tug of war between individual privacy and access to information.

MARVIN: The problem of privacy is always with us, because if you want to prevent crimes, you can just watch everyone all the time—and that annoys people. There's a beautiful book by [award-winning science fiction writer] David Brin, *The Transparent Society: Will Technology Force Us to Choose Between Privacy and Freedom?*, in which he proposes that we now have to choose between two worlds: one where nothing is secret, everyone knows everything, and we have all sorts of protections, and one where privacy is maintained but there are more dangers.*

BRUCE: But the main issue—which is important, because it involves more than just the Internet—is accountability versus privacy. That pertains to the mail, to all other kinds of communication, too. It's just escalated on an enormous scale with the Internet.

BART: This raises the issue of taxation. How will governments be able to tax people's incomes if all they see is that there has been a transfer of money from account A to account B?

---

*Brin offers the controversial proposition that the best way to preserve freedom will be to give up privacy; that privacy, far from being a right, thwarts accountability, which is the true foundation of a civil society.

ROBERT: They should hire you as a consultant.

BART: That won't do the job. I would predict a shift away from income taxes and toward consumption taxes.

MARVIN: We're going to have that anyway. Consider the cost of collection. What fraction of the tax collected is the cost of the tax collection? Not to mention accountants and tax lawyers and the weeks of people's time every year.

ROBERT: Bart, what about the economics of the Internet? Is it really all free?

BART: There's no digital free lunch. There's a price for every bit of exchange on the Net. Every time you send or receive a bit of information, there's a cost associated with it. Historically, the American taxpayer has subsidized the Internet, and we continue to do so to some degree. That will change, and it's a good thing. Otherwise the Internet would be overwhelmed. For example, let's say you, as a user, have a so-called intelligent agent—that is, software that collects information off the Web for you—and that agent creates two agents, and each of those creates two more, and very soon the Internet is saturated. There has to be a cost. Imagine a newspaper of the future tailored for you, where your agent searches all around the planet for the kinds of information you like—arts, entertainment, sports, the news. That agent should probably have to pay microcurrencies—fractions of a penny—for each piece of information. It won't be a free lunch.

ROBERT: George, your company, TriVergence, tracks the strategic moves of Intel and Microsoft. How much of their business is Internet-related?

GEORGE: A lot. Intel and Microsoft realized that a transition needed to be made from personal computing to the Internet. So both companies are using their balance-sheet cash, billions of dollars, as well as the currency of their stock, to stimulate all the economic drivers of the Internet—bandwidth, content, and so forth.

ROBERT: How is the Internet affecting international commerce?

FRANK: It will break down commercial barriers, but it also serves as a challenge to governments, because any political system—liberal democracy, particularly—needs to be based on shared values and perspectives. The Internet has the potential for fragmenting society—not just

The Internet has the potential for fragmenting society . . .

nation-states but local areas—into multiple microscopic communities. It puts you in touch with all three hundred people who are interested in growing gladioli on the upper peninsula in Michigan, but you may have nothing to say to people who like growing roses in southern Florida.

ROBERT: So as groups get more cohesive and don't bother communicating with people in other groups, all these groups grow farther and farther apart.

FRANK: And that has sinister implications. The militias get to talk to one another, and they create a parallel reality that isn't anyone else's reality.

ROBERT: Marvin, doesn't this worry you?

MARVIN: Oh, sure. But the formation of cultures in general worries me. A culture is a number of people all thinking the same way, and most of our troubles come from small cultures. The quandary is that given modern technology, small cultures have more leverage, but I think we're just jumping from one frying pan into another.

ROBERT: This brings up freedom of expression—a major issue, obviously, involving everything from pornography and hate groups to controversial theories in science, politics, and religion. All nonmainstream ideas are subject to criticism.

MARVIN: Right now, pornography is a terrible problem, because we can't face it. But I don't think it's a particularly terrible problem inherently—not if we address it as a society—but I don't know how you deal with these things.

BRUCE: You're saying that pornography is inherently not a terrible problem, that it wouldn't be a problem if we didn't have all the attributes of human society—our language, our mores, and everything else. But then our world would be completely different. Aldous Huxley wrote a book about that; it's called *Brave New World*. But this mix of diversity and tension is what it means to be human.

BART: Think what would happen if Hitler had had the Internet. Or Napoleon. Their reach over humanity would have been greatly extended.

BRUCE: Exactly the opposite. Then all the groups that Hitler and Napoleon suppressed would have been able to use communication against them. The Internet would have leavened the lump.

ROBERT: This is a real dichotomy: on the one hand, dictators can control public opinion with rapid, ubiquitous downloads; on the other hand, subversive information—*samizdat*—can't be suppressed.

BART: The Internet amplifies. It amplifies evil and good.

MARVIN: Yes, there's a serious problem in that people don't understand the difference between popular democracy and representative democracy. The idea of taking a poll five minutes after

---

The Internet amplifies. It amplifies evil and good.

---

something has been publicized is very dangerous. So the most important thing that we can do might be educating people not to make decisions based on the latest news, but I don't know who the "we" is.

ROBERT: We are we. This is it. Bruce, what do you see as the evolution of the Internet itself?

BRUCE: Everywhere you turn, there's conflict—privacy versus accountability, centralization versus fragmentation. It's all going on at once. But I think there's a way out of these conundrums. If you were a sociologist on a planet orbiting Alpha Centauri, looking at this funny, just-discovered planet called Earth, you would see that this period of time, this hundred or two hundred years of human history, is unprecedented. There's nothing like it, nor will there ever again be anything like it—because the trends can't be sustained. For one thing, the world's population can't continue to grow at the same rate. So we're in this remarkable transition—I call it the crunch. And this perspective makes you realize that outcomes are not a simple linear progression of what we see now. There are new alignments emerging—and eventually new belief systems. My prediction, for what it's worth, is that the next major religion will develop over the Web.

ROBERT: Let's get a prediction from everyone. Fast-forward a hundred years. How many hours a day will the average person be online?

MARVIN: I don't want to answer that, because I suspect that within a hundred years there will be artificial intelligence systems on the Net, and you won't have to search it yourself, because they will have read all the stuff and answered all your questions. So maybe you won't have to spend any time at all online. But seriously—it's impossible, as Arthur Clarke said, to predict more than fifty years ahead in technology, because all the things we don't think can be done will seem like magic. Ten years ahead—that's a different story.

BRUCE: The limiting factor will be us. I'm not only a futurist, I'm a geologist, so I've been schooled in the idea that we're an evolved species. Now we're in a very stressful period, because our environment is changing rapidly. In fact, we're at the limit. We could go crazy both individually and collectively, because of this rate of change. So there's a limit to how completely we'll be consumed by a cybersociety, because we're biologically primitive.

GEORGE: We'll maintain a rich blend of the physical world and the Internet world, but I can't go forward a hundred years either. I simply see things moving too quickly and I can't possibly forecast that far.

ROBERT: Bart, you can go a hundred years.

BART: Well, I don't know about that, but as Marvin said, we'll have intelligent software agents doing our work for us, they will always be online, and we'll be in wireless, real-time connection with them. So the answer, relatively soon, will be "twenty-four hours a day." Some part of you will always be in communication with some part of the Internet.

ROBERT: Frank, how do you see communications affecting the political structure of the world?

FRANK: Well, since I've said we were at the end of history, I don't need to see [any further]. But it's probably true that technology will be embedded in everything, exacerbating some social problems—loss of privacy for example. If you want to establish trust with other people, if you want to deal with them on a long-term basis, that's a social problem that isn't solved by technology. In fact, trust gets in the way of privacy, because if you want someone to trust you, you have to reveal something of who you are and establish your credibility. And that's not a problem that can be solved through technology.

ROBERT: What will be the most significant fact, looking back, about the Internet?

MARVIN: People will say, "Well, the Internet was really important until the development of artificial intelligence in 2073." The second event will be the big one.

BRUCE: I think the most significant fact is the point that Frank [Fukuyama] made—that radical change in the political and economic relations of people all over the world is happening because of this unprogrammed advent of the Internet and the Web.

GEORGE: Diverse communities. The ability to have a very wide range of communities come together around special interests—commercial, recreational, educational.

BART: I think, unfortunately, the most significant change will be a form of world government, and the first big step in that direction will happen when the United Nations begins taxing the Internet.

ROBERT: Will everyone have to wear black [as Bart does]?

BART: They may.

FRANK: Actually, there are two parallel revolutions going on—one in information technology and the other in biotechnology. Whatever is going to happen in a hundred years will come out of a fusion of these two.

ROBERT: CONCLUDING COMMENT

The Internet, like most new technologies, brings us a set of conflicts. The benefits are obvious: there's personal choice and empowerment, unlimited information at the speed of light, and the breaking of boundaries of every kind. But the Internet also threatens to fragment society, isolate communities, depersonalize relationships, distort intimacy, erode privacy, and sacrifice reflection to an addiction to speed. Yet such change is only the beginning. The Internet is not a something, it is virtually an everything; and therein lies a deeper, more fundamental issue. The Internet entails such a profound change for human beings that we who embrace it may be setting in motion a new kind of evolution, literally transforming humanity into a new kind of species. Maybe that's science fiction. Or maybe that's closer to truth.

OUTTAKES

MARVIN: It sounded like a good show to me.

BRUCE: Well, you seem to know what you're doing.

ROBERT: It's virtual, not real.

MARVIN: —actually property is a bad idea, and of course we'd have to kill all the lawyers, but it'd be worth it.

MARVIN: There are some people who are very good at influencing public opinion—

BRUCE: —and you can see a change of twenty or thirty percent in the national poll within days.

BART: There is a proposal to tax the Internet in the U.N. But the capacity to have worldwide plebiscites, so that people in other countries can decide if should we invade country X, is frightening.

CHAPTER 20

How Does Technology Transform Society?

W
hat new treats will technology offer us? It's a nice list—prettier television pictures, better diet drugs, no-hassle home shopping on the Internet, instant communications anytime anyplace, gizmos for your kitchen, gadgets for your car. This is technology's public face, but its true transformation lies deeper. What are the traps in this cornucopia of gifts that pulse, packet, and flash? Separately these are just fancy widgets, but collectively they can conceal hidden hazards. Since technological advance is unstoppable, social change is inevitable—and these tectonic shifts in society will affect our lives more than all those fancy widgets combined. Think about how technology has brought sweeping changes in our life at home and at work, and in entertainment, commerce, government, international relations, personal relations. That's our list. Let's see how our thoughtful observers expand on it.

PARTICIPANTS

Dr. Gregory Benford, a physicist at the University of California, Irvine, is a well-known science fiction writer whose novels are acclaimed for their scientific accuracy. Greg assures us that the future will not simply be the past with snazzy new gadgets; serious social change lies ahead.

Dr. Francis (Fred) Fukuyama, an international public policy expert, is the author of several important books on political and social change. Frank discusses how the information revolution has changed society, from labor markets to organizational structure to the feminist revolution.

Dr. George Kozmetsky, founder of the IC² Institute (for "Innovation, Creativity, and Capital"), an entrepreneurial think tank at the University of Texas, Austin, was awarded the National Medal of Technology in 1993. George focuses on the changing nature of wealth and of business.

Dr. Marvin Minsky, a pioneer and champion of the field of artificial intelligence, has made important contributions to machine perception, robotics, and automation. Marvin talks about a disappearing workplace and what will happen when computers get common sense.

Dr. Gregory Stock, trained in biophysics and business, is the director of the Program on Medicine, Technology, and Society at the University of California, Los Angeles. Greg emphasizes three important vectors of change: genetic engineering, artificial intelligence, and space travel.

ROBERT: Frank, your book on the new information society is titled *The Great Disruption.* Why the aggressive title?

FRANK: Well, nobody's interested in reading about a little disruption. It seems to me that the transition to an information society is comparable to moving from a hunter-gatherer to an agricultural society, and from an agricultural to an industrial society, and it would be very surprising if this current transition didn't involve huge social changes in the way we relate to one another.

ROBERT: What are some of these social changes?

FRANK: Labor markets, for example. The feminist revolution was made almost inevitable by the movement into an information society, where you substitute mental labor for physical labor at the margin.

ROBERT: Marvin, have robotics and automation affected the social fabric?

MARVIN: Not too much yet, although robots are used here and there in industry. But they're not very autonomous, so there are usually still a lot of people around. What we're going to have

in the future are much more independent robots, and that means less manual labor. And also what's called telepresence, which means a person in one place—a different state or a different country—can work in another place without actually being there.

ROBERT: How will this affect human interaction—family and social groups?

MARVIN: Right now, many people have two lives, one at home and one in the workplace. But the workplace may start to disappear. On the other hand, people make connections through the Internet and have friends distributed broadly throughout the world. I don't know what will happen to the family under these conditions.

ROBERT: George, you're a pioneer in the relationship between technology and society. You cofounded a technology-based conglomerate (Teledyne), and you were a board member of Dell Computers. How have technology companies affected society?

GEORGE: First, technology companies—the two you mentioned, plus others—have changed the notion of what wealth is. Wealth is now nothing but liquid paper. Second, the best companies have realized that if they treat their employees well, giving them stock options at attractive prices, they motivate their employees. And this has had the effect of distributing the wealth.

ROBERT: Dell and Teledyne have a long history of treating their stakeholders very personally.

GEORGE: They've also given capital to the communities in which their employees live—it's a new resource we call "community cap."

ROBERT: Greg Stock, your book *Metaman* postulates a new world, where humans and machines work together as if they were a global superorganism. Why do you see such a change?

GREG STOCK: There's going to be dramatic change in the near-term future, because extraordinary things are occurring. Three of them are obvious. We're unraveling our own biology, so that we're beginning to be able to manipulate it profoundly, through genetic engineering—altering human design in some way or another, which challenges who we are and what it means to be human. Then there's artificial intelligence, where we introduce a level of complexity into nonliving materials that has up to now been present only in life itself. And then space travel. We're beginning to move off the surface of the planet that has contained and constrained life for billions of years.

ROBERT: But how do these things affect ordinary people just going about their daily lives? How will it affect me today?

GREG STOCK: Imagine the enormous changes that would result just from an extension of the human life span. Virtually everything

about the trajectory of human life, about all our institutions, and about the way we deal with life would be transformed.

ROBERT: Greg Benford, you've written some thirty books in the past twenty years—mostly science fiction related to current science. Has your fiction changed as technology has changed?

GREG BENFORD: Oh, of course. I was once young and naïve, and now I'm old and naïve. But you have to remain that way—you have to be open to possibilities. As Greg [Stock] was just saying, you ain't seen nothing yet. Hold on to your hats. We may even wear hats again in the future—hats would be a good investment.

. . . the future will not just be like the present with a lot of snazzy new gadgets.

You've got to understand that the future will not just be like the present with a lot of snazzy new gadgets. It's going to change the whole way we think about ourselves. But what most interests me is that the grounds of discussion will change. We won't think of problems in the same way. Think back to the 1890s—look at those social discussions and how irrelevant they are today. The same thing will happen again.

ROBERT: Frank, when I mentioned *The Great Disruption*, you immediately brought up the changing role of women. Other people, when they talk about major social transitions, bring up things like genetic engineering or artificial intelligence. Why do you focus on the role of women?

FRANK: That's already one of the big changes that technology has brought about in the last half century. A century ago, the average woman would have died by the time her last child left the household, so she had no life apart from family life. Today, thanks to improvements in medical technology, probably thirty-five to forty-five years of a woman's life are spent outside of either her birth family or the family she raises, and so almost inevitably feminism becomes an issue, because you have to figure out what to do with those extra years. One of the characteristics of an information society is that women have a much more natural place in the labor market, and that affects the family, and it affects the nature of relationships. Sexual harassment doesn't exist as an issue unless women are working.

ROBERT: What's happened to families?

FRANK: Families have become destabilized, because the traditional role that women have played has changed. The change is inevitable, but it's created a great deal of social stress, in

---

Families have become destabilized, because the traditional role that women have played has changed.

---

terms of the welfare of children. It's something that society as a whole has been struggling to fix for the last generation.

ROBERT: Marvin, what other social stresses are there as a result of an increase in technology?

MARVIN: Well, there's the problem of increasing life span, which Greg Stock mentioned.

We're looking at an extra three hundred or four hundred years of life, because rather soon we'll start extending the average life span by one or two years every year.

ROBERT: What will that mean for families? Will marriages go on for three or four hundred years, or will there be serial marriage? We'll need new rules, or what?

MARVIN: People will invent all sorts of things, and a little evolution will find that some of these inventions are acceptable and some of them are intolerable.

ROBERT: What about artificial intelligence?

MARVIN: That really hasn't happened yet, because computers now can't do ordinary commonsense thinking. They don't know enough, but there's going to be a sudden critical point when they will. It could happen in ten years, or fifty, but since hardly anyone is working on giving computers common sense, we can't predict when it will happen. But then everything will change, because no one will have to work.

GREG STOCK: We've had some big changes as a result of a more general sort of artificial intelligence—that is, the kinds of communication we have today. This has resulted in an incredible diversity of subcultures, little clusters of people that have arisen and are distributed across international boundaries. So you have trends manifesting rapidly, diffusing broadly, and then disappearing again. There's a volatile, dynamic environment, which I don't think existed prior to the kinds of communications we have today.

ROBERT: It's fascinating to see the blurring of national and organizational boundaries. What's happening to organizations under the impact of technology?

FRANK: The classic early-twentieth-century organization was hierarchical—the auto factory, for example—and you had a segregated white-collar staff that gave all the orders to a poorly educated blue-collar workforce. In modern organizations, that system is being almost entirely replaced by networks, or with much flatter kinds of structures, as the skills levels of the workers rise. Modern organizations have to become more self-managing. You can't manage a modern organization like Microsoft by operating with a lot of detailed bureaucratic rules.

ROBERT: People who produce knowledge are similar regardless of what kinds of organizations they belong to; these so-called knowledge groups look the same wherever they're found— private sector, public sector, universities, business, government. For example, a university computer science department is more like a software company than that software company is like a steel company. Marvin, as a founder of MIT's Artificial Intelligence Lab, how do you manage this kind of knowledge group?

MARVIN: There are several artificial intelligence laboratories, and they're all trying to make machines smarter in one way or another. But they're not dealing with large amounts of knowledge, and that's what's wrong with them. For a machine to achieve common sense, it probably has to know fifteen million little things about the world—like if you push something round, it will roll, but if you push something square, it won't. No machine knows that sort of thing today. Every child knows it. Children know, I suspect, fifteen million little things about the world: You can pull something with a string but you can't push something with a string, but you can push

something with a stick, and so forth. There are millions of these little things, and no computer knows them. That's why no computer can browse the Web and find out which information is going to be useful to you. But when enough research is done, this will suddenly happen.

GREG STOCK: So, Marvin, when will enough intelligence be internalized in these machines so that they can begin to obtain those millions of little things by reading on their own, essentially—rather than through the laborious effort of codifying all those rules? That's when we'll get an inflection point. How far away do you think that is?

MARVIN: Oh, it could be a thousand years or ten years. I know only five people in the world who are trying to make a system that can absorb more commonsense knowledge. This is the largest industry of the future, and nobody's in it. Fascinating!

GEORGE: What I find happening in the corporate world is that we're dumping information

in the corporate world . . . we're dumping information technology and moving to knowledge.

technology and moving to knowledge. And the first thing we're doing is building knowledge communities in our companies.

ROBERT: What's the difference between knowledge and information?

GEORGE: If I take plain old data and remove the noise, then I'll have information left over.

You need information, not data. If I need to make a decision, for example, I'll have it nice and neatly cut out, so that even a machine can understand it—

MARVIN: That's what I mean by common sense. No machine has the information needed to understand other information.

GEORGE: What I see happening is that we're going to be forming groups to do what Marvin [Minsky]'s talking about. When we begin to understand how we work together to produce the knowledge that generates wealth and prosperity and to distribute it right, then we'll be able to put all that into a machine and go on to the higher levels he's dealing with. And we were talking about how organizations have been transformed by technology. Back in the early decades of the twentieth century, businesses were organized functionally. Then, after World War Two, we had the cold war, and technology came into its own. We had very little experience running large-scale, complex organizations— how in the world do you manage a large-scale program? What we learned was that if you figured out how to do it, they promoted you, and if you didn't, they fired you. So we were led into program management. And then we moved to information technology, and that's gotten rid of what was left of the society's old economic structure. Nowadays you can't really talk about "the service industry" and "the manufacturing industry," because they're so intertwined. And that's the new society we're in. It's a knowledge economy, and the problem now is how to empower people and get them to work together.

ROBERT: Frank, you've studied many different kinds of organizations over the course of your career. You've seen these changes. How does your view accord with George's?

FRANK: Most organizations today are less centralized, less rule-bound, less controlled from the top down. People are self-organizing; they form networks based on shifting coalitions of interest, which change with technology, with time, with environment.

ROBERT: Are these structural changes occurring primarily in high-tech companies?

FRANK: Well, I think this trend is everywhere; it's really spreading. It begins in high-tech, but everybody is high-tech these days. There's not a single product that does not make use of technology, at least as a process.

ROBERT: Technology knows no borders. What's the importance of globalization in generating social change?

FRANK: I think it's having a very disruptive effect. In an advanced country like the United States, if you're a low-skilled worker, all of a sudden you have to compete not just against machines in your own country but against millions of low-skilled workers in Malaysia, India, and Vietnam. Every year a new country comes online, and that basically pushes down your wages; or if you're European, it raises the cost of social protection to keep your job in place.

MARVIN: It lowers the price of things for everyone else.

ROBERT: Yes, so that's good?

MARVIN: It's good and bad.

ROBERT: So do you just let that happen?

MARVIN: I presume you evolve a [wage] floor, but I don't know how you do it.

FRANK: The Europeans have evolved a very high floor, which is part of their problem.

MARVIN: Right. You have to evolve the right floor.

ROBERT: Greg Benford, in your experience as a writer, do you find that as globalization has progressed you have more readers in more countries, and do you get feedback from them?

GREG BENFORD: Certainly, that's happening. I have about a dozen foreign editions, and I get E-mail from people who've read my work in languages of which I have no knowledge whatever. And to some extent, I wonder what they get out of it, because you never know how the Japanese translation, say, is going to work, if you don't speak Japanese. World culture is coming together; that's surely the prospect in the next century. But what worries me is an undercurrent: We've got this hierarchy—here's data, here's information, here's knowledge, and above that there has to be something we would call wisdom. There's a marked scarcity of wisdom, and we certainly haven't automated it yet.

ROBERT: You want to automate wisdom?

GREG BENFORD: Yes, of course. But only on the hundred-year scale. If we start living for two centuries, we might actually acquire some wisdom. That's one of the limitations of the human race.

GREG STOCK: I think this is a very important point. We need whole clusters of planners who will acquire a wisdom about how to manage the future. Only then will we figure out how best to proceed.

ROBERT: Wisdom by committee? Wisdom from the top down?

GREG STOCK: It's a government issue, generally—and it seems to me that we really don't know where our technologies are taking us, how our society is going be transformed. The only way we can gain some sort of wisdom for dealing with the future is by trying—that is, moving forward and learning from our mistakes. A trial-and-error process as we move into the future. And there will be a great deal of conflict about how we do this—how we move forward in this era of increasing uncertainty.

ROBERT: Given such uncertainty, Frank, what will happen to international relations? Do you see turbulence ahead?

FRANK: Technological change always brings turbulence. On the other hand, one of the few rules in political science that people seem to agree on is that democracies don't fight [each other]. And in fact we've got a new set of international relations today, whereby people are pretty much agreed on the basic forms—at least in the powerful, industrialized countries. They're pretty much agreed on the rules of political governance and on the rules of the global economy. And this is a very unusual situation, in that the world is much more peaceful than ever before. There are wars in the Balkans and in Central Africa, but the big powers have not been this peaceful in quite a while.

ROBERT: But doesn't the increasing prevalence of small groups destabilize the world in a new kind of way?

FRANK: It destabilizes the world in small ways, but large world orders have to be created by large great powers. And that's what's different about the world right now—the conflict among the powers seems to have been channeled into economic competition rather than the traditional military struggles.

ROBERT: What are some of the hidden hazards, as technology transforms society?

GREG BENFORD: My fear is the too-comfy future for all the advanced nations. This is a world in which, say, computers animate your desk, your car, your home, and they respond to you personally. You go to the mall, and the buildings address you and tell you about the bargains, and they know who you are—they recognize you on the video camera. This is a world of supercomfortable surveillance and artificiality, in which the city is uniquely nurturing and the natural world is seen as indifferent and even hostile—which is a complete reversal of the stereotype that obtained, say, a century ago.

ROBERT: Does that future scare you, Marvin?

MARVIN: I'm not sure what to be scared about, because I don't see what the role of people will be, once goods are free. But yes, maybe things are too comfortable. I don't see any objection to

---

. . . no matter how comfortable you are, if you don't have other goals, then society is doomed . . .

---

the house and the machines knowing your preferences, because there's always something to grumble about. But no matter how comfortable you are, if you don't have other goals, then society is doomed anyway. Even if society lasts a billion years, if nothing happens, I'm not interested in it.

FRANK: One of the scarier technologies comes out of the life sciences. If we determine that we're genetically programmed to behave the way

we do, what happens to personal responsibility, what happens to the law, and what happens to our ability to think of ourselves as free agents?

MARVIN: Well, we're going to need a theory of personal responsibility, because right now the theories we have are clearly unsound. Someone commits a crime and we argue about its social causes, or the religious people say that the devil got into him—I heard that the other day. But when we understand the brain, then we'll have some real decisions to make—like what level of violence we want in our children.

ROBERT: This brings up the whole issue of social engineering. Should a humane society manipulate its citizens, whether biologically or psychologically, to create a social order that the majority wants?

MARVIN: It already does so to a great extent, by pumping beliefs into us. We have to figure out some way to get enough variety into society so that even if there's a culture with a billion people who all think the same way, and it turns out to be a bad way, there are alternatives available. For one thing, let's spend twenty billion or fifty billion dollars—whatever it takes—to get three or four colonies off the planet Earth.

GREG STOCK: With all the potential danger in the biological sciences, we should do our explorations and make our mistakes now, when our capabilities are just nascent, rather than waiting until these technologies advance to where they can be implemented suddenly and on a large scale.

MARVIN: And you can't take it back.

GREG STOCK: Then technological advance can become very disruptive and create huge errors, and so it seems to me that we have to bite the bullet and move forward as aggressively as

---

. . . technological advance can become very disruptive and create huge errors, . . .

---

we can now, while these technologies are young, and while we can still learn at relatively low cost.

MARVIN: Let me interrupt, because I see politicians noticing that somehow the United States has a big surplus. They don't quite understand how it happened, but it's there and they're trying to decide how to spend it. So some people say, "Let's put it into Social Security, so that Social Security won't go broke in 2030." But by 2030 people will probably be living to a hundred and fifty, and so the Social Security system will really be broke.

ROBERT: There are self-correcting mechanisms.

MARVIN: They'll just raise taxes.

GREG STOCK: Or you can change the pattern of people's work life. Many people past the current retirement age will continue to work and to contribute.

MARVIN: I would put this surplus into the rapid development of a couple of Mars colonies and things like that. I haven't heard a single politician suggest any scheme that would help the human race if we faced a cosmic accident.

ROBERT: Frank, what happens to culture under the onslaught of technology?

FRANK: By one account, culture disappears, because the information revolution moves ideas and entertainment from one part of the globe to another. But I think the actual way this will play out is going to be much more complex, because in a way what people's lives are all about is their culture, and they're going to react against this kind of homogenization. Witness Quebec and Scotland deciding that they're separate nations, right in the heart of a modern technological world.

ROBERT: Aren't cultural groups becoming more numerous, more fragmented, more isolated?

FRANK: At a subnational level, people are saying, "Look, we're not just part of the McDonald's–Coca-Cola global economy. We have values that are distinctive and traditions that we want to keep alive."

GREG STOCK: But at some level, this global homogeneity offers all people a culture much richer than was ever available in the past.

MARVIN: That's what they're rebelling against.

GREG STOCK: Yes, because they're trying to hold on to what's theirs. I think this elevation of ethnicity is a revolt against the future, a protest against the transformations that are taking us into the future. That's why conservative religions have been on the ascendancy. It's as if we don't want to go there, we don't want progress, because it means the destruction of traditional values.

MARVIN: But not everyone rebels, just the vast majority of people who find learning painful.

ROBERT: But doesn't this reflect what human beings really are?

MARVIN: No. Most cultures exist because they've taught their people to reject new ideas. It's not human nature, it's culture nature. I regard cultures as huge parasites. I think each person has a lot of potential, and I find it painful when I'm introduced to somebody, say, in Europe, and when I hear that a man's name is O'Brien, I know he's Catholic. He didn't choose it. His culture chose it. And to me that culture is an evil, mindless force that first teaches its values and then teaches you to fear other values. So, of course it looks like human nature, but it's meme nature.

ROBERT: "Meme" being a term coined by British biologist Richard Dawkins to describe the contagious spread of ideas that replicate like viruses and spread from mind to mind. Memes are inherited, like genes—they're transferred from one person to another by imitation, and they compete as they spread throughout society. They've been described as "mind viruses," caring only about their own propagation.

MARVIN: They're ideas that get into the brain. And the ones that stick best are the ones that are best at killing the other ideas.

ROBERT: Don't you have a culture in Cambridge at MIT?

MARVIN: I have many cultures. Look, the other day I logged on to the Net because a little girl was asking me something, and I found a group of people who collect the whiskers of cats. There are only about fifty of them all over the world. They spend a lot of time collecting these whiskers, and they send little E-mails to each other about how to find them. On a long-haired cat, the whiskers get blown around. . . . Oh, well, forget it. The point is that I'm in a lot of cultures. Every week I find a culture, and I say, "I'm going to get into this."

FRANK: But you're not really part of those cultures. You're just a visitor.

MARVIN: What do you mean, part? You mean it doesn't eat up my whole brain? Thank God, no.

FRANK: But you don't share their norms and values.

MARVIN: I share norms and values with the chemists in our Chemistry Department. That's a little culture. But I don't want ninety percent of my mind eaten up by sharing the norms and values of a bunch of rules that were written thousands of years ago and don't reflect anything good.

ROBERT: Yes, but the fact is that in today's world there's more of this sectarian feeling— cultural, ethnic, religious. It may be a rebellion against technology, against depersonalization, against a strict materialism.

MARVIN: Do you really think there's more of this today than in the past, when whole populations were fanatic about their religions? At least now we're breaking into millions of little cults, most of which won't last. So that's fine with me.

GREG STOCK: It's a futile expression, a dying gasp of traditional cultures. It's not going to slow things down substantially.

GREG BENFORD: This is tribes against the empire. It's been that way for a long time, and the tribes never win. They have some great wars, but the empire always wins. The real problem we'll have is what I call the Alexander Wept problem. Alexander the Great wept because there was nothing left to conquer, no more places to go. What is this society going to do in a hundred years? Stay home and watch the twenty-first century on TV? We really need frontiers. The biggest problem for advanced nations is Alexander's problem.

FRANK: Well, I don't know. I think the people running this empire are getting a little arrogant. There are cultural underpinnings to the empire itself that are very necessary, having to do with tolerance and the free exchange of ideas. These are cultural values that don't just occur to scientists. They're socially inherited and they have to be socialized into the population.

MARVIN: What's so great about tolerance? Do you mean we should teach our kids that all ideas are equal and good?

FRANK: No.

MARVIN: It would be nice to prevent violence, but I don't think that we should tolerate ideas that say, "It's OK—let that poor person have his brain eaten by that set of ideas." That offends me.

ROBERT: Some non-Western people might say that the imposition of American or Western ideals of critical thinking is cultural imperialism.

MARVIN: But [cultural thinking] is a disease, yes? So critical thinking is not exactly an imposition; it's more a cure. Most cultures, although they've defended themselves against other bad theological ideas, haven't found a way to defend themselves against critical thinking very well, and they're terrified.

GEORGE: As we're speaking, the culture is changing. And it's not going to be changed by the people sitting here. It's going to be changed by the youngsters out there.

GREG STOCK: The division between high culture and popular culture is less important, since the substantial change is that culture is really popular culture now. And all other kinds are irrelevant.

ROBERT: Isn't popular culture getting more homogenous around the world?

GREG STOCK: No, I think it's more fragmented in many ways, although it's more extensive geographically; a young person in China has more in common with a young person in the United States than either has with his grandparents. But it's not necessarily homogenous. There's incredible diversity. People within any environment today have far more to choose from than similarly located people had a hundred years ago. So it's not homogenous. I have many more choices. I can go out this evening and select from restaurants that serve the foods of dozens of countries—China, Italy, France, Japan, Thailand, India—or even innumerable fast-food places.

ROBERT: The fact of choice itself is the new global homogeneity. Many people in many countries now have those same kinds of choices that we have here in America.

GREG STOCK: Yes, but usually when people describe culture as homogenous, they think of it as very narrow—for instance, you can eat only fast foods.

MARVIN: Fast food isn't imperialism. If I want to eat in five minutes instead of an hour, well, the fact that McDonald's is all over the world doesn't mean it's a cultural imposition. It means it's a great blessing in time, and lots of people don't want their time wasted by their culture or whatever, and so they eat a Big Mac.

ROBERT: But is it always welcomed in other societies?

FRANK: I just think that there are shared values that constitute communities and allow people to relate to one another. These traditions are very hard to dislodge, whatever outsiders may think of them. They will be very tenacious even a hundred years from now.

ROBERT: Do you think that's good or bad?

FRANK: It's an inherent part of the way humans are constituted.

ROBERT: But some people feel that traditional cultures are impediments to human advancement.

MARVIN: In a culture, people relate to one another to the extent that they think the same thoughts—and so don't have to really think. I don't regard that as a virtue. Maybe lazy humans like it, but I would like to teach them not to be lazy.

ROBERT: Let's look a hundred years into the future and ask ourselves how happy people will be, given the benefit of all this advanced technology. On a scale of 1 to 10, with 10 as the happiest and assuming today is a 5, what's your number?

FRANK: If it's 5 today, it'll be 5 in a hundred years.

MARVIN: Well, I want people to be very unhappy that they don't understand cosmic

theory or something. I hate happiness, because that means you're not interested in anything new.

ROBERT: So if society would be less happy, you would be more?

MARVIN: Yes. If we can get happiness down to a 1, then everybody will be very busy—and happy in a less superficial sense. If we really think that happiness is important, then people will be very happy. But I don't think it's necessarily a desirable goal.

GREG BENFORD: I vote for 6. We're going to get a little bit richer, and people tend to be happier when at least their basic needs are met. But we always return largely to the center. So, a little bit of improvement.

GREG STOCK: There's not necessarily a correlation between people's material well-being and their happiness. People are far better off physically than they were a hundred years ago, and yet they're in many ways unhappier, because there's more uncertainty about life. Sounds like about a 5.

GEORGE: I'll give it an 8, mainly because I have great faith in the ability of human beings to solve their problems.

ROBERT: CONCLUDING COMMENT

Yes, the world is changing. You knew that. But how does technology alter society? By energizing two primary forces of social transformation. On the macro level, it's the blurring of boundaries, smearing borders among enterprises, institutions, sectors, and nations. For example, there's greater collaboration among academia, business, and government, and greater globalization, the increasingly free flow of international commerce and ideas. On the micro level, it's the empowering of the individual, who has been given enhanced reach and strength, buoyed by a confident capacity to make independent choices. We have a new model of society, and companies and countries alike must adapt. But there are potential problems. Does the blurring of boundaries engender mercantile values, promoting profits at any cost and eroding culture? And does the empowered person replace interpersonal relationships with self-gratification? Let's be both delighted and apprehensive, exuberant and vigilant. While the short-term benefits of technology are obvious, the long-term risks are not. Sometimes vigilance alone can bring us closer to truth.

OUTTAKES

GREG STOCK: *People a hundred years from now will still never understand what happiness is.*

GEORGE: *We'll probably be able to manipulate our happiness by then.*

MARVIN: *Then it'll probably be 5 squared.*

FRANK: *Happiness sounds like an economist's idea, like utility, something worth something to someone.*

MARVIN: *It's a bad idea even to use the word, and I don't—except in my forthcoming book [The Emotion Machine], where I make fun of it.*

GREG BENFORD: *Imagine how easy this would be if we all had a script.*

CHAPTER 21

Can We See the Near Future— Year 2025?

Twenty-five years ago, there was an empire called the Soviet Union, and there were no kids surfing the Internet. Twenty-five years from now, what familiar institutions will be extinct and what unexpected innovations will have emerged? From artificial intelligence to genetic engineering, will our burgeoning technology make our lives happy or gloomy, content or confused? Will there be more political freedom in the world, or less? Will there be more cultural and ethnic fragmentation, or a world more integrated and unified? What about competitiveness, confrontations, conflicts, wars? What breakthroughs lie ahead? What surprises are in store? In great part, we could not have successfully predicted the changes of the past twenty-five years. Can we do any better with the next twenty-five? We recruited five forecasters to be our time-travelers to the year 2025. Let's see how they do.

PARTICIPANTS

Edward de Bono, the author of *Lateral Thinking: Creativity Step by Step,* teaches creativity in schools and corporations around the world. Edward hopes that new educational techniques will bring about a better future.

Dr. Edward Feigenbaum, a pioneer in expert systems, is coscientific director of the Knowledge Systems Laboratory at Stanford University. His 1963 book *Computers and Thought* helped launch artificial intelligence. Ed believes that machines will become our valuable assistants.

Graham T. T. Molitor, author of numerous articles and books on the future, is vice president of the World Future Society. Graham sees, along with an enormous increase in the global population, an increase in knowledge and prosperity over the next twenty-five years.

Dr. Bruce Murray, a professor of planetary science and geology at the California Institute of Technology, is a cofounder, with the late Carl Sagan, of the Planetary Society, which fosters public interest in space exploration. Bruce is concerned about unprecedented global stress and seeks sustainability and world governance.

Dr. Bart Kosko, a professor of electrical engineering at the University of Southern California, is the author of the science fiction novel *Nanotime*. Bart's not-all-rosy vision of the future is stamped by computer chips outpowering and outthinking the human brain.

ROBERT: Bruce, you've stated that the greatest drama in man-the-toolmaker's unprecedented evolution awaits us in this new century. Haven't people always said that the time they live in is the most important? Why are we so special?

BRUCE: We're special because these circumstances will never happen again. I'm sure it may have seemed that way in the past. But never have we as a species been surging so out of control. There have been times when whole civilizations have been eliminated, there have been droughts and other natural disasters, but never has the globe as a whole been so stressed. There are objective indicators. Never has the globe held anywhere near as many people as it does now. Never has the globe had this tremendous technological progress you just mentioned. There is an unprecedented use of fuel and the like. If you were an alien looking down at planet Earth now, you could detect our presence simply from the gases in the atmosphere, from the changes in plant life that you could see from space at great distances. It's this combination [of technological progress and overpopulation] that makes the present time unprecedented—and also unsustainable: the planet can't go on like this—and therefore we can't predict the future.

ROBERT: Bart, *Nanotime* is a World War Three futuristic thriller, in which—thirty years from now—computer chips begin to replace brains. How seriously should we take your fiction?

BART: I'd take it with a big fuzzy grain of salt. But the concept behind *Nanotime* will come to pass—in the next twenty-five or thirty years, the power of computer chips will exceed that of the human brain. Whether we can get chips and brains to interact is the question we'll be exploring within the next decade.

ROBERT: Ed, what is artificial intelligence, and what will it be doing for us, or to us, in the next twenty-five years?

ED FEIGENBAUM: We're going to see artificial intelligence techniques ride on top of other waves that are pushing the information revolution along—the wave of communications, the wave of increased computer power, and especially the wave of connectedness. The connectedness generates a great deal of what you might call information clutter in our world—clutter that artificial intelligence techniques may help to sort out for us.

ROBERT: Graham, you're a leading futurist, coeditor of the *Encyclopedia of the Future*. What are the major trends of the next twenty-five years?

GRAHAM: There are so many that it's hard to choose among them. Population is critical. Auguste Comte, the great sociologist, stated that demography is destiny. Truly it is. In the time span we're looking at, there will be a tremendous increase in population. I think the global population ultimately will go as high as sixty billion. The density in this country is about seventy-five people per square mile. In other countries, it's almost a thousand, [but] there's plenty of room for lots more people.

ROBERT: Edward, as a pioneer in creative thinking, can you help us do some creative thinking here? What's the role of education in the next twenty-five years?

EDWARD DE BONO: I want you to imagine a ship on the high seas, in which the engines keep stopping, the lights keep flickering, the crew's very demoralized, and things aren't good. Then we helicopter in a new captain, new senior officers, we fix the engines, the lights don't flicker, morale goes up, but the ship's still going in the wrong direction—and that's education. Education in most countries is really a disgrace. Three key things need to be taught in society. The first is how value is created; this is not taught now. The second is the relevant skills; these are not taught. The third is basic thinking; again, not taught. Education is helplessly out of date.

ROBERT: Bruce, let's get back to the planet. You talk about global sustainability, generational equity, intervention versus market forces. Unify these thoughts for us. What's the ultimate outcome?

BRUCE: The primary impact will be on governance, not government—we'll see a decline in the power of central governments. That's already happened in China, it's happened in Japan, it's happened in Western Europe.

ROBERT: What are the underlying causes?

BRUCE: Increased communications is a big one. And as this decentralization is going on, global challenges are rising: we have to keep order, we have to provide populations with food and supplies. So we have to invent, for the first time, a system of planetary governance that doesn't depend upon an imperial boss or a ruling party or something like that. That's the big challenge.

ROBERT: Is that a pipe dream?

BRUCE: No. It will happen, well or poorly.

BART: Bruce, how can you argue that the power of central governments has decreased? The IMF—the International Monetary Fund—keeps statistics on how much [the governments of] the major countries spend of their gross domestic product [GDP]. In the 1870s, it was about twelve to fifteen percent, and it's risen nonstop, so that at the end of the twentieth century the average large government is spending about forty-seven percent of its country's GDP. There's been no decline whatsoever. Governments seem only to grow over time.

BRUCE: I guess we're looking at different measures. Certainly you can't argue that the Soviet Union hasn't been decentralized.

ROBERT: What about the surge in nationalism, ethnicity, commercial enterprises, social fragmentation?

BRUCE: Right. The fact is that the world is a more diverse place than it was before 1989. In China, economic reform has diversified the society. In Japan, the ruling Liberal Democratic Party collapsed and has not been replaced by a working majority. In Western Europe, there have been minority governments continually for about the last ten years.

ROBERT: If we agree that decentralization is being energized through political processes, the rise of nationalism, and the Internet, what's the end result?

BRUCE: There's a natural tension between a retreat into hatred—a narrowness that shows up in religion and in politics—and a global vision that's sweeping the planet, with people really identifying with people in other parts of the world. These are the two competing pressures.

EDWARD DE BONO: I would say they're not pressures. They're two opposite directions that can coexist. You see the fractionalization of geographic segments into smaller regions, cities, and so on. At the same time, you see unification, like the European Union. Both trends are happening simultaneously. I think nationalistic hatred is a phase that will pass; it won't be a major factor in the future.

ROBERT: You don't think that's Pollyanna-ish?

EDWARD DE BONO: No. What's happening now is that people in most countries—most communities, like the business community—are working toward similar goals, have the same values. Nationalism and ethnic conflicts are remnants, the dying embers of our traditional hatreds.

ROBERT: Bart, what are some myths of forecasting the future?

BART: One myth is the assumption of military stability. It's now becoming cheaper to attack than to defend. I call this a smart war, and it's something new in military history. It always used to cost a lot more to attack; the Greeks had to launch a thousand ships to attack Troy, whereas the Afghan rebels could take a relatively inexpensive stinger missile and shoot down a multimillion-dollar Soviet helicopter. Now as cruise missiles get smarter, as we shift into information warfare, it's easier to attack and it costs less. The average real cost of a cruise missile today is somewhere around a hundred thousand dollars, and as chip densities continue to shrink and other economic efficiencies increase, that real cost will fall in a decade or so to about ten thousand dollars—less than the price of a car. How do you defend against cheap cruise missiles? Just as it's very difficult to find a hidden land mine; land mines cost about three dollars to make and about three hundred dollars to find. All this, I think, will be extremely destabilizing. Maybe there won't be big wars, but one country could decide that it's easier and cheaper to launch a smart attack than to resort to diplomacy.

ROBERT: A multiplicity of countries divided by ethnicity feeds further destabilization.

ED FEIGENBAUM: At the end of the twentieth century, there were some hundred-and-eighty-five member countries in the United Nations. I would think, as countries continue to divide along ethnic and language lines, that by 2025 there will be more like four hundred.

ROBERT: Other estimates of the number of nations in twenty-five years?

EDWARD DE BONO: It depends whether you call them nations or semiautonomous regions.

ROBERT: The defining characteristic is that they're independently governed.

EDWARD DE BONO: I would say about five hundred.

ROBERT: Or that could mobilize their own armies—I think that's the best definition.

EDWARD DE BONO: No, I wouldn't say that. Five hundred able to be pretty independent, OK—but not necessarily to mobilize their own armies.

ROBERT: How many nations will be able to mobilize their own armies?

EDWARD DE BONO: Much lower—because why would people want their own armies?

ROBERT: Why is sadly irrelevant; they just do.

GRAHAM: You have to keep in mind the size of the countries we're talking about. Some of these nation-states have only forty thousand people. Some of them have territories smaller than the neighborhood I live in. Certainly more countries will be coming. After the close of World War Two, there were something like seventy-eight nations. Now there are about two hundred and twenty, depending on who's counting, and it will grow.

BART: Some countries are artificial—they contain different peoples, languages, religions—and they could fragment. Some have borders drawn by colonial powers, particularly the British, hundreds of years ago. The Indian subcontinent. Parts of Africa. Perhaps even China.

ROBERT: Why are wars not included in most studies of the future?

ED FEIGENBAUM: Because futurists are just too optimistic. They're too hopeful; they adopt a

---

. . . futurists are just too optimistic.

---

positive vision in hopes that that will make it more likely to happen.

BRUCE: And I think it's a big mistake. The reason you study alternative scenarios is not to predict—because you can't predict—but to look at the range of outcomes so that you then can get insight into what's likely to be the big driver. And this range of outcomes includes some very messy, unpleasant kinds of worlds ahead of us, even within twenty-five years. Mexico could be out of control; that would be serious for us. The Balkans could lead to a larger conflict.

ROBERT: There are many opportunities for unpleasant surprise.

EDWARD DE BONO: But advancing age is on our side. A lot of people running these countries have grown up in time of war, and their thinking remains that way, but the next generation won't necessarily think that way.

ROBERT: That's been an unfulfilled hope for generations. Let's shift gears. Ed, how do you see artificial intelligence in twenty-five years? Take two fields with which you've dealt, business and medicine.

ED FEIGENBAUM: I just want to start out by saying that I disagree a bit with your opening statement about how difficult it has been to predict the future. The general rule of thumb is, If you want to know what will be out there twenty-five years from now, look in the research laboratories of major universities and corporations. The best example is Moore's law [that computing capacity doubles every eighteen months]; we've had a curve to follow ever since the late 1960s and early 1970s. The bang for the buck in a microchip doubles approximately every eighteen months. Sometimes the rate accelerates to fourteen months; sometimes it slips to twenty-four months.

ROBERT: What's another example?

ED FEIGENBAUM: In the mid-1940s, Roosevelt's science advisor Vannevar Bush published an article in the *Atlantic Monthly* about a machine he called a memex, which has a great deal in common with today's personal computers. And there's [pioneer computer scientist] J. C. R. Licklider's wonderful 1962 essay [with W. Clark, "On-line Man-Computer Communication"] about a so-called galactic network—his tongue-in-cheek term for what we now call the Internet. So we can indeed make predictions.

ROBERT: So predict. We're putting you on the spot.

ED FEIGENBAUM: Right. In the artificial intelligence world, I think you'll see the use of large knowledge bases to [help us negotiate] the World Wide Web. We're deluged with data on the Web. When we request something from a search engine, a ton of stuff comes out that we don't want. Now, if we could only inject some knowledge of the real world into that search engine, it could answer the query that we're really asking—which is for just a small number of relevant items. This will be the major contribution of artificial intelligence to the business world. It will make the use of the World Wide Web for electronic commerce and for individual interaction a great deal more plausible, pleasurable, tangible, and accessible for the average person. In medicine, you have a different story. There you're looking at expert systems, and the question is, Can we gain medical knowledge from practicing experts any faster than we've done in the past? That's been the chief bottleneck in creating expert systems: How do we model human expertise? And here the prediction would be that we're going to see automatic methods to do that. Just as the more knowledge you have the better you can perform a task, similarly the more knowledge you have the easier it is to acquire more. We can use this acceleration effect in learning [software]—for example, programs to read the medical literature and extract knowledge that can be useful in these artificial intelligence reasoning programs.

ROBERT: Graham, as you forecast world economics, do you see the robust, steady climb continuing?

GRAHAM: There are several things to consider here. One is the extraordinary change since the 1920s, when only several hundred thousand people were in the stock market. In 1999, forty-three percent of Americans were in the market, either directly or indirectly through mutual funds, pension plans, and retirement accounts. The amount of equity that average householders have in the stock market exceeds the value of the equity of their homes and real property. So what's driving this? Well, it's the baby-boom generation, which has about another nine years to work its way through its most prolific spending years—upscale houses, second homes, luxury cars, exotic vacations, the furnishings and collectibles, and all that goes with it. The stock market will probably double or triple within the twenty-five-year time frame.

BART: What happens when the baby boomers cash out?

GRAHAM: When they cash out, there's a fantastic series of things that come along. Think about this: The mega-expenditures of the average individual in a lifetime have increased radically. It's expensive to have children these days: It costs about $179,000 to $359,000 to raise a child through age seventeen. Then every kid has to have further schooling, because, as Edward [De Bono] says, educational is pivotal.

EDWARD DE BONO: Is it pivotal or pitiful?

GRAHAM: It's pitiful, but it's also pivotal—both. And that education costs $50,000 to $250,000. Then don't forget that baby boomers are darn sure to give their kids lavish weddings; that's another $10,000 to $100,000.

BRUCE: But you're not talking about everybody in the United States. You're talking about an important group with a lot of money. But there are other groups that aren't so privileged.

GRAHAM: Forty-three percent of the population are in the market.

BRUCE: How do you deal with the poorly educated?

ROBERT: Doesn't the increasing disparity between rich and poor provoke greater fragmentation in society?

BRUCE: It's happening. It's a fact—society is becoming more fragmented.

ROBERT: And that generates serious social pressures.

BRUCE: Right, and in the long run it makes the system unstable, unless you figure out a way—

GRAHAM: I totally disagree. You know, a rising tide raises all boats. The growth trajectory for

---

The growth trajectory for linchpin industries is in place, and it will produce a very powerful economy.

---

linchpin industries is in place, and it will produce a very powerful economy.

BART: In a few years, the disposable income of workers could buy all the stock on all the exchanges.

EDWARD DE BONO: I think in twenty-five years the stock market will just be dead. It's a giant Ponzi scheme.

GRAHAM: That's Social Security you're talking about.

BART: The stock market grows because earnings grow.

BRUCE: What happens when this show is seen in the houses of many Mexican-Americans, African-Americans, immigrants, other people who are not part of this economic boom? They'll say, "What are we hearing? These guys must be from another planet." To ignore the fact that a significant fraction of the people in this country are not sharing in our material success or getting the tools to be effective in the future is delusional.

ROBERT: The accumulation of wealth can exacerbate divisions in society.

BRUCE: Right, and remember, we're in a particularly favorable time. Those tensions are not nearly as manifest as they've been at other times and will be again in the future.

EDWARD DE BONO: That's why education is so important. If it weren't for education, these people would just be playing catch-up. But if we can really improve education—which we can—they'll become much more productive and much less dependent. Without a change in education, though, we're just going to repeat the steps that got us where we are today.

ROBERT: Let's go into space. Bruce, for decades you've been a leader in the American space program. What can we look forward to in the next twenty-five years? Any practical applications?

BRUCE: There'll be a series of utilitarian benefits—there already are. Satellite communications are so common that people take it for granted. What's becoming equally embedded in our social infrastructure is the fixing of locations by GPS—global positioning satellites. It's become another utility.

BART: It's something, by the way, that you could jam during a war.

BRUCE: But it's commercial.

BART: No, the military has to deal with them.

GRAHAM: Even more of a problem when you have thousands of satellites.

BRUCE: Well, you can also set off nuclear bombs [in the atmosphere] and knock out a country's electrical power systems—but that hasn't happened.

BART: Information warfare will undermine these communication structures.

BRUCE: If you go to war, it doesn't make a lot of difference whether you do it on the earth or above the earth. But the real issue about space is

---

Information warfare will undermine these communication structures.

---

not utilitarian; the issue is what it can do for our spirit, not so much for our bodies—how space can inspire humanity.

ROBERT: And what space exploration says about us as human beings. There's no way you can justify going to Mars on an economic basis.

BRUCE: That's right. And obviously one answer to that is pure science. Another is earth science. The more we learn about planetary environments, just as we did on Earth, the more it helps us overall. And that's certainly true with Mars or Venus or other places.

ROBERT: Do you send carbon [humans] or silicon [robots]?

BRUCE: We've been sending silicon, because that's all we can send. I'm not going to answer your question about twenty-five years from now. You know that I'm advocating and trying to make it possible for humans to go to Mars, somewhat the way we first went to Antarctica. But there may be another trajectory. Just as

Moore's law operates in terms of computation speed, it also operates with respect to communications. Communications is an enterprise that's doubling in power about every two and a half years. And it's not the result of government efforts; it's going to happen regardless. So whereas human beings stay about the same—our physical bodies are no better than those of the early polar explorers—there will be more and more capacity on the robotics side. And a fusion between humans and far-more-sophisticated machines is going to emerge that will be unlike anything we've ever seen before, and that's the way most of us are going to see the solar system.

ROBERT: Will that help our collective spirit?

BRUCE: So far it has. I'm the president of the Planetary Society [planetary.org], and we survive at the pleasure of a hundred thousand people who send in their dues every year. We don't have any big aerospace companies backing us, and we don't have any government grants. We survive because we represent hope. We represent a link to the possibilities of the future. We will continue, provided that our space systems bring back new stuff—stuff that's interesting and, most important, interactive. The new phase of space exploration will see humans interacting with robotic systems operating on Mars and other such places.

EDWARD DE BONO: What space illustrates to me is our ability to deal with linear, predictable systems and our inability to deal with nonlinear loop systems. The more we put our efforts into, say, bigger rockets, better robots, and so on, the more we move away from and neglect the more complex social systems, behaviors, and interactions—poverty, crime, and so on. If we put as much intellectual and

financial resources into those areas as we do into the linear systems, we'd make a better world.

BRUCE: You should feel good; we're doing exactly that. We're reducing both the absolute and the relative expenditures on space exploration in this country and in every other country.

BART: And spending more on prisons than ever before.

BRUCE: We're also spending more on consumption, on commercial products.

ROBERT: This contrast marks our human heritage, reaching for the stars while living in the dirt. As Bruce [Murray] said, space exploration feeds our spirit more than our body.

BRUCE: It's an old argument. It's the argument of the sixties. Societies have made their judgments; part of it is decentralization of services, and there's less going into space.

EDWARD DE BONO: You're misunderstanding what I said. I didn't say that there should be less going into space; I said that we should put more into other areas.

BRUCE: Look, the gross national product is doubling every ten years; the space fraction is going down; obviously, resources are going somewhere else.

EDWARD DE BONO: They're not. That's my whole point. If you're spending less on meat, it doesn't mean that you're spending more on milk.

BRUCE: But you're spending on something.

EDWARD DE BONO: If society would give the same priorities to poverty and crime and education as we gave to space, it would make a huge difference.

ROBERT: I think we're all just a bunch of narrow-minded technocrats. Where are the humanists, the theologians, the philosophers who can guide us through the next twenty-five years?

ED FEIGENBAUM: Hey, I'd like to defend the technocrats. I'm a technocrat myself. Take the example of life extension. Average life span increased little by little, until [Scottish bacteriologist Alexander] Fleming discovered penicillin in 1928, until the advent of sulfa drugs, and then there was a dramatic increase in life span from about fifty-nine years to about seventy-two years.

ROBERT: That's a real discontinuity.

ED FEIGENBAUM: We need to look for such discontinuities during the next twenty-five years.

EDWARD DE BONO: Living longer doesn't necessarily improve quality of life. If one old lady living in a small town gets mugged, the quality of life for every old lady in that town is

---

Living longer doesn't necessarily improve quality of life.

---

seriously impaired. Being free from the fear of crime—that is quality of life. Just achieving technological extensions of life is like being bombarded with useless information by E-mail. That's not quality of life.

BRUCE: Let me jump in, because I think the issue of being technocrats is justified. I feel

uneasy about this, but the problem is that the people who specialize in understanding social behavior or history tend to be backward-looking. Let me tell you what I think is the most important diagram of our times. It plots world population from 1750 to 2150, with the explosion starting in the early twentieth century. And I argue that this geometric increase in people is transforming not just the surface of the earth but also—and partly due to technological change—the way we think.

ROBERT: Creating a kind of global consciousness?

BRUCE: Right. We're immersed in a new kind of culture. We're talking here as though we're external from earth, speculating what life will be like "over there" in 2025. The most radical change going on is not the increase in human life span but the changing cultural and social attitudes.

ROBERT: What's happening to privacy amid all this change?

BART: It's diminishing.

ROBERT: Despite all the clever gadgets cluttering up our kitchens and cars and so forth, doesn't the erosion of privacy depress our quality of life?

BART: We leave ever more footprints to be picked up by digital devices manned by friendly and unfriendly sources alike. The government has twelve underground acres of computers at Fort Meade just to crack certain kinds of codes that people don't even know about. We've taken it for granted that we can have a conversation in a supermarket, or on a street corner, that won't be recorded. Soon we won't be able to do that.

EDWARD DE BONO: Why do you care who's listening, unless you've got something to hide? Why does it matter?

BART: Let's put a camcorder into your living room.

ED FEIGENBAUM: If privacy mattered, people would turn on the encryption feature of their browsers when they send E-mails—and nobody does. How many of you have ever sent or received an encrypted E-mail?

BART: I have, and I think more people will, as they learn how to do it.

ROBERT: We don't appreciate how much personal information is being gathered and used already; people aren't sufficiently sensitive to that yet.

BRUCE: Look, instead of saying how we feel about privacy, we ought to agree that it's important to our society and that we have a body of law concerned with it. Other societies don't. Privacy is one of our culturally dependent mores, and it's probably going to be much more difficult to maintain. The Western tradition of privacy is not a free good, and it is certainly at risk.

ROBERT: But is privacy a fundamental human right?

EDWARD DE BONO: Not at all.

BRUCE: No, it's not fundamental in the sense that there are many societies that don't [privilege privacy].

ROBERT: Would you give up privacy in exchange for more gadgetry, more technological comforts?

BRUCE: Not me, but others might.

ROBERT: Twenty-five years from now, looking back, what's the biggest surprise unforeseen today?

BRUCE: The biggest surprise will be something we probably can't appreciate now, because our descendants will have changed in a way we

---

The biggest surprise will be something we probably can't appreciate now, . . .

---

wouldn't recognize. Just as my grandfather and I are separated forever by cultural and psychological differences.

EDWARD DE BONO: I'll be wearing face jewelry.*

GRAHAM: I think what will come to pass are extraordinary advances in human intellect and understanding, with information doubling every five years and knowledge every two and a half years—six to eighteen months in some disciplines—and the ability to acquire knowledge and use it efficiently and effectively for the cause and the course of humanity.

ED FEIGENBAUM: The biggest surprises are going to be biological: on the positive side, gene therapy to cure a range of human diseases, and

---

*In fact, Edward did wear face jewelry on this one television show—a large silver safety pin that was attached prominently to his nose. None of us knew quite what to say or do, which, no doubt, was Edward's point.

on the negative side, a very scary future for biological warfare.

BART: I agree; we'll soon be able to manipulate our genes, at least to some degree. There will be artificial eyes. At the social level—on the small level, we'll have mail on Sunday—and drugs will be legalized, so this massive transfer of wealth from taxpayers to drug dealers will be gone.

ROBERT: CONCLUDING COMMENT

Einstein once said, "I never think of the future. It comes soon enough." One prediction I'm sure about: The future is coming quicker and sooner. Does the year 2025 seem forever in the future? For many of us, the year 1975 seems hardly in the past. The safest way to forecast the future is a standard extrapolation, which means taking what has happened and projecting it forward at the same rate to predict what will happen. For example, since the world is becoming tightly wired, if economic prosperity continues, educational equality will ultimately come to all nations and peoples. But in 1943, Thomas Watson, the chairman of IBM, said that the world market for computers would be "maybe five." So much for extrapolations. The theory behind the study of the future is that if you plan for the future—even if your plans are wrong—you get two benefits:

You can more likely influence the flow of events and you can more quickly react to surprise. Yet here's a hunch; I give it, say, one in twenty that something unexpected—*really* unexpected—will have occurred by the year 2025. As for me, I hope still to be doing this show, with less hair and more makeup, amused at how naïve I was twenty-five years before. And finally, after all that time, I may find myself closer to truth.

OUTTAKES

EDWARD DE BONO: Mark Twain said you should live your life so that when you die your parrot could be given to the village gossip. In other words, what's there to worry about? If an invasion of privacy makes life more interesting for other people, and if it's reciprocal, their lives could become more interesting for you.

ROBERT: Privacy entails something essentially human. How can you not care if unauthorized snoops access your personal records?

EDWARD DE BONO: I don't mind. Access my genome and medical data, too.

BRUCE: Read your E-mail—you don't care?

EDWARD DE BONO: Not in the least!

CHAPTER 22

Can We Imagine the Far Future—Year 3000?

Try imagining what the world will be like in the year 3000. Some serious thinkers are starting to do just that. But can our minds even project that far? How will we work, play, propagate, communicate, worship, wonder? What forms of bodies will we have? What will our cities look like? How many nations will there be? How long will we live? What technologies will be available to us? What about family, business, government, education? How deep into space will humans have ventured? How many people will live on Earth? How strange will it be? Most of us don't know what we'll be doing a year from now; why then should we care about what our descendants will be doing a thousand years from now? It's fun to speculate, sure; but envisioning the year 3000 may be more than an idle exercise or mere amusement. Our time-traveling futurists explain.

PARTICIPANTS

Edward de Bono, the author of more than fifty books on thinking and creativity, teaches new ways of thinking to diverse groups around the world. Edward foresees abbreviated, high-speed language; he also expects a world of all women and no men—or is he playing with us?

Dr. Bart Kosko, the author of *The Fuzzy Future,* is a professor of electrical engineering at the University of Southern California. Bart presents his vision of "Heaven on a chip," along with other startling opinions.

Graham Molitor is the author of numerous articles and books on the future and coeditor of the *Encyclopedia of the Future.* How can Graham forecast details of the next thousand years so confidently?

Dr. Bruce Murray, a futurist and former director of the National Aeronautics and Space Administration's Jet Propulsion Laboratory, is a professor of planetary science and geology at the California Institute of Technology in Pasadena, California. Bruce stresses communications and considers how humanity may join "the galactic community."

Dr. Gregory Stock, the author of *Metaman* and *The Book of Questions,* is the director of the Program on Medicine, Technology, and Society at the University of California, Los Angeles. Greg believes that we are now in an extraordinary evolutionary transition, which he views with excitement and optimism.

ROBERT: Graham, you're the chief spokesperson for the World Future Society and the author of an upcoming book on the next thousand years. Considering the unimaginable advances in the last hundred years, how can you be presumptuous enough to predict the next thousand years?

GRAHAM: The answer is simple. All of the recorded history of humankind—and even pre-history—is nothing more than an evolutionary, step-by-step march down a path of progress, and the ideas that shape tomorrow cast long shadows and leave lots of footprints in the sands of time. The path may meander, but it has a certain sequence through which it passes and which is easy to discern. There are many ways of conceiving, tracking, and timing trends that are inevitable but not foreordained.

ROBERT: Aren't you ignoring discontinuities?

GRAHAM: Discontinuities simply indicate that people haven't done their homework.

ROBERT: We'll be challenging that later. Bart, you've stated that our brains—which you politely call "meat"—don't communicate very well, that brains are just nature's first flimsy attempt at using meat to compute, and that biology is not destiny. Are electronic chips our destiny?

BART: I don't know that [present-day] electronic chips are, but some sort of chips—I'd guess maybe plastic. Our three-pound brain is definitely a marvel, perhaps the greatest marvel of natural biology, but from an engineering point of view it's a fiasco. In this coming century,

---

. . . chips are our destiny.

---

we'll be reengineering the brain a piece at a time, initially with implants and other supplements and ultimately engineering an outright replacement. There's no question that in the distant future we'll play the music of the mind on instruments different from the current ones. So, yes, chips are our destiny.

ROBERT: Bruce, you're president of The Planetary Society, which is the largest public-participation organization concerned with space, and you're a leading advocate of space exploration. A thousand years from now, where will humanity be in space?

BRUCE: Well, of course, we don't know in a narrow sense, but we can envision the possibilities. Certainly the limitations of the corpus that we carry around with us will have been overcome in many ways, on earth as well as in space.

But how far out into space we go as corporal beings is anybody's guess. I'm a geologist by training and a fairly conservative person, so I have a hard time seeing much beyond Mars. But the potential is enormous, whether we go physically or robotically.

ROBERT: Greg, you're a biophysicist who studies the impact of technology on society. Your book *Metaman* sees the merging of humans and machines into a global superorganism. You're an optimist about the next thousand years. Why?

GREG: I'm optimistic because I think the prevailing view—that we're out of balance with the natural world and heading toward some sort of deadly reckoning—is absolutely wrong. Modern technology is a very robust development, of extraordinary evolutionary significance. I think we're in the midst of an evolutionary transition as significant as the one that occurred when single cells joined together 700 million years ago to form multicellular organisms. Things occurring now are unprecedented in the history of life—space travel, genetic engineering, artificial intelligence.

ROBERT: And this show.

GREG: Well, I don't know about this show, but this is an extraordinary moment to be alive as observers, participants, and architects of the future.

ROBERT: Edward, for decades you've been showing the world how to think more creatively, how to break the bonds of traditional thinking. Are we seeing the year 3000 too simplistically, almost as if it were just the year 2000 on steroids?

EDWARD: The answer is yes. In 3000 perhaps the biggest difference from today is that there

will be no more men. Females can have female children, without any need for men. In about ten years, we'll find the hormone cocktail that women can take to have female children. There'll be no need for men at all.

ROBERT: Will the world be a better place?

EDWARD: Oh, yes. And this show will be archival material. Women will take it out of the video store and say, "Look, those are men; aren't they funny?"

ROBERT: We can go even further than female and male. How about carbon systems versus silicon systems, biological life versus robotic intelligence? Bruce, you've thought some about this.

BRUCE: Yes. What's going on in our own lifetimes—the extraordinary development of computing and communications, things that operate in silicon, with capabilities similar to those of human beings—these are some of those footprints in the sand. The Antarctic explorer Ernest Shackleton was probably as good an explorer as any that ever lived, but with the computational and communications tools we have today, to say nothing of the biomedical ones, Shackleton's reach can't compare with ours. Clearly, we live in a time of human-machine fusion. The pictures we have of Mars, say, come from machines (silicon) but make sense only to people (carbon). When we see Martian landscapes with our own eyes, in real time, we're somehow transported there. And that's just the very beginning of this extraordinary period, which is at most only a few decades old.

ROBERT: Bart, take us out to the end of that period. Give us your rendition of Heaven on a chip.

BART: What is Heaven? Heaven's a place where you can create worlds at will, and the ideal Heaven is where you run the whole thing yourself. The current means of getting to Heaven involve various supernatural systems for which, at this point, there's no scientific evidence. So I think we can reduce Heaven to an engineering project, which we're doing. The demand for Heaven is great—witness the desire of every human heart, from the people who built the ancient pyramids to modern society, to live beyond one's biologically allotted time. Our plan is ultimately to transfer human consciousness from the brain to bits of information in a computer chip, or some other kind of computational medium, so that just by thinking—that act of volition—we'll be able to create our own personal world. And I think the first stage of Heaven will be the sensory world, and beyond that I think we'd hit a higher, spiritual plane.

ROBERT: So we download our personalities into silicon, into electronic chips enormously more sophisticated than anything imaginable today, so that we can then live as hardwired, superdense circuitry, virtually forever?

BART: Just take the example of your past. You can't remember a great deal of what you did three years ago. But if you had the detailed richness of that experience wholly embedded in a chip, you could not only relive it at will, you could edit it at will, modifying it thousands of times in innumerable creative ways.

GREG: Maybe you wouldn't want to.

BART: Maybe you wouldn't want to.

ROBERT: But you could. It's all about options—that's Bart's vision.

EDWARD: The emphasis on machines and chips is a possibility. But there's so much more to do with what I call human software. Human language at the moment is incredibly slow and primitive. One of the things I've been working on is a language that's twenty times as fast as normal language and could go up to fifty times as fast. Human-being-to-human-being communication, with no chips involved. We're below the potential of our biological systems, way below. We're stuck in old-fashioned, crabby ways of using our minds.

GREG: We have two processes going on at the same time: our biology is becoming determined by design and more mechanized, and our machines are becoming more complex; we're breeding complexity into them so that they're becoming more lifelike. And so which side will win is really—

ROBERT: Is this a competition?

GREG: Well, it's not a competition, in that there's a symbiosis and we have all sorts of machine extensions. But the ultimate question

---

What will become the central core: expanded human biology or transformed intelligent machines?

---

is, What will become the central core: expanded human biology or transformed intelligent machines?

BRUCE: I'm a little concerned about the drift of this conversation, because it sounds kind of technocratic—the world as seen by a bunch of physicists or biologists or electrical engineers—and I don't think we all feel that way. I certainly don't, because there is the intuitive dimension and the moral [and existential] issues of why we're here—and these issues aren't going to go away. None of them are affected by technology, though the questions and answers may become more complex. So I think we ought to separate the issue of what form our humanity will take—separate that issue from the power we'll have, intellectually and otherwise, through the use of our machines.

ROBERT: But the technocrats' argument is that their high-tech world becomes so powerful and so dominant that it simply overpowers moral or existential issues.

GREG: Humanity is being ripped free from its past.

ROBERT: Free from the constraints, superstitions, and intellectual hypocrisies that shackled humanity for thousands of years. This is also part of the technocratic argument, and I use the term nonpejoratively; it's also the humanistic argument. And I'm not saying that it's all true or good, but there is surely some truth and goodness there.

GREG: There's going to be a tremendous loss. It's going to be a traumatic time that we're moving into, because such change does not come easily. We have a huge population being torn free from their past, and that will produce stress.

EDWARD: There are things that we can make available to masses of people to help them make better use of their brains. We just haven't made any effort to do this. We put billions into space travel; if you put that amount into developing human software for the brain, you could transform the human race.

GREG: Take an example. If you could extend the human life span, if you could double it, would you do it?

EDWARD: I don't think that's so important. The better use of what we underuse is what's important. It doesn't matter whether you live long or don't live long.

BART: Edward [de Bono], we're talking about a thousand years from now, not a hundred years from now.

EDWARD: In a thousand years, we could communicate in ten seconds what now takes thirty minutes.

GREG: So what?

EDWARD: We could communicate much higher concepts, better ideas, more human languages.

GREG: That's all we get for a thousand years?

GRAHAM: Let me go to a different level here. The man-machine interface and biotechnology—all that will work OK, but the real key when you're looking ahead a thousand years is to take an anthropological look at the biometrics of human development. If you trace back to our earliest ancestors and project forward, the average weight for an adult male by the year 3000 is likely to be 180 to 210 pounds, which means a bigger biomass to feed.

EDWARD: What's the basis for that? How do you get that?

ROBERT: Aren't you just extrapolating—projecting what might happen in the future based on what did happen in the past?

GRAHAM: Nothing wrong with linear progression. It's not extrapolation—there's a difference. There's a continuous thread of development that ties together human height, weight, life expectancy, cranial capacity—all of these things—so that you can make some judgments about the future of the human species.

EDWARD: But within one generation, we could halve human size. Then you'd have about four times as much space in the world, eight times as much food. How do you do it? There's something on the surface of the cell that absorbs growth hormone. We can produce antibodies so that it won't.

GREG: Anybody here want to be half his size?

EDWARD: We'd have four times the space, eight times the food.

GREG: You can say we'd have four times the space as a society, but what individuals would want to be half their current size? None!

ROBERT: A fundamental issue—open to challenge—is Graham's thesis that we can forecast the future based on some sophisticated methods.

BRUCE: I don't know what the world or the solar system are going to be like in a thousand years—much less our descendants. What I do know is that we're living through an unprecedented period of time right now; our parents did, to some extent, and our children certainly will. It happens once in the history of the world, when the population saturates the earth, when humans become a perturbing force on the

planet, changing it as a consequence. It happens only once, and we happen to be living in that period. And so that's the big news. We're going through a cultural transformation, a viewpoint transformation; that's why I don't go along with taking some kind of average pattern for the past and trying to project it forward. It's obviously not going to work. Everything goes off the scale if you're just projecting linearly.

ROBERT: You've talked about humanity maturing and, in your words, joining the galactic community.

BRUCE: Right, right.

ROBERT: Do you mean this metaphorically, or do you think there are literally other civilizations out there waiting for us to grow up?

BRUCE: I mean it literally, but of course it's intuition. I cannot imagine, out of all the possible habitats for beings like us throughout the universe, that there's just one success and we happen to be it. But that's a possibility; it can't be ruled out until we get definitive evidence [of alien intelligence]. I predict we'll get that evidence within fifty years.

BART: But even without extraterrestrial contact, humans will tend to expand exponentially in all directions. We're surely going to conquer the solar system, and once we've done that we're going to conquer—

BRUCE: Who's the enemy?

BART: By "conquer" I mean taking it over, controlling it, living on it. I think the first [space colonists] will be the conquistadors of science—and then we'll get beyond that. Maybe it'll be robots or their intellectual offspring that will venture farther out into the galaxy. Whether we find any alien life or not—and it may be better if we don't—humans historically do tend to expand their sphere of habitation, in a mathematical sense, very quickly.

GREG: The real question is, How are we going to deal with so deep and profound a transformation? It's going to be very, very challenging to all of our institutions—to everything that has gone before.

ROBERT: A thousand years, this incredible time of transition, is really a very short period, cosmologically speaking. The universe, it seems, will stretch on for thousands of billions of years and still, cosmologists say, it won't even have reached adolescence [current estimates are that all the stars won't burn out for about 100 trillion years; see Chapter 27]. That's the deep fascination.

EDWARD: And just the last hundred years have seen unimaginable change.

ROBERT: That's the point.

EDWARD: So another thousand years is not a short time; it's a long, long time.

ROBERT: Sure, it's unthinkably long on our personal timescale, but it fits between single heartbeats on the universe's timescale. We just can't imagine it.

GREG: It's boggling even to look out a thousand years, because most of the changes we're speculating about will take place just within the next century.

BRUCE: Let me try a different cut at this. I wrote a book once—it's a rare but not valuable book— called *Navigating the Future*. I wrote it back in 1975, and I looked at a range of extreme scenarios, the outermost situations I could imagine— the idea being that as you imagine maximum shifts you can get deeply inside of the present. And it turned out that there was a natural structure that emerged. One was what I called the crunch—the exponential-growth model we're now living through, with uncontrolled changes and social dislocations. And then you have to believe that something happens after that, which I called the "afterward." However these forces are resolved, pleasantly or not, the model levels off, because it's physically impossible to keep growing like this; the instability would tear the biosphere apart. So what all this says to me is that the key to the future is governance—that is, how humanity learns to govern itself.

BART: So government is destiny?

BRUCE: Not government, governance.

ROBERT: I have a specific question. A thousand years from now, how many nations will there be in the world? These are your choices— orders of magnitude—one, ten, a hundred, a thousand, ten thousand?

EDWARD: Ten thousand.

BRUCE: Probably a federation of a hundred and fifty to two hundred. Or zero, because the concept will have disappeared. I'll give you zero.

GREG: I agree. The idea of nations is being transcended and there will be all sorts of levels of control, from local to global.

EDWARD: Like the human body.

BRUCE: Governance will be distributed in many ways. For example, your letters move around the world, and airplanes fly around the world, without any one polity being in charge. There are agreements, for these and many different functions.

BART: Bruce, you don't have mail on Sunday. You have this crude merger of church and state and it still exists at the height of the information age.

BRUCE: So big deal.

BART: The power lust is so strong in humans—about ninety-eight-plus percent of our DNA is identical to that of chimpanzees—that as we increase computing and communication power [and its ubiquitous dominance of humankind], that power lust is going to go right along with it, and the outcome may be one big world government. If government can rule you, it will rule you; that's always been true throughout human history.

EDWARD: But if you look at the human body, there are billions of cells; each one is autonomous, has its own energy, is affected by certain hormones, yet they all work together. I think we'll separate into thousands of little nations, where there's a city, a village, or an autonomous region. There'll be some system of communal communication—like the bloodstream carrying hormones—but each unit will be self-sufficient and capable of managing its own affairs.

GREG: I think the real kinds of questions for a thousand years from now are, What will humans be? How human will we be? Will we even *be* human?

ROBERT: Genetic engineering is so powerful and the acceleration of technology is so dramatic that those are legitimate questions.

GREG: We're at a point where we need only a few decades to seriously alter our own genetics. How, then, can we even imagine where we will be in a thousand years?

BART: Humans are political animals—that's a polite way of saying we love power. I wish I could share your optimism here, but from the evidence of the twentieth century and what I've seen of the past, I can't.

GREG: This is the longest period without a major international war between major powers—

BART: As we tape this show right now, there are something like forty wars going on in the world.

GRAHAM: There are some hundred and sixty armed conflicts.

ROBERT: One could argue that there's more turmoil today than ever before. But I'm tired of war; and since we've already dealt with the future of love [see Chapter 9], let's go to the future of work.

EDWARD: Work is going to be interesting. Already in the United States there are more people employed in the fast-food industry than in the whole of manufacturing.

BART: But fast food is manufacturing.

EDWARD: Fast food is a service industry.

BART: It's hamburger manufacturing.

EDWARD: It's a service industry.

ROBERT: And I'm trying to get agreement on a thousand years from now?

EDWARD: The point is that all of our manufacturing production will be automated and robotized. A few people will be involved in service industries. In the European Union, it's estimated that within ten years one percent of the working population will be employed in call centers, just sitting there taking orders for sweaters or hamburgers. In other words, we're going to end up like the [ancient] Greeks, whose greatest joy in life was writing vindictive speeches about one another while slaves did all the work.

GRAHAM: Edward's right in his vision but wrong with his numbers, and that makes a difference when you're projecting the present to forecast the future. Two hundred years ago, over ninety percent of the American workforce was involved in agricultural or extractive industries. Today, the number on the farm is down to two percent or less, and even so, seventy to eighty percent of many of our crops are exported. We have this prodigious output, thanks to our technology. The same trends will continue. All our basic needs—food, shelter, clothing, education—will be satisfied in a thousand years.

ROBERT: Are we forgetting reality? Maybe we should invite Dr. Pangloss to join us. Bart, what do you think about all this optimism?

BART: Well, I'm an optimist, despite my pessimism about human nature. I think in the end it will work out, which means that most of us will achieve some kind of Heaven in a chip.

GREG: It's important to remember how long a thousand years really is. The black death—the bubonic plague—killed forty percent of the population of the known world in the fourteenth century. That seems a distant shadow now. So even if humanity has to endure severe

trauma in the next couple of centuries, it won't have a large impact ultimately.

EDWARD: I think we'll sit in corners letting designer drugs stimulate our pleasure centers, hallucinating, while technology does all the work.

ROBERT: That would be an awful world.

EDWARD: It will be an awful world.

BRUCE: I see a somewhat different trend. Hominids, as distinguished from other animals, have been toolmakers. Man the toolmaker— that's what has led to both the good and the bad. And what are the tools? First they were mechanical, then they made use of various energy sources, then—

EDWARD: Language, language, language.

BRUCE: Language, actually, was developed in response to these tools—writing, too. My point is that the key technology that runs through all of this is communications. Humans, in essence, are a communicating organism. We started as a

---

. . . the key technology that runs through all of this is communications.

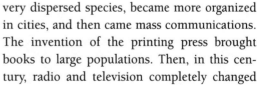

---

very dispersed species, became more organized in cities, and then came mass communications. The invention of the printing press brought books to large populations. Then, in this century, radio and television completely changed the psychology and social setting of most of the world's people.

ROBERT: And now, of course, the Internet.

BRUCE: And now we're on the verge of what I think is a millennial kind of event—interactive communications and education. The former stuff has all been one-way, blazing out at you. Now it's becoming interactive, two-way: the Internet itself is bottom-up, self-organizing, self-adapting, very powerful. Society is undergoing profound change in response to the Internet. What's ahead a thousand years from now, with even better communications, more miniaturizing? I see human society much more together, with an almost literal planetary consciousness—and I hope we'll also be communicating with other societies elsewhere in the universe.

ROBERT: Greg, in a thousand years will we be having regular communications with alien civilizations?

GREG: The real question is, Why haven't we had it to date? If life is as present in the universe as many imagine it is—which seems reasonable—consider this. Our galaxy is only a hundred thousand light-years across, so if an intelligent species were to take even a thousand years to move out just one light-year [and colonize], they would [geometrically expand and] fill the whole galaxy within a hundred million years, which on a universal timescale is a very short period. So why no contact? The most obvious possibilities are either that (1) such an advanced species is already here but are so transformed that we can't recognize them; or (2), they're staying home watching TV—meaning that virtual realities have become so compelling that it's not meaningful for them to expand into the universe, because there are much more inter-esting and entertaining things going on at home.*

EDWARD: What you're saying is, If they're stupider than we, they can't communicate; and if they're more intelligent, they don't want to.

BRUCE: No, I think you're missing the real point. Assuming that there are alien civilizations and they do wish to communicate, the last way they would do it would be to send a spaceship with someone or something inside of it. The most efficient means of intergalactic communications is by some kind of electromagnetic signal—not just radio or infrared, maybe something else. That's the obvious way to communicate.

ROBERT: You haven't found any signals yet.

GRAHAM: But we're looking, though our methods are still primitive compared to all the possible—

BART: It's too soon to say.

---

*There are other possible explanations why there has been no alien contact. For one, the development of intelligent life—as opposed to organic chemistry or even simple life-forms—may be so exceedingly improbable that there might not be another example in our galaxy or even in the communicable universe [see Chapter 28]. For another, it would take several billion years for a technologically adept species to develop—witness our own evolution. There would be no reason to suppose that such other civilizations would have developed more or less at the same time we did, either. They may have arrived in this area before our solar system formed (unlikely, but possible). They may arrive two billion or five billion years from now, by which time we hopefully will have gone somewhere else.

BRUCE: Yes. This is the great exploration. If we continue the search for a hundred years and still don't detect any alien signals, then maybe we are alone. Within a hundred years, we will have imaged Earth-like planets of nearby stars and tracked billions of frequencies from all over the universe. And if out of all that there's nothing, the answer may be that we truly are alone, and then there may be a biblical return.

ROBERT: You'll be applying to a seminary?

BART: I think Greg made the key point here, which is our fascination with entertainment and what I see as the movement toward becoming high-tech couch potatoes—whom we'll inevitably call "chip potatoes," not to be confused, of course, with potato chips. Our consciousness just may be in such chips, and once we've been uploaded, we can communicate directly with other consciousnesses in other chips. Right now, minds can't converse directly with one another, except by means of crude verbal vibrations, because skulls get in the way. It will be very different when we've been uploaded into a chip in some form and complex collections of chips interact. At a minimum, it would be like allowing the ants crawling around in an airplane to have a sense of what the airplane is and how they all fit into the global economy. I just don't think we can accommodate those kinds of thoughts in our three pounds of [cerebral] meat right now.

EDWARD: Why would we want to communicate? You communicate because you think someone is going to tell you something useful. Well, we'll have all our material needs taken care of technically. You communicate because it's going to give you pleasure. If we can stimulate our pleasure senses directly, why should we bother to communicate?

BART: For example, there's never been a multi-authored symphony. It requires just too much focused, concentrated thought. I think there'll be all kinds of collectively created art and science and other things. It's just not physically feasible to do that now.

GRAHAM: Let me suggest a statistical dimension. Our galaxy, relatively minor on the scale of things, has an estimated 200 billion to 450 billion stars. There are something like 100 billion galaxies in the [observable] universe. Many of

---

The statistical probability of life elsewhere is so enormously probable . . .

---

these individual stellar systems may have up to twenty or thirty planets with lunar-type satellites and asteroids. The statistical probability of life elsewhere is so enormously probable that—

ROBERT: But that makes the question "Where are they?" that much more compelling. We should also differentiate between the probability of life and intelligent life [see Chapter 28].

BART: The volume of space is so vast—just as the volume of the ocean is much vaster than the surface, because it's in three dimensions rather than two—that we haven't begun, in any statistically interesting sense, to search it. On the other hand, there may be nothing to search for.

ROBERT: Is speculating about the next thousand years more serious than merely an evening's good fun?

BRUCE: I think it is. It's also fun, of course, because it's unlimited. But we're in this enormous transformation, and things that we do or don't do in our own lifetimes will have very far-reaching effects. For example, in a thousand years there may be no natural world left at all. There may be no primitive languages recorded any more. The past may be completely gone. That would be a tragedy; we might have a stable world, but we wouldn't have a rich world. So why we worry about these things is to be sure that we act as visionaries in this present period of time. We're consuming like mad, bulldozing everything—

BART: And innovating like mad to balance it.

ROBERT: Do you really care about what will happen that far in the future?

BART: Sure I care! But we're innovating at a rate that seems to exceed our consumption.

GREG: And these images of the future reflect back and alter the present—which is a problem. Some of the current images, which suggest that we're moving toward some sort of a reckoning, that our development is not robust, that we're out of sync with the natural world—these sorts of images are very destructive. I don't think that's the case at all.

EDWARD: What we forget is that millions of years ago the dolphins met in the sea and said, "Look, why do we want to go back on land? We've got to support our own weight, we've got to make tools, we've got to learn new tricks to survive, we're much better off where we are." In

other words, a decision that development is not necessarily the best direction to go.

GREG: But to act as though that's a decision, an intentional decision, is ludicrous.

EDWARD: Why? Why?

GREG: I mean, we're embarked upon an evolution . . .

EDWARD: Why?

GREG: Because dolphins *didn't* sit around in a huddle and say, "We're going to stay in the water because—"

EDWARD: How do you know that? How do you know that?

GREG: We're essentially caught on a treadmill: Our technologies are creating all sorts of problems that can only be dealt with by our technologies.

ROBERT: What happens to traditional religion over the course of this new millennium?

BART: I would argue that religions will survive the onslaught of science. There'll be great competition among them. If I had to predict the winner a thousand years from now, I'd pick Buddhism. People like how the Buddha enjoyed life—feasts and all that—and then broke through to the other side.

ROBERT: Fast-forward a thousand years for predictions. What characterizes human life in the year 3000?

GRAHAM: Economics is the linchpin that holds society together. I think it'll go through five phases. Communications will dominate for twenty years, and then it'll be the recreation-entertainment industry complex. Next will be life sciences; beyond that nanotechnologies, the manipulation of atomic matter. Along the way, energy, including solar and nuclear fusion. Finally, extraterrestrial contact at around the year 3000 as we move out into the universe.

BART: I think some safe predictions are that English will be the dominant language of the solar system, if not beyond. We'll have conquered death, solving the engineering problem that it really is. So if you die, it will be by your choice—or the choice of the government that runs your computer. You [or they] can flip your switch on or off at will. And, as I said, I think we'll have achieved some form of Heaven in a chip. Whether you'll want to stay there is another matter.

EDWARD: Back to what I said in the beginning. No men; women sitting around bitching and taking designer drugs.

GREG: I think the dominant trend is going to be diversity. I don't know what shape humans will take, but a transformation will occur. And when those future beings look back, they will see that the very basics of their lives are being laid down right now—by genetic engineering, artificial intelligence, and space travel.

BRUCE: Communications. The essence of individuals will be their ability to communicate with an enormous array of entities, many of which we can hardly imagine.

ROBERT: CONCLUDING COMMENT

If in the year 1000 the smartest people had predicted what the world would be like in the year 2000, it would have seemed a joke. We think we're much smarter today—more in tune with the universal music of truth. So we now imagine the year 3000. Life spans of hundreds of years, with homegrown body parts and chips for brains. Abundant, clean energy from the sun and a safe, inexhaustible source of power in nuclear fusion. Computers doing all the work—unobtrusively, thank you. Colonies on a greened Mars or perhaps on planets of nearby stars, with intergalactic ships heading out into the great beyond. Who knows? But what I find more fascinating is that we humans seem compelled to imagine the far future. We are beings who comprehend time and its flowing passage, who project our mind's eye and envision epochs long before our births and long after our deaths. That such a time-sensitive, self-aware being exists at all somehow makes me wonder about the far future. Could something unexpected, really unexpected, occur before the year 3000? I'd give it—just a hunch here—a three out of ten: thirty percent. I guess I won't be doing this show, but that would be expected, wouldn't it? One wonders whether Y3K will find humanity any closer to truth.

OUTTAKES

BART: *—chips for brains?*

ROBERT: *I had to be very careful reading that line.*

BRUCE: *Are you serious about the female thing, Edward?*

EDWARD: *It's certainly a realistic possibility.*

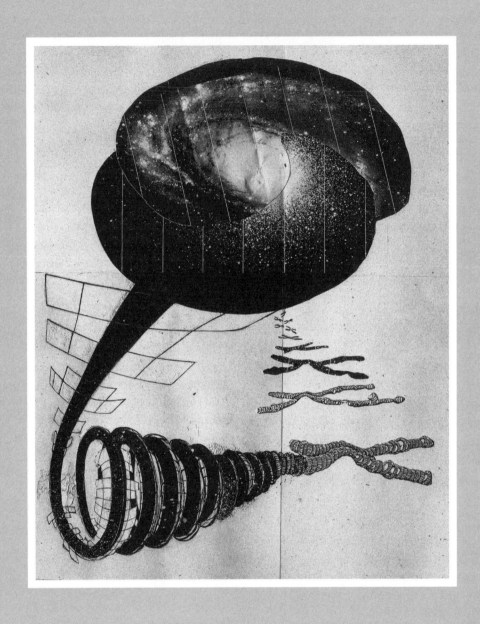

PART FIVE

UNIVERSE & MEANING

Neurocosmology. (Courtesy of Todd Siler.)

CHAPTER 23

What Are the Grand Questions
of Science?

How about a grand tour, not of the continents, but of science? We seek truth, where it may change. We view the cosmic spectrum of science, the Big Picture—of the fundamental structure of matter and energy, the beginnings and ends of the universe, the global changes on our planet, the evolution of life, and the essence of brain and mind. What discoveries lie ahead? What surprises are in store? Grand science requires grand questions. We brought together five leading scientists and thinkers and asked them to make a list.

PARTICIPANTS

Dr. Francisco Ayala, who is sometimes called the Renaissance man of evolutionary biology, is a geneticist and philosopher at the University of California, Irvine. For Francisco, biology poses the most interesting and diversified questions.

Dr. Patricia Churchland is a professor of philosophy at the University of California, San Diego, where she focuses on neuroscience, the study of the brain. Her books include *Neurophilosophy: Toward a Unified Science of Mind-Brain*. Pat cautions that before we deal with the large questions of brain and mind, we need to understand how nerve cells work.

Timothy Ferris is an award-winning author, a filmmaker whose *Life Beyond Earth* was a PBS special, and a consultant to the National Aeronautics and Space Administration (NASA) on long-term space policy. His best-selling books include *Coming of Age in the Milky Way* and *The Whole Shebang: A State-of-the-Universe(s) Report*. Tim sees physics and astronomy, which together reach from the subatomic to the cosmological scale, as embracing the grand questions.

Dr. Steven Koonin is vice president and provost of the California Institute of Technology (CalTech), where he is a professor of theoretical physics. He has also written on subjects as diverse as Earth's atmosphere and the human genome. Steve explains how the process of science works and draws a distinction between questions of fundamental physics and those of biology.

Dr. Neil de Grasse Tyson is the director of the Hayden Planetarium of the American Museum of Natural History, in New York, and the author of several popular books on astronomy, including *Just Visiting This Planet*. Neil shows how the fun of science is as much process as results—and that the answers we find often lead to new questions.

ROBERT: Steve, as provost of Caltech, one of the world's great scientific institutions, you are responsible for overseeing all kinds of research. Do great questions drive great scientists?

STEVE: Yes, they do. Science is about figuring out how the world works, and there are really two kinds of science. One is where you know the rules but have to figure out how they apply in specific situations. The other is where you try to figure out the rules themselves. In this second category there have been revolutions—such as thermodynamics, quantum mechanics, relativity, the genetic code—that change the whole game. My late colleague [Nobel Laureate] Dick Feynman used to say, "Once you know the rules, everything else is just chess." The great questions lie in figuring out the rules.

ROBERT: Your own research ranges broadly from computational physics of atoms to global phenomena like the earth's magnetic field and the composition of the atmosphere. What drives you?

STEVE: Gee, what does drive me? Interesting questions, I think, and the possibility of being able to answer them. But you can't ask questions that are too far out there.

ROBERT: Neil, you're a public scientist: why are the grand questions of science important for the public to know about? And how important are they in the day-to-day conduct of science?

NEIL: First of all, few scientists ever have the privilege of addressing, much less answering, the grand questions of science, but these are the carrots, the intellectual carrots, that seduce people into wanting to do science in the first place. And these questions do keep you going throughout your career-long journey. But often the fun of doing science is the path you take along the way, the progressive exploration that gets you closer to the machinery of how the world works.

ROBERT: What happens to the ambitious aspirations of these idealistic young scientists?

NEIL: You learn that once you've solved one question, there's another on the far side of it. So don't be fooled by how close you seem.

ROBERT: Tim, you've written a number of elegant and insightful books on astronomy. Why astronomy?

TIM: Well, it's perhaps the oldest science. Long before history began, people were looking up at the night sky—and until quite recently, of course, most people had access to the night sky on clear nights. The tremendous urbanization and lighting up of the Western world is a recent phenomenon, and it has really hampered amateur astronomy and ordinary people's appreciation of the wider universe. Astronomy was my original interest—after all, it's the science of everything there is, on the largest scale.

ROBERT: Why do so many of the grand questions have to do with physics and astronomy?

TIM: They have to do with physics because physics looks at the foundations and structure of matter, the very smallest things on the smallest scales, and with astronomy because astronomy looks at the structure of the universe, the very largest thing on the largest scale. Within this framework is every phenomenon that we know about and that we are.

ROBERT: Francisco, Pat, how does that sit with you? Have physics and astronomy subsumed the bulk of the grand questions, or are these questions moving toward the life sciences?

FRANCISCO: Only after Darwin—after that major breakthrough in the nineteenth century—could we ask fundamental questions about biology. Before Darwin, there were no

---

Only after Darwin . . . could we ask fundamental questions about biology.

---

explanations of why birds had wings, say, or humans had lungs. These things were attributed

to the Creator. Since Darwin's theory of evolution by natural selection, we have been able to ask all the important biological questions—questions about where we come from, why we function as we do, how we relate to one another.

ROBERT: Aren't an increasing number of the grand questions biologically based?

FRANCISCO: Absolutely. With all due respect to physicists and astronomers, biological organisms are the most interesting and diversified phenomena in the world. That's why we study them.

ROBERT: Pat, you're one of the leading thinkers about what's traditionally known as the mind-body problem [see Chapters 1 and 2]. I'm revealing my bias here, but could you tell us why the brain and the mind are among the grand questions of science?

PAT: Two major questions need to be distinguished here. One has to do with whether psychological states—our mental life of remembering, thinking, creating—are really a subset of brain activity. And on that major question, although there are residual problems, I think most people agree that it's all only the brain—that there isn't anything in addition to the brain, such as a nonphysical soul.

ROBERT: Most people agree? Or most scientists agree?

PAT: Scientists do, by and large. And I think that's the way the evidence stacks up now, in neuroscience. It's possible that there is a nonphysical soul, but it doesn't really look like that's the way things work. The other major question you need to ask, given that [materialist] framework, is, How do high-level psychological processes come about from basic neurophysiological effects? How do these brain cells, orga-

---

How do these brain cells, . . . give rise to my watching

---

nized in this complex way, give rise to my watching something move, or seeing color, or smelling a rose? These are the kinds of questions that preoccupy me.

ROBERT: Let's try enumerating the grand questions of science by category, from the most fundamental to the most complex. And let's start with physics.

STEVE: There are several interesting questions at the forefront right now. One is that we have a picture of how the physical world is constructed at the most fundamental subatomic level. It's called the Standard Model and it includes quarks [the constituents of protons and neutrons, which themselves make up the nucleus of the atom], it includes electrons, it includes bosons [particles that carry the fundamental forces, or interactions]. And the question is, To what extent is this Standard Model valid? So far it has proved maddeningly valid. Everywhere we look to test it, it seems to be right. But it has some free parameters in it that we have to measure. We would like to know how many free parameters there are. What are those values? Are they all related in some way? And can we get them all into the Standard Model [see Chapter 25]?

ROBERT: Tim, what are some quantum questions in physics?

TIM: Physics at the beginning of the twenty-first century is composed of quantum physics and relativity. One problem is that they're not quite compatible. Another is that there are aspects of the quantum world that are very difficult—even confounding—to understand. Some physicists feel that these problems won't ever be of any functional importance. Others feel that through this keyhole there may be a great deal to be learned. If you look at the whole universe in quantum terms, it's interesting to think about light traveling vast distances over eons of time and then striking your eye and suddenly turning into something different—that is, into a kind of perception, or knowledge. And when we try to understand the two ends of this spectrum, the questions that naturally arise—and they're equally important—center on how the whole thing originated. How did the universe originate—and, completing the loop, how did human intelligence originate?

ROBERT: "Loop" is a good metaphor for thinking about these questions—better than the traditional hierarchies or levels. Francisco, I know physics is not your field, but what questions do you ask about physics?

FRANCISCO: Not very many, because as a biologist I assume that the atoms are stable, the molecules react, and the laws of physics apply. And then I can start asking my kinds of questions—I don't have to know the details.

ROBERT: I see. You don't need to reduce biology to physics to enable you to answer very sophisticated questions.

FRANCISCO: That's right.

STEVE: These are different kinds of questions. The biological questions deal with complexity, operate at a higher level. As an analogy, in order to build a computer I don't need to know the internal makeup of each of its parts—that is, the fundamental physics. But I do need to know how its constituents are interconnected and work together—that is, the engineering.

ROBERT: Neil, talk about the implications of the Copernican revolution for the grand questions of astronomy.

NEIL: In the sixteenth century—just to remind us—Copernicus restored the sun to the center of the known universe, and that dislodged our perception of our planet as the center and ourselves as so important. Earth became merely one of a number of other planets in the solar system. And later we learned that the sun is not the center of the universe, either, but just one of hundreds of billions of stars in a galaxy, which is itself one of perhaps a hundred billion other galaxies. Each time we thought we were special, scientific discovery demonstrated that we are in fact not. Every step has led in this direction—we're ordinary. Maybe one day this message will no longer apply, but it seems to work at every step we take.

ROBERT: Is there a limit to this process of demotion?

NEIL: No, I don't think so. I think it will continue even to the very chemistry of our bodies. We're carbon-based life, and carbon is one of the most abundant elements in the universe, formed in the crucible of high-mass stars that explode and spill their guts across interstellar space, generating all the stuff that makes planets and life and people. This commonality is a testament to the universality of the laws of physics. If the laws of physics were one way here and another way there, or one way this minute and something else

the next, we'd all be out of a job. We'd have nothing to study.

ROBERT: Commonality being a fundamental principle of science.

NEIL: It's a fundamental principle, but not because we like it that way. Evidence throughout eons has demonstrated it.

ROBERT: It seems that we've merged seamlessly from questions of physics to questions of astrophysics—from fundamental particles, in other words, to cosmology.

NEIL: And that trend will continue.

ROBERT: It's the trend of the past thirty years or so. You can't explain the origin of the universe without referring to elementary-particle physics and the forces that operate on these particles—and it's becoming increasingly difficult to do the reverse, that is, study the most fundamental properties of particle physics without referring to the origin of the universe.

STEVE: That's right. We can't get to the scales needed to explain fundamental physics unless we look back at the initial conditions of the Big Bang. We don't have accelerators powerful enough to generate the required energy.

TIM: Biology and neuroscience are going to be increasingly embedded in these questions, too.

... the future of biology will involve looking at the environments on other planets ...

Biology began, as it were, on a tabletop—on one planet existing in a wider context about which very little is known. I think the future of biology will involve looking at the environments on other planets and determining to what extent the way things are here on Earth are accidents and to what extent they could not have been otherwise.

FRANCISCO: Why would that be interesting? I'm much more interested in studying life on this planet. And I know that we're not accidents. So I'm not so interested in what is happening all over the universe. Not at first.

TIM: But wouldn't you be interested in knowing whether evolution, for instance, is a universal law or a law peculiar to this planet?

FRANCISCO: Well, I'm not particularly interested in that. I'm much more interested in evolutionary questions right here.

STEVE: If we discovered an instance of life on another planet—say that we found that life there had a different chemistry, different cell structure, different body structure—wouldn't that be extraordinarily interesting?

FRANCISCO: Oh, it would be interesting, but I have many more interesting questions about life right here on this planet.

NEIL: But comparative studies can be critical. Take our study of the solar system: For the longest time the only planets we knew were the ones in our own system, so theorists came up with models that explained why, say, you have a big planet here, a small planet there, rings here, moons there. You construct your whole paradigm based on the example of one system. That can be extremely limiting. Whereas just by looking over the fence, you can find other examples—in my analogy, other solar systems—so that a whole new field of comparative planetary science is born.

FRANCISCO: But that's the difference precisely. You can't compare simple, inanimate systems like solar systems with complex, living organisms like human beings. I don't expect to find human beings, or any intelligent life, over the fence—anywhere else in the universe. That won't be repeated [see Chapter 28]. I want to understand what's happening here; I get all my universes, so to speak—as many as I want for now—here on this planet.

ROBERT: Let's stay with the universe. Neil, what's happening with the expansion of the universe, certainly one of the great questions of science?

NEIL: Well, we're expanding, and we've been expanding, and it looks now as though the expansion is a one-way trip. For decades, theorists felt that a philosophically attractive universe would be one in which we would expand and collapse and then expand again [in some infinite cycle], because that took away the worrisome issue of there being only one beginning to the universe. But it looks as if things are moving outward, never to reverse and come back into a Big Crunch. And it may well be that the universe is not just expanding but that its expansion is accelerating [i.e., the longer time goes on, the faster the flying apart becomes—though evidence is still equivocal and the question remains unresolved]. The temperature of the universe is dropping, the density of matter is diminishing, and it would seem that we're headed for what we call a thermal death, where everything falls to the same extremely cold temperature—close to absolute zero, which is the temperature at which all motion virtually stops.

ROBERT: Are you depressed about that?

NEIL: It's a few hundred billion years away.

ROBERT: Actually, cosmology is becoming even more complex. Tim, tell us about the theories of multi-universes and inflation. There's a whole new realm of reality out there.

TIM: The original models of the Big Bang, after the expansion of the universe was first discovered [in 1929 by astronomer Edwin Hubble], lacked an explanation of why the universe should be expanding in the first place. The inflationary models contain physically plausible mechanisms that could have caused space itself to expand, which is indeed what seems to be happening in the actual universe that we inhabit.

ROBERT: The inflationary model solves several problems inherent in the Big Bang, such as the horizon problem, the quandary that the universe appears the same in all directions even though light hasn't had enough time since the Big Bang to travel across the universe and link the horizons [see Chapter 26].

TIM: In the various inflationary models, the universe began as a small bubble of space. These models are rather beautiful, and they seem to imply that the bubble occurred in pre-existing space of some sort. And this raises, to me, the marvelously stimulating notion of there being ensembles of many universes, of which ours is only one example. In that case, a question arises in cosmology similar to Jacques Monod's question about chance and necessity in biology: Which aspects of our universe are chance and which ones had to be the way they are because that was the only physically possible outcome?

ROBERT: And with regard to chance and necessity in biology, there are some questions about to be answered by the Human Genome Project: the massive, multiyear effort to sequence our DNA, the three billion chemical bases arranged into some hundred and forty thousand genes—the number of genes keeps changing. DNA is resident in the nucleus of virtually every cell of our bodies from where each gene—each working hereditary unit—determines an aspect of our physical mechanism.* How is this enormous project faring at the moment?

STEVE: We're getting the list of the parts—if you like—of the human genome. We'll have most of the sequence soon. But we also need to understand the configuration of all those parts, how they fit together and work together.†

FRANCISCO: The sequence of the genome will give us very interesting and important information, but this is only the beginning. The genome is a linearly organized molecule. Information is conveyed in the same way as in the sequence of letters in a sentence of English. You have a sentence, you read can it, but now you have to go

---

*The Human Genome Project, coordinated by the United States Department of Energy and the National Institutes of Health, is an international initiative to discover all the human genes (the human genome) and make them accessible for biological and medical study. A genome is all the DNA in an organism, including its genes.

†The Human Genome Project estimated (at year-end 1999) that the working draft sequence of the entire human genome would be ninety percent finished by mid-2000 and the final, high-quality sequence completed by 2003. It's become a race among competing scientific groups, accelerating the original timetable, so that the final map of the human genome—filling in the gaps—could come even sooner.

from there to create the whole organism—that's where biology comes in. A human being, or any other kind of organism, is organized in four dimensions—the three spatial dimensions plus time. How an organism develops and changes over time is surely one of the grand questions.

ROBERT: Pat, what are some of the core questions of neuroscience?

PAT: The thing to remember about neuroscience is that we don't yet have what you might call an explanatory framework, and in this sense neuroscience really differs from physics, astronomy, and even cell biology. Neuroscience is still very, very young. We don't have the strong, established paradigms within which the general explanations fit. Now, this makes brain research very exciting, but it also means that we can't expect from neuroscience the kinds of [coherent models] we can expect from physics.

ROBERT: What kinds of fundamental questions are we dealing with? Questions regarding cognition? Memory?

PAT: I like to think about the field in a slightly different way. Of course there are all those kinds of questions. But first you have to know what the basic structural units are. And it looks like neurons—the nerve cells in the brain—are those basic structural units. But there's a lot we don't really understand about a single nerve cell. So when we contemplate the larger questions—such as the nature of consciousness and the biological mechanisms for decision making—we still have not satisfactorily answered the question of how individual neurons work. In particular, we don't know how neurons code information. There are a number of hypotheses; some of them look plausible and some have explanatory strength. But it's a fundamental

question for which we have no answer. When you're thinking about the brain, you have to avoid going immediately to the grand, sexy questions and expecting good answers. It isn't going to be like that. Ultimately, I think we'll have an understanding of the neurobiological mechanisms for consciousness, for decision making, and so on. But in the meantime we have to understand how individual neurons work and how they cooperate with other neurons. It's not a grand, sexy question, but it is a grand question.

ROBERT: Steve, are there any grand questions about our own planet Earth?

STEVE: Sure. For example, questions about the fluid earth—the ocean, the air, the various layers of the atmosphere. What is the extent of the natural variability of these systems? What causes that variability? What makes ice ages is one specific question we don't understand yet. Similarly, we don't understand what's going on in the deep oceans, which are an important component of the earth's atmospheric system. All this affects the long-term climate of the earth, which is obviously of great interest to us.

TIM: We don't even know where the oceans came from.

STEVE: That's certainly true. I remember asking that question in third grade: Where did the water come from?

NEIL: It came from where everything comes from. We've had comets streaming throughout the solar system, and they've got tons of water in them. That's one way that the earth's oceans could have been brought here, though there are still unresolved problems with isotope ratios. But I beg to differ that questions related to Earth are in the category of grand questions, because Earth is just one planet. When I think of grand questions, I think of questions that apply everywhere, involving the future and evolution of the universe.

ROBERT: But if there were a massive glacier creeping down toward your new planetarium in New York—

NEIL: Don't get me wrong. I love Earth—it's our home.

STEVE: Well, there are questions about Earth that are generic questions. Ice ages are an example because they elicit questions regarding the origin of planetary magnetic fields.

NEIL: Good, there you go.

STEVE: Some planets have magnetic fields and others don't. The earth's magnetic field reverses about every hundred thousand years or something like that. We don't understand how that happens. So it's a grand question of sorts. But I also think that climate is a grand question—for one thing, because we really care about the answer.

NEIL: I'd think of the climate question not so much as it applies to Earth, but how it's generalized to conditions on other planets. Why, for instance, has Jupiter's red spot survived for at least three hundred years?

STEVE: You may get very different answers on different planets. Planetary science is going to be like biology; there's a different answer in each system.

NEIL: You hope not. But on the other hand, if some phenomenon on other planets requires a different explanation from that here on Earth, that's critical to know.

ROBERT: Francisco, what are the grand questions in biology?

FRANCISCO: I'd say there are three. The ape-human transformation. The gene-soma [cell] transformation. And the brain-mind transformation. What I mean by the ape-human transformation is, Why is it that we are so similar to apes and yet something happened in our evolution to produce our minds and our culture? By the gene-soma transformation, as I touched on earlier, I mean, How does the linear information in the genetic code generate highly complex, multidimensional organisms, with innumerable parts and always changing? As for the brain-mind transformation, Pat [Churchland] can answer that one much better than I can.

NEIL: As you were talking, I was thinking that physics has counterparts to these deep transformation questions. For example, as we understand the laws of physics, there's a reversibility in the laws of motion in terms of collisions of molecules. Yet if a drop of ink falls into a glass of water, that ink doesn't reassemble itself into a drop. It's dissolved, never to return to the drop it once was. So things change as you go to different scales. These transitions from how things work at microscopic levels to how things work in their complex forms at macroscopic levels are fundamental.

STEVE: That is perhaps the pervasive character

How do you go from small pieces to large phenomena?

---

of all these grand questions. How do you go from small pieces to large phenomena?

ROBERT: A stunning example is, How can a hundred billion neurons generate the grandeur of consciousness—or, in the vernacular, How can meat make mind? This is the first time in history when we can even begin to answer this question.

PAT: There are a number of reasons why it took neuroscience a lot longer to get going than, say, astronomy. In astronomy, you could make certain fundamental observations with very simple devices, very simple technology—like a ground lens. In neuroscience, you need much more knowledge. You need to understand electricity; you need to understand cell biology; you have to have the technology to put something under a microscope and see all the tiny bits and pieces. If you want to understand neuron function, you need very advanced technology to probe these very, very tiny cells. And so we had only a sort of speculative psychology for a long time, and not much neuroscience, because other science and technology had to be in place first. We now see remarkable developments in the study of the brain, because the technology is coming online. But there are still fundamental things we haven't been able to do. For example, although imaging is a set of great new technologies, it still gives us only broad portraits. This picks up on what Steve [Koonin] said about going from small pieces to large phenomena—in this case, between what single cells [neurons] do and what [brain] imaging shows us. We have no technology for accessing this gap in function.

NEIL: As we know, physics has had a long string of greats, like Newton and Galileo, who laid a foundation for centuries of discoveries. Could it be that neuroscience needs a counterpart?

PAT: There was a lot of physics before Newton. In order to have great insight and great synthesis, you've got to have lots of bits and pieces, and that's especially true in neuroscience. We're seeing tremendous progress in neuroscience at all levels of organization. But ultimately we'll have some great figure or figures, I suppose, who will put it all together and tell us what the fundamental principles are.

STEVE: You can't have Newton before you have Kepler.

PAT: You can't have Newton before you have Galileo.

FRANCISCO: There's another issue here. We're never going to find a universal law or simple equation like $f = ma$ [force equals mass times acceleration] for the human brain. We're going to need much more complex explanations.

TIM: How do you know we'll never find a Newtonian-level law for the function of the brain?

FRANCISCO: That's a very interesting question, because I never like to say "never" in science.

ROBERT: He does anyway.

FRANCISCO: It's the complexity.

STEVE: How do we describe complexity? A gas, for example, consists of billions of molecules—

FRANCISCO: It's not only complexity, it's the complexity of the brain. I can have simple laws to explain complexity, but how can I explain the brain?

STEVE: Ultimately we'll have simple laws to explain it.

NEIL: The solar system was complex, too, before its laws were discovered.

ROBERT: But the kind of complexity Francisco [Ayala] is talking about in the brain is orders of magnitude greater than that of planetary motion.

PAT: Here I think I do disagree. It simply depends on how things go in our study of the brain. At the moment, it's hard to see what the fundamental principles are going to be, if any. But I'm not so sure there aren't going to be fundamental principles. Bear in mind that before the discovery of the structure of DNA, many people said we'd never be able to get a fundamental principle that explained the inheritability of traits.

FRANCISCO: But we've already discovered that. Biology has already had its Galileo and its Kepler. Mendel discovered the laws of inheritance—how genes act—before we even knew that DNA was the genetic material and how it acts.

PAT: We do have comparable discoveries in neuroscience—fundamental discoveries we can build on.

FRANCISCO: Yes. I think you're downplaying the brilliance of many great neurobiologists who have made many important discoveries.

TIM: I've been listening to this, and I'm struck by a thought that hadn't occurred to me before. Two of these great questions that we've been describing involve codes or inscriptions. One is genetics, which is simply a linear molecular code that manifests itself in complex, living organisms. It occurred to me that coding is also an issue of intelligence. In searching for extraterrestrial intelligence, for example, we define intelligence pragmatically—as the ability to send an encoded message. We're the only species on Earth, and probably in the history of the earth, that's had that ability. So our one species came about from an encoded system and now uses an encoded system to signal or discern intelligence. So these two great questions are quite closely related, aren't they?

FRANCISCO: In the first case, genetics, we're using the concept of information metaphorically. In the second case, communications and language, we're talking about real information. The relationship between the genetic code and the organism—what I've called the gene-soma question—is really a chicken-and-egg question.

TIM: There's also a case at the intermediate level. How is information encoded in the brain? How do our synapses "remember," for example?

FRANCISCO: Here's what I mean by the chicken-egg question: If you put the DNA into the world all by itself, it's never going to produce a human being, not even the tiniest insect. To activate the DNA, you need the information provided by the mother in the egg.

TIM: All codes are context-determined.

FRANCISCO: That's right, and in this particular case calling DNA a code is purely metaphor.

ROBERT: Some physicists claim that information is more than metaphor—that it's actually more fundamental than matter or energy. But let's switch to practical questions. What are the grand questions of science that have practical applications?

STEVE: About fifteen years ago, people discovered a new class of superconductors—high-temperature superconductors—with all sorts of interesting applications: everything from better MRI [magnetic resonance imaging] machines to faster trains to more efficient power plants to better stereo speakers. And we still don't understand how these superconductors work, or what the highest temperatures can be. Another potentially practical area is stable atoms with superheavy nuclei. People have hypothesized that there could be nuclei with a charge of about 114, stable and heavier than any of the known elements. Do they exist, and if so, are there interesting applications?

ROBERT: How about quantum computing, where the physics is different from digital computing? In digital computers, the so-called logic elements are bits, which can be in one of two states, either on or off. But the logic elements in quantum computers are something called "qubits," which can be in both states at the same time?

STEVE: That's right. The superposition principle of quantum mechanics allows a quantum computer to be in many states at once—at least until you ask it for the answer—and therefore it can explore a tremendously large set of solutions.

ROBERT: Just how much more powerful could a quantum computer be?

STEVE: Well, we already know that quantum computers can in principle solve problems that aren't solvable by digital computers. Among these are problems whose difficulty increases rapidly with problem size, such as factoring large numbers.

ROBERT: How about potential applications?

STEVE: The factoring I just mentioned is important in encrypting data to provide security.

Theorists have produced quantum circuits for this task and also for looking up entries in a table. However, you should realize that these applications will require dealing with hundreds of qubits to be useful, and so far it's an experimental triumph to get just two qubits to work. The major task facing the field is finding the right quantum system that can be rigged to compute, whether it be atoms, electrons, nuclear spins, or something else. Dealing with the inevitable imperfections in a real system is also going to be a major challenge. But I think it's something that's going to happen in the next few decades.

ROBERT: What about the prospects of biological computing, using the chemical bases of DNA molecules as logic elements for the massive parallel processing of information?

STEVE: We've seen two demonstrations already of DNA computing. One is where all possible solutions to a problem were encoded in DNA molecules, and then chemical techniques were used to fish out the correct one from the test tube. A second is where small, specially constructed DNA molecules were induced to self-assemble into a large structure embodying the solution. While both of these demonstrations are extraordinarily clever and provocative, they run afoul of the fact that you can put only so much DNA into a reasonable volume of liquid. So I think DNA-based computing, like quantum computing, will be a niche technology. However, there's a very interesting potential application of the self-assembly of DNA. That is, you can induce DNA to self-assemble into a three-dimensional scaffolding, and that structure can then be turned into wires and electronic elements by suitable chemistry. So we'll soon have the ability to assemble 3-D circuits [circuits built vertically upward from the surface of a microchip] on the tiniest scale.

ROBERT: How do you see the development of computers and computation power in the new millennium?

STEVE: Obviously, we're going to ride silicon and Moore's law [i.e., the storage capacity of a microchip doubles about every eighteen months] for all they're worth—probably for another ten to fifteen years for a factor [gain] of five hundred to a thousandfold. Important steps will be ever-finer chip features, although there are fundamental limits there, and some exploitation of the third dimension. There are also new physical phenomena to explore, including the spin degrees of freedom in semiconductors.

ROBERT: And beyond that sort of obvious evolution?

STEVE: There will be increasingly broad searches for new substrates to make computers. Bucky tubes and Bucky balls [complex molecular assemblies composed of carbon-based hexagonal structures, also known as fullerenes, for their resemblance to the geodesic domes designed by the visionary architect R. Buckminster Fuller], individual organic molecules, quantum dots, and other devices might let us make smaller and faster computers. And even farther out would be ways to induce biological systems to compute. We know that information flow within a cell is important. Suppose we could somehow encode a problem in the chemicals of a bacterium and then let the bacterium reproduce under the appropriate selection pressure to evolve toward the solution. The possibility has already been demonstrated using artificial digital organisms, but we don't know how to do it with living organisms. Then, apart from the hardware, there's the very real challenge of learning how to exploit all this power: with the best algorithms, the right sort of storage and visualization, high-

speed communication, usable software, and so on. Using computers effectively requires a lot more than just having great hardware.

TIM: Quantum computing is a possibility. Biological computing is also an interesting possibility. And if you take seriously the idea that the brain is a computer—and I'm not sure I do—it's by far the best computer we've ever encountered. So why not try to simulate it?

ROBERT: Pat, what do you see out there in the medical world, particularly in neuroscience?

PAT: There are a number of diseases we're working on but which are still without a cure. One, of course, is Alzheimer's. And there are the various addictions, such as alcohol and drugs. It's also very important to get to the bottom of schizophrenia; roughly one percent of the population has a schizophrenic episode at some point. I think the practical implications of advances in neuroscience are going to be tremendous. But much more work needs to be done.

ROBERT: What needs to be done now is to ask a final question. If each of you could be given the absolute answer to one grand question, but only one, which one would you want it to be?

STEVE: How did life begin? Is there life elsewhere in the universe?

TIM: How did intelligence originate? Because until I know that, I don't know whether Francisco [Ayala] is right in assuming that intelligence is rare in the cosmos.

FRANCISCO: Pat [Churchland]'s sexy question: How is the brain-mind transformation effected? How, out of all these neurons, with their electrical signals and chemical flows, do we get a mind that can think, write poetry, appreciate music?

PAT: Francisco [Ayala] has stolen my question. Out of meat, how do you get thought? That's the grandest question.

NEIL: There are some grand questions on which I don't want to risk wasting my allotted opportunity, because they may be dead ends. But one that isn't a dead end is, What is the nature and what are the properties of dark matter in the universe? Dark matter is ubiquitous—there's more of it than all other matter put together—and yet we're in a state of complete ignorance about it. We know it's there, because its gravity manifests itself, but we know nothing else about it. Dark matter is the ultimate tangible frontier.

ROBERT: CONCLUDING COMMENT

The grand questions of science are compelling and overarching, awesome and exhausting; they provoke our curiosity, creativity, intellectual rigor, speculation, and even fantasy. They embrace subatomic structure and multi-universal inflation; the enormous diversity of biology; the prodigious capabilities of the human brain, the most complex organization of matter known; and the marvel of the human mind, creator of art and science and seeker of purpose and destiny. The position of our species in the universe is oddly extreme. On the one hand, humankind seems completely meaningless, an insignificant accident on an inconsequential galactic outpost among billions of galaxies; on the other, the universe is, to some thinkers and in some sense, human-centered—something the ancients thought obvious and we moderns think ancient. It's thrilling to skim the bits and pieces of heroic thinking; it puts one's own life into perspective. As for my own favorite questions, I'll pick two. First, what is the extent of reality—are there multiple universes? Second, can everything in the mind be explained by something in the brain? Whether the universe is grand design or random accident, our investigation of it amounts to an imperative; from consciousness to cosmology, our instinct is to get closer to truth.

OUTTAKES

FRANCISCO: *You get so emotional about this.*

PAT: *Was that half an hour?*

CHAPTER 24

What Are the Next Breakthroughs in Science?

Breakthroughs are those magic moments when a new way of thinking becomes suddenly clear. Consider some of the major breakthroughs in the various sciences: in astronomy, an expanding universe; in physics, wave/particle duality; in geology, plate tectonics (continental drift); in biology, the structure of the DNA molecule; in neuroscience, electrical impulses in the brain. None of these advances were accepted easily when they were first introduced; most are now taught in high school. How are current beliefs challenged in science? Twigs snap at their weakest points; the same is true in science. Take a theory, test it, see where it fails; this is what leads to a better theory. What are the newest ideas floating around? What radically different scientific concepts will dazzle or perplex us? What can we expect in astronomy, physics, biology, brain science, behavioral science? You never know where or when a breakthrough will occur, but we invited a diverse group of distinguished scientists and thinkers to give us their best guesses.

PARTICIPANTS

Dr. Francisco Ayala, a leading evolutionary biologist and philosopher at the University of California, Irvine, is a former president of the American Association for the Advancement of Science. Francisco discusses the importance of Darwin's theory of natural selection to the science of biology, both its explanatory powers and potential overuse.

Dr. Patricia Churchland, a philosopher at the University of California, San Diego, focuses on neuroscience and has written a number of books on the mind-body problem. Pat discusses some important issues about the brain, embedded within her top-ten list of unanswered questions in neuroscience.

Timothy Ferris is the best-selling author of nine books, including *Coming of Age in the Milky Way,* which won the American Institute of Physics Prize, *The Mind's Sky,* and most recently *The Whole Shebang.* Tim reflects on the scientific process and the nature of learning.

Dr. Rochel Gelman is a professor of psychology at the University of California, Los Angeles, where she studies the thought processes of infants and young children. She is on the board of directors of the American Psychological Society and in 1998 was a recipient of the William James Fellow Award. Rochel discusses the process of cognitive change.

Dr. Neil de Grasse Tyson, an astrophysicist at Princeton University and the author of *Universe Down to Earth,* is the director of the Hayden Planetarium in New York. Neil looks forward to an era of great breakthroughs in astronomy.

ROBERT: Neil, as a working astronomer and also as director of the Hayden Planetarium, you keep watch on the progress of your science. In the next ten years, how will breakthroughs happen in astronomy?

NEIL: Well, I'm not sure how the other sciences move ahead, but in astronomy and astrophysics we get together as a community once per decade to prioritize—to advise Congress how money should be spent on such things as space science and new telescopes. We're living in a time when very few breakthroughs are made just by somebody who sits down with pencil and paper. Breakthroughs nowadays come from the frontiers of technology—from building bigger telescopes to see clearer and farther, better detectors to capture parts of the electromagnetic spectrum that haven't been searched before. So we have to plan our breakthroughs, because of all the expensive hardware we need.

ROBERT: Paid for by each of us.

NEIL: That's right; tax money pays for nearly all of it. So we're all participants in this cosmic discovery process. But that's nothing new. The discoveries in astronomy that turned the world upside down came through progressively bigger telescopes, so we can predict where breakthroughs might take place. For example, the Space Interferometry Mission [SIM], when it's launched in 2005, will enable us to observe the location of stars with unprecedented precision. This means, among other things, that we'll be able to detect slight wobbling in a star's position—which may indicate the presence of a planetary system.

TIM: Exactly, because the gravity of a planet influences the motion of its host star.

ROBERT: SIM will measure a given stellar distance from two separate locations, and that's what enables your unprecedented precision?

NEIL: That's correct. Images from two space-borne telescopes separated by specific distances—a long baseline—interfere with each other, and when you combine that information it's as though you had a huge telescope with a diameter equal to that baseline, which produces very high resolution. It requires a substantial investment.

ROBERT: Francisco, you've been called the Renaissance man of evolutionary biology, a well-deserved appellation. Why do you think that the theory of evolution by natural selection is the single most important discovery in the history of science?

FRANCISCO: Because it opened up the explanation of organisms. Before Darwin's formulation, we did biology largely descriptively [i.e., morphology and classification] with some empirical work [e.g., Mendel's genetic experiments]. The really fundamental questions

---

The really fundamental questions started with Darwin.

---

started with Darwin. His insight has made it possible to ask why organisms are organized the way they are, how they develop, how they change. As I like to say sometimes, it's the completion of the Copernican revolution. Copernicus, Newton, and others made physics into a science; Darwin did the same thing for organisms. After Darwin, we can do biology.

ROBERT: Now people are taking the next step, talking about evolutionary psychology and using biological evolution to explain everything from music and art to altruism and romantic love. Can you explain human psychology that way?

FRANCISCO: Oh, yes, you can explain much of human psychology. There's a kind of altruism—parental love and sacrifice, for example—

which can be explained biologically. Now, true altruism—doing something that benefits others at a cost to me—may be outside of biology.

ROBERT: But some people are trying to account for every human emotion and behavior using technical evolutionary arguments—

FRANCISCO: Right, and I spend a lot of my time refuting those arguments.

ROBERT: I'd rather not be on the opposite side from you. Pat, as a leading theorist in the neurosciences, you've been developing a top-ten list of core questions about brain and mind. Assuming you're not competing with David Letterman, can you give us a few?

PAT: One that may surprise you is why we sleep and how we dream. It's a remarkable fact that we spend about a third of our lives asleep. Why we do it, what the mechanism is, and why it's so important isn't really understood. Why the brain needs to sleep remains a puzzle, though we know that keeping an animal awake for a long period of time—even for only two or three days—can lead to its death. [Similarly, preventing humans from dreaming can cause psychological disturbances.] Another question concerns the nature of neural development: How does the fertilized egg mature into a fully developed human with a fully developed brain?

ROBERT: How does each of our hundred billion neurons find its thousands of specific connections? Think of the possible permutations there!

PAT: We're learning that the old argument over nature versus nurture, of which much was made, turns out to be a lot more complicated. As you know, most of our DNA does not code for proteins; most of it is regulatory. And much of what happens in our development depends on this regulatory DNA, which governs when certain genes are turned on. And the environment, both within the organism and outside it, also has a big influence on when genes are turned on and how the organism develops. Of course, once the organism is born the environment plays an even larger role.

ROBERT: Tim, in addition to being a distinguished author, you're also a generalist scholar and something of a polymath. Let's talk about the process of science. Is there a difference in the creative process in big science—the large particle accelerators, the Hubble Space Telescope, the Human Genome Project—versus the fabled solitary scientist working alone?

TIM: Sir Fred Hoyle had a nice way of putting it. He said that the trouble with running a big laboratory is that you can't go fishing on Friday afternoon, because you have meetings scheduled—and that's a pity, because it's when you're out fishing that you come up with the good ideas that carry the research forward. I don't think there's anything inherently wrong with big science, but, as [the theoretical physicist] Freeman Dyson likes to say, it's a little like an ecosystem—a healthy science should contain some big projects, some middle-sized ones, and some small ones. The most dangerous kind of project, as Dyson notes, is the big project in which national prestige has been tied up to such a degree that the nation cannot afford for it to fail. An experiment that can't fail is usually a mistake, since it must be either absurdly expensive or inappropriately cautious in its design.

ROBERT: When it's more politics than science, it's almost nonscience. Rochel, as a cognitive psychologist, you've expanded our knowledge

of how children think and babies count things. Analyze our scientific colleagues here—not that they're children and we'll assume they can count. Does cognitive psychology provide any insights on how science develops and theories change?

ROCHEL: Yes, it does. The short answer is that change comes with great difficulty where scientific theories are concerned. The mind is a learning machine, such that it has structures it prefers to use, like any biological entity. In other

---

. . . change comes with great difficulty where scientific theories are concerned.

---

words, when you already know something in an organized way, it's easy to learn more about it.

ROBERT: To learn more about the same thing in the same way?

ROCHEL: Well, it needn't be exactly the same thing. For example, if you know something about numbers, it's easy to learn that there's another number. But if you don't know anything about, say, negative numbers, it's very hard to learn about them. The reason is straightforward: these are different structures. The human mind prefers structure—and likes it. If you don't have some structure to start with, you've got this enormous problem of erecting a new conceptual framework without any data. It's a sort of chicken-and-egg problem then: How do you get to the middle of the lake without a boat? So it's very hard to bring about scientific change of the kind Newton made.

ROBERT: Let's talk about how breakthroughs happen in science. But first, let's define what a breakthrough is.

NEIL: I think there's an important distinction to be made here. Yes, there are, in the history of science, breakthroughs that constitute shifts in our worldview, and we all know what they are—Copernicus, Galileo, Newton, Einstein, Bohr, Schrödinger. However, a different kind of breakthrough also occurs in science that doesn't necessitate discarding a pre-existing framework or unthinking something we've thought before. And that's because there *was* nothing to think before—the breakthrough is simply something new. For example, Tim [Ferris] mentioned Sir Fred Hoyle, who played an important role in discovering that the heavy elements in the universe are formed in the middle of stars, which blow up and spread this material around in interstellar space—a process leading to the formation of planets and life. That realization didn't require any shift in paradigm; it didn't bury some previous conception. We just didn't know where the heavy elements came from; then we got the data, and there it was.

ROBERT: That was a real breakthrough?

NEIL: It was a tremendous breakthrough, but it didn't entail this problem that Rochel [Gelman] refers to, about having to acquire new structures in order to receive the new idea. It was received because it made perfect sense. We had no previous concept to contradict.

ROCHEL: That helps, but—

NEIL: And I submit that most scientific discovery unfolds in just this way.

ROCHEL: I understand, and I'm inclined to agree with you. For one thing, it means that scientists don't change theories very quickly.

ROBERT: That's good.

ROCHEL: That is good. Science shouldn't be in a rush to throw away a theory on the basis of one experiment that doesn't work. But there's a different point of view on this, which involves the transmission of knowledge to the young. They have difficulty coming to understand what we, sitting here, know are breakthroughs in science.

ROBERT: Why is that?

ROCHEL: Well, for example, the natural way to think about the way things move in space is rather close to an Aristotelian theory of motion [i.e., that a constant motion requires a constant cause, that as long as a body remains in motion a force must be acting on that body]. This is so foreign to modern scientific thought about motion [i.e., Newton's first law, that a body in motion remains in motion unless slowed by external forces such as friction] that what you have here are two conceptual structures that have no overlap. You not only have to get rid of one, you have to establish a new one, and change the meaning of terms.

TIM: Compounding that is the strange conservatism of our lower schools. Even though relativity is no more intrinsically difficult to understand than Newtonian mechanics, every generation is first taught Newton and then, later on, relativity. It's something like the doctrine of original sin—all students have to recapitulate the historical process by which we got to relativity. I have no idea why, except that there are very few high school teachers who are equipped to teach relativity.

ROCHEL: It's a bad reason, of course, but it's a fact. There are occasional shifts in the educational system. Here's an interesting case in point. In the seventeenth century, Pepys wrote in his diary about how proud he was that he was teaching himself long division. It used to be that you had to go to Cambridge or Oxford to learn long division. We teach it now in the fourth grade—but I can assure you that that doesn't mean the kids can understand it.

FRANCISCO: I have a very simple definition of a breakthrough in science. A breakthrough is a solution to a problem—but it's a solution that opens up new questions that either we haven't thought of asking before or had no way of answering before. But breakthroughs come in many sizes: A major breakthrough opens up major questions; a small breakthrough opens up small questions. And of course there are the kinds of incremental discoveries that don't open up anything but just fill in details.

ROBERT: Let's go through some fields of science and talk about breakthroughs that you'd like to see. Start with physics.

NEIL: There are many small breakthroughs that together become something big. Take the precession of the perihelion of Mercury, the closest planet to the sun. Over an extended period of time, astronomers realized that there was a slight discrepancy between Mercury's actual orbit and what was predicted by Newton's law of gravitation. The last time they'd faced this problem was with disturbances in the orbit of Uranus, the seventh planet. Back then, people said, "Well, Newton has been right for so long—maybe there's some other planet out there influencing Uranus." And there was, and that's how Neptune, the eighth planet, was discovered. OK, now what about Mercury? A new planet had

worked before—how about trying that again? There was speculation that another planet existed inside the orbit of Mercury, and this mystery planet was even given a name—Vulcan—but there was no Vulcan. Mercury's orbit, sure enough, required a whole new paradigm. It was Einstein's general theory of relativity that precisely predicts this observed behavior of Mercury's orbit. So a slight discrepancy, one that presumably could have been swept under the rug or just explained away by some traditional means, became part of a true breakthrough.

ROBERT: What's coming next?

NEIL: I'm expecting an ocean on Europa, the fourth-largest satellite of Jupiter—one of the moons originally seen by Galileo. We have almost incontrovertible evidence for the presence of a subsurface ocean. Europa is covered in ice, yet when you look at the surface of the ice you see flow patterns and fracture patterns, which indicates that something liquid is below. In the old days, we used to think that sunlight was the sole source of energy, but this concept has been broadened. We know that Europa is being pumped with energy because of the variations in gravitational force as it orbits Jupiter. It's like what happens when you play squash or racquetball for a long time—the ball gets hot if you hit it hard and often enough. A similar action is taking place on Europa; that action is an energy source, and you may have liquid water beneath the ice. Anyplace on Earth where you've got liquid water and a source of energy, you've got life. It's tantalizing to think that Europa might harbor alien life. At the very least, we'd have liquid water on another world. I can't wait.

ROBERT: Francisco, what breakthroughs do you anticipate in the life sciences?

FRANCISCO: Well, if I knew what the next breakthrough was going to be, I'd make it myself. One of the few cases where biology has become big science is the Human Genome Project, which is the monumental effort to sequence every component of every gene of the DNA of human beings [see Chapter 23]. It will give us lots of answers—and lots of questions—concerning disease. It's also going to open up new areas, including the functioning of the nervous system. Many discoveries will be made as a consequence of completing the genome. Of this much I'm certain.

ROBERT: Rochel, what do you see on the horizon in the behavioral sciences?

ROCHEL: My best guess is that we're going to learn a fair amount about the right way to describe cognitive architecture. Cognitive architecture has to do with how the brain organizes itself to process information coming in from the outside, in a way that gives it meaning.

ROBERT: Could this revolutionize education?

ROCHEL: There would certainly be major consequences—no question. However, we could probably revolutionize education just by understanding how some conceptual changes occur as a result of development and experience.

ROBERT: Thomas Kuhn—my namesake, no relation, though I did audit his course at MIT—wrote a famous book entitled *The Structure of Scientific Revolutions,* and in it he developed the concepts of paradigm and paradigm shift, which have had great influence on the philosophy of science.

NEIL: What Kuhn meant by "paradigm" is simply the prevailing scientific attempt to understand the world, which is usually some landscape [or framework] that emerges to which everyone gets attached. And the longer that landscape is in place, the more embedded it becomes—whether or not it's in fact the ultimate landscape you're looking for. That's the

---

A paradigm shift is a scientific revolution.

---

paradigm. And a paradigm shift is when the prevailing scientific landscape is abandoned for another landscape someplace else—in other words, not just a redesign of the one you're inhabiting. A paradigm shift is a scientific revolution.

ROBERT: Like the shift from Newtonian to relativistic physics?

NEIL: Yes. Classical physics to modern physics—relativity, quantum mechanics—was such a shift. So, too, was plate tectonics [commonly known as continental drift] in the earth sciences. Who could imagine that pieces of the earth's surface would be moving around? Although the continents do look like pieces of a jigsaw puzzle in some places. But when the evidence [such as seafloor spreading] accumulated [in the 1950s], that enabled the paradigm shift. Some people accepted it more quickly than others—students quite easily. Older scholars who were invested in the original framework were often resistant.

FRANCISCO: Let me pick up the matter of plate tectonics. Most of the geology we had before the theory was accepted continues to be valid science. The theory of plate tectonics is now well-established and a major advance, but I don't see it as a leap, as it were, from one hill to another. Likewise, in biology we've had a few major discoveries, like natural selection, genetic inheritance, the structure of DNA. But that doesn't mean that everything that went on before no longer applies.

ROBERT: But evolution by natural selection was a paradigm shift.

FRANCISCO: I wouldn't call it that. What happened with Darwin is that biology then took on its modern meaning. Before Darwin, as I've said, we didn't have modern biology in a fundamental sense. You can call these things paradigm shifts; I prefer to call them major advances.

ROBERT: There was a classic paradigm shift in geology, with the replacement of catastrophism by uniformitarianism in the early nineteenth century, thanks to the work of men such as James Hutton and Charles Lyell. Uniformitarianism is the theory that all geological phenomena are produced by forces that have operated uniformly and gradually throughout the history of the earth. Before that, people still believed that the earth had been sculpted once and for all by the Noachian flood as described in the Bible. Catastrophism has re-emerged recently, in that cataclysmic events are now also seen as contributing to the earth's natural history—like the giant asteroid impact that's thought to have altered the world's climate enough to kill off the dinosaurs. For years, any form of catastrophism was ridiculed; now it's accepted. So that's a double paradigm shift—and utterly new results.

FRANCISCO: But [the extraterrestrial cause of the Cretaceous extinction] was a major discovery, not a paradigm shift. I don't see that it changes the overall way of thinking in science.

NEIL: It most certainly does if you're interested in how planetary systems are altered. Here, floating around the solar system, are these large objects, and here on Earth is the fossil record, showing major extinction episodes; and this particular extinction matched the evidence of an impact.

FRANCISCO: The other mass extinctions aren't explained yet.

NEIL: There is one extinction, of course, where we have the smoking gun—the crater and the deposits [at the Cretaceous-Tertiary boundary]—the famous impact that took out the dinosaurs about sixty-five million years ago. All I'm saying is that we do know the sizes of objects flying around the solar system and we [have some statistical idea] of how often we can expect them to hit the earth. So I tell you, the biologist, that I'm going to hand you a 4000-megaton explosion every certain amount of years, and then you decide what it will do to the surface of the earth. I promise you there will be major biological effect.

FRANCISCO: I agree that it will have a major effect, and I don't want to underestimate the value of that discovery. But I still have to account for the origin and the extinction of the millions of species that once existed on Earth. Impacts [or other catastrophic events] may account for a good part of those extinctions, but I still need other data.

TIM: The term "paradigm shift" doesn't really help much, in my view. All such changes can be accounted for by the single word "learning." If you start out as a freshman in college and your goal is simply to graduate knowing more about the things you already know, you will not have had a very good education. You should come out as a substantially different person, because you've learned entirely different ways of thinking as well as lots of new facts. The same is true in science, but again it's just learning. There's a recent tendency, among some people in the humanities, to claim that science is what they call "socially conditioned"—which means either that science is done by human beings and human beings interact socially, or that social conditions affect how scientists think.

ROBERT: Is this deconstruction of science accurate or meaningful? And is it important or trivial?

TIM: It's important only if, as a result of such social conditioning, experimental results are skewed in some fundamental way, or are fabricated or falsified—but those cases are so rare that in the end it hardly seems worth basing such extravagant claims on them. So observations that science is socially conditioned are accurate or meaningful only insofar as they're trivial.

ROCHEL: Wait a minute. To say that all change is just learning is to beg the question, because exposure alone doesn't guarantee the acquisition of an organized new knowledge.

TIM: Then you haven't learned.

ROCHEL: Well, it's not clear that you haven't learned anything. You may have learned a bunch of facts that you may not understand. And learning with understanding is very different from just learning.

TIM: I don't call it learning if it doesn't include understanding.

ROCHEL: Well, a lot of people do. It's really not trivial to focus on the fact that the word "learning" itself has different meanings in different conceptual systems. I don't care if people want to call [these ways of thinking] paradigms or not. But conceptual systems do organize the meaning of our technical terms.

NEIL: I think there's an important point here. There are certain things about the world around us that *don't* make sense but are nevertheless true. Take quantum mechanics, for example, which describes nature as behaving in ways that are counterintuitive—that have no counterpart in our normal, macroscopic lives. You can never understand quantum mechanics, in some sense. All you can ever do is grow accustomed to it and accept it for what it is, knowing that it works. Who can really understand how something can be both a wave and a particle at the same time? There are many things that you just accept without actually understanding them.

PAT: Rochel [Gelman] is clearly right here, in that there are superficial ways of adopting knowledge, and there are also ways that indicate a true understanding. Let me give you an example. I came across a Betty Crocker cookbook that told you how a microwave oven worked. Here's the explanation [as closely as I can recall it]: The microwaves come into the oven and they cause the water molecules to move faster and faster. Well, she should stop there, right? If she [or more likely her ghost writers] really understood what temperature is, she should stop. But she continues: . . . so that they rub against one another more and more, creating more and more friction, and that makes more and more heat. Now, this is a good example of what Rochel means. The writers of that cookbook profoundly do not understand that temperature is really just the motion of molecules. But in science education we do want students to appreciate things at a deep level—which is partly why we have them do experiments as well as just memorize facts.

NEIL: Yes, but today it's technology that exposes the universe to us, by taking us farther and farther beyond our five natural senses—until we get to the point where it's nearly impossible to say to students, "I want you to take this home and comprehend this," when in fact what they'll be doing is manipulating equations. A predictive capability is not the same as true understanding.

PAT: It's no different from learning by doing anything. If I try to explain to people how to paddle a canoe, they're not going to be able to do it; they have to actually get in the canoe and they have to learn the feel of the canoe.

NEIL: But to get into an atom, to get the feel of an atom, you have to be an electron.

PAT: No, no, you just have to learn to do the experiment.

FRANCISCO: We do depend on our senses, but these often give us only a kind of superficial knowledge. True knowledge comes from discovery. Discoveries arise from hypotheses, and hypotheses are creations of the mind. To imagine what is possible—this is removed from the senses. But that's where great science comes from.

ROCHEL: I have no quarrel with that, but you can't just say to people, "Go out, do an experiment, and discover." It helps to know what you're doing, to know that the experiment is a good one.

FRANCISCO: So there's learning and there's

learning. For me, profound learning is generating new ideas and making discoveries.

ROBERT: That's Tim [Ferris]'s idea of learning, in its largest sense. But let's turn to something more profound. There was once a professor who had a cute theory about the relationship between the amount of time a species spends mating and the relative importance of that species. Francisco, as our resident biologist, what's your take on that?

FRANCISCO: I'm all in favor of that theory, because I like to do research with *Drosophila,* the little fruit flies that live for two weeks. When they mate they stay at it, passing sperm for half an hour. Lower organisms like paramecia, little single-celled creatures, mate even longer—for twenty-four hours.

ROBERT: Twenty-four hours spent mating? How long do they live?

FRANCISCO: Oh, just a few more hours—paramecia mate for most of their lives. And so I wonder why humans are called higher organisms.

ROBERT: Could this be a breakthrough in international as well as personal relations? Now, please pick a field of science and a favorite breakthrough you'd like to see before the end of your lives, which I trust will be long ones.

NEIL: What's underappreciated is the role of high-performance computing as a frontier in scientific discovery. Not only does it enable us to model systems in ways that weren't previously possible, it can even be the source of discovery of new theories. High-performance computing can become as important to us as telescopes and microscopes were to past generations.

PAT: I'd like to see better, easier, more efficient methods of contraception.

TIM: That's a good one, a hard act to follow. But I'd like to see a breakthrough in what's probably the biggest idea of the twentieth century, which

---

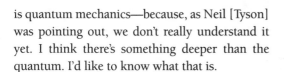

I'd like to see better, easier, more efficient methods of contraception.

---

is quantum mechanics—because, as Neil [Tyson] was pointing out, we don't really understand it yet. I think there's something deeper than the quantum. I'd like to know what that is.

ROCHEL: I'd like to see a successful way to stop our bones from deteriorating and breaking as a function of use.

FRANCISCO: I'd like to understand the fundamental biology of the parasite that causes malaria. Five hundred million people a year suffer from malaria; one million children die in tropical Africa alone from this disease. It would be wonderful to put an end to it.

ROBERT: Any other breakthroughs, desired or expected within your lifetime?

NEIL: Another go-round? Well, the Human Genome Project, as Francisco [Ayala] pointed out at the start of the show, will give us tremendous insight into disease and other enemies of human life. We can almost talk now about living

to the age of 150. Let's try for 500—why not? In fact, one of my regrets with regard to my inevitable death is that I won't be around to see some stunning scientific development or other. Every week, I look forward to reading *Science* and learning what's happening in different fields. And I love every minute of it.

PAT: Although the brain seems in some ways to be an input-output device, in fact it's not. It does get input, of course, and it does have output. But far and away the brain's greatest activity— what we sometimes call spontaneous activity— is the seemingly random [but surely not meaningless] electrical activity that involves neither input nor output. We really don't have the right concepts to think about something that's intelligent, that solves all kinds of problems, that perceives, makes decisions—but isn't an input-output device. This means that we need not only breakthroughs in basic neuroscience but also a certain kind of conceptual innovation just to imagine what that intelligent non-input-output device may be.

TIM: It's of course inherently difficult to predict a real breakthrough. A great breakthrough in science is like a great work of art—that is, it's intrinsically creative and therefore unpredictable. My definition of a breakthrough is that it changes not *what* you think but *how* you think. But if I have to back another horse . . . it would be information theory. If we had a proper information theory, it could deal with complicated things like living organisms and the brain. I'm speculating here, because we don't have that theory yet. But what attracts me about the idea is that so many things can be analyzed in terms of the transmission of information. Even evolution, for instance, can be viewed as a sort of communication channel.

ROCHEL: How is it that human beings do so many simple things that computers can't? For example, we have no trouble walking around and not falling down. We have yet to build robots that can do that. We have no trouble understanding speech, whereas speech machines and generators are not all that terrific. So what I'm looking forward to is a deeper understanding of the great accomplishments of human beings.

FRANCISCO: What in our biology makes us human? I'd like to see the answer to that question in my lifetime, which will require that I live many, many years. The answer no doubt relates to our genes. Yet we're so different from other animals: we have language, culture, technology; we do all sorts of things that other animals cannot. What in fact is the critical difference between humans and other animals and what happened in evolution to cause it? What makes us human?

ROBERT: CONCLUDING COMMENT

Breakthroughs in knowledge are a perennial passion of the human imagination. Even the search is glorious. The very word "breakthrough" evokes the notion of dramatic scientific change—it has the right sound—even though real progress is almost always progressive, not radical. When data begin not to fit the current scientific model, a kind of stress builds up; it's then that the twig snaps and old theories in, say, astronomy or biology, can't be reconciled or repaired but must be replaced with new theories. Breakthroughs are rare and risky; they are initially unacceptable to most, but ultimately obvious to all. Some have said that we are at the end of science, with no more breakthroughs coming. Does that sound right? You keep watching and we'll keep watch; that's how we'll get closer to truth.

OUTTAKES

ROCHEL: *The show's over? I thought we'd just started.*

ROBERT: *Francisco, fifty years from today we'll do another breakthroughs program. I hope our other friends will be back, but you and I will surely be.*

FRANCISCO: *Let's plan our fiftieth anniversary.*

ROBERT: *This is show number 28—the last taping of our first season. [The order of taping related to participants' schedules and has no relationship to the order of television broadcasting or book chapters.]*

CHAPTER 25

Why Is Quantum Physics So Beautiful?

Beauty, elegance, charm; flavor, color, vibration; string, symmetry, strangeness. These are the actual words that physicists use to portray the most fundamental natural phenomena. Their field, quantum physics, describes how the world *really* works, from the minuscule microstructure of atoms to the cosmic macrostructure of the universe. What they envision is breathtaking. Quantum physics may seem like fantasy—or magic—because quanta don't behave like anything you're familiar with. An electron can be in two places at once. Subatomic particles, in fact, cannot really be said to "be" anywhere in particular, unless they are measured—that is, observed—to be there. If you think quantum physics sounds hard to understand, unfortunately it's even worse than that. Quantum physics is, to say the least, counterintuitive, and the Danish physicist Niels Bohr, one of its founders, is supposed to have remarked to his German colleague Werner Heisenberg that if it doesn't make you *schwindlig* (dizzy), you haven't really understood it. Nobody in his right mind, my friends warned me, would dare do television like this. So there I was, doing it, because quantum physics is real and relevant, and because every literate person can appreciate its profound beauty. We invited five physicists to provide us with their impassioned portrait of this new reality. So tilt your head and it won't be so hard. Stick with us. My bet is that you'll get it and like it. Who knows? It may forever change the way you think about the world around you.

PARTICIPANTS

Dr. Gregory Benford teaches plasma physics and astrophysics at the University of California, Irvine, and is also a leading writer of science fiction. Greg says the world is not as ordinary as it seems, and he uses poems and paintings to illustrate how strange it really is.

Dr. Charles Buchanan, a high-energy experimental physicist, teaches a course at the University of California, Los Angeles, called "Science and the Human Condition," which brings quantum theory and cosmology down to earth. Chuck notes that quantum theory is fundamental for biology as well as physics.

Dr. Steven Koonin is vice president and provost of the California Institute of Technology [Caltech], where he is a professor of theoretical physics known for his work in computational and nuclear physics. Steve gives us examples of quantum physics in action and tells us about Schrödinger's cat.

Dr. Leon Lederman, director emeritus of the Fermi National Accelerator Laboratory [Fermilab], in Batavia, Illinois, was awarded the Nobel Prize in physics in 1988 for his contributions to the body of evidence that revolutionized our understanding of the subatomic world. Leon describes a quantum and its history and explains why it seems spooky.

Dr. Andrei Linde, a Russian professor of physics now at Stanford, is a principal inventor of the "chaotic inflationary" model, which describes the universe as a meta-universe, continually and randomly giving birth to new universes in a series of what he likes to call "Pretty Big Bangs"—a process generated by quantum physics.

ROBERT: Leon, pretend I'm your grandchild; how would you explain what you do for a living?

LEON: Look, kid, listen closely. I try to solve some of the mysteries—things we don't understand—about the world. We want to understand how the universe works, why things happen the way they do. We work on little pieces at a time. Sometimes we have a simple problem, like how did the world begin. Now, Andrei's the expert on that, but there are a lot of things he has to know first.

ROBERT: I heard you were there at the beginning.

LEON: I was there, that's right. I'm here because I was there. I knew the Dead Sea before it was even sick. But to answer these questions it's important to have evidence. We do know that the universe began and at the beginning it was all particles, and particles are what we do in our laboratories. I do my research at Fermilab, thirty miles west of Chicago. Everybody's invited, it's an open lab, and scientists from all over the world come to address issues having to do with the most primordial building blocks of matter and energy. A city might be made of bricks and cement, but what are the bricks and what is the cement? A library is composed of books, but the books are composed of letters and the letters, ultimately, are composed of [information] zeros and ones. There are rules by which you put the zeros and ones together to represent the letters, and rules of spelling to make the words, and rules of grammar to make the sentences of all the books in the library. My job is to ask, What are the zeros and ones of our universe?

ROBERT: Steve, your research interests at Caltech are very broad, ranging from nuclear astrophysics to global climate change. What's so special about quantum physics and what are some of its practical applications?

STEVE: There are many incredible things about quantum mechanics, and one of them, at least to me, is that it really works. It's the theory of the universe. It describes what's happening here on earth and what's happening across the whole cosmos. When we think about how those building blocks that Leon just mentioned fit together to make the world around us, we use quantum mechanics to describe [the nature and behavior of] nuclei, atoms, molecules, and light. Because quantum mechanics is the theory of the world, it's not surprising that we see everyday occurrences and applications: for example, the lasers used in compact-disc players, or the MRI [magnetic resonance imaging] images of medicine. The lines of research that lead to developments like these began decades ago with basic quantum science.

ROBERT: Chuck, your teaching at UCLA is interdisciplinary, and you integrate the physical sciences with the biological and social sciences. How do your undergraduate students from other disciplines deal with fundamental physics?

CHUCK: Well, it's a lot of fun. We take the sorts of things you've been discussing and try to communicate that excitement to a broad group of undergraduates. One course I particularly enjoyed recently was an honors collegium—a seminar entitled "Science and the Human Condition," which I taught with two biology professors, one from molecular biology and one from

genetic evolution. The question that framed the course was, Where do we come from and what are we? We started with the beginning of the universe and proceeded through the formation of the heavy elements in supernovae [exploding stars], the formation of our solar system, the evolution of life on earth, and on up to human beings. It's fascinating how those heavy elements, formed under such extreme conditions, are absolutely essential for life.

ROBERT: Could you relate that to quantum mechanics?

CHUCK: Quantum mechanics is everywhere throughout this whole process.

ROBERT: Andrei, quantum cosmology theorizes about the role of elementary particles in the early universe. How can stuff so unfathomably minuscule have affected something that is now so unfathomably gigantic?

ANDREI: Years ago it would have seemed impossible that quantum mechanics could have any relationship to the universe, because quantum mechanics is supposed to be important for only very, very small particles. Well, over the last twenty years the study of cosmology has changed. To the standard Big Bang theory we are now applying something else, called inflationary theory, which claims that the entirety of the universe began from a tiny spot smaller than an elementary particle and then expanded incredibly fast. In analyzing this expansion, small quantum fluctuations, though initially invisible, become huge and build galaxies—and they are continuing to build different parts of the universe.

ROBERT: So the quantum mechanics of elementary particles, the smallest things there are, is directly responsible for creating the entire universe and its macrostructure, the largest thing there is.

ANDREI: Yes. Indeed, you can't understand galaxy formation if you don't understand quantum mechanics.

ROBERT: Today, particle physicists look to cosmology almost as a virtual experimental test of quantum mechanics. Greg, you've studied exotic areas of astronomy, like quasars, the extremely distant and incredibly energetic objects thought to be the nuclei of very young galaxies, but you're also a poet. How does the poet, not the physicist, see quantum physics?

GREG: Well, think of quantum mechanics as being like a French impressionist painting—luminous, vibrant—of, say, a cow, but the miracle is that real cows give milk. Painted cows don't. The universe is better than any metaphor we can imagine, even though we trade in them.

STEVE: To quote an old song, "There's nothing like the real thing, baby."

GREG: Right. And you were asking how we can explain the huge universe with tiny quantum mechanics, which acts only on very small scales, but you have to remember that once the universe was extremely small, too. As I said in a poem once, "All that bang and sass/Beneath an eyelid's underpass." Everything was once ruled by quantum mechanics, not the categories of physics we exaggerated chimpanzees are used to today. Sticks and stones are OK if you're hunting down game on the African savanna a million years ago, which is when our physical ideas began. But they're crude approximations when you go down the scale to where physics does its heavy lifting. So we say that an electron is like a particle—a stick or a stone—and it's also like a

wave, which in fact means that it's neither of these. It's something for which we don't have a good category. It's as if quantum mechanics is

"All that bang and sass/Beneath an eyelid's underpass."

saying to us, you humans may be great chimpanzees, but you're not ready for prime time as far as our metaphors go.

LEON: I just want to add that particles are studied in large accelerators, which the media calls atom smashers. The Big Bang was an atom-smashing laboratory with a totally unrestricted budget. (That's the budget we'd like.) Out of that lab came the beginning and all subsequent events—oceans roiled, and out of oceans things crawled, and eventually here we are, wondering how the universe began.

ROBERT: Leon, define a quantum. Remember, I'm still your grandchild.

LEON: Yeah, I know—go clean your room. Quantum theory characterizes the difference between the subatomic world and the common world we know—the classical world that was

. . . nature prefers discreteness to continuity. Things come in pieces.

clarified by Isaac Newton in the seventeenth century. Quantum mechanics began in the 1920s, and what it showed is that nature prefers discreteness to continuity. Things come in pieces. The word "quantum" arose from a study of electromagnetic radiation. When you heat up a body, it radiates energy, and around 1900 that radiation was discovered not to be smooth—*zzzzzzzzzz*—but to exist in discrete packets.

ROBERT: *ch, ch, ch, ch, ch . . .*

LEON: That's very good—a terrific simulation of quantum theory. There are so many of these packets, these radiating pieces, that collectively they give rise to what looks like a continuum, a smooth beam of light, whether from the sun in our sky or lightbulbs in our living rooms. But when you get down to individual processes within individual atoms, these are discrete events. Envision an atom as a flight of stairs, with nothing in between each step.

ROBERT: You're either on one step or another, never in between. Everything happens in steps or pieces, and each distinct unit of energy is what's called a quantum.

LEON: That realization utterly changed our view of the world. The quantum world is very different from the world we know. Everything we see is composed of billions and billions and billions and billions of atoms, and this is what makes for the apparent smoothness. If you were to watch from afar someone pouring a stream of fine sand from one bucket to another, the stream of sand would look like a liquid—a continuum—to you; but if you got close enough, maybe with a magnifying glass, you would see tiny, discrete grains. And it's an understanding of the nature and behavior of those grains that has so remarkably changed our view of the microworld.

STEVE: One of the beautiful aspects of quantum theory is how this discreteness, or quantum nature, merges eventually into the classical behavior that we see all around us. It's the so-called semiclassical regime, where, instead of things just becoming smooth, what actually happens is these discrete units oscillate faster and faster, so that the average of all of them melds into the familiar laws of Newton.

ROBERT: Let's talk a little about probability in quantum physics. You've written papers on what's called Monte Carlo simulations. Are you a gambler?

STEVE: In many senses, scientists are gamblers in their work. But here's the story on Monte Carlo. One of the things that quantum mechanics tells us, beyond the fundamental discreteness of nature, is how particles travel. If I'm a particle, and I want to go from here to there, Newton [and common sense] would advise me to go in a straight line. But what quantum mechanics does is to let the particle explore all possible paths from here to there—Dick Feynman was the first to express it this way. So the particle can go in a straight line, or it can take a big curve, or it can follow zigzag paths, and so on. If you want to model such uncertain routing, it's impossibly hard, even in a computer, since you'd have to count up all those innumerable possible paths, adding this one and that one and on and on—because in quantum mechanics the particle takes all of the paths, and you can't tell which one it actually took unless you measure it. So we choose those paths at random with a computer. First we take this one, then that one, then another one in a very random way. We can't take them all, but if you judiciously choose a few, you can get the total effect. It's like taking a poll of only a few voters to predict the outcome of an election.

ROBERT: So you have a probabilistic analysis of what happens in the subatomic world, which seems totally different from the apparent certainties of the real world.

STEVE: The subatomic world *is* the real world. It's just that our everyday experience is an imperfect image of it.

ROBERT: Good point. Leon, why is quantum mechanics spoken of as "spooky"?

LEON: Oh, it's very spooky. First of all, probability by itself is spooky. Let me illustrate how probability enters the system. You walk past a store window and see an image of yourself reflected there—hmmm, you're looking good, for a man of your age. The guy in the store window who's arranging the mannequins sees you at the same moment that you're seeing yourself. What's happening here? A stream of photons from the sun bounces off your face, heads for the window—let's consider a single one of those photons. It has a choice: It can go right through, so that the guy behind the window can see you, or it can be reflected back from the window and into your eye so that you see your own reflection. So some fraction of the innumerable photons are reflected, and some fraction go through. What determines the fate of each particular photon? Countless such examples have taught us that the outcome [for each photon] is random, it's a throw of the dice, and that's what led to Einstein's famous statement that he didn't believe that God plays dice with the universe.*

---

*Einstein apparently made several references to dice, such as a remark to Niels Bohr: "You believe in the dice-playing god, and I in the perfect rule of law." Alice Calaprice (in *The Quotable Einstein*) quotes from an Einstein letter to Cornelius Lanczos, one of his biographers: "It is hard to sneak a look at God's cards. But that He would choose to play dice with the world . . . is something that I cannot believe for a single moment." And in a letter to Franck: "But that there should be statistical laws with (in)definite solutions, i.e., laws that compel God to throw dice in each individual case, I find highly disagreeable."

At every instant, for that single object, for every quantum object, we have probability; we do not have certainty. That gives us an indeterminate world, which in some sense frees us from the old classical world of Newton, where everything is predetermined, everything goes according to forces and positions, so that in principle the entire world could be predicted by some all-knowing mind or super-supercomputer. In classical theory, if you knew all the data, you could toss a coin and predict the outcome with certainty. But now we know that's not so. There is a fundamental quantum nature that in some sense frees us from this determinism.

ANDREI: Well, I do not quite agree. The question is about free will. Classical theory says that everything is determined by something that happened in the past, even a million years ago. Quantum theory says that you can never know for sure what will happen in the future. But nothing is determined by anything other than your past. So if your will is not completely determined by things that were before [i.e., because of the uncertainty of quantum mechanics], but it is not determined by anything else, then you can't have free will unless you assume that your will (and your consciousness) is something separate and additional, that it has its own degrees of freedom.

ROBERT: What's fascinating is how quantum mechanics has the broadest applications, from the beginning of the universe to the freedom of the will to the lasers at your supermarket's checkout counters. We're not talking about something esoteric here, but something that affects everything that has to do with human life. Yet it has all these tortuous problems.

LEON: Scientists wrestled with these terrible problems through the 1920s up to 1930. Real data was coming in from the atom; finally they realized that here was something absolutely new and counterintuitive to human experience. Most experimentalists appreciate the fact that it was the experimental data which we had to rub in the faces of these itinerant theoretical scientists like Einstein. At times, some of those theorists would say, "We're going to get out of physics." [The Austrian-born particle physicist] Wolfgang Pauli once said, "I'm going to go and become a stand-up comic, because this business doesn't make any sense."

ROBERT: And quantum mechanics is one of the most remarkable achievements of human endeavor.

LEON: Absolutely!

STEVE: And very beautiful.

CHUCK: This is where much of the beauty comes from. We were used to a relatively rational, understandable world of Newtonian

It's bizarre, it's elegant, it's mysterious, it's surprising.

mechanics, and then quantum mechanics came along. It's down underneath everything else. It's bizarre, it's elegant, it's mysterious, it's surprising. It's all these things and yet it really works.

ROBERT: How do you differentiate between elegance and beauty?

LEON: I'll take a shot at that. Quantum mechanics is elegant in that it is a wonderful solution to

incredibly difficult experimental data that looked contradictory. As for beauty . . . hmmm. Well, when you see someone else's theory and you don't like it, you say, "Boy, that's a beauty!"

STEVE: I think elegance is economy of expression. It's being able to write down a short, fundamental equation that can express and predict all these implications that we've been talking

. . . elegance is economy of expression.

about [such as the Schrödinger equation for quantum mechanics]. That's elegance. Beauty is when you work out the implications and it matches what we see in the real world.

CHUCK: Beauty is also mysterious.

STEVE: Right. A different dimension.

LEON: Beauty is in the eye of the beholder. A theorist's theory is beautiful; it's his child, it has to be beautiful.

GREG: Truth is beauty; beauty is truth.

ROBERT: Let's apply some beauty and elegance to what's known as the Standard Model—that is, our current understanding of the elementary particles and the fundamental forces, or interactions, of nature. There are four of these interactions: the strong nuclear force, the weak nuclear force, the electromagnetic force—those two unified as the so-called electroweak force—and gravity. Gravity has not yet been incorporated into the Standard Model. So let's define each of these. Gravity I think people know about—the attraction between masses. Gravity structures the universe, from the shapes of galaxies to the earth's orbit around the sun to keeping our feet planted firmly on the ground. It's the easiest one to describe but the hardest one to explain; in fact, the Standard Model has to pretend that gravity doesn't exist. How about the electroweak force?

CHUCK: The electroweak force combines, in a very elegant theory, the electromagnetic interaction—which is manifested by both electricity and magnetism—with the weak nuclear interaction, which governs the kind of radioactivity known as beta decay [in which a neutron decays into a proton, an electron, and a neutrino]. The weak interaction, which is the hardest one to grasp, describes what happens when a particle decays and it disappears, and in its place two or more new particles appear. The sum of the masses of the new particles is always less than the mass of the original particle.

ROBERT: Research in radioactivity first suggested the existence of the weak interaction.

CHUCK: As for the strong force, this is what binds the quarks together inside nucleons— that is, the protons and neutrons in atomic nuclei—and holds the nucleons themselves together in the nucleus. The theory of the strong force is known as QCD, for quantum chromodynamics.

ROBERT: Now let's define quarks, which are fundamental components of the Standard Model.

STEVE: As far as we know, quarks are the most elementary building blocks of protons, neu-

trons, mesons—the stuff that makes up most of the matter in the universe.*

ROBERT: How many kinds of quarks are there, and how do they bind together?

STEVE: Six. They come in six flavors, which we've named *down, up, strange, charm, bottom,* and *top*—well, "flavors" here simply mean different kinds—and three colors: red, green, and blue. "Color" here doesn't mean real colors, of course; the term is simply an analogy with the way the primary colors mix to make real colors. Quarks have charges of one-third or two-thirds that of an electron [which has a negative charge of −1] or a proton [which has a positive charge of +1], and thus quarks can be positive or negative. They have spin; they whirl around like little tops, and the spin is characterized as "up" or "down." The quarks are bound inside the proton or the neutron by quantum chromodynamics. QCD is very interesting in that we think we understand the theory but we can't make it explain how the strong-force attraction between the quarks actually works. Although we use the term "gluon" to describe what is exchanged to

---

*A proton consists of two up-quarks and one down-quark; a neutron consists of one up-quark and two down-quarks. The existence of quarks was proposed in the early 1960s, by Murray Gell-Mann, then at the California Institute of Technology, and independently by George Zweig, then at CERN (the European Center for Nuclear Research, in Geneva). Gell-Mann named them, borrowing the quirky term from a phrase in James Joyce's novel *Finnegans Wake,* "three quarks for Muster Mark." Quarks are extremely small, occupying a minute fraction—perhaps only a billionth—of the volume of the particles they comprise. No one has ever observed a free quark, because they are inextricably bound inside their protons, neutrons, and other particles, but there is strong evidence for their existence.

effect this interaction among quarks, we don't quite know how they hold the stuff together.

ROBERT: Now we come to what is called the Theory of Everything, or TOE. What do we have to do to get it?

GREG: Wow, lots! You have to stitch all of this fabric together and somehow make a suit that people want to wear. I don't work in the field, and so I'm sort of an informed skeptic about it. The current hot topic, of course, is string theory.*

LEON: Four of the principal string theorists came out of Princeton. They were four great guys, and they're known as the Princeton String Quartet.†

GREG: String theory is certainly the most complex physical theory ever advanced. And you can tell, because all these brilliant people are having a visibly difficult time with it—

---

*String theory is the most viable candidate for a Theory of Everything. Based on complex abstract mathematics, string theory claims to integrate gravity with the Standard Model and general relativity with quantum mechanics. It replaces the numerous point-like particles with ultratiny strings, coils, or loops, whose vibrations are manifested as particles—something like the way musical vibrations are perceived as distinct notes. The way these vibrations occur is through compacting or curling up six extra dimensions of spacetime—a state difficult to imagine and impossible to visualize—in addition to the usual four dimensions. The size of the strings would be at the (effectively invisible) scale of quantum gravity, which is about 10^{-33} centimeters. There are many string theories, each targeted at separate phenomena, and an attempt to combine them all is known in some quarters as M Theory, as in "the Mother of all theories."
†David Gross, Jeffrey Harvey, Emil Martinec, and Ryan Rohm.

which is encouraging, since a really great theory that tells us everything ought to be really hard; it shouldn't come to one person in a weekend. It's the best clue that we may be on the track of something large. But what we're on the track of is still very mysterious. The idea that particles are not little dots but strings that vibrate sits at the core. Of course, that's another chimpanzee metaphor [a currently accepted concept or category of physics conceived by us "exaggerated chimpanzees"]. But the implications are huge: It goes from Andrei's cosmology to the fundamental way you glue all these particles together.

LEON: The Standard Model is a powerful theory that explains all the data coming out of all the accelerators since Galileo dropped those two "students" [weights, actually]—one fat, one thin—off the Leaning Tower of Pisa. But one of the problems with the Standard Model, as we've touched on, is that gravity has not been incorporated into it gracefully. And the Standard Model itself is ugly. Six quarks, three colors each; six leptons [the electron, the muon, the tauon, and their neutrinos]; the bosons, or force carriers, like the photon and the gluons. The Greeks promised us aesthetic simplicity, a beauty and an elegance that we don't have. We can't even fit all these particles on a T-shirt.

CHUCK: But the Standard Model is incredibly elegant compared to what preceded it in the 1960s, which was a mess.

STEVE: And it's a powerful synthesis of many phenomena and data.

LEON: We want a T-shirt embroidered with one thing, or group, that does everything.

CHUCK: That's TOE [Theory of Everything].

STEVE: You know, we've seen this pattern repeat over and over in science. Look at the periodic table. In the nineteenth century, when people were organizing the elements, it was a mess all right. There were ninety or so elements, and you really couldn't understand this, and there was certainly nothing you could put on your T-shirt. And then came the periodic table.

LEON: The Standard Model is the physicists' version of the periodic table. And we know that there's something simpler, some underlying simplicity or unity. We're looking for missing pieces, like the Higgs particle, or the Higgs boson, and we tried to build this humongous machine [the superconducting supercollider] in Texas in order to find it—but the Congress didn't let us. Scientists must rededicate themselves to a massive effort at raising the science literacy of the public. Only when citizens have reasonable science savvy will their congressional servants vote correctly. But we'll eventually come to terms with something that must be simpler than the Standard Model. Our belief in simplicity and elegance, which has not disappointed us over the centuries in which we've done good science, tells us there's better to come.

ROBERT: Why should the public fund this search?

LEON: Oh, well, because it's beautiful, because it's elegant, and because we want to know, to understand, something about the world we live in. And because, according to some absolutely closer-to-truth testimony I gave before Congress, quantum mechanics accounts for 37.9 percent of the gross national product, or some number like that.

ROBERT: Thanks for the plug, but how do you get that percentage?

LEON: Well, I made up the number, but it's plausible. You get it by tallying up what we have thanks to our understanding of the quantum theory. Without that understanding, we would never have had transistors and therefore microprocessors, and the whole microelectronics revolution wouldn't have taken place. Our computers wouldn't be what they are. The biotechnology revolution was catalyzed by Watson and Crick's discovery of the structure of DNA in 1953, which was stimulated by a book by Erwin Schrödinger on the quantum theory of large molecules. The core products of twenty-first-century technology—electronics, computers, biotech—all relate directly to an understanding of quantum theory.

ROBERT: Steve, let's look deeper into the bizarre essence of quantum mechanics. Tell us about "Schrödinger's cat."

STEVE: There are a lot of bizarre things, and people work hard trying to understand them. One of them is that although we know that subatomic particles exist only in discrete states, they can exist in several of those states at the same time, and only when you look at them— that is, take a measurement—do they collapse into a single state. Schrödinger's cat is a famous thought experiment [conceived, in a moment of frustration, by Austrian physicist Erwin Schrödinger, whose famous equations form the foundation of quantum mechanics]. You put a cat in a box with a capped bottle of poison gas and close the box. You can't see inside it—and you don't peek. There's also an apparatus in the box that will uncap the bottle of poison gas—and thus kill the cat—but only if one particular radioactive atom in the box decays. Quantum theory dictates that this atom must exist simultaneously in two states—that it is both "decayed" and "not decayed" until it is measured. But since you can't do this measuring without opening the box, while the box remains closed, the cat must be both dead and alive at the same time. And you don't know which one it is, *not even in principle,* until you open the box to check it.

ROBERT: But is the cat alive or dead?

STEVE: It's neither . . . and both. While it's in the box it's in some combination of both, and only when you do the measurement—when you open the box up and look, thus collapsing the atom's dual state into one state, "decayed" or "not decayed"—does the cat become alive or dead. The point is that the cat does exist in those two states until you open the box—and only when you open the box up will probabilities determine whether the cat is actually dead or alive.

ROBERT: Leon, does that make any sense?

LEON: It doesn't make any sense. It's one of the bizarre features that derives from the fact that quantum mechanics denies the possibility of knowing, for example, how a particle moves from point A to point B. If you try to find out by experiment, you spoil the experiment. It's like trying to measure the precise temperature of a small cup of water by taking a big, fat, hot thermometer and thrusting it into the cup, splashing out the water and heating it—you'll never know the original temperature. Denying the possibility of knowing how a particle goes from A to B leads quickly to the notion that it has no path between A and B, and then the mathematics says to try all paths. But fundamentally we can't know, and therefore we deny the reality of the

particle's transit from point A to point B—and that's bizarre. Einstein never accepted the fact that we can't know the particle unless we look at it. He asked, "Does the moon disappear if we don't look at it?" Well, the moon is a macroscopic object, as is the cat. In quantum mechanics, we sort of accept the notion that since we can't predict the properties of a particle, we give up the possibility that it has those properties—until we measure them. But requiring the intervention of human consciousness is very upsetting to scientists.

ROBERT: Andrei, if we don't look at the universe, does that mean it doesn't exist?

ANDREI: This is one of our main challenges. With Schrödinger's cat, the question is whether the cat was really dead or really alive before we opened the box. The answer that quantum mechanics gives you, as Steve [Koonin] said, is that it was neither dead nor alive—at least in the standard Copenhagen [Bohr-Heisenberg] interpretation of quantum mechanics. Now assume that when you open the box you see that the cat is dead, then the most you can say is that *everything looks as if* the cat was dead before you opened the box; or if it is alive, you can say that *everything looks as if* the cat was alive before you opened the box. So when you look at the universe, the maximum that you can possibly say is that *everything looks as if* the universe has existed for some billions of years.

ROBERT: But it may not have?

ANDREI: Oh, it may not have, and that's the main challenge. You think you are describing reality, but then the whole concept of reality becomes dependent on an observer—which brings you to the nature of consciousness, and this is something dangerous.

LEON: The problem gets worse if you say, "I'm not going to look in the box, but I have a camera that takes a picture inside the box." Now what happens to the cat? Say the film isn't developed. Or if the film is developed, it's viewed only by a computer. Quantum mechanics leads to incredible conundrums.*

STEVE: So you can see why people got all tangled up when they tried to understand or interpret what was going on.

LEON: We should emphasize that almost all working physicists ignore these questions [and just get on with their calculations, which consistently say that quantum mechanics is right].

ROBERT: Greg, I'm asking the science fiction writer, not the physicist: Why is reality structured this way?

GREG: Why is the world the way it is? Gee, give me an easy one. We have simple categories, analogies, and metaphors that we make about the world, but the world is more sophisticated than we are—and in fact it's alien, it is truly strange. That's really the essential message of quantum mechanics—that there is a strangeness to the world and it does not respond at every level to our chimpanzee categorizations of it. It's as if you were viewing wonderful French

impressionist paintings at a museum, and then you slowly discovered that the paintings changed in response to whether or not you were looking at them. That's how strange quantum mechanics is.

ROBERT: But all this very indeterminate small stuff we study yields all this very ordinary stable stuff we see.

BENFORD: The world isn't as ordinary as you think. We just get used to it, and we don't inspect the stuff that's really strange.

ANDREI: And also, when you ask this question you are assuming that the world is everywhere the same. But in fact our new theory of inflationary cosmology [see Chapters 26 and 27] tells you that our universe must be incomprehensibly huge, and it may be divided into many, many regions, all of which may be absolutely different from one another. So there are some regions where the world is absolutely bizarre and you cannot live there, and there are some regions where everything is ordinary and you can live there. That's why you can have science.

ROBERT: And since we can only be conscious where we can be alive, then that's the only kind of universe we can observe.

ANDREI: Right.

LEON: Yes, but once you understand the processes and the confusion and the indeterminacy, understanding leads to control. Everything is made of molecules, and molecules are made of atoms. We can zoom down into atoms and examine their properties. So we learn that electrons in a certain kind of atom can move

---

*In a talk at the California Institute of Technology, Sidney Coleman of Harvard continued the serious fun. Suppose you look in the box and see that the cat is alive, but you're alone in your lab. You want to tell someone, but as you reach for the phone you have a heart attack and die. Is that cat now back to being alive and dead at the same time? It's a joke, half a joke, or both a joke and not a joke, depending on whether you were the one looking in.

around in a certain kind of way, and out of this can come the invention of a transistor. And even some of the most bizarre consequences of quantum theory can be used in the frontier work of quantum computing, which [because of the opportunities for parallelism] will be unimaginably more powerful than anything we have today.

STEVE: I think we'll see a quantum computer in the next ten to twenty years. We don't quite know how we'll make it, whether with atoms or with the spins of nuclei, but we will make it. (See Chapter 23.)

ROBERT: Won't quantum computers be limited to certain kinds of problems?

STEVE: Well, they'll probably solve all kinds of problems, but they'll be most efficient and effective for a certain class of problems, at least as we understand it. For example, the factoring of large numbers—decomposing 6 into 2 × 3 but amplified to hundreds of digits.

ROBERT: So someone with a quantum computer can eventually steal my credit card?

LEON: My grandson can do that now.

ROBERT: It's not worth stealing. A prediction please. A hundred years from now, will there be a Theory of Everything that will be complete, unassailable, and forever immutable?

LEON: Immutable? Yes.

ANDREI: No, I don't think so.

CHUCK: Yes, I do think so. Look at how far we've come in the last hundred years.

GREG: I believe so, but remember, even a Theory of Everything won't actually tell you everything.

LEON: Not how to avoid a traffic jam in Chicago or cure the common cold.

ROBERT: Or why you wore that tie.

STEVE: I think we'll have a Theory of Everything to account for what we now observe. But it's likely that we will observe new things that won't quite fit into that theory, and then we'll be back to where we are right now. That's one of the joys of science.

ROBERT: CONCLUDING COMMENT

The great mystery of quantum physics is that it works. Really weird stuff at the subatomic level forms rather ordinary stuff at the human level, so that the uncertainties and probabilities of the quantum world produce the certainties and absolutes of our normal world. The experimental data is now overwhelming in its scope and captivating in its elegance. Quantum physics is simply the way everything had to be, explaining the behavior of the small zoo of subatomic particles that make up the atoms of the hundred or so elements that in turn make up an unlimited multiplicity of molecules. But the Standard Model remains incomplete: Gravity must be integrated with the strong nuclear and electroweak forces to yield a Theory of Everything, the Holy Grail of physics. The best current idea drops down a level lower and envisions seemingly mystical, minuscule strings, all wrapped up in ten dimensions, whose vibrations may make the universe sing. It gives a chill to reach so deeply into reality. But quantum physics has made people queasy from its inception. If you're unconvinced of its truth, don't feel bad—you're in good company. Albert Einstein never accepted it either. Which just demonstrates how very difficult it is, sometimes, to get closer to truth.

OUTTAKES

LEON [to ROBERT]: *By the power vested in us, you now have a master's degree in quantum physics.*

ROBERT: *If nobody watches this show, does that mean that it doesn't exist?*

ANDREI: *Everything would look as if it doesn't exist.*

CHAPTER 26

When and How Did This Universe Begin?

The creation question is humanity's ancient and perpetual fascination. When did it happen and what caused it all? We may finally be getting some real answers. Cosmology is the study of the origin and outcome of the universe, and it is a young science: Its revolutionary discoveries have been relatively recent. The accepted theory is known as the Big Bang; it holds that the universe began a number of billion years ago, when an infinitesimally small point expanded majestically and cooked up space, time, energy, and matter in a colossal cosmic stew. Formulated in the middle decades of the twentieth century, the Big Bang had to compete for a while with another cosmological theory known as the Steady State universe. Steady State theory envisioned the universe as without an origin—that is, as having always existed—and as expanding while maintaining a constant average density. This theory posited the continuous creation of matter, with new stars and galaxies forming at the same rate as older ones became unobservable due to the cosmic expansion. A Steady State universe had no beginning or end in time, galaxies of all possible ages were intermingled, and the picture of the universe on a grand scale, viewed from any position, remained essentially the same with respect to the average density and arrangement of galaxies. Big Bang theorists found the continuous creation of matter an unappealing idea and preferred to have all creation concentrated in a single moment. Proponents of the Steady State argued that it eliminated the need for an unexplained beginning of the universe, and a few were gratified that it undermined the foundations of various creation-based theological models. But observational data over four decades have remarkably and consistently supported the Big Bang and laid the Steady State to rest. One of the more powerful corroborations of the Big Bang was the discovery in 1965 of the cosmic microwave background radiation, a lingering remnant of the primordial explosion, which permeates the universe at the predicted temperature of about three degrees above absolute zero. However, recent research now suggests that the Big Bang, awesomely, may have been far bigger than that: The Big Bang may have been followed immediately by a period of short-lived but exponential inflation—a theory that seems to solve a number of cosmological puzzles. There have been various versions of inflationary theory; one of them, known as *chaotic inflation,* proposes that the universe resembles a huge, rapidly multiplying fractal—an irregular, self-similar pattern (like clouds or coastlines) in which each part appears as a reduced-size copy of the whole. This mega-universe would consist of many separate universes (in only one of which we live), each undergoing episodes of initial inflation and producing new universes randomly, ad infinitum. Its evolution has no end—and may well have had no beginning. But how can we draw such fine-grained portraits of the universal origin? What methods can reach back over many billions of years? And how many billions? The proposed cosmic life span has been variously pegged at ten, twelve, fifteen, or twenty billion years, and cosmologists are closing in on the number. Why should we care? Because beyond just knowing—which is important enough—what happened so very long ago may carry very great meaning for human understanding today. Heated debate is still a part of cosmology, and we invited some people who care deeply about ultimate matters to tell us why they think so hard about when and how the universe began.

PARTICIPANTS

Dr. Wendy Freedman, an astronomer based at the Observatories of the Carnegie Institution, in Pasadena, California, is the principal investigator for a Hubble Space Telescope project to determine the age of the universe. Wendy takes us back to the very beginning of time and gives us the latest firm date.

Dr. Leon Lederman, a Nobel Laureate in physics, is the founder of the Illinois Mathematics and Science Academy for gifted high school students. Leon reflects on how the origin of the universe intersects with particle physics and why this is important for all of us.

Dr. Andrei Linde, a professor of physics at Stanford, is one of the originators of inflationary theory, developed while he was still in Russia. Andrei believes that the idea that the Big Bang was a single fireball is incorrect, that this observable universe is not the only one, and that as a result of a series of random inflationary episodes the universe is incomprehensibly larger than it appears.

Dr. Nancey Murphy, theology division chair and a professor of Christian philosophy at Fuller Theological Seminary, studies the relationship between science and religion. Nancey describes how theologians try to keep up with the rapid changes in cosmology.

Dr. Frank Tipler, a professor of mathematics and physics at Tulane, is coauthor (with the British astronomer John Barrow) of *The Anthropic Cosmological Principle.* Frank wonders why our universe is so astonishingly well suited to bring forth life.

ROBERT: Wendy, let's start with a number—the age of the universe. You measure distances to galaxies as a way of assessing the rate at which the universe expands. How old is the universe, and why does its expansion rate matter?

WENDY: We're finding the age of the universe to be about twelve billion years old. Expansion matters because, since we observe our universe expanding now, we know that the galaxies must have been closer together in the past; and we can rewind that picture back to the very origin of the universe, and thus see how long the universe has been expanding—and that's its age. It's like playing a movie in reverse.

ROBERT: What methods do you use to observe this expansion?

WENDY: We use the Hubble Space Telescope to measure the distances to galaxies. This is the first time we've been able to make these measurements above the earth's atmosphere, and to do it very precisely for a large number of galaxies.

ROBERT: The age of the universe used to be wildly uncertain.

WENDY: That's right. The range has been something like ten billion to twenty billion years. Obviously it's difficult to measure cosmic distances; we can't use a yardstick. We have to come up with approaches that allow us to use light from galaxies. We've done the measurement five different ways, and that's how we've convinced ourselves that we under-stand [the confidence limits and] the uncertainties.*

ROBERT: Andrei, inflationary cosmology has been hailed as one of the most remarkable scientific theories in the history of science, extending the scope of reality beyond comprehension. How would you explain inflationary theory to a high school student?

ANDREI: Well, this is a tough one. Inflationary theory describes the very early stages of the universe, and its enormous, though short-lived, expansion. The standard Big Bang theory held that the universe began as a very, very big explosion—an expanding fireball. But then we found that this big explosion was not big enough to explain everything we see in the universe. At the end of the 1970s it was proposed that the early universe came through a stage of inflation, an exponentially rapid expansion in a kind of unsta-

---

*Several independent techniques are used to measure distances in the universe; each has limitations, and the process can be tricky. For example, the parallax method, which can be used only for distances to close stars, is a direct calculation of a star's apparent motion against a more distant stellar background as a result of the earth's orbit around the sun. The luminosity method measures the brightness and periods of variable stars (e.g., Cepheids) and exploding stars (novae and supernovae); these are called "standard candles," in that if their absolute luminosity (energy output) is known (a key assumption), then their apparent brightness is directly related to their distances (an appropriate method for nearby galaxies, but not distant ones). The red shift method, which uses a spectrograph to assess light from rapidly receding stellar or galactic objects (Doppler effect), assumes that receding velocity is related to distance as indicated by the Big Bang theory of the expansion of the universe.

ble heavy vacuum-like state (a state with large energy density but without elementary particles). A vacuum-like state in inflationary theory is usually associated with a scalar field, which is often called "the inflation field." So instead of imagining the beginning of the universe as very hot, we imagine it at the beginning as this kind of an unstable vacuum-like state that did not contain any elementary particles but which did contain this scalar field. It is totally empty, without any particles, but still has a lot of energy. And I will be in trouble if I try to explain it in any more detail without using jargon of quantum field theory and general relativity. [See Figures 1 and 2.]

ROBERT: There's nothing but a potent sort of potential energy?

ANDREI: Yes, the potential energy of the scalar field. And then, a fraction of a second after the Big Bang, a region of this scalar field starts expanding exponentially. This is our universe,

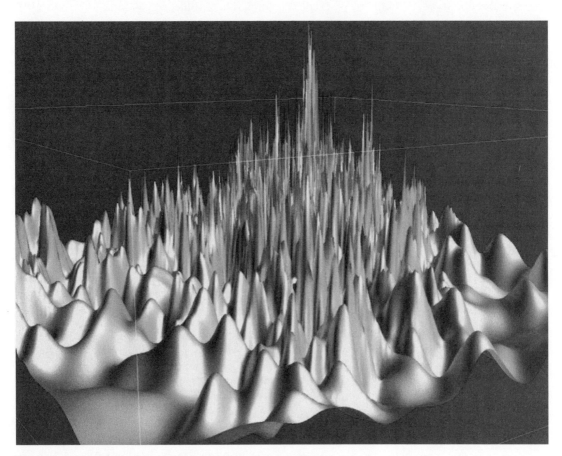

Figure 1   *SELF-REPLICATING INFLATIONARY UNIVERSE*
Domains of the inflationary universe with sufficiently large energy density permanently produce new inflationary domains. Due to quantum fluctuations, new regions of very large density (new mountains) appear all the time, which puts the universe into a regime of eternal self-reproduction. Calculation of the volume of the parts of the universe corresponds to the peaks of the "mountains." (Andrei Linde)

Figure 2   *KANDINSKY UNIVERSE*
The universe after inflation becomes divided into many exponentially large regions with different laws of low-energy physics (shown by different shades) in each of them. The domains are so large that for all practical purposes each can be considered a separate universe. (Andrei Linde)

and at this stage it expands much faster than in standard Big Bang theory, and eventually—after another fraction of a second—the scalar field decays. And after that, the evolution of the universe and the formation of elementary particles can be described by standard Big Bang theory. [See Figure 3.]

ROBERT: Leon, you've helped elucidate the Standard Model of particle physics and you're a pioneer in science education in America. Why is the origin of the universe an important question for nonscientists?

LEON: Well, for one thing, the age of anything is very sensitive to me personally. Fundamentally, almost all human beings who think at all

---

. . . almost all human beings who think at all think about origins.

---

think about origins. Where did I come from? Where did my world come from? These questions are natural—not like questions about my

Figure 3   *EXPLODING UNIVERSE*
Different parts of the inflationary universe expand with different speeds. (Andrei Linde)

quarks [see Chapter 25]. By the way, you stopped Andrei [Linde] just as he was about to make quarks in his universe. People are fascinated by the whole story of the universe—how we got from there to here. They also have a morbid interest in endings—where we're going.

ROBERT: We'll get to that in the next program [see Chapter 27].

LEON: Unless we know how we started, it wouldn't make much sense to wonder where we're going. So to me, the origin of the universe is one of the easiest topics to get interested in.

ROBERT: Frank, you're the author of two fascinating books: *The Anthropic Cosmological Principle* and *The Physics of Immortality*. Let's start with the more modest controversy: What is the anthropic principle?

FRANK: The anthropic principle starts by saying that there are many different types of universes. Take Andrei [Linde]'s eternally inflating universes, which you spoke about in the introduction. Some of them would inflate very rapidly and survive for long periods of time; other universes would have other characteristics, perhaps not inflating as fast and therefore collapsing before intelligent life had time to evolve. So what you have, in effect, is a selection process among all these possible universes. Only those universes that will admit life, that have just the right collection of physical constants and cosmic conditions to allow life to evolve, will have intelligent life able to ask questions like "How old is the universe?" Only in those universes where this question can be asked will it be asked. All other universes will never have intelligent life, so no such issues will ever arise.

ROBERT: The idea sounds almost trivial, a tautology—only in those universes that allow for intelligent life will there be intelligent questions. What are you adding?

FRANK: The anthropic principle asks why the universe has one value [for a given physical parameter] rather than another, since a complete range of values is possible. For example, take the cosmological constant, which results in a universal vacuum field that causes an accelerated expansion. The natural value that we theoretical physicists have computed is something like a hundred and twenty orders of magnitude larger than what is actually seen by observational astronomers. So there's a gigantic discrepancy between our theory and experiment. Now, we would expect other universes to have very different cosmological constants. But only those universes that have a cosmological constant very close to zero would be capable of giving rise to intelligent life.

ROBERT: So the anthropic principle's notion is that there's something about our universe specially suited for intelligent life. That's not trivial. Nancey, the book you cowrote with George Ellis, *On the Moral Nature of the Universe,* interrelates theology, cosmology, and ethics. Is modern cosmology compatible with traditional Judeo-Christian views?

NANCEY: That's a difficult question to answer, because cosmological theories keep changing so quickly. Those of us who specialize in the relationship between theology and science complain that since theological books get published so slowly, by the time they come out the science has often changed on you. But there are many interesting points of contact, not necessarily of agreement, that make for interesting dialogues.

ROBERT: What are some of these points of contact between theology and cosmology?

NANCEY: Well, one of the questions has to do with the infinity of the universe. A traditional Christian claim about the universe is that somehow it must be less than God. And so theologians speak in terms of the universe being finite in time, finite in size, or at least having a contingent origin or existence. But it seems to me that if some of Andrei's theories about a universe of universes are true, then we may be looking at an ensemble of universes that is potentially infinite in time, infinite in space, and perhaps necessarily existing. And that idea begins to tread on theologians' toes.

ROBERT: Are you uncomfortable with multiple universes?

NANCEY: If the universe turns out to be that way, Christian theologians are going to have to do some more homework to ask in what sense they can maintain those traditional claims about finiteness and contingency.

ROBERT: That's good justification for next season. Wendy, let's get back to the age of the universe, where your work has been extremely important. In recent years, astronomers faced the apparent contradiction of a universe younger than some of its stars.

WENDY: Scientists have two ways of measuring age. One is to observe the oldest stars in our own galaxy and assess their ages as determined by their masses. More massive stars burn up their fuel more quickly, and so by gauging how long a star has been burning its fuel you can estimate its age. And the estimates from the oldest stars gave us an age of about fifteen billion years.

ROBERT: That's older than your twelve-billion-year-old universe.

WENDY: Yes, but recent measurements from a satellite called Hipparcos have revised those stellar ages down to about twelve billion years. The other way that astronomers have of measuring age is one I mentioned earlier—where we look at the expansion of the universe and extrapolate backward. To determine the age from the expansion, however, not only requires us to know how fast the universe is expanding, which is what we do with the Hubble Space Telescope, but it also depends on knowing how much matter there is in the universe, because the more matter there is, the more gravity there is, and the more the expansion is slowed down.

ROBERT: Meaning that you can't simply run the movie in reverse, since the speed of the film today—if I've got the analogy right—may have been different from the speed in the past.

WENDY: Right. So when we take all that into account, including estimates of the matter in the universe, we deduce an age of about twelve billion years. So now, both measurements—oldest stars and universal expansion—appear to be compatible within a margin of error.

ROBERT: And the ages are derived from independent measurements.

WENDY: Completely independent—nuclear burning in the stars and the [rate of] expansion of the universe.

ROBERT: Andrei, let's talk some more about inflationary theory. The standard Big Bang theory has a series of intractably complex problems which inflation claimed to solve. One is the homogeneity or extremely even distribution of matter in the universe on a larger scale combined with the large clumps of matter called galaxies at a smaller scale.

ANDREI: Initially, inflation was considered as an intermediate stage of the evolution of the universe, which was necessary to solve many of these cosmological problems. At the end of inflation, as I said earlier, when the scalar field decayed, the universe became hot, and its subsequent evolution could be described by the standard Big Bang theory. Thus inflation was a part of the Big Bang theory. Gradually, however, the Big Bang theory became a part of inflation

---

the evolution of the universe, . . . has no end and may have had no beginning.

---

cosmology. Recent versions of inflationary theory assert that instead of being a single, expanding ball of fire, the universe looks like a huge, rapidly multiplying fractal. This fractal-like universe consists of many inflating balls that produce new balls, which in turn produce more new balls, ad infinitum. Therefore the evolution of the universe, as you mentioned in your introduction, has no end and may have had no beginning.

ROBERT: The size scales intrinsic to inflation theory are far beyond anything ever conceived.

ANDREI: After inflation, the universe becomes divided into different exponentially large domains, inside of which properties of elementary particles and even the number of dimensions of space-time may be different. Thus, the new cosmological theory leads to a considerable modification of the standard point of view on the structure and evolution of the universe and on our own place in the world.

ROBERT: How does the size of the universe in inflationary theory help solve some of the problems of the Big Bang?

ANDREI: The total size of the observable universe—the part of the universe we see right now—can be described by the number 10^{28} centimeters, which is 10 followed by 28 zeros, 10 to the 28th power, a pretty huge number on the human scale. Well, the question is, Why is the universe so large? We needed a theory to explain these great dimensions. There was also another question: Why don't parallel lines intersect? At first, this seems kind of stupid—everyone knows that parallel lines do not intersect. But Einstein told us that the universe is curved, and in a curved universe parallel lines eventually may intersect. So why has no one ever seen parallel lines intersect? And there are many other questions like that, such as why different parts of the universe started to expand simultaneously, and why we see the homogeneity you referred to—that is, everywhere we look in the universe, it looks very much alike. These were the problems, and we got the answers.

ROBERT: That's why you're here; if you didn't have the answers, you wouldn't be here.

ANDREI: But these problems are kind of metaphysical. People could be excused for not even addressing them. They could say, "Well, the universe is given to us and we study it, but we don't ask questions that begin with 'Why'—the universe is just the universe, and this is the way it is." Inflationary theory, however, does give us a simple answer to all of these questions simultaneously. When you get the answer, you cannot forget it.

ROBERT: We're all listening. Give us some sense of the enormity of inflation.

ANDREI: The answer is that the universe expanded extremely fast in this vacuum state. The main difference between inflationary theory and the old cosmology becomes clear when you estimate what the size of the universe should be after the expansion. You get, not 10 to the power of 28, which is the current size of the observable universe, but 10 to the power of one trillion—or even greater than that, depending on the model.* So you have this small piece of space that expands enormously. If we draw an analogy between the universe and the earth, we can appreciate the parallel-lines problem. On Earth, lines of longitude meet at the South Pole and the North Pole. Why don't we see these longitudinal lines converging? Well, it's because we live on an extremely tiny patch of the earth, far from the poles. For the same reason, we don't see parallel lines intersect in the universe, because what we actually see of the universe is only a very small sector of the totality.

ROBERT: Hubble [Space Telescope] has taken some remarkable pictures revealing breathtaking panoramas of galaxies, even when it's pointing at some apparently unremarkable areas of the sky. The universe seems the same no matter in which direction we look.

ANDREI: The standard Big Bang theory has what's known as the horizon problem. That is, opposite sides of the observable universe have the same physical properties—density and temperature—to a degree of accuracy better than one part in ten thousand, even though when light decoupled from matter [about three hundred thousand years after the Big Bang], they were already too far apart [perhaps fifty million light-years in some models] to become homogenous. Even at this moment, they still can't communicate with each other, because they're separated by a distance very much greater than the speed of light multiplied by the age of the universe [and such communication is necessary to make densities and temperatures of different parts of the universe the same].

---

*The scales and orders of magnitude in inflationary theory are astonishing and they are critical to appreciate its ultimate significance. During the universe's fleetingly brief inflationary era (perhaps only 10^{-35} to 10^{-32} seconds), it is said to have increased in size by a factor of at least thirty orders of magnitude (10^{30}) and perhaps far more. According to some inflation models reported by Linde, the universe could have expanded to $10^{10^{12}}$ centimeters—that's ten to the tenth to the twelfth power—to the trillionth power, a trillion orders of magnitude. It is impossible to conceive of a physical representation of this number. For comparison, the size of the observable universe containing a hundred billion galaxies is 10^{28} centimeters. So what kind of number is $10^{10^{12}}$ centimeters? Let's say you wanted to draw such a line. Assume that you had all the time needed; also assume that you could draw the line no thicker than the diameter of a hydrogen atom, and finally assume that the entire observable universe is filled with ink. Your problem is your ink: The universe of ink would run dry long before you had drawn a tiny fraction of that line. What's equally interesting, as Linde likes to explain, is that it doesn't matter what the units are—whether centimeters or kilometers or light-years or even radii of the observable universe. A number this large is virtually the same irrespective of all human-devised units. Linde says that even if the universe at the beginning of inflation was as small as 10^{-33} centimeters, after 10^{-35} seconds of inflation, this domain acquires an unbelievable size. So rather than being expressed in specific units, numbers such as $10^{10^{12}}$ usually express the relative expansion—the increased orders of magnitude that the universe inflated. These numbers depend on the models used, but in most versions the size is many orders of magnitude greater than that of the observable universe.

ROBERT: It's fascinating that these areas on the edge of the universe don't, in effect, know about each other's existence—whereas we do.

ANDREI: Yes. In some sense, we're at the center of the action, but so is everything else. The real point is to explain why the right and left edges of the universe look the same. And inflationary theory does that. Just after the universe was created, in the pre-inflationary moment, all parts of the universe could see one another, so to speak, and information could pass between them. All parts of the infant universe were thus able to come to a state of equilibrium. And then inflation began, and the horizon expanded exponentially.

ROBERT: Since the speed of inflation vastly exceeded the speed of light, after that transitory inflationary moment, it would be impossible for separate sides of the universe to ever again communicate, thus producing the situation we observe today.

ANDREI: Indeed, we will never see some very distant parts of the universe. But it is very important to keep their existence in mind if one wants to understand his or her own place in the world.

ROBERT: So your theory asserts that everything we see—everything that Wendy [Freedman] sees with Hubble—is an infinitesimally small part of all there is?

ANDREI: Yes.

WENDY: And the observable universe is all we have that's accessible to us, given the age of the universe and the finite speed of light.

ROBERT: Right. Most people assume that nothing can go faster than light—this is part of Einstein's special theory of relativity. But Andrei is saying that space expanded enormously faster than the speed of light, and that because there was no matter, relativity didn't apply.

ANDREI: Einstein's relativity applies to light. It does not apply to the speed of expansion of the whole thing—all space-time. By way of analogy, suppose you send a signal along a membrane, and the signal moves at a constant speed. Next, paint two dots on the membrane. Now stretch the membrane. There is no upper bound on the increase in distance between these two dots if the distance between them is large, even though the signal still travels at the same speed along the membrane. Likewise, there's no upper bound on the speed of inflationary expansion in the early universe, even though light still travels at the same speed. Inflation theory tells how fast the whole of space expanded.

FRANK: I want to claim that if you look at the coupled equations of gravity and the Standard Model, and also throw in all the important quantum mechanics, these equations collectively have only one solution. And that solution is, the closer you get to the beginning, the more isotropic and homogenous the universe has to become.

ROBERT: Leon, you told me you're old enough to have been there at the beginning. Do you believe in any particular theory of origin?

LEON: My high school students would say, "Gee, this is very interesting, but we weren't there and no one's ever going to be able to verify that any of this took place." So they'd ask whether there was another way to account for the creation of the world—whether there was an alternative explanation.

FRANK: Yes. Andrei mentioned this scalar field, this vacuum field, but he neglected to mention that you have to invent it *ab initio*. It exists only in the theorists' minds. I prefer to use fields that people like Leon [Lederman] have already seen. So if you just use standard physics—that is, relativity and quantum mechanics and the Standard Model of particle physics [see Chapter 25], which involves fields we've actually observed, then there's a unique solution to how the universe began. And it began in a singularity [a point of infinite density], out of which sprang gravitation and all the other laws, energy, and matter of the universe. Now, there *is* an energy field—what we call a gauge field, which we're all familiar with as theoretical physicists. That's the only field we have in our normal experience. One way for you to think about it is as something like light. It's not quite light but something resembling it.

ROBERT: And all of this gives you a solution that amounts to a single universe?

FRANK: Yes, a unique solution.

ROBERT: And what you mean by a unique solution is that the one universe that Wendy sees is the only one there is?

FRANK: Yes.

ROBERT: Nancey, from a theological perspective, what is your view of inflationary theory's multiple universes versus the Big Bang's unique universe?

NANCEY: Well, it's a disappointment to me that inflationary theory has taken off so well, because it undermines the argument that George [Ellis] and I developed in our book [*On the Moral Nature of the Universe*]. We started out with the anthropic principle that Frank [Tipler] talks about, and we reasoned that if there's only

one universe—and we know the cosmological constant in this one—then it had to have been designed by a brilliant mathematician. And so it looked like we had grounds for a new design argument.

ROBERT: A resurrection, as it were, of the so-called argument from design, which was one of the classical arguments for the existence of God.*

NANCEY: Exactly. Other such arguments [for the existence of God] usually last for a hundred, a hundred and fifty years or so, before someone like Darwin comes along and destroys them. But it looks as though Andrei [Linde] has come along and destroyed ours in two years flat.

ANDREI: This was not my purpose.

NANCEY: I know.

ROBERT: He had to invent new physics to do this.

NANCEY: But he's never embarrassed about doing that.

ROBERT: Do you have a preference? Which creation model, single-universe Big Bang or multi-universe inflation, would better support an argument from design affirming the existence of God? Or can you handle it either way?

---

*The argument from design, also known as the teleological argument (explaining things by their ends or purposes), is largely and long discredited. The argument is based on analogy: Put simply, since a watch was created by a watchmaker, the universe was created by a Universe Maker. Fallacies include the nature of probability theory and the absence of external comparisons against which we can judge the putative design of the universe. But debate still rages on this most fundamental question of existence.

NANCEY: It's not clear to me yet. At this point, I'll refrain from answering that question. I like the idea that [experimental or observation] data will decide.

ROBERT: How do you do that?

WENDY: I think it's important to make the point that our conception of the universe has changed radically over the last four hundred years. We originally thought that the earth was the center of the cosmos, then the sun, then our Milky Way galaxy. Even in this century, we thought that the sun was at the center of the universe. We now know that the sun is one star of hundreds of billions in our Milky Way. And

---

Some may think theory will ulti-mately decide. I'm for experiment.

---

our galaxy is one of at least a hundred billion other galaxies. We're really at the forefront of cosmology now; we're talking about matters that haven't been subjected to the same kinds of experimental test. Some may think theory will ultimately decide. I'm for experiment.

ROBERT: You've got to see it.

WENDY: Most people want to see it to be convinced, and in Andrei [Linde]'s favor there are a lot of observational data supporting inflation.

ROBERT: Inflation is an unbelievably creative solution to some very complicated problems.

LEON: It's consistent.

WENDY: It's consistent with other data we have.

LEON: I'm waiting for the Standard Model to pop out of these guys' theories. I want to see all the particles, masses, strengths, and couplings. Why are there six quarks and six leptons? Why all the rest of the stuff? Basically, some of these guys are arrogant. When I was director of Fermilab [the Fermi National Accelerator Laboratory in Batavia, Illinois] I preached against arrogance and they took me seriously. I heard this one guy say, "Dear Lord, forgive me the sin of arrogance. And Lord, by arrogance I mean the following. . . ."

ROBERT: Andrei, let's go back to your scalar field. You say that inflation was energized by the potential energy intrinsic to the scalar field. Where did that potential energy come from?

ANDREI: First of all, I should say that we did not invent the scalar field for the purposes of cosmology. Such fields and the fact that they may have energy is a necessary part of the Standard Model of electroweak interactions. Several Nobel Prizes have already been awarded for developing this theory.

ROBERT: But it's a question of initial existence, to begin with. Some theorists speak of a "quantum foam," out of which all the initial stuff of the universe—energy and matter—emerged into existence. Spontaneous eruptions, if you will, of matter and antimatter, the vast majority of which instantly annihilated right back out of existence.

ANDREI: Sure. Then the question is, Why was the scalar field in the early universe large enough to provide enough energy to create [inflate] the whole universe? Well, look at it this way. Suppose you have a small universe, just being born, but it does not contain a sufficiently large scalar field. So then—sorry!—it dies very young [collapsing back and annihilating itself, a universal stillbirth]. Only if you have a scalar field large enough can the universe become exponentially large and enter the process of stellar production and have sufficient time to engender beings who are capable of asking questions, so—

ROBERT: —the problem becomes self-solving. This leads us back to the anthropic principle, which apparently comes in two flavors, weak and strong. Frank, what's the difference?

FRANK: The weak anthropic principle is simply that the universe must be consistent with the

---

The strong anthropic principle says that the universe must give rise to intelligent life at some point in its history.

---

evolution of intelligent life. The strong anthropic principle says that the universe must give rise to intelligent life at some point in its history.

ROBERT: "Must be consistent with" versus "must give rise to"—a significant difference. The weak anthropic principle sounds like the situation Andrei was describing: Only those universes that have all the conditions necessary for intelligent life will have intelligent life, and we must therefore be living in one such universe—because in all the innumerable universes that do not have these conditions, there is no intelligence around to ask or do anything.* The

strong anthropic principle sounds causative— that this universe was required to spawn conscious life as if by necessity. Is that what you mean?

FRANK: Yes.

ROBERT: Leon, does all this sound like philosophy?

LEON: That's the point. I just want to make clear that this is not physics. It's not even science in my opinion. It's philosophy. Now, many people respect philosophy—

ROBERT: But not physicists?

LEON: Not physicists—generally, that's right. But it doesn't matter whether you respect philosophy or not. You have to make a clear distinction. This is not something that is subject to the traditional tests of science, where you propose a theory or a model, do an experiment, get data, verify [or falsify] the theory or model, predict results of future experiments, and so on. In fact, you can never prove a theory right. You can prove that maybe it's right, or you can prove that it's wrong, which is more fun.

ROBERT: Andrei, cosmologists generally don't spend much time worrying about the anthropic principle?

ANDREI: Well, unlike many cosmologists, I like the anthropic principle very much. But there's a good reason why cosmologists gener-

---

*The weak anthropic principle may seem obvious, which it is, and a tautology, which it is not. Assuming that one doesn't accept the strong anthropic principle—of one single universe that must give rise to intelligent life—then the weak anthropic principle seems consistent with the multi-universe idea. Because without the strong anthropic principle, reality would seem to need multiple universes to enable the self-selection of universes whereby intelligent life would exist in only those universes where intelligent life could exist.

ally don't like it, because some people use it without really understanding it, just to give an easy answer. If you use the anthropic principle carefully, then it's a powerful weapon, but if you use it indiscriminately, then it hurts all of us.

ROBERT: Nancey, how do you use the anthropic principle? In terms of understanding theology, that is.

NANCEY: Well, it certainly did look like good evidence that the universe had to be designed. Frank [Tipler] says that the universe had to be the way it is so that it would permit intelligent life. Then when you ask what's the basis of that "had to be," you're getting into the question of why there is a universe.

LEON: I think there's a universe because somewhere, way back, there were the laws of physics. The laws of physics said there had to be a universe. The laws of physics were there. Now Nancey [Murphy]'s going to ask me who put the laws of physics there.

NANCEY: Exactly.

LEON: I'll think about it for a while.

ROBERT: It's what we call an infinite regress—seeking causes of causes of causes ad infinitum.

ANDREI: One may ask this question in a different way. If you say that first there were laws of physics but no universe, then where were the laws of physics written? If first there was the universe without the laws of physics, then how could the universe exist without the laws of physics? And so it looks like we must have a universe together with the laws of physics. They pop up simultaneously. But who tells you that they pop up? Well, we're telling you, because

we're observing. So it looks like we have three entities bound together: the laws of physics, the universe, and us.

FRANK: I also want to remind Leon [Lederman] that living beings are a physical phenomenon and must be taken into account when you are trying to explain things. Actually, the anthropic principle has led to experimental predictions. For example, the British cosmologist Fred Hoyle realized that carbon atoms—upon which life is based—would not have significantly existed unless there was a resonance, as it's called, in a certain nuclear reaction. He predicted its energy, and experimenters found it where he predicted it to be.

ROBERT: Wendy, is there a danger that theory can run too far ahead of hard data?

WENDY: I think that's right. It may be that ultimately, as Leon [Lederman] was saying, we'll have a complete theory that will explain the numbers of quarks and all other experimental data. But we may never be able to test directly whether or not there are many universes, and so we may have to rely on something like the anthropic principle, which is unsatisfying to many people. But it comes back to the fact that we're now at the forefront, asking questions that have never before been addressed by science. And while Andrei [Linde] has said that there were many questions the Big Bang theory didn't answer, there are also many questions that the Big Bang theory does answer.

ROBERT: What are some questions that the Big Bang has answered?

WENDY: For example, when we look in any direction and we measure the cosmic microwave background radiation, we see that it is uniform across the sky. This uniformity of residual radiation is predicted by the Big Bang theory. There are no other explanations for the cosmic microwave background at this point. Here's another example: When we consider the abundance of the lightest elements, like hydrogen and helium, we can predict how much would have been formed during the Big Bang. Then we can go and observe, as experimentalists, and see how much there is.

ROBERT: How close are you?

WENDY: Very close. To within a few percent. Better. Our data confirms what's predicted by the Big Bang theory.

LEON: That's another success, which segues into the anthropic principle. We're all charmed by these accidents [or coincidences]—for instance, if the charge of the electron were a little different from what it is, life would be, if not nonexistent, at least very different. But in our accelerator collisions, where we're trying to replicate the early universe, we make equal amounts of matter and antimatter.

ROBERT: Antimatter being matter with the opposite charge. So if they occur together—

LEON: If they occur together, they annihilate. So, if nature makes both and prefers neither, the big question for fifty years has been, Where's the antimatter? *We're* here, and we're matter. We look at the solar system, no antimatter; we look at our galaxy, no antimatter. It's a mystery. What happened to the antimatter? About thirty years ago, an important experiment showed that the symmetry between matter and antimatter isn't perfect. There's a very small deviation from symmetry, and that deviation, in combination with the Big Bang theory, means that this symmetry

wasn't perfect at the beginning either and that there were slightly more quarks than antiquarks in the early universe, and that made all the difference! In a perfectly symmetric universe following the Big Bang, all matter and all antimatter would have annihilated—all would be radiation—and we wouldn't be here to speculate why.

ROBERT: But since that didn't happen—

LEON: It didn't happen because in the cooling process, to put it as simply as possible, a slight excess of quarks over antiquarks was left over—and those became us.

ROBERT: Are we living in a unique time for cosmology? The Hubble Space Telescope's pictures and data are approaching tantalizingly close to the origin of the universe. Will the next ten to fifteen years be really special, or have people always thought that their own time was special?

WENDY: I'm sure people have always thought that, but this really is a unique time in cosmology and astronomy. With Hubble above the earth's atmosphere, we can look farther back in time than we ever could before. We also have new satellites that will measure the background radiation from the Big Bang to .001 percent accuracy, which will enable us to test all of these theories again with new data—they all make predictions for this increased degree of accuracy. And besides the satellites, we also have more powerful accelerators and large ground-based telescopes linked together with advanced electronics and software. All these different technologies, never before possible, are closing in on the ultimate target. So it's not an exaggeration to say that this time is special.

ANDREI: I would compare cosmology at this time with the development of geography in pre-

Columbian times. Europeans didn't know that America existed. After the New World was discovered, it was done—you had a map of the earth. So in the next ten to twenty years, perhaps we will have a map of the part of our universe that we can see—which is about twenty or so billion light-years away. For billion of years into the future, irrespective of what happens to humanity, this map of the universe is not going to change. So we are participating in an event for which the universe has been waiting, in a sense, for billions of years. Just wait—another ten years or so and it will happen.

FRANK: Let's not forget that there are parts of the universe that may be forever outside our purview.

ROBERT: Unless we engage in some other method, which Nancey might recommend.

NANCEY: Well, let's just remember that although this program was introduced as a discussion of creation, what we've really been talking about are the conditions at the very beginning, whether or how that included the laws of physics, quantum foam, scalar fields, or

---

Why is the universe here? Why is there something rather than nothing?

---

whatever. And that's not answering the question of creation. Why is the universe here? Why is there something rather than nothing?

ROBERT: That, Nancey, is my favorite question [see Epilogue]. In a hundred years, will the multiworld interpretation—that is, many universes,

all budding off from one another—be commonly accepted?

ANDREI: Oh, yes.

LEON: I tend to be optimistic; I will say yes, but I won't bet much on it.

NANCEY: Let me give you a theological rationale for saying that it will be. In the fifth century, Augustine developed what he called the "principle of plentitude," and that was his explanation as to why we have the sorts of beings in the world that we don't particularly like, such as mosquitoes, as well as the ones that we do, such as dogs and horses. And I think that that same principle, when you think about it, leads you to expect that there would be more universes than just the one we can observe and measure.

ROBERT: That's an expansion of traditional theology.

NANCEY: Yes, if there is a God, and God cares about creating, then why would God stop with just this one little bubble?

FRANK: I'll agree that there will be a general belief in many universes, simply because it's an automatic consequence of quantum mechanics. However, I don't think the inflation model that Andrei is defending will be around, because I don't think you need it to explain the universe. All you need are the standard laws of physics.

WENDY: I think many universes are quite possible. And it will be important to put this theory to experimental test, which will be difficult. But in the same way that we've moved our thinking from the sun to the galaxies to the universe, it doesn't necessarily make sense to stop with just one universe. I'd like to see experimental data, though.

ROBERT: CONCLUDING COMMENT

Regarding the beginning of this universe, I guess there are only three little questions: *When? How? Why?* It is the dawn of a new millennium and the time is good to ponder ultimate issues. We started with *when,* and we came up with its creation at twelve billion years ago. But I'd like to compare this number with the human life span of about a hundred years. I am fascinated by this awesome mismatch, in light of the fact that humans can envision and perhaps pinpoint the creation event, and I wonder whether it's at all related to the anthropic principle, which defines the incredibly precise universal values required for human existence. I also marvel at inflationary cosmology, which would allow for multiple universes beyond our wildest imagination, disrupting forever our attempts even to imagine the totality of existence. Are there other universes, perhaps an infinite supply, existing outside our own, with different physical laws? It's a new com-

plication and, be assured, not a minor one. As for *how* the universe came into existence, the current candidate is random fluctuations in the quantum foam, energized by the laws of physics—but where did the foam and the laws come from? Which brings us back to the anthropic principle and the question of whether our universe was specially constructed to produce sentient life. Is that *why* this universe began? Sometimes only silence . . . gets us closer to truth.

OUTTAKES

WENDY: *With astronomy, you see history unfolding live, because you're always looking back in time. Geologists don't have that on earth—nor do archeologists.*

LEON: *Our machines are time machines. Telescopes and particle accelerators are time machines.*

CHAPTER 27

Will This Universe Ever End?

Will this universe ever end? If so, how? There are two basic theories, neither pleasant. One is that the Big Crunch is coming: At some point, the universe, which had been expanding, will begin contracting, rushing inward, so that all matter and energy will eventually squash together into a singularity, where mass has no volume and space and time stop. The other is known as the Heat Death (i.e., heat dies): The universe, with its continued expansion, flies more and more apart, so that all matter and energy will dissipate and all will become the ultimate cold void. But startling new challenges throw it all up for grabs. A key question is the amount of matter in the universe. Are there enough stars, planets, gas, dark matter, and exotic particles of one sort or another for gravity to reverse the current expansion and in the end implode the universe in the Big Crunch? Another key question is whether or not the expansion is accelerating—and if so, how much and why? And if this universe does end, might another take its place? Are other universes already in existence, perhaps an infinite number of them, furiously expanding? There's a lot loaded into our titular question—from the geometry of the universe to the existence of multiple universes. There aren't many people who get paid to ponder the end of all things. Fortunately, we have gathered some of the best.

PARTICIPANTS

Dr. Wendy Freedman, an astronomer at the Carnegie Observatories, provides key data to determine the age of the universe. Wendy explains why the amount of matter in the universe is important in determining its ultimate fate.

Dr. Leon Lederman, author of *The God Particle,* was awarded the Nobel Prize in physics in 1988 for his work on the Standard Model of particle physics. Leon's insight and humor illuminate and leaven these ultimate questions.

Dr. Andrei Linde, a professor of physics at Stanford, invented the concept of chaotic inflation, which has redefined the beginning of the universe. Andrei believes that there may well be myriad universes, each giving birth to new universes, and that this birthing process will go on forever.

Dr. Nancey Murphy is a professor at Fuller Theological Seminary; her book *Theology in the Age of Scientific Reasoning* won several awards. Nancey wonders that if this universe ends—by freezing or frying—what is God going to do for the rest of eternity?

Dr. Frank Tipler, a physicist and mathematician at Tulane, is the author of *The Physics of Immortality,* in which he speculates that the dead will be resurrected and live eternally (time being a subjective concept) just before the Big Crunch.

ROBERT: Leon, what are the kinds of questions about the end of the universe that you want high school students to think about?

LEON: I'm not a cosmologist. I'm the token noncosmologist.

ROBERT: We need diversity.

LEON: High school students are obsessed with the present and not so concerned about the future. But these ultimate questions are fascinating and could awaken their interest. The universe began with a Big Bang; will it end with a whimper? And if so, when? A guy once asked a cosmologist, "How many years?" And the cosmologist said, "Fifty billion." "Oh, thank God!" the guy said. "I thought you said fifty *million.*" I'd sort of like to be around and see what happens.

ROBERT: Frank, you claim that at the penultimate moment before the Big Crunch—which you have called the Omega Point—everyone who ever lived will be resurrected, and that the Omega Point is God. Why should we believe it?

FRANK: Because it's the only alternative allowed by the firmly tested laws of physics.

ROBERT: Why would we like it?

FRANK: Because you'll be brought back into existence near the end of time, and you will exist forever, right before the Big Crunch occurs at the very end of time—this is the Omega Point.

ROBERT: That "forever" is really only a very small fraction of a second, but it's supposed to feel like forever?

FRANK: We'll have new life forever, on a more reasonable timescale.

ROBERT: Sometimes this show feels like forever.

FRANK: Let's remember that it's a big mistake to try to apply human concepts to the universe as a whole. Our concept of time arose in our present environment, on Earth. A far more reasonable timescale is *experienced* time. There will be an infinite amount of experienced time between however close you are to the end of time and the actual end of time.

ROBERT: Nancey, you're a Christian theologian who is not threatened by all these cosmologists. Are discussions of the end of the universe based on physics and cosmology important for people who believe in the Judeo-Christian Bible?

NANCEY: I think they're important, but more for negative than positive reasons. When Christians talk about the end of the world, or about last things, what they mean is what happens after the phase of history that this universe belongs to is over—after the end of physics. So anything that physicists could predict about how this universe is going to close down is, in a sense, irrelevant to what Christians are talking about in terms of last things.

ROBERT: The New Heaven and the New Earth, from the Book of Revelation.

NANCEY: That's right.

ROBERT: That would take place after the end of this physical universe.

NANCEY: That's right. There's supposed to be personal continuity: I am still "I" in some sense when I'm resurrected afterward. But the afterward occurs following whatever our cosmologist friends can talk about. If the prospects for the physical universe are, in colorful terms, to freeze or to fry [Heat Death or Big Crunch], then that's good motivation for asking whether there is some sort of hope for human life beyond either of these scenarios.

ROBERT: Now, if I wake up in some resurrection, am I going to know whether I'm in Frank's Omega Point or your New Heaven?

NANCEY: I think so. But we'll probably have to talk about that later.

ROBERT: Frank, am I going to know the difference?

FRANK: Well, from the traditional Christian and Jewish descriptions, no.

WENDY: Eating and drinking and all of that good stuff?

FRANK: Certainly.

ROBERT: Wendy, I need to get back to some hard data here—my head's spinning from the Omega Point and the New Heaven. What kinds of observations could help us understand what will happen at the end?

WENDY: There are two primary things we need to understand to address this question of the ultimate fate of the universe—how fast the universe is expanding and how much matter

---

There are two primary things we need to understand . . . how fast the universe is expanding and how much matter there is in the universe.

---

there is in the universe. These are two very active areas of investigation. We need to know how much matter there is, because if there's enough, the expansion could be slowed down by gravity and possibly reversed.

ROBERT: The more matter, the more gravity; and the more gravity, the more the expansion is slowed.

WENDY: Yes. We also need to know whether the universal expansion is in fact accelerating. And we need to know accurately the values for these parameters.

ROBERT: These data recast all the old questions.

WENDY: And they can now be answered empirically.

ROBERT: They are no longer theoretical questions, whether for cosmologists or theologians.

WENDY: Correct. You need both theory and experiment.

ROBERT: Andrei, what are the implications of inflationary theory for the end of the universe?

ANDREI: The answer to this question may not be quite what you expect, because people in general think that the universe everywhere is the same as it appears in our vicinity—and therefore that the question about its future can be answered once and forever by looking at our part. But inflationary theory says that most probably the universe consists of many different parts, some of them still in the process of being created [see Chapter 26]. And new life may appear in different parts of the universe, all over again. So our part of the universe may collapse, or may become cold and unsuitable for life, but simultaneously other parts of the universe will appear that will be able to support new life.

ROBERT: So whereas our sector of the universe may be subject to either the Big Crunch or the Heat Death, there's far more to the totality of reality, in which vast new things may happen.

ANDREI: Yes. This is analogous to the fact that while individual humans are mortal, the human species is immortal. Though each of us will die, our children will give rise to their children, and humanity as a whole may exist forever. So it seems with the universe.

LEON: Is that encouraging?

ANDREI: It depends on your personal perspective. If you want a personal immortality, I'm afraid that so far science doesn't allow us this.

FRANK: In your theory, our particular civilization and our particular lines of descent will become extinct.

ANDREI: Yes, that's probably so.

LEON: There's a metaphor I like for whether or not the universe, in the simplest case of the Big Bang theory, will expand forever. The metaphor is the launching of a rocket, and in fact the mathematics of it are similar to the mathematics describing the future of the universe. If you launch a rocket on an austere budget, reflecting NASA's impecunious state, it might go up for a while, but then it will fall back. That's like the Big Crunch.

ROBERT: Sometimes that happens with a big budget, too.

LEON: True. But if you have a well-funded rocket, and you put a lot of fuel in it, then it will escape from the earth. It might go into a permanent orbit around the earth—or, with huge thrust, it will escape completely from the solar system and go on outward forever. So the three things that can happen after the launch of a rocket—falling back to earth, orbiting the earth or the sun, and escaping from the solar system—are analogous to the three possibilities for the future of the universe—closed, flat, and open—unless we've left out something that we don't know about, something that happens after the launch.*

ROBERT: To summarize: Originally cosmologists had two competing theories, each of which claimed to explain the origin of the universe: a Steady State theory, which requires the continuous creation of matter, and a Big Bang theory, in which matter was only created at a momentous initial event. Experimental data has consistently supported the Big Bang. So assuming the Big Bang started it all, what's the end of it all? Will the universe ultimately crunch together? Or will it continue flying apart? Are there multiple universes? And in any case, is there any deeper meaning or theological implications? Certainly, there's wishful thinking. Now let's get to some hard data, particularly the total density of matter in the universe.

WENDY: Well, the question comes down to— as Leon [Lederman] was just figuratively explaining—the mass density of the universe. If we live in a low-density universe, then the uni-

---

*A closed universe is finite, and will one day stop expanding and begin collapsing to an ultimate crunch. An open universe will expand forever; the energy of the expansion is always greater than the gravitational energy. A flat universe is the exact boundary between the two. In a flat universe, the average mass density is exactly enough to keep the gravitational energy equal to the kinetic energy of the expansion; such a universe will also expand forever, but at an ever-slower rate. Note that the Steady State theory [see Chapter 26] is not the flat universe option of the Big Bang theory.

verse will continue to expand forever. If it's a high-density universe, then in theory the expansion would slow, halt, and reverse, and everything would come back to the Big Crunch. So astronomers have been looking very hard, for decades now, to see how much matter there is in the universe. And early in the 1970s, when people were trying to pin this number down— determine the average density of matter in the universe—it seemed that there was not enough matter to halt the expansion.

ROBERT: How do you determine the average density of matter in the universe—density being the amount of matter in a specific volume? Where do you look?

WENDY: You can look on very different scales, so let me give you an example. In our own galaxy, say, you can look at the outermost stars and determine how fast they're moving around the galactic center. You'd predict that they would be moving more slowly than inner stars; if there's not much mass out there, then the velocity is going to fall off even further. [The velocity of stellar movement is a good test for the amount of matter, since velocity is energized by gravitation, which is directly related to the amount of matter.] This is true of our own solar system; you see it in planetary motions. But when people were able to make these sensitive measurements, they found that the stars on the outskirts of galaxies were actually moving quite rapidly.

ROBERT: So you concluded that there had to be more matter in our galaxy than met the eye. Astronomers had to postulate new stuff?

WENDY: People began to postulate the existence of matter that we can't see. Dark matter— matter that doesn't emit light. But we can infer its presence because of its gravitational effect, which is increasing the velocity of stars—and these are motions that we *can* see.

ROBERT: But even with all the dark matter in the universe, there's still insufficient mass to achieve the so-called critical density (or closure density), which is a term astronomers use to define the total amount of matter needed to balance the force of the expansion. Anything *above* that value will eventually cause the universe to stop expanding.

WENDY: That's right. When we add up all the mass we can see, we can only get to about one percent of the critical density. Then we estimate how much dark matter there may be in the universe. As we go to larger scales—more and more galaxies, then clusters of galaxies—the more evidence you find of dark matter. There was a hope, especially in the 1980s, that when we got out to the largest scales, we'd find sufficient dark matter to achieve the critical density—since the universe seems to behave as though it's flat. But this hasn't happened.

ROBERT: What might dark matter be? There are several options and no consensus.

WENDY: Dark matter could be a number of things. It could be exotic particles, left over from the early formation of the universe. It could be failed stars [i.e., nonluminous brown dwarfs, star-like bodies whose low mass is insufficient to sustain thermonuclear reactions]. It could be neutron stars or black holes, although that doesn't seem to work.

ROBERT: How much dark matter have astronomers found relative to the critical density?

WENDY: We estimate that the total amount of matter in the universe is something like thirty percent of what would be required to achieve the critical density—most of it is dark matter; visible matter is only a small component of that. So, if our universe is at the critical density, then there's an extra seventy percent unaccounted for.

ROBERT: So what about that extra seventy percent?

ANDREI: Recent observations suggest that it may be in the form of a cosmological constant, which is actually vacuum energy—

LEON: Spooky matter.

ROBERT: Didn't Einstein say that the cosmological constant was his greatest mistake?

ANDREI: Yes.

ROBERT: Einstein imagined a cosmological constant as sort of a universal fudge factor, which he needed as a repelling force—of unknown origin—to balance the attractive force of gravitation, to prevent the universe from collapsing.

WENDY: Einstein did his work before we recognized the expansion of the universe.

FRANK: Einstein's equations clearly show that the universe had to be expanding. He did not accept his own equations, and so he adapted them to make the universe the way he wanted it philosophically.

ROBERT: So he put in a cosmological constant to balance gravity, to keep the universe on an even keel. What happened to the cosmological constant?

ANDREI: Many people tried to understand what the interpretations of this cosmological constant could be. The conclusion was that it was the energy of empty space, of the vacuum. Empty space, as strange as it sounds, may still have some energy density hidden in it. This is not forbidden by the laws of physics, so people tried to measure it. Well, this is the first kind of

> *Empty space, as strange as it sounds, may still have some energy density hidden in it.*

cosmological measurement where we are trying to calculate this energy of nothing, and it seems that it is not exactly zero. Although we can't be sure of the exact percentage right now, it looks like we may have the missing seventy percent of matter in this hidden state.

ROBERT: We talk as if the universe has a spring to it—a springiness, as well as a spookiness.

FRANK: If the cosmological constant were there, it would be pushing the universe apart faster and faster.

ROBERT: And that's what the data seem to show—that the expansion rate of the universe has been increasing over time.

WENDY: Yes. If you take the recent data at face value, that's what you'd conclude.

FRANK: In fact, I'm very dubious about taking the data at face value.

WENDY: We're working on the frontier, and we should stress that. These are very difficult measurements, and it will take a while before they're conclusive.

ROBERT: But isn't this recent data a major surprise? Astronomers seemed to like the notion of a harmonious universe finely balanced between rapid dissipation and compaction. But instead of showing what you might expect—that is, that the expansion is gradually slowing, because of the effects of gravity—the data seem to indicate that the expansion is actually getting faster and faster. How do you determine that?

WENDY: What happens is that we can look back in time. As we look farther away in distance, we are looking farther back in time. The more distant the object, the earlier the moment.

ROBERT: You're looking at history.

WENDY: Yes. And when we look locally—out to about sixty million light-years, say—we can see clearly that the universe is expanding. As we look farther out, we continue to see this expansion, and if we look back far enough, we should be able to see what the universe was doing early in its history. So if there's sufficient matter generating sufficient gravity, the universe will have been slowing down—decelerating over time because of gravity. However, if there is this cosmological constant, then the universe's expansion would actually be accelerating, and as a result the objects that we see further back will be dimmer than they would be if there were no acceleration. So what astronomers have done is to compare supernovae [i.e., very bright stars that exploded at the end of their lifetimes] in the far-distant universe with those in the nearby universe. And the distant supernovae do appear dimmer than you would expect if there hadn't been an acceleration of the expansion.

ROBERT: That's remarkable. Now, Leon, regarding the end of the universe, one phenomenon that physicists look for is the possible decay of stable elementary particles, such as protons.

LEON: The lifetime of a proton? At the moment, we don't know what it is, but we do have a limit to it.

ROBERT: Meaning that it's not less than such-and-such?

LEON: That's right. Protons seem to be much more stable than theorists would like. They'd like to see one decay, but they haven't.*

ROBERT: So that would indicate that protons, at least, will exist for a very long time, if not forever.

LEON: Well, the lightest particles are supposed to be stable, so electrons ought to be around forever, however long that is. But to return to the

---

Protons seem to be much more stable than theorists would like. They'd like to see one decay, but they haven't.

---

expansion rate—I think scientists are driven by the notion that they *want* the mass of the universe to be equal to the critical density.

WENDY: If the universe does not have enough mass (or density), it will continue to expand

---

*The lowest estimate for the half-life of a proton (the time it would take half of a given amount of protons to decay) is not less than 10^31 years (and rising in recent experiments)—or a thousand billion billion times the current age of the universe.

forever. If the mass (or density) is large enough, the expansion will be halted and the universe will ultimately collapse. The critical mass (density) is the mass (density) between the two [where the universe will *just barely* continue expanding forever, but at an ever-slowing rate— i.e., a flat universe].

LEON: The inflationary people like Omega to equal 1.

ROBERT: What is Omega?

FRANK: Omega is the symbol representing the density parameter in the universe; it's the ratio of the amount of matter actually present to the critical density.

ROBERT: OK. So if Omega is 1, then the universe is at the critical density.

LEON: But in order to get Omega to equal 1, they have constructed a fantastic cocktail. They say, "OK, there are stars, that's part of it. Then there's dark matter, which would include dark stars, planets, and exotic particles. Maybe we'll find some of those exotic particles in our accelerators." And even with all this dark matter, they still don't have enough matter to achieve the critical density, so they seize on Einstein's blunder, the cosmological constant.

WENDY: The other important point to make is that when you calculate what that cosmological constant should be, it's much bigger than what's being observed. The natural value is smaller than you would infer from calculating it.

ROBERT: Andrei, how does Omega, the density parameter, relate to the multi-universe theory of chaotic inflationary cosmology?

ANDREI: What we've been talking about is the energy density in [the observable] universe. The multi-universe picture is somewhat different. The question goes back to where and how the universe began. Our new picture of it is inflationary cosmology—an extremely fast expansion of the universe in a kind of vacuum-like state, driven by a specific form of energy called a "scalar field." The energy of this scalar field had the same kind of outward force as Einstein's cosmological constant. As it [this scalar field] slowly decreased, some quantum fluctuations in [it] were responsible for later galaxy formation. But what inflation also predicts is that sometimes these quantum fluctuations become so large that they increase the local body of this cosmological constant, so to speak. And by increasing it, they make the universe [in that local region] expand exponentially faster. These events are also exponentially improbable, but once you jump, you are exponentially rewarded by [a vast amount] of new space, which you get. [See Chapter 26, Figures 1 and 2.]

ROBERT: And each one of those exponentially improbable jumps can breed a new and different universe?

ANDREI: Right.

ROBERT: Frank, how can multiple universes be compatible with your Omega Point—your theory that the universe will come back to a final singularity and just before that everyone will be resurrected? Won't we get lost?

FRANK: Well, multiple universes directly contradict the Omega Point. If Andrei is right, then I am wrong. That's the way physics is. If one of us is right, then one of us is wrong.

ROBERT: Of course, you both could be wrong. In fact, the only thing we know for sure is that you both can't be right.

FRANK: Yes. It's interesting that we now have theorists and experimentalists on each side. I keep whirling around. The data will eventually correct all of us. But if the expansion of the universe is accelerating, then of course the universe

---

> *If Andrei is right, then I am wrong. That's the way physics is.*

---

will never come back to a final singularity. I think it's something of a misnomer to call that a Big Crunch, or a "fry," as Nancey termed it, because that's looking at the universe from an anthropocentric point of view.

ROBERT: That's what it looks like to me.

FRANK: If humans were there, building things, that's what it would look like, but we have to remember—

ROBERT: If you were there, what would you see?

FRANK: If I were there, I would be vaporized and tossed into nonexistence. But that's if I were there at what we call in computer science the lowest level of implementation [i.e., in the flesh].

ROBERT: You'd never get caught like that.

FRANK: What would happen is that as the universe contracted, things would get hotter and hotter. But it would be possible for [far-advanced intelligence] to use the energy of contraction itself to build devices that survive the unlimited heat. So, from the point of view of a more reasonable timescale, the actual experiences that life would have between the resurrection and the final state would be literally infinite. Now, the reason I'm very dubious about an ever-expanding universe—besides the fact that it contradicts my theory—is that if you have an ever-expanding universe, you will have black holes evaporating.* Now, the problem with having black holes evaporating *to completion* is that it violates a fundamental law of quantum mechanics called unitarity.

ROBERT: Nancey, is your theological perspective compatible with an infinitely growing universe and/or with an ultimately contracting universe?

NANCEY: You started out by asking why high school students, or people in general, should care about all of this. And what we're asking from a theological perspective is, Why should the human species care? Most of these scenarios are so far beyond what we can project for the longevity of *Homo sapiens* that they're irrelevant.

ROBERT: But they're not irrelevant to our conception of what human beings are and what our purpose may be in the cosmos.

---

*Black holes are the densest conceivable form of matter, formed by the gravitational collapse of large stars in their final stages. No imaginable force can stop their contraction and the gravitation force is so strong that not even light can escape. All the mass of a black hole is concentrated into a single point, called a "singularity," where mass has no volume and space and time stop. Black holes were conceived by theory but confirmed by observation. It is believed that supermassive black holes, perhaps with the mass of a billion suns, sit in the center of galaxies. Black holes are thought to evaporate in a process known as Hawking radiation, but there is disagreement over whether or not they are immortal.

FRANK: I've argued the very promise that we'll be blown back into existence [at the penultimate moment just before the Big Crunch].

NANCEY: Right. Frank's point of view is in fact relevant to that [why-should-we-care] question. But the more general questions raised in cosmology—about whether the universe is open and expanding or closed and contracting, or whatever—are fairly irrelevant to the human species.

ROBERT: Well, I disagree. Endtime cosmology may be irrelevant to what happens to us individually, but it may help classify, clarify, limit, enhance, or purge human purpose or position in the cosmos. If we define progress as progression toward truth, even nullification of human purpose or position would be progress.

NANCEY: But if we simply cease to exist—literally go out of existence, without any trace left of us—it doesn't really matter how that happens, does it?

ROBERT: If we ultimately vanish and that, indeed, is the last out of the last game, then, sure, nothing else really matters. But the fact that we human beings may soon understand what actually happens at cosmology's ultimate end would mark us as unique beings—participants, in a way.* And that, I think, may be terribly relevant.

---

*Lawrence Krauss and Glenn Starkman speculate in their article "The Fate of Life in the Universe" (*Scientific American*, November 1999) that about one hundred trillion years from now, the last conventionally formed stars will wink out, that black holes will consume galaxies in about 10^{20} years (10^{30} years after the Big Bang) and that galactic black holes dissipate in about 10^{88} years.

NANCEY: Well, yes, but that doesn't have any particular theological significance over and above what most of science does. Another way to ask the question is, What does all of this cosmology look like from God's point of view?

ROBERT: I won't ask Frank; I'll ask you.

NANCEY: I'm attracted to Andrei [Linde]'s conception of multiple universes, because one would be tempted to ask what happens to God if

---

What's God going to do for the rest of eternity?

---

our little universe ceases to exist. Or, if it ceases to have any life in it, with whom would God interact? What's God going to do for the rest of eternity?

LEON: Unemployment. He will want to avoid that at all costs.

NANCEY: That's right.

FRANK: But what bothers me about Andrei [Linde]'s universe is that it seems to be a resurrection of the Steady State theory, in which on the largest possible scales nothing much happens. Everything is sort of constantly reproduced.

ROBERT: Andrei, you've now had someone claim that your multiple universes are a God-sent remedy for God's own ennui and someone else allege that it's just the outmoded Steady State model dressed up in modern language. You're the man—what does it look like to you?

ANDREI: First of all, I should perhaps take a more modest position and say that this is not my

universe. This is the standard prediction of the standard inflationary theory, which is widely accepted by many cosmologists who actually work in this field.

LEON: Just because Frank [Tipler] is in the minority doesn't mean he's right.

FRANK: Nor does it mean I'm wrong.

ROBERT: Andrei, are all of your universes, however many fractal bubbles there may be, the totality of reality?

ANDREI: That's a very hard question. Our discussions here are using the language of normal particles. Meanwhile, over the last fifteen years or so, we've started to learn that maybe nature should be discussed in terms of string theory, and this could produce quite unexpected outcomes. For example, suppose that our universe is collapsing and it comes to a state of singularity, a single point, which would mean the end of everything. From the point of view of string theory, it could mean the beginning of a different phase.

ROBERT: String theory being that minuscule, vibrating strings are theorized to be the fundamental stuff underlying all energy, matter, and forces, including gravity—

ANDREI: Yes, instead of the universe consisting of point-like objects, it fundamentally consists of these extremely tiny string-like objects. And when the universe is collapsing, the question is whether the collapse is the end of everything or just the end of the stage where you can easily apply the old prestring theory. Now, with string theory, when you come close enough to this point of singularity, you see there is no singularity. There are some people who call this the pre–Big Bang theory. My point is that when we speak about the end of the universe as a whole, we can run into trouble if we use simple language rather than the mathematical models of physics.

ROBERT: Nancey, cosmologists are now talking about the beginning and the end of the universe—things that theologians have talked about for thousands of years. Doesn't that excite you?

NANCEY: Yes, it does, because it gets people thinking about human destiny and raises the sorts of questions that religion sets out to answer. But most of what's being said here is genuinely irrelevant to what Christians have been saying over the centuries, because Christians are talking about the way this whole universe, however the physicists describe it, is going to be transformed afterward.

ROBERT: And that afterward would occur when?

NANCEY: Well, that's not clear. The scriptures, which are all we've got to go on, speak about last things in highly imaginative picture language and don't set out any chronology of events. The Bible doesn't tell us how long the human race is going to last—a million years, or a thousand years, or whatever. It just tells us that it's all going to end up good. And we have rich, literary descriptions of what that goodness consists of. But no account of the time line.

ROBERT: Does this all sound pretty good to you, Leon?

LEON: Sounds wonderful, though it's somewhat above my salary level. But it seems to me that we have a working theory of the origin of the universe that is somewhat consistent with the data. We have lots of things we have to learn about it, and we will learn them. Our progress has been very good, and in a hundred years from now, maybe the Theory of Everything will tell us how the universe began and how the laws of physics dictated this particular expansion and brought us eventually to galaxies and stars and one inconsequential solar system, with one minor planet out of whose oceans we crawled. If all of this emerges from the Theory of Everything, that theory also ought to be able to predict the conditions at the end of the physical universe. Humanity will not be around to bear witness to it, because all kinds of rather unpleasant things will happen first.

ROBERT: That's the Standard Model, if you will, of current cosmology.

LEON: That's the Standard Model. But I don't think that means we should be discouraged, because everything we've created—our institutions, our passions, our loves, our enthusiasms—will continue for the foreseeable future.

ROBERT: Wendy, do you ever think about theological issues when you're looking at photographs and data from the heavens?

WENDY: I think when you look at the heavens, it's hard not to have a sense of wonder and amazement that we live in a universe that we can describe by physical laws, and we can ask questions and make predictions about its origin and ultimate state. I agree with Leon [Lederman]; ultimately we may come to a theory that will allow us to describe those things. I don't like the name—the Theory of Everything—

because it will describe only a particular set of things and will have to be linked to other unsolved problems such as consciousness.

ROBERT: Do you discuss these issues with theologians or people interested in the nature of consciousness or religion?

WENDY: Yes, I do. It's an area where there's still room to interpret things as you would like to interpret things. And so we ask them, What came before? Where were the laws of physics? What was the universe? Science doesn't offer an answer to those questions, but what's interesting is that we're at a point where we can come to these questions in very different ways.

ROBERT: Project forward a hundred years. It's not quite Frank's Omega Point, but genetic engineering has enabled us to reconvene. Will there be a final theory of what will happen at the end of the universe?

FRANK: I think there will be. Obviously, I'm going to think that we'll have moved toward acceptance of the Omega Point theory. The reason is that Andrei [Linde] and his colleagues are inventing new forces in physics to accomplish his inflation mechanism, whereas tried-and-tested physics—actual forces that Leon [Lederman] has seen in the lab—leads inexorably to the Omega Point theory. The known laws of physics are sufficient to tell us what the future of the universe will be. If the universe were to expand forever, then black-hole evaporation would give rise to a violation of a very fundamental law of quantum mechanics. I'm sure that can't happen. That's why I'm confident that the universe will expand to a maximum size and then contract into a final singularity.

NANCEY: I'm intrigued by the fact that Frank [Tipler]'s book is attacked as vehemently by theologians as it is by scientists.

FRANK: Not by Wolfhart Pannenberg, the famous German theologian.

NANCEY: Quite right. But I'm not sure whether to judge cosmological theories on the basis of their theological acceptance or rejection. This is not something that a theologian can speak to—unless, of course, the end of the world in my sense of the term comes sooner than a hundred years from now, but I doubt it.

ANDREI: If we want to understand the end of everything, then we should first understand the end of each and every one of us. In particular, we need to understand the nature of consciousness, which has been outside the bounds of our discussion [but not of other discussions; see Chapters 1, 2, and 3]. I do think that scientists must attack the problem of consciousness much more seriously than they do right now and not insist that in order to describe consciousness the only thing we need to know is how to describe electrons and protons, and so forth.

ROBERT: *Closer to Truth* oscillates between cosmology and consciousness, because these are the two critical questions of human understanding.

ANDREI: First of all, I don't think that the universe as a whole is going to collapse. Second, it seems to have little practical consequence for us personally, because our part of the universe must disappear one way or another. And this may require that we consider other things, ideas that Nancey [Murphy] thinks about. After all, even all the multi-universes may still not be the whole thing. What about our perception of the universe, our consciousness, our life? From my perspective, these are much more difficult phenomena to understand than the universe and perhaps, in some specific sense, may encompass it.

WENDY: As a scientist, I can't predict the future, other than anticipating continued incremental solutions to many of these unsolved problems. I don't know what the timescale will be for solving them; it may be a hundred years, it may be a thousand years. If I were to take a guess, the question of how the universe will end may be one of the questions we will debate for a long time, because I think we're getting to the point where many of these ideas can't be tested—where you can propose theories or make predictions that aren't amenable to scientific test. However, we're now addressing questions that weren't even possible to conceive of a hundred years ago. Our ideas about the universe have changed that dramatically, and I think we'll continue to learn dramatic things about the universe.

LEON: I'm close to that. At the moment, if you take all the data and the best synthesis, the expansion will continue, entropy will increase, heat will die. On the other hand, in a hundred years, if our educational system improves, we'll have thousands of brilliant scientists who will think hard about this question, so that maybe there will be some alternatives. There are already fragmentary ideas about totally different alternatives for the future.

ROBERT: So you want to make a lot more Wendy Freedmans.

LEON: I'm in favor of that.

ANDREI: There are some theories about the possibility of creating a universe in a laboratory. And that's not science fiction.

LEON: Be very careful.

FRANK: It involves laws of physics that have never been seen.

LEON: One of the things we're leaving out is the scientific design of human evolution. This growing knowledge of our biology is going to have an impact on all facets of our understanding, including how much we find out about the universe. It's unforeseeable, so I'm not going to say any more about it.

ROBERT: CONCLUDING COMMENT

The fate of the universe: it's the question that makes you take a deep breath. Current theories seem clear enough. Either there is enough matter for gravity to reverse the universe's expansion and cause the Big Crunch, compacting everything back into a singularity, or there is not enough matter, and the universe will expand forever, evaporating into nothingness. The latest data not only supports the unstoppable expansion but also suggests an accelerating expansion. Space, it seems, has some spring to it, increasing the outward rush. And just when we think we cannot be any more astonished, cosmologists whack us again, this time with multi-universes—perhaps an infinite number of universes, each bringing forth new universes, continually, endlessly, all of them somehow co-existing in the totality of reality. Remember what Einstein said about the universe: "Make it as simple as possible, but not simpler." Cosmological problems are overwhelming, but I'm oddly preoccupied with something else. How is it that we humans have such vast understanding after only a few thousand years of historical consciousness and a scant few hundred years of effective science? Maybe it's still too early in the game. Maybe answers have been with us all along. Some say that the more we learn about the universe, the more pointless it becomes. Not me. The further we look, the closer we get to truth.

OUTTAKES

LEON: *What's the crew laughing at?*

WENDY: *That was such a funny line.*

CHAPTER 28

Will Intelligence Fill the Universe?

In the fullness of time, there are three megaquestions that speak directly to the issues of human uniqueness, purpose, and destiny. 1) Does intelligent life exist anywhere else in the universe? 2) Will human beings ultimately spread across the galaxies and colonize the cosmos? 3) Is it an accident or a necessity that conscious, self-aware creatures like us have appeared in this universe? No questions carry greater meaning. Any real answers would change us forever. And here to suggest answers are people who know what they're talking about. But be prepared for some surprises from our distinguished guests.

PARTICIPANTS

Dr. Francisco Ayala, the Donald Bren professor of evolutionary genetics at the University of California, Irvine, is a leading thinker in biology and philosophy. Francisco believes that human-like intelligence is a unique event that will never repeat itself in the history of the universe.

Dr. Gregory Benford brings the dual perspective of a working astrophysicist and a leading science fiction writer to the question of life in the universe. Greg envisions the human species colonizing the galaxies.

Dr. Leon Lederman, who is the author of *From Quarks to the Cosmos,* received the Nobel Prize in physics for his work on the fundamental structure of matter. Given the odds, Leon thinks the existence of intelligent alien life is likely.

Dr. Bruce Murray, a professor of planetary science and geology at the California Institute of Technology, is president (and cofounder with Carl Sagan) of The Planetary Society. Bruce believes that intelligent life exists elsewhere in the universe—and that we should and will find it.

Dr. Frank Tipler, a professor of mathematics and physics at Tulane, has often written on questions of universal purpose and destiny. Frank believes that human beings are special and that if other intelligent beings existed, they would have reached us by now.

ROBERT: Greg, as an astrophysicist and science fiction writer, you must often think about space travel. Do you believe that it is the destiny of human beings to colonize our galaxy and ultimately the whole universe?

GREG: Pretty much. Our species has always, as its main virtue, tried to move into new territories, take up new life sites—and I don't think anything's going to stop that.

ROBERT: Bruce, The Planetary Society supports the search for extraterrestrial intelligence, or SETI. What's the likelihood that intelligent life exists anywhere in the universe? And will we ever make contact?

BRUCE: I certainly think it must exist elsewhere; we're not some kind of scientific miracle here. That's an intuitive belief that I can't justify analytically. As far as whether we'll make contact—in the fullness of time, certainly.

ROBERT: Leon, why do most astronomers believe that intelligent life must be abundant in the universe?

LEON: It's a question of numbers—stars, planets, the likelihood of life formation, and so on— the workings of sheer chance with innumerable possibilities, even though our own existence on this planet is miraculous, in the sense of its low probability. Our judgment is that there are enough opportunities out there that intelligent life, broadly defined, is very likely.

ROBERT: Francisco, you're an evolutionary biologist who tracks the flow of genetic information. Why is the question of alien intelligence usually addressed by physicists and astronomers? Why aren't we biologists asked? Don't the physicists think we're smart enough?

FRANCISCO: Because when we answer, we answer no—that's why they don't ask us. For me it's an easy no, since intelligent life is a biological improbability. My answer would be like Leon [Lederman]'s—it's the numbers. The numbers make human beings a unique historical contingency that will not repeat itself in the history of the universe.

ROBERT: You're saying that the numbers—the probabilities—support the notion that human beings are unique, and Leon is saying, representing many physicists and astronomers, that the numbers suggest that there must be other intelligent life.

FRANCISCO: No, the numbers we're using are not the same numbers—mine are a different order of magnitude.

ROBERT: Frank, you're a cosmologist and co-author [with British astronomer John Barrow] of *The Cosmological Anthropic Principle,* in which you claim that the universe is uniquely suited for self-aware life. Define the anthropic principle in the context of alien intelligence.

FRANK: The anthropic principle has several different meanings, one of which is just as a selection principle—that is, obviously we have to live in a universe that permits our sort of life to exist (see Chapter 26). But I have to agree with Francisco [Ayala]; even though I'm a physicist, I think he's correct that the likelihood that intelligent life has evolved elsewhere in the cosmos is very small—in spite of the huge numbers that Leon [Lederman] correctly mentions. The number of stars in the visible universe is about one to the twenty-second power [a one followed by twenty-two zeros]. But in spite of the gigantic size of this number, if you multiply it by the probability of intelligence evolving on a planet orbiting any one of them, you still get a number substantially less than 1.

ROBERT: Francisco, what is it about intelligent biological systems that makes their improbability exceed the gigantic number of opportunities in the universe?

FRANCISCO: Start thinking about what we are and how we came about. The history of life in the universe is like a colossal bush, and we are a teeny-weenie twig at the extremity. Life on Earth began more than three and a half billion years ago. It was microscopic for most of its history—up to about one billion years ago. Then multicellular organisms came about, and for ninety percent of their history there were no mammals. Then came the mammals, and for 99.9 percent of their history, there were no human beings. So you have thousands and thousands of branches dependent on millions and millions of events. If any one of them were changed along the way, we would not be here.

ROBERT: Could other branches and events have produced a different kind of intelligence?

FRANCISCO: They didn't.

ROBERT: Certainly not here.

FRANCISCO: So that proves its improbability. We are here because we happened. And all prior events happen to have happened, and had to have happened.

ROBERT: That's the one thing we know for sure.

FRANCISCO: But any change in this long chain of contingent events would not have produced human beings—or beings of any kind that we would recognize as intelligent. You have the immense improbabilities—on the order of 10^{-22}, multiplied again and again and again. So no matter how many stars there are in the universe, and how many universes there are, there are no other human beings.

BRUCE: I'm a geologist, so I'll give the geological perspective compared to the biological; and from my point of view this progression you mentioned of the development of different life-forms results in a couple of conclusions. One, there are no scientific miracles at all; we don't see anything that requires some kind of special event, like two stars passing close together. Everything we see is plausible, including the formation of the earth itself, now that we have space and meteorite information. And second—and I think this is an overriding perspective—we ourselves appear very early in the process. Let me give you an analogy. If I'm out hiking, and I see a bunch of ants crawling around, the ants seem to have a kind of intelligence, they have behavior patterns, they may have some kind of self-awareness. But there's no way that an ant could imagine the kinds of things in my mind and heart. I have far more awareness of the way the world is, of what's out there. Yet I consider myself a very primitive being—an ant, as it were—compared to what's really out there, to what's really necessary to understand things. The consequence of this is twofold. First, there's humility. But second, you become very suspicious of closed arguments—that is, "I know all there is to know, and therefore I can prove x is impossible." We're not smart enough to make that statement.

ROBERT: Greg, what is the Drake equation?

GREG: It's a basic argument that predicts the likelihood of intelligent civilizations in the galaxy by multiplying together a bunch of probabilities, all of which, of course, are crude estimates. Start with the number of stars that form, multiply that by the probability they'll have planets, multiply that by the probability that a planet will give rise to life, and so forth.* We've become increasingly tough in our estimates of the last term in the equation, which is how long civilizations last. Ours has lasted a few thousand years—I hope that's not the upper bound.

ROBERT: Francisco, which of the terms do you attack?

FRANCISCO: The ones that go from simple life to intelligence and civilizations. I'm willing

to accept simple life in many places in the universe, but not intelligent life.

ROBERT: So you differentiate sharply between the existence of life and the presence of intelligent, self-aware life.

FRANCISCO: Right. The existence of life I'm willing to accept. But the existence of intelligent life, the kind with which we could communicate, is what I object to. The reason is that it's so highly improbable. You know, Bruce [Murray] was speaking of scientific miracles. I'm not speaking about any miracles. We aren't a miracle, we're just highly improbable. He was saying that I'm therefore concluding that alien human-level intelligence is impossible. It's not impossible, it's just highly improbable. But the probabilities against it are so high that no matter how many universes are there, you still won't have it.

ROBERT: Greg [Benford] is the one guy here whom I haven't yet interrogated about whether he believes in the existence of intelligent alien life.

GREG: I noticed that. I think there may be a very large number of intelligent—

---

*The Drake equation, a way to estimate the number of technologically advanced civilizations in our Milky Way galaxy that might be broadcasting signals, was conceived by Dr. Frank Drake, a radio astronomer who is now president of the SETI Institute, headquartered in Mountain View, California. The equation is given as $N = R_* \cdot f_p \cdot n_e \cdot f_l \cdot f_i \cdot f_c \cdot L$, where N is the number of communicative civilizations whose radio emissions would be detectable; R_* is the rate of formation of suitable stars in the galaxy with a large enough "habitable zone" and long-enough lifetime to allow for the development of intelligent life (estimated at between two and twenty per year); f_p is the fraction of suitable stars with planetary systems

(recently increased to fifty percent, encouraging SETI people); n_e is the number of Earth-like planets located within a habitable zone (where the temperature would allow water to exist as a liquid, assuming it's essential for life); f_l is the fraction of those planets on which life actually begins; f_i is the fraction of these life-bearing planets on which some form of intelligence arises; f_c is the fraction of those intelligent species that develop sufficient technology and are able and desirous of communicating with alien civilizations; and L is the average number of years (lifetime) that a communicative civilization broadcasts detectable signals into space. The terms $f_l, f_i, f_c,$ and L are the most difficult and controversial to estimate.

ROBERT: Not just to promote your science fiction books?

GREG: Oh, sure, it's that too. But seriously, one of the numbers we forget about is that Earth is a young planet, and that most of the stars in the galaxy formed before our sun. Planets around those other stars have had more time to work on the evolution of higher intelligence. If there's a certain down payment you have to make for intelligence, you have to develop a significant nervous system. On Earth, we didn't get into this brain game until roughly half a billion years ago. But other parts of the galaxy may have been players five billion years ago.

ROBERT: Therefore?

GREG: They've had a lot of time to work on this problem, meaning that chance has had a much longer run there than it has here. Based on the numbers, intelligent alien life is just not doubtful.

FRANK: We can use those same numbers to conclude the exact opposite, because if those other stars and planetary systems are billions of years ahead of us, and if what you say is correct, then because interstellar travel isn't particularly difficult, those beings would have reached us long ago.

BRUCE: That's another argument. I'll take you up on that.

FRANK: I've got two arguments, one entirely from physics and one from biology.

LEON: No, your argument is weak, because if we're talking about intelligence, then they may have decided they didn't want to come here.

FRANK: Well, they wouldn't have the choice. The number-one feature of life itself, arising from its exponential growth, is the desire to expand.

LEON: Lower life-forms may want to expand, but more sophisticated life may not.

FRANK: But intelligent life, in order to survive, has no choice. For example, our sun is going to leave the main star sequence in five billion years. That means the sun will expand outward and consume Earth. If future beings have not left Earth, they're going to be destroyed. So because the crucial behavioral characteristic of life is survival—

ROBERT: —they must seek to travel in space, assuming they exist. Bruce?

BRUCE: I come at this from a different point of view, having been involved in deep-space programs. And I've had to ask myself, What are the limits? How far out in space can we go? And it turns out, because the universe is so thinly populated with stars, that [to get anywhere] you have to travel at speeds approaching the speed of light.

ROBERT: Easy, for civilizations with millions or even billions of years' head start.

BRUCE: Well, it's not been easy so far. It gets to be a complicated, energy-intensive process. And where are you going to go? We just got through saying that there are billions of stars out there. You can't just go from one to another the way they do in a TV movie. No. You're only going to go—*if* you go at all—to a place that you already know is inhabited.

FRANK: Advanced civilizations could use self-replicating probes. They would send a robot probe to a nearby star to explore that solar system and also make copies of itself. These robot copies would go to other solar systems and replicate again, which would then produce other copies to send to other solar systems [and thus geometrically expand the volume of exploration relatively rapidly].

BRUCE: How do you know it has to happen that way? There's no way of knowing. No, of

---

How do you know it has to happen that way? There's no way of knowing. No, of course not! You have no way of knowing.

---

course not! You have no way of knowing. There's absolutely no way that process would work.

FRANK: Just as you can tell that our Earth is an inhabited planet from a hundred light-years away, by means of the strong [spectrographic] oxygen line, advanced intelligent life, when it moves out, would start to control the environment [in places that it landed]. Robots would obviously not need to create oxygen, but they would start to remake the solar systems in various ways.

ROBERT: Some people have said that you can make the assumption that it would take an intelligent civilization about a thousand years to travel one light-year. Does that seem to make sense? One thousand years for every light-year of distance?

BRUCE: I think that number may come from a different calculation. That's the idea that the

species itself is spreading out and occupying new sites. Not just sending probes.

ROBERT: OK, if that's true, then consider that our current galaxy, with a few hundred billion stars, is about seventy thousand light-years in diameter. So in about seventy million years—seventy thousand times a thousand; say a hundred million, to round up—any civilization in our galaxy, theoretically, could have visited us. And in galactic history, a hundred million years is a small fraction of the available time.

FRANK: Even with current rocket technologies, a thousand years per light-year is doable, so that, as you say, in only about a hundred million years an exploratory, self-replicating civilization would have covered the galaxy.

ROBERT: But that doesn't prove your point, Frank—the negative evidence of visitations doesn't justify the positive assertion that alien intelligence doesn't exist. As Leon said, they may not want to come here, especially after they've seen this show.

LEON: Extrapolation won't work. What Frank [Tipler]'s neglecting are technological advances beyond anything we can now imagine that might change this intelligent system in such a

---

It's much easier to communicate than it is to travel.

---

dramatic way that travel would be one of these obsolete customs you see in ancient movies. It's much easier to communicate than it is to travel.

FRANK: Still, there are limited resources in any planetary system.

ROBERT: I want to get a biologist's take.

FRANCISCO: We have six billion people in the world. Let's assume that we have six billion times six billion people, and let me ask the following question. What is the probability that two human individuals, born from two unrelated sets of parents, will be genetically identical? I can make that calculation, and the probability is effectively zero. The probability that intelligent life would arise independently of the way it has arisen on Earth is even less probable than that. So what I conclude is that it's zero.

ROBERT: But aren't you limiting your definition of intelligence to human-like life and basing your calculations on DNA sequences?

FRANCISCO: That's right. I have defined intelligent life as the kind that we can communicate with and understand. They'd need self-awareness and some kind of language.

ROBERT: Certainly our form of intelligent life does want to explore space. The only arguments are over what we can afford and how we allocate limited resources. The issue, Bruce, that you've addressed often is, Should it be carbon or silicon? Should we explore space with human beings, who are very expensive to take on space rides, or with robots?

BRUCE: Both are involved so far. And that's natural, because we have barely become civilized on a geological timescale, so we're basically the same kind of animal that once hunted on the plains of Africa. Physically doing things, going out and exploring, is deeply embedded in our genes and will continue to be. But now our brains have produced, in just this remarkable century, an enormous breakthrough in informa-

tion technology and robotics. Robots are better at this than the best of our astronauts—by at least a factor of 2. So there's no question what the future holds. The future is mostly robotic, controlled by our intelligence, our attitudes, and our command systems.

FRANK: Imprinted in the robots themselves? Artificial intelligence?

BRUCE: Perhaps. But in any case it's a symbiotic relationship between us, as highly evolved animals, and these new things, these intelligent machines.

ROBERT: Project into the future.

BRUCE: I'm talking about the future. Earth itself will get more like this, intermixing humans and machines. We're in the middle of an enormous transition, I think the most significant, in an anthropological sense, in human history—that's my gist. But when you say that there's no one out there because they don't come flying across the universe the way they do in our science fiction movies, I just say that you have a very limited view of the future, because it's much easier to use robotics and communications.

ROBERT: You're doing that, though. You're actually involved in listening. Tell us about SETI.

BRUCE: Right. Good point. So after we've debated whether intelligent alien life exists, after we each give our gut feelings, after Francisco [Ayala] and I disagree, then we do the experiment, then we search for real data. Well, the experiment is just beginning. First of all, because star systems are so very far apart, the only kind of signal we could receive is one that is intended to be received. It must be a beacon. It can't be an accident. We're not going to get random interstellar communications; we're not going to get the *I Love Lucy* version on Alpha Centauri. What we'd get would be a civilization that wants to communicate with us—one that has spent a lot of its money to build an omnidirectional beacon, for example. That's what people are looking for now, with the microwave. An omnidirectional beacon. It's a very inefficient way to go, so an alien civilization could easily say, "Let's wait another hundred years; these people will get smarter, have more receivers in space, and know a lot more about communications. And then they'll find the signal that we want them to find"—if they want us to find them at all. It could be a primer for entry into the galactic community. So the assertion that since we haven't had any alien visits, therefore there isn't any alien intelligence—when there are so many other possibilities—means nothing.

ROBERT: Frank, how do these two questions relate to the anthropic principle—whether there's intelligent life elsewhere in the universe, and whether human beings will ultimately colonize the cosmos?

FRANK: I think that what science will tell us is that Francisco [Ayala] has given the correct biological answer—that we are alone in the cosmos. But I also think that life will expand out from this planet—particularly robots, which although primitive now will ultimately be the form of life that will spread out into the cosmos—and ultimately take over the universe.

ROBERT: How does that reflect back on the anthropic principle? Is there some precursor design working here?

FRANK: Well, this eventual colonization of the universe is actually locked into the laws of physics; in other words, the laws of physics are

such that this will inevitably happen. I think that you have to have intelligent life near the end of the universe for the very consistency of the laws of physics themselves.

ROBERT: That's a controversial position, to be polite.

LEON: Yes, it is. Ask Francisco [Ayala] what the influence of natural selection would be in this context. Even if you believe that there's a huge reservoir of life in the universe, wouldn't natural selection [play a critical role]? Assuming the laws of physics are the same out there as they are here, which we believe, then even if the circumstances are very unusual, that makes physics conducive to the evolution of life, which would be everywhere.

ROBERT: Must natural selection and the abundance of life ultimately produce some kind of human-level intelligence?

FRANCISCO: No.

FRANK: Why are you so equivocal?

FRANCISCO: Natural selection is only part of the story. Some organisms reproduce more than others, and those that do will, so to speak, conquer the earth. But what directs natural selection to make some organisms reproduce better than others? There's a tremendous diversity of genes, which is what I was taking into account in considering the improbability of having two identical human genotypes. And then you have the additional complexity of the environment; each minute of each environment is different, and it's different everywhere in the world. You have different genetics, different environments. So you cannot possibly have the same intelligence anywhere.

ROBERT: But couldn't we find a different kind of intelligence in the cosmos? Are we being too humanocentric?

FRANCISCO: Yes. But it would have to be a kind of intelligence with which we can communicate. It would have to have some kind of nervous system comparable to ours and some form of language.

ROBERT: It has to be able to communicate, sure, though its nervous system doesn't have to be comparable.

BRUCE: That might be a transition phase also.

ROBERT: What would an alien civilization need so that you could detect its signals on your current systems?

BRUCE: They'd need a technology capacity and the motive and will to build a communication system whose broadcasts can be received by our enfeebled early-detection devices here; they'd have to use some obvious signals, so we'd know it wasn't background noise. Signals that would be enough to demonstrate that they exist.

ROBERT: What kind of signals would be obviously artificial?

BRUCE: Our favorite is a very-narrow-band frequency, because any natural process with any natural temperature will generate broad frequencies. And they'd have more sophisticated elements. I'd put a funny modulation on there: on, off, on, off, off, off, on, on. That's not likely to happen normally.

ROBERT: What about consistent signatures of matter identical throughout the universe, such as emission lines, that any intelligent civilization would recognize as a signal?

GREG: There's an argument that you should look near natural frequencies, like hydroxyl or water lines—things like that.

BRUCE: Carl Sagan did this with the images sent out on *Voyager* [i.e., two spacecraft, launched in 1977, that toured the outer planets and then became the first human-made objects to escape the solar system and journey into deep space]. The assumption is that hydrogen-line emissions would be known by any intelligent civilization, and so all other information, such as numbers, are set in relationship to it.

FRANK: Let me say something about sending signals. This proposal was made a hundred years ago, by an astronomer at Harvard named Pickering. He wanted to communicate with Martians, who everyone thought were there. They were going to build a huge dish, a mile across, to send light pulses. Now the problem, of course, was that there were no Martians. In recent years, as we know, we've sent robotic probes to Mars with great advantage. The robot probes can tell you something about your target systems that signals can't.

ROBERT: Leon, can there be noncarbon, nonbiological intelligence?

LEON: Conceivably there can be, though we can't evaluate the probability. And there are neutron stars—collapsed cores of exploded stars—that are vast accumulations of very, very dense nuclear matter. Processes in these neutron stars take place a million or more times faster than in our chemically based biological systems. Could these enormously fast reactions possibly generate enough complexity to begin the evolution of intelligent life? Surely, such intelligence would be radically different, and although they might have interesting ideas, they'd be hard to communicate with, because one second of our time would be many, many, many generations of their time—so while we're discussing something, they would have the rise and fall of the Roman Empire.

ROBERT: Rapidly spinning neutron stars called pulsars broadcast enormously strong signals.

GREG: I used to work on pulsar radiation. And everyone was always wondering if in fact they were artificial beacons. They are very powerful.

BRUCE: The important point that Leon [Lederman] brings out is that there could be systems in which natural evolution might work a million times faster than in this creaky old biological world of ours. And because the rates of processes are much higher, the probabilities of producing intelligence are also much higher on any given timescale. So we ought to realize how ignorant we are before we close out possibilities. I want to pick on ignorance, because that's what we have to start with: We must recognize how little we understand, compared to all there is to understand. And we've been futzing around in this discussion, talking about a miraculous Earth-centered life. That's the biblical view of the origin of life.

FRANCISCO: No. It's not what I was saying—

BRUCE: What you're both [Francisco Ayala and Frank Tipler] arguing is that intelligence only happened here. That it has happened nowhere else. If that's not the religious view, it bears extreme similarity. Don't reject what I'm saying. Leon [Lederman] is saying, "Well, maybe we can have other kinds of thinking things evolving." And that's all right, in some sense. The point is—what *this* is, really—is an argument about God. This is about meaning, about the whole enchilada. And my point of

view is that we are so primitive ourselves—as recognizing, thinking machines—that we shouldn't expect to come up with strong answers to these questions. But the fact that we can conceive of some universal principle, or some universal connectedness, and sense some meaning in it, is itself a reflection of our basic approach—whether as a religious believer, or as a nuclear physicist, or as a geologist. It's the same sense that there must be something here that's larger than us, in our current primitive scratchings.

FRANCISCO: The problem I have, Bruce [Murray], is that I know how to multiply. And I have to multiply with probabilities, which has nothing to do with miracles, nothing to do with religious views. It does have to do with the example that I gave you: What is the probability that two human beings, engendered by separate parents, will be genetically identical? Zero. It makes no reference to religion, none to miracles. It's just simply a matter of probabilities.

ROBERT: What I find fascinating, Francisco [Ayala], is that people take what you say—which is clearly nonreligious, nonmiraculous—and interpret it to suggest religious overtones. Doesn't this suggest that we are beings who crave meaning? Wherever it comes from, this search for meaning is pandemic. I crave that. Do you crave that?

FRANCISCO: Absolutely. But you see, meaning is something that we need sometimes. And that's wonderful.

ROBERT: Just because we need meaning doesn't make it less real. (Or more real.)

FRANCISCO: Absolutely. I don't think science is all there is to the universe. There's art, aesthetics, ethics, all sorts of other things that are real—and that's what I crave.

ROBERT: There's nothing miraculous about art, aesthetics, ethics, but they are all based on human consciousness and self-awareness, which are the instruments of search for such meaning. Project forward, how will this human craving—this search for mearning—develop?

GREG: Well, certainly Bruce [Murray] is right. We are searching for meaning, but this is the first inning of the game, and I, too, have a dislike of arguments that close out possibilities. We ought to realize that it's a big universe out there, it's been around a long time, and our knowledge of even the rates of processes is so primitive that we can't eliminate options. So in fact I do think that, say, a billion years from now the galaxies are going to be packed. But probably packed with us, because—you know—we're ugly, we're mean, we're ornery, and we're damned hard to kill.

FRANK: I think it's better to say "our descendants," since I don't think we'll still be *Homo sapiens.*

GREG: Well, I was hoping that this panel might stick around till then.

FRANCISCO: I'll have proved my point by then.

GREG: Francisco [Ayala] knows how to multiply. And on this show, he also knows how to divide—politely, of course.

ROBERT: What kind of descendants, Frank?

FRANK: Our descendants in the far future will be more like artificial intelligences. One possibility is what we call human downloads, mapping our consciousness into a computer. Alternatively,

we might create actual artificial intelligences. That's the form of life able to exist in the harsh environment of space. We are a species adapted to this particular planet, filled with water and oxygen. It's an utterly different environment out in space. Machines, however, can adapt to anything—even perhaps to neutron stars.

LEON: Here's another approach. Our planet is gifted with supplies of iron and copper and other heavy elements, all of which came to us from supernovae—vast explosions of stars in distant galaxies. And we know that organic molecules also exist throughout space. So what's the possibility that this miracle of intelligent life— this low-probability event that happened here on this planet—might propagate?

ROBERT: Would that be a miracle?

LEON: Yes, to me a miracle is a low-probability event.

FRANCISCO: First of all, I recognize the possibility of many other kinds of life—for example, based on silicon. Second, I don't have a problem with the origin of life and with life being common in the universe, as I've said. But once you consider the kind of intelligent life that we've been speaking about—life that we could communicate with—that's where I have the problem. It's the power of probability.

ROBERT: By the year 2100, will Bruce [Murray] and his colleagues in SETI, or their descendants, have detected alien intelligence?

GREG: Yes. And I'll be right here to cheer them.

BRUCE: I don't think we can answer that question definitively, because it may take a thousand years.

ROBERT: What's your guess on a hundred?

BRUCE: I sure hope so.

ROBERT: If human beings are around for a million years?

BRUCE: Definitely.

FRANK: We will never detect alien intelligence.

ROBERT: Even in a million years?

FRANK: No, we will never detect alien intelligence anytime in the future, because they're simply not out there to be detected. And what's the reason we know that they're not out there? As we can see, no probes have ever arrived here.

FRANCISCO: In a hundred years, will we have detected life in the universe? Yes, because life is not rare, considering the size of the universe. But we will not be communicating with any of this life, because none of it is intelligent—there is no other intelligent life in the universe. However, I'm an optimist; I believe that one hundred years from now, we will have found intelligent life on Earth.

LEON: Will we detect life? Absolutely, yes. I think.

ROBERT: CONCLUDING COMMENT

Let's restate our three megaquestions: Does intelligent alien life exist? Will humans colonize the cosmos? Did the universe "expect" conscious beings to emerge (the anthropic principle)? As you might have guessed, opinions are divided, with physicists, astronomers, geologists, and biologists lining up on both sides. What I've thought is that these killer questions may be related. Better is what the British geneticist J. B. S. Haldane thought: "The universe is not just queerer than we suppose, but even queerer than we can suppose." My purpose, here and throughout the *Closer to Truth* series, has been to spotlight fundamental issues of existence, dissect them, enjoy them, and link them, if that's possible. In coming seasons, we'll continue to go after human uniqueness, purpose, destiny. Count on it; we won't stop asking these questions. Their pursuit alone is satisfaction sufficient. Can obsessiveness like this get us closer to truth?

OUTTAKES

ROBERT: Closer to Truth *is framed by consciousness and cosmology. I just love this stuff.*

Epilogue

I was normal until I was twelve. That summer, between seventh and eighth grades, I was kidnapped. No ransom could redeem me; what was abducted was my mind.

I was at summer camp, where my slice of society had determined that I should compete in athletics for two months, just as I should compete in academics for the other ten. In the fashionably austere A-frame cabin, there were eight of us, well-off suburban kids, roughing it; the toilets weren't private and I didn't like making up marine-tight beds. I did like Debbie Reynolds' dreamily romantic ballad *Tammy*, which resonated with awakening hormones.

My bed was third down from the green wooden door, on the left. I was tucked in one perfectly ordinary night, taps had sounded, and I was falling asleep, when a sudden realization struck such terror in me that I strove desperately to blank it out, to eradicate it as if it were a lethal mental virus. My body shuddered with dread; an abyss had just yawned open in front of me—four decades later I can feel its frigid blast still. I struggled to repress the intrusive thoughts that crowded in, only to discover that the more you try not to think about orange monkeys, the more they dominate your mind's eye.

> Why not Nothing? What if everything had always been Nothing? Not just emptiness, not just blackness, not just the barrenness of emptiness forever, not just the thickness of blackness forever, but not even the existence of emptiness, not even the meaning of blackness, and no forever. Wouldn't it have been easier, simpler, more logical to have Nothing rather than Something? Why not Nothing?

I think I must have finally dozed off, because by morning the fright had faded—but an unease lingered. Like a low-grade chronic fever, that moment would become my life partner, never disruptive though always disquieting, the ultimate question against which all others would be put into context. *Why Not Nothing?* is the core of *Closer to Truth*.

Perhaps it was coincidental, but when my physical growth stopped early, pre-
cluding varsity athletics, my career musings began. Daydreaming as a high school
sophomore, I oscillated between particle physics and cosmology, the former
reaching down into the microstructure of everything, the latter reaching up to the
macrostructure of everything. In 1960 the theoretical unity of the fields was not
yet widely apparent.

The quandary was resolved by a mental shift of high-speed excitement: How
could I even contemplate these two universes? Through what extraordinary
mechanisms could human beings apprehend the sweeping spectrum of existence,
from the subatomic to the cosmic? *Only through the brain.*

What a realization! Though obvious now, it was startling when fresh. Only by
studying the human brain could one encompass all science, all thought, all
knowledge. The human brain was how physics became conscious, how the cosmos spawned witnesses to appreciate its wonders. The human brain—the most
complex form of physical law, matter, and energy in the universe. As far as I knew.
And as far as I know.

I had found my focus, a robust intellectual hub that would last a lifetime. In
this brain-centered construction of reality, human awareness and comprehension
emerged as the omnipresent common denominator. The brain is our only connection with everything, our only contact with anything, our only bridge to existence.

You know, I'm starting not to like this annoying early teen, buttoning up all
reality for the rest of us. In real life, I wasn't so pompous. I still played stickball,
struggled with basketball, hung out with my peers, started lifting weights, skipped
Hebrew school, listened to Elvis, wrote notes to girls, had a crush on one who was
dating a senior. Be kind: it was a guileless grandiosity fueled by youthful exuber-
ance.

With naïve insouciance, I assumed that becoming a neurosurgeon was the
clearest path to an understanding of the human brain. (This was just before the
Ben Casey television series made neurosurgery, for a time, a pop profession.) The
bubble burst when I witnessed the chief resident in neurosurgery at a major medical center prepare a basic lecture on how the spinal cord worked by consulting an
introductory textbook that even I, a lowly undergraduate research assistant, had
read. Soon thereafter, a prominent brain scientist informed me that he wouldn't
give a nickel for an M.D. degree. The medical momentum was still strong, however, and I entered a new five-year program at Johns Hopkins Medical School two
months before turning eighteen. The basic life sciences were what I sought, not
the clinical sciences or health care, and when after two years I took a leave of
absence to do a Ph.D. I knew I would never return for the M.D.

Though I maintained clandestine interests in philosophy, religion, and even
parapsychology, my doctorate was taken in the rigorous sciences at the Brain
Research Institute (Department of Anatomy) of the School of Medicine at the

University of California, Los Angeles. Of course, the scientific study of the brain rapidly loses its initial grandeur and settles into a series of specific problems to be solved, just like any other scientific discipline. Nonetheless—here comes my prejudice—because the brain is always the interface between our awareness of reality and the essence of reality, the brain researcher may be more sensitive to the distinctions between perception and substance, and thereby may sit a little closer to ultimate truth.

I learned "neuro-" everything: how to study the brain with the tools and methods of functional academic disciplines—anatomy, physiology, biochemistry, biophysics, psychology, psychiatry, mathematics, computer simulations, and the like. I became absorbed, as must all graduate students, in the ultra-specific problems of my thesis. My research methodology was neurophysiology, which focuses on the bio-electrical activity of the nervous system. My research target was the cerebral cortex, which is the thin outermost part of the brain—the folded, undulating matrix within which conscious activity is generated.

I thought I discovered some important stuff; no one else quite did. What I did attain was more personal growth than professional usefulness: I acquired an appreciation for scientific experimentation and methodology, the rigors of clear analysis, the subtle mechanisms for teasing out truth.

My first experiment was a comic exercise in humility. I was trying to find the locus for learning in the brain, and I had devised an elaborate experiment requiring the simultaneous recording of electrical responses from five different areas of the brain of a partially anesthetized (though conscious) cat during a simple learning task. Of course, I couldn't even fit more than two of the bulky electrode holders onto the laboratory apparatus, nor could I get, that first day, either of the tortuously implanted electrodes to record anything at all. Forget about teaching a barely awake animal any sort of learning task, "simple" or not.

It was clear I was headed for another life but I never escaped the lure of the brain. My doctorate was followed by long excursions into all kinds of pursuits that seem strange sitting on the same list: theology, foundation and concert management, academic business, entrepreneurship, investment banking and finance, advisory work in China, writing and editing, and television production. I pursued each of these, sometimes in series, sometimes in parallel, with a dogged intensity but without any real sense of freedom or fun. Though for decades it appeared otherwise, even to family and friends, I never lost that all-consuming passion for the fundamental questions of consciousness and cosmology, of purpose and destiny, and all that is subsumed by them. Every day these quandaries haunted me: on the subway going to teach corporate strategy in the M.B.A. program at New York University, on the freeway driving to my merger-and-acquisition company in Southern California, on the plane to Beijing. I've never ceased wondering about existence, just as I had at summer camp; such thoughts have been the single most defining characteristic of my life.

Closer to Truth is the product of forty years of existential fascination, scientific methodology, philosophical musings, theological concerns, worldly awareness, and professional experiences, with no small injection of obsessive wonder and fluctuating frustration. Producing and hosting the shows of the series, on which this book is based, was a great treat. It was a self-imposed requirement, but, for the first time in my life, it also brought a certain kind of freedom and a new kind of fun—though if you had observed me preparing for the shows, you would occasionally have doubted that I actually liked what I was doing.

Producers didn't choose the guests; I did. Associate producers didn't pre-interview the guests; I did. Writers didn't suggest my questions or script my comments; I did. I did it all, because I love this stuff. It's the content that drives me—drives me crazy and drives me happy—a more-than-metaphorical return to my bunk at summer camp, where, frankly, I am still just as awestruck.

Producing the series and arranging for the appearances of fifty-five distinguished (and very busy) guests on twenty-eight shows was a Desert Storm of scheduling and logistics. At an early viewing of a rough-cut show, my editor at McGraw-Hill commented, in reference to the scientists, scholars, and artists who appear, "Are all of these people your best friends?" They weren't, but getting to know these great thinkers, before and during the tapings, learning what they believe and how they think, sensing what they consider meaningful and what they deem irrelevant, was pure joy.

Then, there were moments of odd juxtapositions, exposing delightful combinations of the majestic and the mundane that are so wonderfully human. After finishing our show on longevity, where the anti-aging strategy was diet and calorie restriction, we found that the studio had provided a hearty lunch of fried meat swimming in cream. And during the technology shows, our air conditioning cut off.

I was not immune from such irony. In the midst of this logistical and intellectual whirlwind, and through my struggle to get current on, say, enough multi-universe cosmology to be reasonably facile with the likes of Linde and Lederman, the workaday world would often dissolve. How dull the details of gasoline and groceries in the penumbra of bubbling universes and their blinding incandescence. And, yet, the mundane held fast—as it somehow always does.

Back home, in that same Long Island, New York, house where as a young teen I had first encountered consciousness and cosmology, my elderly parents fell victim to a covetous neighbor. While their backs were turned (visiting my sister in Arizona), he tore down their forty-five year-old fence and expropriated a few feet of their property, to make room, it turned out, for what looks to be a poolside cabana. My parents were demeaned but not daunted, insulted but not cowed, and they decided to fight, calling constantly for my counsel during the protracted and tortuous legal maneuverings.

The last thing I wanted to do after a day spent in the hurly-burly world of mergers and acquisitions was to allocate my cherished evenings for surveyors' reports and lawyer machinations instead of my preparations for *Closer to Truth,* which were so important and gratifying to me. So there I was sacrificing grasp and feel of the farthest reaches of Space only to tangle and squabble over a few feet of Earth. I am not proud that I was not always so pleased when my parents would call.

In the end, a court order gave my parents their property back, a new fence, and more importantly their honor. Perhaps my greatest insight of this whole adventure was that doing something as "mundane" as helping my parents with their old fence was closer to truth than understanding all the multi-universe cosmology one can imagine.

Pasadena, California
New York, New York
March 2000